Mario Dunkel, Sina A. Nitzsche (eds.)
Popular Music and Public Diplomacy

Popular Music

Mario Dunkel, Sina A. Nitzsche (eds.)
Popular Music and Public Diplomacy
Transnational and Transdisciplinary Perspectives

Bibliographic information published by the Deutsche Nationalbibliothek
The Deutsche Nationalbibliothek lists this publication in the Deutsche Nationalbibliografie; detailed bibliographic data are available in the Internet at http://dnb.d-nb.de

© 2018 transcript Verlag, Bielefeld

Cover layout: Maria Arndt, Bielefeld
Cover illustration: designritter / photocase.de

Print-ISBN 978-3-8376-4358-9
PDF-ISBN 978-3-8394-4358-3
https://doi.org/10.14361/9783839443583

Table of Contents

Acknowledgements | 7

Popular Music and Public Diplomacy
An Introduction
Mario Dunkel and Sina A. Nitzsche | 9

PART I: COMPETITION AND COLLABORATION

Music in Transnational Transfers and International Competitions
Germany, Britain, and the US in the Nineteenth and Twentieth Centuries
Klaus Nathaus | 29

The Paradoxes of Cultural and Music Diplomacy in a Federal Country
A Case Study from Flanders, Belgium
Alessandro Mazzola | 49

Dervish on the Eurovision Stage
Popular Music and the Heterogeneity of Power Interests in Contemporary Turkey
Nevin Şahin | 69

PART II: INFILTRATION AND APPROPRIATION

Between Propaganda and Public Diplomacy
Jazz in the Cold War
Rüdiger Ritter | 95

"Liberated from Serfdom"
Willis Conover and the Tallinn Jazz Festival of 1967
Maristella Feustle | 117

A Musical Inquisition?
Soviet 'Deputies' of Musical Entertainment in Hungary during the Early 1950s
Ádám Ignácz | 133

PART III: EDUCATION AND PROMOTION

Dancing in Chains
Why Music Can't Keep the World Free
Martha Bayles | 155

Becoming a Blue-Collar Musical Diplomat
Billy Joel and Bridging the US-Soviet Divide in 1987
Nicholas Alexander Brown | 175

Music Trade in the Slipstream of Cultural Diplomacy
Western Rock and Pop in a Fenced-In Record Market
Sven Kube | 197

National Flamencoism
Flamenco as an Instrument of Spanish Public Diplomacy
in Franco's Regime (1939-1975)
Carlos Sanz Díaz and José Manuel Morales Tamaral | 209

PART IV: REPRESENTATION AND PARTICIPATION

The Ethics and Politics of Empathy in US Hip-Hop Diplomacy
The Case of the Next Level Program
Kendra Salois | 233

**Popular Musicking and the Politics of Spectatorship
at the United Nations**
James R. Ball III | 255

From Sons of Gastarbeita to *Songs of Gastarbeiter*
Migrant and Post-Migrant Integration through Music and German Musical
Diplomacy from the 1990s to the Present
Gesa zur Nieden | 277

**Public Diplomacy and Decision-Making
in the Eurovision Song Contest**
Dean Vuletic | 301

List of Contributors | 315

Index | 321

Acknowledgements

This book results from a larger research project between TU Dortmund University and the Carl von Ossietzky University Oldenburg which started with an international conference on "Popular Music and Public Diplomacy" in 2015.

We would like to thank institutions and people who made this project possible. The Deutsche Forschungsgemeinschaft (DFG), the US Consulate in Düsseldorf, the TU Dortmund Society of Friends, and *Oxford Music & Letters* provided grants that enabled us to finance the initial conference. We would also like to express our gratitude to our colleagues at the English and music departments of TU Dortmund University and the music department of the University of Oldenburg. Walter Grünzweig and Holger Noltze supported the initial conference. Our Conference Advisory Board, consisting of Rebekah Ahrendt, Mark Ferraguto, Damien Mahiet, and Daniel Stein, helped us to plan the conference program. Our panel moderators Eric C. Erbacher, Elena Furlanetto, Randi Gunzenhäuser, Sibylle Klemm, Peter Klose, Iris-Aya Laemmerhirt, Cyprian Piskurek, and Gerold Sedlmayr created an inspiring and productive conference atmosphere. Bileam Kümper managed the technology equanimoulsy while Steven Wulf provided an innovative conference design. Matt Lockaby helped us to refine the book proposal. Terence Kumpf proofread the book manuscript and commented on individual chapters. Finally, we would like to express our gratitude to our students who not only assisted us in organizing the project, but also provided valuable perspectives on the topic. Our assistants Kassandra Beckmann, Tanja Ferreira, Thuy-Vy Nguyen, and Hanna Rodewald supported us tirelessly during the conference. Björn Jeddeloh and Léon Raschen helped us in the final stages of the editing process. Our students' enthusiasm, reliability, and commitment were fundamental to the success of this project.

Mario Dunkel and Sina A. Nitzsche
Oldenburg and Dortmund, October 2018

Popular Music and Public Diplomacy
An Introduction

Mario Dunkel and Sina A. Nitzsche

Every year since 30 April 2013, the official date of UNESCO's International Jazz Day, the event's so-called global concert has ended with a jam. After about two hours of live performances by individual artists, all of the musicians involved in the event share the stage for a ritualistic, final performance of John Lennon's "Imagine." The global concert's version of this song builds on Herbie Hancock's 2010 adaptation on his record *The Imagine Project*. While some musicians keep playing throughout the performance of "Imagine," others sing individual fragments of the piece. Some instrumentalists are assigned short sections for solos, while others provide backings toward the end of the performance. "Imagine" ends on a scat riff, which is again based on Hancock's earlier version. Sung by several musicians on the syllables "ba" and "dap," the final unisono motif draws on the shared practice of imitating musical instruments, reaffirming the event's central rhetoric that frames jazz as a "universal language." Launched in 2011, Jazz Day officially celebrates the "diplomatic role" of jazz in uniting people around the world ("About"). It has been hosted by the US (2012 and 2016), Turkey (2013), Japan (2014), France (2015), Cuba (2017), and Russia (2018). The 2019 event will take place in Australia. Barack Obama hosted Jazz Day at the White House in 2016 while the Russian Ministry of Culture supported the global concert in 2018 when it took place at the Mariinsky Theater in St. Petersburg, Vladimir Putin's home town. In addition to this involvement of several national governments, International Jazz Day has been funded by large corporations such as United Airlines and Toyota.

That an event such as Jazz Day has become significant for some of the best-known jazz musicians as well as for state leaders, large corporations, and audiences testifies to the significance of this volume on the interaction between popular music and public diplomacy. Undoubtedly, jazz and its mediations hold significant cultural capital both for governments and corporations. Over the last two decades, questions concerning this political significance of music in international relations have been raised in different disciplines. Political scientists and historians, such as Andrew F. Cooper, Lisa Davenport, Penny von Eschen, Jessica Gienow-Hecht, Simo Mikkonen, Frédéric Ramèl, among others, have tended to emphasize the significance of different types of cultural practices, including music, in international relations by looking at the manifold ways in which these practices and their mediations contribute to public diplomacy and become politically effective (Eschen; Gienow-Hecht, *Sound Diplomacy*; Davenport; Cooper; Ramel and Prévost-Thomas; Mikkonen and Suutari).

At the same time, musicologists, literary scholars, art historians, and other academics interested in the study of cultures have begun to inquire about the ways in which the diplomatic politicization of music and musicians reverberates in the cultural sphere (see Fosler-Lussier, *Music;* Ahrendt, Ferraguto, and Mahiet; Bauer; Street; Kemper et al.). The politicization of music can have a great array of resonances and repercussions, ranging from the marketing of musicians to the branding of genres and the transformation of musical practices and aesthetics. Integrating perspectives from history, political science, but also musicology and popular music studies, the present volume therefore understands the relationship between popular music and diplomacy as multidirectional rather than unidirectional or reciprocal, raising questions that are relevant for cultural, musical, social, economic, and political developments in a globalized world.

POPULAR MUSIC AND MUSIC DIPLOMACY RESEARCH

This book illuminates the interconnectivity of popular music and public diplomacy from transnational and transdisciplinary perspectives. Fourteen scholars with diverse national and disciplinary backgrounds provide individual chapters, guaranteeing a wide range of perspectives on the topic. Except for the first chapter, which provides the historical background to the topic, the chapters assembled in this volume take a focused look at one specific aspect and time period in music diplomacy. By concentrating on popular music after World War II, they provide additions and amendments to individual debates on music diplomacy. The book's narrow focus regarding time period and musical practices, then, facilitates an otherwise vast approach to the topic.

The authors' focus on *popular* music rather than music per se results from several considerations. First, popular music has tended to be sidelined in the study of music diplomacy, as initial studies of the role of the arts in propaganda focused mostly on European concert music. Only recently have researchers begun to dedicate more attention to diplomatic practices that include popular music. The work of Penny von Eschen on the US jazz ambassadors programs may be regarded as a door opener for studies exploring musical practices and genres beyond the canon of European art music that have emerged over the last fifteen years (Eschen). This anthology contributes to closing this gap in music diplomacy research.

Second, the inclusion of popular practices and genres in public diplomacy is closely associated with questions of cultural representation, participation, and power. Looking at processes by which different musical practices have been included and excluded in public diplomacy raises questions about larger phenomena, such as social, cultural, and political participation. Music diplomacy has a unique power to reaffirm, maintain, and intervene in what Stuart Hall calls "regimes of representation" (232). One example of exclusion in music diplomacy is the negligence of popular music in music diplomacy programs of the 1950s, for instance, when the period's most successful music, rock 'n' roll, played only a marginal role in official music diplomacy programs. While the diplomatic use of popular music was initially limited to such "semi-popular"[1] practices as jazz, the second half of the twentieth century saw a growing presence of various popular genres in diplomatic contexts, including country, bluegrass, rock, punk, reggae, and hip-hop. Two events indicate how understandings of national representation and popular culture were changing fundamentally in the 1950s: Dizzy Gillespie's 1956 tour to the Middle East, Turkey and the Balkans on behalf of the US State Department; and the launching of the Eurovision Song Contest (ESC) in the same year. As Dean Vuletic details, the ESC has redefined what popular culture means for the forging of European identities (Vuletic; see Vuletic in this volume). In a way, both events fundamentally questioned the politics of representation in music diplomacy, suggesting a more participatory and democratic practice of musical representation.

Third, the reliance on political archives in the field of public and cultural diplomacy entails a tendency to de-emphasize the perspectives of audiences—the ostensible recipients of public diplomacy—and musicians while overemphasizing the views of government officials. This tendency has been critically interrogated by ethnographic studies that have emerged over the last ten years (see

---

1   According to Danielle Fosler-Lussier, the term "semi-popular music" was actually employed by United States Information Agency (USIA) officials who defined it as "music that 'has achieved a degree of permanence,' including band and glee club music" ("'The State's Canon'").

Aidi; Bayles; Fosler-Lussier, "Cultural Diplomacy"; Salois). Despite these efforts, the inclusion of audiences' perspectives in public diplomacy research remains one of the great challenges within the field. By focusing on popular music and popularization processes, this volume seeks to decenter exclusively government-oriented perspectives. The participatory orientation of popular music and popular culture in general encourages academics to ask questions about reception processes and the manifold cultural repercussions of music diplomacy rather than reducing the field to the study of cultural policies.

The inclusion of popular music is thus more than a question of genre. In fact, attempts to define popular music as a genre have failed repeatedly (Shuker). Within the framework of this book, the "popular" in popular music is less about the nature or essence of music than about the particular ways in which music is practiced and mediated. Consequently, this volume is concerned with ways in which music can help—and, indeed, has helped—to *popularize* by rendering complex messages accessible, appealing, and enjoyable. In the case of Jazz Day, for instance, the shared participatory performance of an extraordinarily popular song such as "Imagine" can make jazz accessible to audiences beyond jazz's otherwise limited circles of devoted listeners. It is this interest in popularization, then, that ties together highly diverse kinds of music, ranging from the Hungarian light popular music discussed by Ádám Ignácz to the Turkish pop music investigated by Nevin Şahin and the US hip-hop performances analyzed by Kendra Salois in this volume. This use of music in order to popularize always works both ways: If music diplomacy musicalizes the political, it also politicizes the musical. The use of popular music practices in public diplomacy, consequently, impacts popular music and the understanding of cultural frames as much as it shapes diplomatic practices. If diplomacy has to do with branding and re-branding (Dinnie), then this re-branding affects musical brands as well as national and corporate ones.

In addition to being culturally powerful, music diplomacy is never dissociated from the social world. Popular music diplomacy, from its beginnings, has been about social as well as cultural participation. The first US jazz diplomacy tours occurred in the midst of the Civil Rights Movement, and the representation of the US by African American jazz ambassadors cannot be separated from the movement's call for equal civil rights and social justice (Eschen; Monson). This underlying presence of a larger social reality within music diplomacy is obvious at Jazz Day, too. When he hosted the event at the White House in 2016, Barack Obama drew on the historical association of jazz diplomacy with the Civil Rights Movement. In 2016, Jazz Day's global concert at the White House framed jazz as an African American cultural and artistic contribution to the world's cultural heritage. If African American music was a "gift" to the United States, as the sociologist and civil rights activist W. E. B. DuBois claimed in 1903, then this gift could be used in order to demand social equality (see Radano). In this way, an event such as Jazz Day not only functions in an international arena, but it also negotiates the social and cultural position of social groups within a respective society. As the contributions to this volume by Nevin Şahin, Gesa zur Nieden, and Kendra Salois demonstrate, contemporary musical ambassadors likewise use popular music in various countries in order to draw attention to similar questions regarding the participation of minorities in the representation of culture.

POPULAR MUSIC AND DIPLOMATIC PRACTICE

As the range of musical practices included in music diplomacy has expanded, so has the understanding of the practice of diplomacy itself. Over the last fifteen years a number of studies have dealt with various sorts of cultural practices and their diplomatic significance. Researchers have begun to consider the role not only of popular musical practices in public diplomacy, but they have also looked at the ways in which larger popular phenomena impact diplomatic practices. Cooper's studies of celebrity diplomacy, for instance, investigate the symbiosis between popular icons and diplomatic activities, ranging from Audrey Hepburn to Bob Geldof and Bono (Cooper). Other studies have investigated the roles and experiences of non-professional musicians and their musical practices in music diplomacy programs (Fosler-Lussier, "Cultural Diplomacy").

At the same time, the understanding of what constitutes diplomacy has changed. International Jazz Day, in fact, exemplifies this. Although it is a UNESCO event, Jazz Day is organized by a US institution: the Thelonious Monk Institute of Jazz. A nonprofit organization based in Washington, DC and Los Angeles, the Monk Institute had already been involved in US jazz diplomacy initiatives before becoming the chief organizer of Jazz Day. In the 2000s, the US State Department directly funded the institute in order to launch several international jazz diplomacy programs. As von Eschen, Davenport, Fosler-Lussier, and others have demonstrated, the practice of US jazz diplomacy goes back to the 1950s, and is intimately interwoven with the history of the Cold War, or the cultural Cold War (Mikkonen and Suutari; Gienow-Hecht, "Culture"). As tensions between East and West were increasing in the 1950s, the US State Department sent jazz ambassadors abroad in order to gain the goodwill of foreign populaces. Many of the most famous US jazz musicians participated in these programs. From a US-government perspective, Jazz Day is an attempt to build on the success of these tours.

While the US State Department used to directly fund the Monk Institute to conduct jazz diplomacy programs, private donors have taken on the role in recent years that used to belong to the US government. One of the institute's main sponsors, for instance, is the military contractor Northrop Grumman. Although it is a private corporation, Northrop Grumman is closely tied to the US administration as the company derives more than 83 percent of its business from contracts with the government alone (Dunkel). While Northrop Grumman is interested in creating goodwill with the US government, the government, in turn, has an interest in promoting US culture throughout the world. Even though the multiplicity of stakeholders at work here obscures political and corporate investments in the event, Jazz Day still functions in a way that is not entirely dissimilar to jazz diplomacy programs of the 1950s, promoting African American music in order to ameliorate the global image of the US.

This complex structural set-up of Jazz Day has to do with one of the major changes in the development of music diplomacy in the twenty-first century: It has become increasingly difficult to identify the actors who are invested in diplomatic initiatives. Funding is distributed in ways that are highly elusive. If US jazz diplomacy during the Cold War was clearly framed as a US initiative, organized by the US State Department, stakeholders are now much less transparent. One of the key concepts for understanding this shift in music diplomacy is the "new public diplomacy" as political scientist Jan Melissen described it in 2005:

The new public diplomacy is no longer confined to messaging, promotion campaigns, or even direct governmental contacts with foreign publics serving foreign policy purposes. It is also about building relationships with civil society actors in other countries and about facilitating networks between non-governmental parties at home and abroad. Tomorrow's diplomats will become increasingly familiar with this kind of work, and in order to do it much better they will increasingly have to piggyback on non-governmental initiatives, collaborate with non-official agents and benefit from local expertise inside and outside the embassy. (*New Public Diplomacy* 22)

This expansive definition of public diplomacy entails a stronger focus on the ways in which cultural and artistic practices function within international relations, including their use by non-government organizations. In the context of this volume, it has the advantage of allowing us to raise questions that concern the complex interplay of politics, culture, media, commerce, and music in diplomatic practices.

Melissen further argued that this type of public diplomacy had become globally dominant:

> Public diplomacy is becoming less national, not only in terms of the actors involved but even when considering the themes that states pick to tell 'their story.' National governments always have their own interests in mind but, when practicing public diplomacy, they increasingly emphasize common interests as well as global public goods. (*Beyond* 21)

It seems that the resurgence of nationalism and the emergence of such terms as "Twitter diplomacy," "undiplomatic diplomacy," and "me-first diplomacy" since 2016 once again provide challenges to understanding how diplomatic practices are transforming. With its focus on polylateralism and non-government actors, however, the concept of a new public diplomacy remains significant as an analytical approach, as it accounts for the continuing multidimensional complexity of diplomacy.

As the exercise of power through digital and algorithmic diplomacy is becoming increasingly significant (Melissen, "Fake News"), this recent shift also affects music diplomacy. In fact, Jazz Day illustrates how techniques of digital control have amended more traditional communication strategies in music diplomacy. Strategies of mediation range from the event's direct framing in speeches by musicians, UNESCO ambassadors, celebrities, and politicians at the global concert, which are then re-mediated across various broadcast and transmission platforms, to their negotiation in digital media and social networks.

On the one hand, the series of performances by musicians at the global concert, for instance, is framed by a number of speeches that are held in between musical performances. At the 2018 global concert in St. Petersburg, UNESCO jazz ambassador Herbie Hancock said:

> Now more than ever before, the world needs International Jazz Day. A vision for the future of humanity, International Jazz Day champions the connectedness of all people. And this evening, an all-star cast of culturally diverse musicians have assembled here in St. Petersburg and will demonstrate that jazz has the power to unite all world citizens as one race—the human race. (United Nations)

This part of Hancock's speech frames Jazz Day in a language of urgency ("now more than ever before"), global solidarity, transracial diversity, and heroic purpose. At the same time, Hancock's statement is ambiguous enough to allow for various readings. The first sentence alone can be read in a number of ways, demonstrating that music diplomacy can be a balancing act that involves the fabrication of ambiguous messages. Why, one wonders, does the world need jazz more than ever? Does this have to do with the confrontational politics of the Trump administration? Or is Hancock alluding to Russian military aggression? The answer remains unclear: either message can be read into Hancock's statement.

Speeches by politicians involved in the event tend to me more specific. Sharing a stage with Hancock, Mikhail Yefimovich Shvydkoy, special representative of the Russian President Vladimir Putin, for instance, emphasized the great national contributions of Russia to the flourishing of jazz and the arts generally:

It is highly symbolic that this year the forum takes place in St. Petersburg. Russia is rightfully famous for a galaxy of talented artists, composers and directors, true masters of the jazz art who perform at the best concert venues and win over audiences with their original talent, virtuosity and splendid improvisation. Due to their creative energy and genuine commitment, our country has been doing much for the professional development of young musicians and implementing outstanding projects in the field of international humanitarian cooperation. The reputation of the Russian jazz education is growing. (United Nations)

Clearly, the struggle over the ownership of jazz is an elementary aspect of the event. It exemplifies a wider debate on claiming popular music practices that has informed this book (Ritter on jazz; Sanz Díaz and Morales Tamaral on flamenco, Salois and zur Nieden on hip-hop, Şahin on dervish performances). This struggle over ownership does not end with the speeches, but it continues in the wider mediation of popular music performance. Jazz Day may appear to be something quite different to the few thousand viewers who actually attend global concerts than to jazz enthusiasts who follow live streams of the event. It also reaches audiences differently who search appearances of individual artists at the global concert on *YouTube* than viewers of abridged versions of the original stream on jazzday.com, the event's official website. Other jazz aficionados may have participated simply by registering their own Jazz Day event on jazzday.com, where a map of the world indicates locations and venues that host Jazz Day events ("2018 International Jazz Day").

Considering the mediation of music diplomacy, then, means investigating how actors seek to control this large variety of ways in which audiences and participants experience a musical event such as Jazz Day. Although Hancock frames Jazz Day as a celebration of peace, harmony, and global solidarity, a closer look at the global concert's mediation in fact reveals an underlying level of competition between different stakeholders. For the 2018 Jazz Day in St. Petersburg, the Russian Ministry of Culture created its own website (jazzdayrussia.com)—despite the fact that Jazz Day has always had one general website representing the event. Jazzdayrussia.com is clearly modeled after the original website—its structure and design are almost identical. Yet, its contents differ fundamentally from the original. The original website, jazzday.com, which is run by the Thelonious Monk Institute of Jazz, portrayed the 2018 celebrations as a double event that simultaneously took place in St. Petersburg and New Orleans (jazzday.com). The website's main page featured two videos, inviting visitors to "watch the International Jazz Day 2018 concerts from St. Petersburg and New Orleans." In previous years, the website had only featured the global concert that took place in the event's respective host city, which in 2018 would have been St. Petersburg. By emphasizing a simultaneous jazz day event in New Orleans, the website thus reasserts US ownership of jazz while downplaying the significance of St. Petersburg as the host city. By contrast, jazzdayrussia.com does not mention the New Orleans concert, inviting viewers to watch the St. Petersburg global concert only ("International Jazz Day"). Obviously, US and Russian stakeholders mediate the event in different ways, with each side emphasizing their own achievements and sidelining the contributions of the other. These differences in the mediation of Jazz Day testify to the digital competition for musical ownership between different actors invested in the event.

STRUCTURE OF THE BOOK

Both in the digital and non-digital realm, the interconnection between popular music and public diplomacy, then, is characterized by several continuing tensions. It is "pushed and pulled," as Danielle Fosler-Lussier puts it, and has the power to push and pull ("Music Pushed"). This volume, therefore, is separated into four parts dealing with different tensions that have shaped the practice of popular music diplomacy. The chapters of Part I, "Competition and Collaboration," investigate the ways in which tensions between competition and collaboration impact music diplomacy. According to Klaus Nathaus, competition has been a key factor in the historical development of music diplomacy in the nineteenth and twentieth centuries. The studies included in this part illuminate the extent to which popular music diplomacy can be understood as a practice that oscillates between international competition, on the one hand, and transnational collaboration, on the other, in various cultural settings and political contexts.

In "Music in Transnational Transfers and International Competitions. Germany, Britain, and the US in the Nineteenth and Twentieth Centuries," historian Klaus Nathaus emphasizes competition as one of the major forces behind the development of music diplomacy in the Western world. He claims that while the transfer of culture in general and music in particular has attracted increasing attention among historians in the last 25 years, studies discussing imperialism, resistance, and appropriation commonly frame cultural relations between nations as cooperative and bilateral. Nathaus's chapter suggests a slightly different interpretative angle as it understands these relations as competitive and prestige-oriented. His approach raises questions of how such diplomatic and cultural relations can be studied, understood, and evaluated. Analyzing both classical and popular music performances, practices, and discursive strategies by musicians and music critics, Nathaus identifies continuities in the institutionalization of transnational musical competition since the early nineteenth century.

Alessandro Mazzola argues that Belgium's musical diplomacy cannot be understood without taking into consideration the country's historical, political, linguistic, and cultural divisions. Unlike federal states whose self-governing components adopt policies that converge and cooperate at an international level, Flanders and Wallonia—the Dutch- and French-speaking communities of Belgium—do not seem to coordinate on this matter. According to Mazzola, popular music is the principal field where the two communities adopt very different approaches and end up competing for resources and international visibility. "The Paradoxes of Cultural and Music Diplomacy in a Federal Country: A Case Study from Flanders, Belgium" showcases how Flanders, in particular, supports self-representation strategies that produce and circulate images of a singular and homogeneous "Flemish nation." Cultural institutions seem to focus on an autonomous nation-building project rather than situating the community in the larger national—Belgian—context.

Closing out the first section, Nevin Şahin's chapter, "Dervish on the Eurovision Stage: Popular Music and the Heterogeneity of Power Interests in Contemporary Turkey," unravels the diplomatic and power struggles behind Turkey's performances at the ESC. In 2004, the popular singer Sertab Erener merged popular music with traditional dance when she performed amidst a group of whirling dervishes, triggering a lively debate between the Ministry of Culture and Tourism, Sufi organizations, and the audience over the representation of Mevlevi Sufism. The image of the whirling dervish at the ESC performance is still vividly debated and contested today. Having collected data in a 15-month ethnographic field research project, Şahin examines the dynamics of competition and collaboration between state, commercial, and religious interests in the practice of music diplomacy.

Part II, "Infiltration and Appropriation," focuses on tensions between sender- and receiver-oriented approaches to the practice of music diplomacy. In *Music in America's Cold War Diplomacy*, Danielle Fosler-Lussier describes the Eisenhower administration's strategy of cultural "infiltration" as a unidirectional, top-down process in which music served as a carrier of American ideas and values that could be "pour[ed] . . . into the minds of the foreign public" (4). By contrast, later concepts of appropriation and exchange emphasize the agency of recipients who defy strategies of cultural infiltration by actively developing their own meanings and cultural practices. While Fosler-Lussier focuses exclusively on US music diplomacy, this part investigates the role of infiltration and appropriation in various settings on both sides of the Iron Curtain.

As Rüdiger Ritter and Maristella Feustle demonstrate, strategies of infiltration and persuasion had unexpected consequences, leading to open or hidden person-to-person diplomacy which often facilitated individual cooperation and exchange. In his chapter "Between Propaganda and Public Diplomacy. Jazz in the Cold War," Rüdiger Ritter argues that scholars of music and diplomacy need to reconsider the similarities and differences between US and Soviet music diplomacy. According to Ritter, jazz was an instrument in the struggle for cultural supremacy not only for the US, but also for the Soviet Union and its satellites. US officials intended to destabilize Socialist societies by introducing jazz via radio broadcasts or by sending jazz musicians as jazz ambassadors while their adversaries in the Eastern Bloc used the music for their own purposes by integrating it into a Soviet-Socialist model of culture. As Ritter argues, US-actors called their efforts cultural diplomacy, while the Eastern Bloc countries simply called their own activities propaganda. Both Eastern and Western actors used jazz to promote their values, and they both tried to benefit from the weaknesses of the other. Ritter concludes that the two ideological adversaries both succeeded and failed: Neither did the West provoke a collapse, nor did the East succeed in diminishing American popular music in their countries. However, as both Cold War opponents undertook intensive efforts to strengthen the Eastern Bloc jazz scenes and to promote jazz contacts, those collaborations facilitated a mutual jazz exchange after the fall of the Berlin Wall.

Maristella Feustle explores Willis Conover's famous jazz broadcast, *Music USA*, which was arguably one of the most effective uses of American "soft power" in the mid-twentieth century. As Feustle argues, the jazz diplomacy of Conover's program depended on the integrity ensured by his independence as a contractor as well as his insistence that the music speak for itself. Accordingly, the Voice of America radio station could talk repeatedly about a free society's advantages, but jazz succeeded in showing those qualities in action, realized in artistic moments which could be efficiently transmitted over the airwaves. Feustle's contribution "'Liberated from Serfdom'. Willis Conover and the Tallinn Jazz Festival of 1967" uses primary source materials from the Willis Conover Collection at the University of North Texas to demonstrate the impact of Conover's approach.

Ádám Ignácz illuminates another unexpected consequence of strategies of infiltration during the Cold War. As he shows, the Hungarian government ended up appropriating and translating mechanisms of Stalinist musical diplomacy in the field of popular music in Hungary. "A Musical Inquisition? Soviet 'Deputies' of Musical Entertainment in Hungary during the Early 1950s" details how communist elites strove to create a jazz-free Hungarian "national dance music" modeled after Soviet musical traditions. While American music diplomacy targeted the people in the Warsaw Pact states during the early Cold War through what the Eisenhower administration referred to as cultural "infiltration," the Soviet Union created its own strategies. With the increased Sovietization of the occupied countries in the late 1940s, Ignácz argues, the USSR had growing motivation to "help" with the cultural revolutions conducted by the local communist parties and to directly command, supervise, and monitor the required changes. Music was an important instrument in this intervention as Soviet musical diplomats visited Hungary to suggest how local cultures could be protected from Western popular infiltrations.

Part III, "Education and Promotion," examines the conflict between two antagonistic purposes of music diplomacy. The rhetoric that surrounds state-funded music programs abroad often implies that music diplomacy seeks to empower foreign audiences by contributing to their musical and cultural education. This perspective on music diplomacy as a benevolent intervention is, however, challenged by the commercial and political interests that underlie such programs. This section exemplifies how the interests of interdependent actors in politics and entertainment industries complicate claims of neutrality and educational motives in the practice of music diplomacy.

Musicians and music managers have often used the alignment of music with politics and politicians as a marketing device (Cooper). At the same time, politicians and political institutions have profited from their association with celebrity musicians. Martha Bayles's chapter, "Dancing in Chains: Why Music Can't Keep the World Free," is specifically concerned with how US popular music becomes a force for repression. She describes how US pop and rap stars such as Erykah Badu, Mariah Carey, and Kanye West performed in authoritarian countries, thus privileging monetary considerations over humanitarian and ethical ones. Bayles contextualizes what she sees as the romantic notion of music as a liberating force with the post-World War II jazz ambassadors program. Bayles explains how the political, media, and socio-cultural transformations after the fall of the Berlin Wall have affected public diplomacy in Europe and Asia. Discussing various transnational examples of jazz, rock, pop, rap, hip-hop, and country music, Martha Bayles demands that Western nation-states reconsider the relationship between politics, the music market, and the music industry in order to reconfigure the role of popular music in public diplomacy.

Nicholas Alexander Brown analyzes how American singer Billy Joel staged himself during the performances in Moscow and Leningrad in the late 1980s. In his chapter, "Becoming a Blue-Collar Musical Diplomat: Billy Joel and Bridging the US-Soviet Divide in 1987," Brown explores how Joel cleverly fashioned himself as an American working-class musician. This identity construction resonated well with the white male-dominated working-class ideology of the Soviet regime and the experience of Soviet audiences. Brown demonstrates that Joel's lyrics address the concerns of the "common man" who is dissatisfied with his government's politics—an issue that spoke to audiences both inside and outside the USSR. Brown's chapter illuminates how Billy Joel's blue-collar diplomacy was situated between American exceptionalism and Soviet *glasnost* politics while ultimately fulfilling commercial objectives. Even today, Joel continues to repackage and repurpose his iconic concert tour in documentaries and album releases by building on his legacy as an American artist who allegedly helped to destroy the Iron Curtain.

Approaching the East German record industry as a space of relative independence from the Socialist government, historian Sven Kube also sees the popular music industry as a liberating force in authoritarian states. "Music Trade in the Slipstream of Cultural Diplomacy: Western Rock and Pop in a Fenced-In Record Market" argues that the constantly intensifying presence of Western music in the GDR heralded liberalization in the realm of culture that fueled the demand for political change. Based on personal interviews with former managers, executives, agents, and officials, this chapter investigates how the Deutsche Schallplatten, East Germany's only record company, operated between the official socialist state ideology, popular tastes, and capitalist production mechanisms. Ultimately, Kube interprets Deutsche Schallplatten as a space of relative freedom in a restricted country, but he also points out that Socialist officials profited from the popular music exchange by gaining foreign currency in order to stabilize the shaky GDR economy.

Carlos Sanz Díaz and José Manuel Morales Tamaral illuminate how Francisco Franco's regime used flamenco diplomacy as an instrument to promote tourism, trade, and, ultimately, challenge Spain's isolated position on the global diplomatic and economic stage. Presenting a new angle on the phenomenon of "national flamencoism," which has been researched by cultural studies scholars and social historians mainly with regard to identities and aesthetics, the authors approach flamenco as a diplomatic practice which is deeply embedded in the Spanish economy, culture, and politics. "National Flamencoism. Flamenco as an Instrument of Spanish Public Diplomacy in Franco's Regime (1939-1975)" presents a close reading of unique historical sources, such as embassy documents, letters, reports, and international news clippings. Discussing two case studies from West Germany and the Soviet Union during the Cold War, Sanz Díaz and Morales Tamaral show convincingly how flamenco, originally a popular, commercial, vernacular, and transcultural art form, was homogenized by Spanish officials in order to promote a homogeneous national identity. The chapter details how flamenco diplomacy was largely organized by private companies, individual managers, and private actors in cooperation with official diplomatic institutions during the Cold War, demonstrating that the program's official, educative intent was enmeshed with underlying commercial and political motives.

Part IV, "Representation and Participation," finally foregrounds how the politics of participation in music diplomacy reconfigure established modes and mechanisms of representation. The chapters in this part investigate participation on both an interstate and an interpersonal level. Not only do national politics of participation influence how nations are represented on the global stage, but participatory processes in person-to-person diplomacy have also provoked a shift in diplomatic practices. In addition, politics of participation have impacted the ways in which minority groups are represented on the international stage. As such, they have affected discourses on the social and cultural locations of minorities within their respective nations. This section asks where and how participation becomes politically effective by intervening in the politics of representation, both on an interpersonal and an international level.

Kendra Salois's chapter, "The Ethics and Politics of Empathy in US Hip-Hop Diplomacy: The Case of the Next Level Program," examines the US State Department's so-called Next Level program. Launched in 2014, this diplomatic initiative connects activists, teachers, emcees, deejays, dancers, and beatmakers. According to Salois, Next Level marks a turning point in the State Department's longstanding promotion of American culture abroad since the jazz ambassadors program. It emphasizes person-to-person diplomacy guided by empathy, emotion, and mutual understanding between American teachers and foreign artists relabeled as students. Analyzing musical performances and interviews with organizers and participants, this chapter makes a case for research which reconsiders the role of music, emotion, and affect in public diplomacy.

In his contribution, "Popular Musicking and the Politics of Spectatorship at the United Nations," James R Ball III investigates the role of subjectivity and emotion in the public diplomacy of the United Nations. The author shows that popular and folk music performances can have quite opposite effects besides the intended objectives of freedom, mutual understanding, and solidarity. Analyzing former Secretary General Ban Ki-moon's participation in the United Nations' International Day of Happiness and in a concert by Serbia's Viva Vox Choir, Ball III demonstrates how Ban's involvement in these performances can create feelings of alienation and frustration among his intended audiences and render diplomatic spaces as highly contested ones. Combining feminist scholarship on abject theory and emotion, Ball III joins Bayles in interrogating the myth of popular music as an expression of freedom and humanism in diplomatic settings.

Similar to the US hip-hop diplomacy program investigated by Salois, the participatory aspects of hip-hop culture have been crucial to recent developments in German music diplomacy. In her chapter, "From Sons of Gastarbeita to *Songs of Gastarbeiter*: Migrant and Post-Migrant Integration through Music and German Musical Diplomacy from the 1990s to the Present," Gesa zur Nieden analyzes how migrant and post-migrant musicians have increasingly been included in the promotion of (West) German culture abroad over the past 30 years. Discussing Sons of Gastarbeita, a local multi-ethnic rap group based in the Ruhr Area who toured Goethe Institutes across France, this chapter elaborates on the development of an educational concept to present German migratory hip-hop culture to French students of German as a foreign language. Zur Nieden's case study exemplifies how musicians emphasizing experiences of migration open up important spaces for cultural institutions to reconsider national representation in an international arena.

Dean Vuletic's contribution on the political significance of the ESC, "Public Diplomacy and Decision-Making in the Eurovision Song Contest," finally explores the ways in which EU and non-EU states reconfigure their public image by participating in this popular music spectacle. Established in 1956, the ESC is one of the most prominent examples of what one might call European popular culture. Organized by the European Broadcasting Union, this contest has enjoyed a high popularity in many states across the political spectrum ranging from liberal democracies to authoritarian states since the end of World War II. The final chapter of this volume looks at the contest's multifaceted history. Because the event is based on reconfigurations of the nation-state, studying Eurovision performances and discursive strategies allows Vuletic to draw important conclusions about how European nations use the ESC to promote themselves and attempt to gain competitive advantages over other states. As Vuletic examines how audiences perceive those performances, his chapter is an important contribution to the formation of European identities at a time when Europe's political landscape is increasingly fragmenting.

Taken as a whole, the chapters in this volume detail the complex and multifaceted interrelationships between popular music and public diplomacy. The authors' manifold, transnational and transdisciplinary perspectives on the topic demonstrate how the investigation of popular music and public diplomacy is in itself a political practice. The terminology we employ for understanding this relationship—from propaganda to cultural and public diplomacy—is loaded and has been subject to political struggles (see Ritter in this volume). Far from seeking to provide an all-encompassing account, this book highlights individual examples and hopes to open new pathways for research at the interface of popular music and public diplomacy.

WORKS CITED

"2018 International Jazz Day Event Map." *International Jazz Day.* Web. 10 July 2018. <jazzday.com>.

"About." *International Jazz Day.* Web. 23 Aug. 2018. <jazzday.com/about>.

Ahrendt, Rebekah, Mark Ferraguto, and Damien Mahiet, eds. *Music and Diplomacy from the Early Modern Era to the Present.* New York: Palgrave Macmillan, 2014. Print.

Aidi, Hisham D. *Rebel Music: Race, Empire, and the New Muslim Youth Culture.* New York: Vintage Books, 2014. Print.

Bauer, Gerd U. *Auswärtige Kulturpolitik als Handlungsfeld und „Lebenselixier": Expertentum in der deutschen Auswärtigen Kulturpolitik und der Kulturdiplomatie.* München: Iudicium, 2010. Print.

Bayles, Martha. *Through a Screen Darkly: Popular Culture, Public Diplomacy, and America's Image Abroad.* New Haven, London: Yale UP, 2014. Print.

Cooper, Andrew F. *Celebrity Diplomacy.* Boulder: Paradigm, 2008. Print.

Davenport, Lisa E. *Jazz Diplomacy: Promoting America in the Cold War Era.* Jackson: UP of Mississippi, 2009. Print.

Dinnie, Keith. *Nation Branding: Concepts, Issues, Practice.* New York: Routledge, 2014. Print.

Dunkel, Mario. "'Jazz Embodies Human Rights': The Politics of UNESCO's International Jazz Day." *Forum for Inter-American Research* (forthcoming).

Eschen, Penny M. von. *Satchmo Blows Up the World: Jazz Ambassadors Play the Cold War*. Cambridge: Harvard UP, 2006. Print.

Fosler-Lussier, Danielle. "Cultural Diplomacy as Cultural Globalization: The University of Michigan Jazz Band in Latin America." *Journal of the Society for American Music* 4.1 (2010): 59-93. Print.

---. *Music in America's Cold War Diplomacy*. Oakland: U of California P, 2015. Print.

---. "Music Pushed, Music Pulled: Cultural Diplomacy, Globalization, and Imperialism." *Diplomatic History* 36.1 (2012): 53-64. Print.

---. "'The State's Canon': The United States Information Agency and American Music Abroad." Sounds and Voices on the International Stage: Understanding Musical Diplomacies Conference. Sciences Po, CERI, Paris. 21-22 Apr. 2016. Conference Paper.

Gienow-Hecht, Jessica C. E. "Culture and the Cold War in Europe." *The Cambridge History of the Cold War. Vol. 1.* Ed. Melvyn P. Leffler and Odd A. Westad. Cambridge: Cambridge UP, 2010. 398-419. Print.

---. *Sound Diplomacy: Music and Emotions in Transatlantic Relations, 1850-1920*. Chicago: U of Chicago P, 2009. Print.

Hall, Stuart. *Representation: Cultural Representations and Signifying Practices*. London: Sage, 1997. Print.

"International Jazz Day to be Celebrated Worldwide on 30 April." *International Jazz Day*. Web. 10 July 2018. <https://jazzdayrussia.com/en/>.

Kemper, Dirk, et al., eds. *Literatur und Auswärtige Kulturpolitik*. Munich: Wilhelm Fink, forthcoming.

Melissen, Jan. *Beyond the New Public Diplomacy*. Clingendael Paper No. 3. The Hague: Netherlands Institute of International Relations Clingendael, 2011. Print.

---, ed. *The New Public Diplomacy: Soft Power in International Relations*. Basingstoke: Palgrave Macmillan, 2008. Print.

---. "Fake News—and What (Not) to Do About It." *Clingendael Alert* (2018): 1-5. Web. 23 Aug. 2018. <https://www.clingendael.org/sites/default/files/2018-02/PB_Alert_Fake_News.pdf>.

Mikkonen, Simo, and Pekka Suutari. *Music, Art and Diplomacy: East-West Cultural Interactions and the Cold War*. New York: Routledge, 2016. Print.

Monson, Ingrid T. *Freedom Sounds: Civil Rights Call Out to Jazz and Africa*. Oxford, New York: Oxford UP, 2010. Print.

Radano, Ronald M. *Lying Up a Nation: Race and Black Music*. Chicago: U of Chicago P, 2003. Print.

Ramèl, Frédéric, and Cécile Prévost-Thomas. *International Relations, Music and Diplomacy: Sounds and Voices on the International Stage*. New York: Palgrave Macmillan, 2018. Print.

Salois, Kendra. "The US Department of State's Hip-Hop Diplomacy in Morocco." *Music and Diplomacy from the Early Modern Era to the Present*. Ed. Rebekah Ahrendt, Mark Ferraguto, and Damien Mahiet. New York: Palgrave Macmillan, 2014. 231-50. Print.

Sheafer, Tamir, and Itay Gabay. "Mediated Public Diplomacy: A Strategic Contest over International Agenda Building and Frame Building." *Political Communication* 26.4 (2009): 447-67. Print.

Shuker, Roy. *Understanding Popular Music Culture*. New York: Routledge, 2013. Print.

Street, John. *Music and Politics*. Cambridge: Polity, 2012. Print.

United Nations. "The International Jazz Day Global All-Star Concert (St Petersburg, Russia, 30 April 2018)." *YouTube*, 2018. Web. 23 Aug. 2018. <https://youtu.be/IKiWqkw4AuA>.

Vuletic, Dean. *Postwar Europe and the Eurovision Song Contest*. New York: Bloomsbury Academic, 2017. Print.

Part I:
Competition and Collaboration

Music in Transnational Transfers and International Competitions
Germany, Britain, and the US
in the Nineteenth and Twentieth Centuries

Klaus Nathaus

The film *Fitzcarraldo* (dir. Werner Herzog, 1982) tells the story of Brian Sweeney "Fitzcarraldo" Fitzgerald (Klaus Kinski), an Irish entrepreneur who, in the early twentieth century, dreams about building an opera house in the Peruvian Andes. He hopes to finance his vision with profits from the rubber boom. With money from his brothel-operating girlfriend (Claudia Cardinale), he acquires a claim that the other rubber barons believe to be inaccessible. Fitzcarraldo's daring plan is to avoid the rapids of the river Pongo by steering a ship up on a second river to a point where the two streams are only separated by a narrow ridge, and then transport his vessel over land to the Pongo to reach the rubber trees downstream. To get to this ridge, however, he needs to cross an area that is populated by indigenous people who are known to be extremely hostile to intruders. When his crew realizes what they are in for, most of them abandon ship. But as he is left behind by his hired hands, Fitzcarraldo establishes contact with the natives who seem strangely fascinated by this man in a white suit playing arias on his phonograph, the horn directed at the jungle.

For mysterious reasons, the natives help Fitzcarraldo haul the massive steamer over the hill. A drunken celebration follows, and while the crew is asleep on board, the natives sever the ropes that hold the ship in place. As the steamer tumbles through the rapids and Fitzcarraldo desperately tries to stop it, the natives on board reveal that they believe the vessel had been sent to them by the gods to sail into a better future. With a dozen beaming Indios on board his battered ship, Fitzcarraldo returns to the point of his departure. To fulfill his opera dream at least in part, he sells the steamer and hires an ensemble that performs Vincenzo Bellini's *I Puritani* on board the heeling ship, to jubilant Peruvians lining the shore.

Fitzcarraldo lends itself as a metaphor for cultural transfers. Defiance against incredible obstacles illustrates the effort required to transport culture across borders. The fact that Fitzcarraldo plays his arias to people who remain inscrutable even as they come into touching distance reveals the openness of first encounters for productive misunderstandings. As Fitzcarraldo's opera treat is ultimately financed by profits from prostitution, the film also shows that money is essential to art and may come from less respectable sources. In addition, the film's soundtrack blends various cultures, cumulating in an Italian opera about Scottish Puritans performed by a European cast in Peru. Non-diegetic music by the German rock band PopolVuh (a Guatemalan term) counters Caruso's opera recordings.

In the last twenty-five years, historians have become increasingly interested in such cultural transfers. They have explored them mostly in view of transatlantic encounters and the possible Americanization of Western Europe. Focused on the political economy of mass media and the allure of consumer culture, some authors propose that the American senders effectively shaped European culture to a large extent (De Grazia; Malchow). While these studies look at Fitzcarraldo's record player and the seemingly mesmerizing effect of his broadcasts, a revisionist position shifts the view to the natives, pointing out that they productively "misinterpreted" arias and incorporated them into their own culture. These studies argue that European consumers of culture (often described as marginalized and hostile, similar to Fitzcarraldo's Indios) appropriated American popular culture, including jazz, rock 'n' roll, hip-hop, and Hollywood movies, to their own needs (Maase; Poiger; Jackson). The debate between cultural imperialism and creative appropriation is echoed in more recent research on musical diplomacy. Again, the focus is mostly on the transatlantic relationship, and interpretations are centrally concerned with the question of the political efficacy of the cultural message. Such studies take music as a reflection of international relations and countries' political aspirations and now commonly dismiss the notion of cultural imperialism in favor of "pull factors" and the agency of audiences (Gienow-Hecht, *Sonic History*; Eschen; Fosler-Lussier).

All this research usually takes a transnational perspective and perceives musical transfer as a dyadic relationship between a more or less powerful sender and more or less active recipients abroad. The following chapter suggests a different approach. Drawing on sociologist Tobias Werron's concept of global competitions for "soft" goods (Werron), it assumes that musical diplomacy—defined here as the promotion of music across state borders in the name of a nation, sometimes administered, but rarely initiated by government agencies—was essentially a form of participation in an international prestige competition, comparable to sending a soccer team to the World Cup competition. This assumption brackets the concern whether music managed to win hearts and minds abroad and leads to the question of how the musical tournament came to be established in the first place. It substitutes the dyadic model of communication with the triadic structure of competition, thus highlighting the genuinely international dimension of musical diplomacy.

In this chapter, I take a long-term view of both classical music and popular genres to show that musical diplomacy has followed a recurring pattern since the early nineteenth century: Against a backdrop of commercial, transnationally traded music, interested groups in one country began to mark a particular style of music as both intrinsically "valuable" and representative for their nation. This initiative was subsequently taken up in other countries by intermediaries and what we may call "prestige entrepreneurs" who pursued their own, not always musical aims. The adoption of the idea that a certain kind of music is a form of art led to the global proliferation of similar institutions and aesthetic standards. Conservatories, concert halls, awards, and music journalism in turn created an international structure for the comparison of musical achievements of nations, and musical "experts," such as critics and musicologists, have acted as referees in the prestige competition.

This chapter traces the establishment of international tournaments in music in two parts. The first section looks at the rise of classical music as the standard for musical excellence during the nineteenth century, a development that originated in Germany and was adopted in different ways in England and the US. The second part moves on to the twentieth century, when America and Britain took the lead in transforming first jazz and then rock into art, while Germany went through the options available to a late-comer. The conclusion will return to the question of music's efficacy in transnational relations, addressing it against the backdrop of the prestige competitions. While I agree in principle that music can afford social transformation, I regard this potency to be limited in the case of musical diplomacy. I argue that music which is acknowledged as "valuable" by experts and bureaucrats shapes listeners' responses in that it forecloses the openness of those first encounters in which ships may be carried over mountains.

NATIONALISM AND ARTISTIC EXCELLENCE: THE ORIGINS OF AN INTERNATIONAL MUSICAL COMPETITION IN THE NINETEENTH CENTURY

Seen from today's perspective, the musical landscape around 1800 lacks clear contours. To be sure, the terrain had been cultivated by the standards of tonality, tuning, and tempi; fenced in by a system of notation as well as conventions about instrumentation and genre. But concerts still featured heterogeneous repertoires, and musical taste was thought to be rooted in the general public rather than monopolized by expert critics (Weber). Operas were creolized to be marketed to diverse audiences in different countries (Sorba). Distinctions of artistic merit were still largely absent, and philosophers regarded music as inferior to other symbolic expressions such as literature. Musicians on the whole had a relatively low social status, and the few who received handsome returns and were adulated as stars—like castrati or violin virtuosos—stood outside the system of occupational and social hierarchies.

One hundred years later, the overall picture had changed dramatically, and the musical landscape of the "civilized world" was fully mapped. It had a distinct topography of "serious" summits and "popular" lowlands and was segmented along national boundaries. It was populated by sharply defined figures like critics, composers and conductors, professionals, amateurs, and knowledgeable listeners. These figures moved in and out of concert halls and conservatoires, read music journals, studied musicology and formed musical societies. Such institutions gave music a history, permanence, and media for evaluation (Blanning; Osterhammel).

Concomitant to the transformation of music's meaning and value, music turned into a medium for an international prestige competition. Two interrelated developments made this possible: Firstly, music became intrinsically valuable, thus generating prestige (and the fear of losing it) as an incentive to compete. Secondly, music became associated with the nation.

These two developments started first in the German territories, where musical nationalism was initially promoted by musicians, who at the start of the nineteenth century faced a collapse of their labor market. The sharp decline in the number of courts and the financial problems of towns under French occupation reduced job opportunities for musicians and forced them to find paid work elsewhere. Few were able to sustain themselves only with concerts and compositions. Aggravating the situation, the commercial bourgeoisie, a class that patronized the arts in other countries, was relatively poor in Germany and less inclined to invest in culture. As alternative income streams were narrow, forward-looking musicians were turning to the state as their potential paymaster (Applegate, "German"; *Bach in Berlin*).

To this end, musicians sought to rub shoulders with bureaucrats and tried to convince them of the spiritual value of music. Taking the lead of writers, who were already acknowledged as artists, musicians insisted on artistic autonomy to include music into the canon of the arts. They stressed "good" music's "seriousness" by drawing a sharp line against music written "merely" for popular appeal, and they claimed that "serious" music had educational value and an integrative effect on the community. In this way, they made music compatible with the visions and aims of "the university-going, state-serving, journal-writing, association-joining mostly men of the educated stream [who] were at the same time the makers and shapers of German-ness" (Applegate, "German" 287).

Historian Celia Applegate presents Carl Friedrich Zelter as an example of a master mason who changed his trade for the insecurity of a musician's life. As a first step to forge a career, he participated in and then led the Singakademie (an amateur choir), where he made contacts with Berlin's bureaucratic elite. Subsequently, he befriended Goethe, who was interested in Zelter possibly because he thought he should be in touch with a practitioner of music, this upstart art form. In any case, Goethe's friendship bestowed prestige on Zelter and, by extension, his music. Goethe also endorsed Zelter's proposal to incorporate music in the Prussian Academy of Arts, a bold suggestion by a non-member. In subsequent years, Zelter's efforts to promote the cause of "serious" music in the name of the German community bore fruit. He became an honorary member of the Academy and the first professor of music at the Humboldt University in Berlin; he was supported in setting up institutions such as music schools and a choral society (Liedertafel) that provided the model for similar amateur choirs throughout Germany (Applegate, "German" 289-95).

Musicians' calls for acknowledgement found resonance not least because they were amplified by a new music press that took music seriously. Financed by music publisher Gottfried Christoph Härtel and edited by musician-turned-writer Friedrich Rochlitz, the *Allgemeine Musikalische Zeitung* (*AMZ*, General Musical Newspaper) was launched in 1798 and became the flagship of music criticism in Germany during its fifty years of existence. While older journals covered concerts as society events, the *AMZ* promoted informed judgement about the music itself. It demanded for music a place among the established arts and promised to educate its readers about its value. Publishing articles from Hamburg, Berlin, Vienna, and other cities, the *AMZ* gave evidence of a coherent and lively musical nation. It ensured its widely dispersed readers that anonymous others were concerned with the same issues, offering them a sense of being part of an "imagined community," as Applegate explains in reference to Benedict Anderson (Applegate, *Bach in Berlin* 86-104).

The claim to produce art in the service of the nation was at first aimed at the domestic elite. However, given the transnational connections of the music trade and music journalism, by the second half of the nineteenth century the initiative showed effects in other countries. As German musicians formulated their claim to "seriousness" in opposition to the commercially successful Italian and French repertoire, they disregarded its popularity as superficial and demanded that music be judged by its artistic and spiritual value. For musicians in smaller European nations, the German example offered a model of how to establish their own successful traditions of national music. Composers like Norwegian-born Edvard Grieg or Czech-born Antonín Dvořák who went to Germany for education returned home with the cachet of having been to "the land of music."

The transfer in both directions made use of an existing infrastructure of cultural exchange that became increasingly dense and effective from the mid-century on. The music press of numerous countries took notice of musical activities abroad. Correspondents reported home and articles were culled from foreign publications to be translated for domestic readers. Transfer routes could also be circuitous. The readers of London's *Musical World*, for instance, got much of their information about German music from *Dwight's Journal of Music*, published in Boston between 1852 and 1881. Dwight in turn received his information from German texts that he translated for his American readers (Cohen). European music publishers also expanded their operations across borders by opening branch offices or collaborating with publishers abroad. Copyright reforms and new technologies of printing facilitated this expansion, as did the growing demand from choral movements and amateur pianists (Boorman et al. 370). From mid-century onwards, the cultural capital generated by German musicians and critics became convertible into economic capital, and German music rose to dominate the market for orchestral works.

The increasing integration of the transnational music trade and music journalism transformed musical nationalism into an international prestige tournament. Many small and emerging European nations were eager to take part in it, but the entry of England and the US into this tournament is particularly revealing. It hints at a different motivation than the expectation to win the hearts and minds of a global audience.

With Scotland and Wales priding themselves on their own musical traditions, it was up to England alone to join the fray of competitors. England participated in the prestige tournament by announcing a Musical Renaissance that took until the 1880s to gestate. The main reason why the country was late to show interest in musical nationalism was the fact that it had, with London, the most developed market for music, which made it less likely for musicians to turn to the state for recognition or support. Tellingly, the most prominent propagators of the Musical Renaissance were not musicians but self-appointed prestige entrepreneurs who gained recognition by making their country's participation in the musical tournament a matter of national pride. The project to create an English national music developed from the 1851 World Exhibition and was first conducted by Henry Cole, a civil servant and former railway administrator. After that, the metaphorical baton was taken up by George Grove, a gifted proselytizer, but not a musical practitioner (Stradling and Hughes). The basic claim of the Musical Renaissance was that music, while neglected in modern England, had had an important place in Elizabethan times. This implied that English musical excellence actually preceded the blossom of German music and provided a historical reference point for a present generation of English composers. Grove worked hard to win the support of music critics, some of them of German origin, for this argument (Hughes).

England's established musicians had less reason to be enthusiastic about the Renaissance. It is indicative that the country's most famous composer, Arthur Sullivan, who had studied in Leipzig and was regarded as the greatest musical talent at the time, ended up outside the Renaissance movement, blamed for having wasted his gift. To be sure, Sullivan wrote "serious" music throughout his career. But he had made his name and his money with musical comedies, and that ruled him out of the competition. An obituary published in *The Times* captures both the critics' disappointment with a composer who had been groomed to carry the musical hopes of his country and the idea of the prestige competition that informed this verdict. The article bemoaned that Sullivan

did not aim at consistently higher things, that he set himself to rival Offenbach and Lecocq instead of competing on a level of high seriousness . . . . If he had followed this path, he might have enrolled his name among the great composers of all time. He might have won a European reputation in addition to his fame at home. (qtd. in Hughes 116-17)

Apparently, commercial success gained the composer domestic popularity, but kept him out of the international pantheon. By the turn of the nineteenth century, Sullivan's versatility had become an untenable quality for a "serious" composer.

Compared with England, the US had even greater difficulties in qualifying for the musical prestige tournament, but made an effort nevertheless. The country was generally regarded as lacking in cultural refinement, and its concert scene up until World War I was dominated by German Romantic repertoire and

German musicians. Between 1890 and 1915, over sixty percent of all music performed by symphonies in the US was of German origin (Gienow-Hecht, "Trumpeting" 599).

German music was accepted as superior by Americans who cared. Urban elites in the East had financed conservatories and symphonic orchestras since the middle of the century, but initially with the belief that art music needed to be imported from Europe and Germany. So while influential figures like music critic John Sullivan Dwight lobbied for the acknowledgement and financial support of "sacred" music, they also castigated domestic composers for lacking "seriousness" (Levine 143; Davidson). Others eventually came to see the lack of homegrown art music as a cause for national embarrassment and took an important step toward a remedy when founding the National Conservatory of Music (initially American School of Opera) in New York in 1885, modeled on the Paris Conservatory and paid for by New York's wealthy elite (Ogasapian and Orr 73). In 1891, the conservatory hired Antonín Dvořák with a mandate to teach Americans how to create their own national music. In line with earlier initiatives by Thomas Wentworth Higginson and William Francis Allen, the Czech composer recommended that American music be based on domestic "folk" traditions, i.e. the music of native or African Americans. While there was some experimentation in that direction (Pisani), the attempt to create a national music from domestic folk styles took another half century to bear fruit, and it would not be Native American sounds that provided the basic ingredient for it.

Compared with the English Musical Renaissance, American attempts to create a national music remained a private affair; state authorities were not involved. Another difference is that commercially successful English composers had problems with the musical uplift campaign, whereas their American colleagues like George Whitfield Chadwick and Amy Marcy Cheney Beach had little to lose in terms of recognition and may have found it easier to follow the call for a national music (Ogasapian and Orr 67).

An Anglo-American comparison also reveals that in the US, white middle-class women often gained from an involvement in music. Women were not only among the prestige entrepreneurs; there were also female artist managers, indicating that the growing importance of art music in the US created career opportunities for women (Broyles 231). Finally, American women found that German concert music afforded them access to public spaces and opportunities to experiment with emotional display. The art music conventions gave female patrons the license to be overwhelmed by the passion of famed German musicians. They threw flowers with concealed personal messages on the stage and showed admiration in ways not entirely dissimilar to the behavior of later-day boy band fans, as historian Jessica Gienow-Hecht argues ("Trumpeting"; Newman 307-08).

The adulation from "matinee girls" was one of those forms of reception that ignored the conventions of art music and may remind us of Fitzcarraldo's transformative encounter with the Indios. Similar occurrences happened outside the Eastern cities, where touring musicians experienced audiences sometimes as mysterious, irritating, or even threatening. Familiar with minstrel troupes, provincial patrons expected European musicians to give a parade and a free open air concert and wondered why none of them painted their face black when performing. Concert-goers did not always find it necessary to dress up for the occasion, and instead of sitting silently and listen attentively as European audiences had learned to do, they stamped their feet and brought barking dogs. Listeners demanded that quiet passages be played louder so that they could be properly heard, showing no understanding for conductors who insisted on the "pianissimo" (Gienow-Hecht "Trumpeting"; *Sound Diplomacy*).

This cursory glance at the making of music into art and a marker of national identity shows that these processes resulted from local projects in which agents with different aims deployed music and its ideology as resources. In turn, different local constellations made for different power relations between musicians, critics, prestige entrepreneurs, and listeners within the respective nations. Due to the scope and integration of the transnational music trade and music journalism, national initiatives had repercussions abroad. They led to the establishment of an international framework for competition that gave small nations the chance to punch above their weight and put pressure on bigger countries to make an effort. The contest allowed contenders to excel on merit, but also created the risk of failing expectations. Finally, the rise of "serious" music stimulated the proliferation of concert halls, conservatories, and canons, creating institutional isomorphism (DiMaggio and Powell). As a consequence, critics around the world applied similar standards of excellence and encouraged composers and musicians to aspire to similar goals. Slowly but surely, audiences were guided to behave in similarly silent and predictable ways.

REVERSING DIRECTIONS, BUT STILL MOVING UP: COMPETITIONS IN JAZZ AND ROCK IN THE TWENTIETH CENTURY

Moving on to the twentieth century, we see striking similarities between the rise of classical music and the emergence of "valuable" popular genres. As in the case of classical music, the development started from adverse conditions, this time on the other side of the Atlantic. Before the 1890s, the US had been a net importer of music, including popular songs. The last decade of the century saw the emergence of a domestic popular music trade producing inexpensive sheet music mainly of soppy ballads. The emerging American popular music business owed its success to the new pop publishers' innovation of integrating the printing of sheet music with its promotion on the vaudeville stages and its sale in department stores (Suisman).

The popular repertoire was stylistically heterogeneous, did not claim to have artistic value and was mainly written and traded by poor recent immigrants from Central and Eastern Europe. Songs were either functional (dancing or marching) or topical (mother or disaster songs), and while part of the repertoire suggested ethnic specificity, the concept of popular music being "authentic" still had to be established. Performers were expected to be "versatile," not "real." "Negro," "Dutch," or "Chinese" acts were obviously masquerade, and no one thought of them as "fake." Just like the creolized operas of earlier years, popular music did not bind performers to a fixed identity. Neither did it make any pretension to be more than entertainment.

All this was beginning to change in the 1910s. As the makers of popular music strove for respectability, certain genres became more "valuable" than others, and the repertoire was differentiated along national and ethnic boundaries. To begin with, the recording industry introduced into commercial music what music historian Karl Hagstrom Miller calls the "folklore paradigm," matching sounds with ethnically and racially defined listeners. American and European gramophone companies had been trying to sell machines and records around the globe since the early days of the industry. Initially, they had advertised the gramophone as a serious music medium by associating it with "good" music. Like Fitzcarraldo, they were bringing art music to the musical periphery. Unlike the film character, however, they found that while classical music left their potential customers cold, these people could be interested in local music, recorded by traveling salesmen with mobile equipment. From the 1910s, American firms applied their insight from global promotion to the domestic market, pitching ethnically defined sounds to musically untrained listeners. In the process, they invented "authentic" popular music like blues or country (Miller).

Meanwhile, black musicians also capitalized on the perception that music was hardwired in ethnic identities and racialized bodies. Banned from most recording studios, shunned by musicians' unions and with only limited access to vaudeville theaters, black musicians concentrated on the labor market for dance music and used "authenticity" as an effective sales argument. In 1910, bandleader James Reese Europe founded the Clef Club of New York City as an employment agency for black musicians. The club not only provided potential customers an address to contact bands, but also showcased the skills of Clef Club members in concert, supporting the claim that black musicians had a special feel for dance rhythm. James Europe and his collaborators thereby reaffirmed the racist stereotype that African Americans were natural-born dance musicians in order to enhance their occupational status (Gilbert).

While the concept of "authenticity" got traction in popular music, songwriters strove to escape the short-termism of the song business and its relentless pressure to produce hit after hit. To this end, a number of songwriters shifted from vaudeville to Broadway theaters, which became possible as World War I halted the influx of European musical comedies and operettas. Some of these songwriters were also involved in the foundation of the American Society of Composers, Authors and Publishers (ASCAP) in 1914, a society that collected money from music users like radio stations and theaters and, by the late 1920s, enabled its more prominent members to bridge hit-less periods. Whereas before they had only received a one-time payment or a percentage from sheet music sales, songwriters now could receive additional performance royalties and thus consolidate their careers. This source of income became increasingly important, as sheet music sales declined and radio appeared as a new music medium. In its early years, ASCAP was fiercely attacked by music users as a monopoly. Both ASCAP's fight for legitimacy and Tin Pan Alley's move from Union Square up to Times Square reinforced the propensity of songwriters to strive for respectability (Ryan).

Irving Berlin exemplifies the upward mobility of the American music business. With impeccable timing, he wrote his first musical comedy in 1914 and was among the figureheads of ASCAP. The former singing waiter from the Lower East Side became part of the Algonquin circle of intellectuals and married the daughter of a wealthy industrialist. In 1925, Berlin's journalist friend Alexander Woolcott published the first biography of the songwriter, confirming the impression that Berlin, who never learned to play the piano in more than one key, needed to be taken seriously (Woolcott). At the same time, Berlin was also hailed as one of several "kings" of jazz, a musical genre whose practitioners tried to leave its lowly and tumultuous ragtime origins behind (Wald).

As popular musicians aspired to respectability, they also associated their product with the American nation. Irving Berlin, who received American citizenship and was drafted into the army in early 1918, made good use of his time with the military by producing the patriotic revue *Yip Yip Yaphank* (Magee 69-82). The affiliation of popular music with the nation also helped to wrestle syncopated dance music out of the hands of black musicians, because it substituted ethnic "roots" with American modernism. This future-oriented tradition provided the white denizens of Tin Pan Alley, many of them with a background of recent immigration, low-status occupation, and poverty, with an entry ticket into the American middle class.

While by the mid-1920s jazz had gained respectability, it was not yet considered art. As in the case of classical music in Germany, it took the blessing of music criticism to achieve that transformation. White proselytizers of "symphonic syncopation" like bandleader Paul Whiteman found radio and sound film a profitable environment while the music remained squarely commercial. Music journalists writing for new jazz periodicals like *Down Beat* took over the leadership of the musical uplift campaign in the 1930s and 1940s. They fought over the credibility of jazz, both in terms of its artistic value and its social ownership. A consensus was formulated in the 1950s by literary professor and jazz scholar Marshall Stearns, who skillfully navigated the threat of McCarthyism and the notoriety of substance-abusing be-boppers (Dunkel, "Marshall Winslow Stearns"). To further the status of jazz as art, he offered his services to the State Department, who in turn appointed him as a special consultant to accompany Dizzy Gillespie's band on a tour that the US government hoped would enhance America's image around the world (Eschen 33).

Long before state-sponsored bands won sympathies for themselves and, possibly, for the US, the transfer of jazz abroad after World War I had had transnational repercussions by stimulating its institutionalization outside the US. Initially, the term "jazz" was taken up rather freely in Continental Europe. In Germany, early adopters of the American moniker embellished their performance of frantic dance music with all sorts of gimmicks and stunts to capitalize on an existing expectation that American entertainment offered something spectacular and improvised that German musicians who rigorously stuck to their play lists could not muster. Just as American musicians in the nineteenth century had acquired German pseudonyms and honed German accents, German "jazz" musicians crafted their stage personas on a largely imaginary American model. Their bluff was called by the German musical establishment the moment the first American bands came to Germany in the mid-1920s. As Paul Whiteman and Sam Wooding introduced symphonic syncopation to Germany, the sophisticated style was embraced by those German musicians who had been upstaged by "fakers" and were now glad to see that "truly" American jazz required the skills of formally trained instrumentalists (Nathaus).

The transformation of jazz from cabaret to conservatory made rapid progress in Germany. Already in 1928, Hoch's Conservatory in Frankfurt offered a class in jazz. The further institutionalization was interrupted by Nazi authorities who pushed this allegedly "degenerate" music underground, including its critical reception (Kater). After World War II, jazz made a quick return, as dedicated jazz bandleaders and instrumentalists staffed the ensembles in the West German regional broadcasting stations (Scharlau and Witting-Nöthen). Music journalists with a penchant for jazz were given opportunities to promote their favored music, not least over the airwaves. Dietrich Schulz-Köhn ("Dr. Jazz") featured jazz music in his broadcasts for the NDR (North German Broadcasting) and the WDR (West German Broadcasting). In Munich, the Bayrischer Rundfunk (Bavarian Broadcasting) employed Hans Ger Huber, Jimmy Jungermann, and Werner Götze who aired jazz music and were, like Schulz-Köhn, active in the organization of local jazz clubs and the German Jazz Federation. The most prominent jazz critic was "jazz pope" Joachim-Ernst Berendt, who wrote and presented radio and television programs for the SWF (South-West Broadcasting) in Baden-Baden. He also published his influential *Jazzbuch* in 1952 and organized jazz concerts in Germany as well as abroad (Wright Hurley).

State-employed, politically-minded, and scholarly critics like Berendt and Stearns distinguished jazz from German schlager and rock 'n' roll, the commercially popular genres of the day. In this way, they opened up alternative sources of funding that allowed jazz to develop outside the marketplace. They helped define jazz as a universal musical language, a living tradition that grew from African American roots in all directions where it found liberal, tolerant, and democratic conditions. On that conceptual basis, the West German government eventually sent its own jazz representatives abroad (Dunkel "Jazz—Made in Germany").

Like in classical music, the transnational proliferation of promotional publications by jazz critics and the founding of conservatories and festivals made jazz canonic and academic. Again, we see the emergence of an international critical consensus that provided a framework for competition where late-coming nations could punch above their weight and pioneers could be challenged. The institutionalization of jazz did not lead to a homogenization of the music itself, as the stylistic diversity of jazz was constantly advanced by musicians. But it stabilized the rules of its reception and, by separating the expert from the indiscriminate listener, primarily addressed an educated middle-class (DeVeaux). Like classical music, artistic jazz silenced the audience, or, to be more precise, made it whoop and clap in the right moments.

The transformation of rock from rock 'n' roll into art followed the pattern set by the institutionalization of classical music and jazz. Before rock 'n' roll resonated with critics who established conventions and a canon, the initiative was first taken by musicians who prepared the ground for an international prestige competition. To cut a long story short (see Wald), the Beatles pioneered this uplift campaign as they used the leverage of their unexpected fame to forge a career that diverted from the usual pop band trajectory. They recorded their own material and took time to experiment with new studio technology. Like other early rock bands that followed them quickly, they left their cuddly appearance behind for uncompromising public personas that communicated artistic ingenuity. Rock bands experimented with longer and more complex songs, unusual instruments, new sounds, and meaningful lyrics, culminating in the progressive rock of Genesis and others in the late 1960s. In the course of this experimentation, musicians found allies in other, more established branches of the arts. Just like Zelter benefited from his friendship with Goethe and Irving Berlin from his involvement with New York intellectuals, rock bands substantiated their artistic aspirations by cultivating contacts with the art scene (Braun).

Most importantly, a music press in search of a new readership turned their attention to the beat bands soon after the Beatles' breakthrough in 1963/64. Among the first, Britain's *Melody Maker*, a jazz magazine with a dwindling circulation, covered the aspirational sounds on musical terms. It found aesthetic categories to assess emerging rock bands' achievements and separate the artistic wheat from the commercial chaff. Further journals followed, then books, so that by the end of the 1960s one could seriously study the genre (Lindberg et al.).

As in the case of classical music and jazz, rock proliferated not only as sound and performance but also as ideology. Music writers and journalists took care of the latter and used it to further their own professional and political goals. In West Germany, rock ideology was imported by young writers who based their status on their knowledge about the Anglo-American rock scene. A growing number of German publications on leading bands, canonical albums, and the history of the genre catered to an audience of better-educated, politically-minded, university-going, mostly male readers who went on to become the shapers of a new liberal-democratic Germany (Rumpf).

The position of German rock critics was stronger than that of domestic bands who, by conceptual default, lacked the "authenticity" of Anglo-American originals. This was beginning to change as British and American critics looking for something different and unique took notice of rock music coming from peripheral countries like Germany. Their discovery of so-called krautrock bands shows that national specificity was not exclusive, but compatible with rock as a universal institution. Occupying a privileged position, tastemaker-critics in the UK and the US opened up the field for contributions from outside the Anglo-American core (Simmeth). Journalists in countries at the periphery of rock music like Germany continued to reserve "authenticity" for British and American bands as it bolstered their authority. Krautrock bands had to negotiate this tension and found it advantageous to frame their contribution to the international rock repertoire in national terms. Kraftwerk's Ralf Hütter, for instance, clad his music in German clichés, especially when talking to foreign critics. In 1975, he told American music journalist Lester Bangs:

We cannot deny we are from Germany, because the German mentality, which is more advanced, will always be part of our behavior. We create out of the German language, the mother language, which is very mechanical, we use as the basic structure for our music. Also the machines, from the industries of Germany. (qtd. in Adelt 396)

Hütter's positioning of krautrock as the product of a German mentality presupposed an international critical institution, a "third party" that acknowledged national specificity in a global repertoire of rock. The fact that such statements were printed and taken seriously shows that this international institution was firmly in place by the mid-1970s.

While we see in the history of jazz and rock an older pattern of musical uplift reoccurring, musical diplomacy at the end of the twentieth century took a different turn. When in 2000 Germany hosted the World Exhibition "Expo," the government did not ask Kraftwerk, or a band with similar artistic standing, but rather the Scorpions to represent the country to the world. The band received official confirmation of the title "ambassadors of rock," which MTV had bestowed on them in the 1980s. Opening the event, they shared the stage with the Berlin Philharmonic and Jon Bon Jovi, members of the aristocracy of classical music and a US superstar of global pop-rock. The Scorpions' Expo performance can be regarded as indicative for a larger trend in which musicians became musical diplomats not because of their artistic reputation, but their world-wide popularity (see Bayles in this volume; Cooper). Apparently, there has been a shift in popular music diplomacy from art to celebrity at the end of the twentieth century, which would be worthwhile studying further at another occasion.

THE POWER OF MUSICAL PERFORMANCES AND INSTITUTIONS: A CONCLUSION

Looking at the history of classical music, jazz, and rock in Germany, Britain, and the US, this chapter has tried to show how these musical genres became arenas where nations competed for prestige. It has identified critics and prestige entrepreneurs as key actors in this development and the fear of inferiority as its major impulse. Moreover, it has pointed to the importance of musical institutions like conservatoires, critical journals, and aesthetic standards for the global prestige tournament.

As sociologist Motti Regev argues in view to pop-rock music and as this chapter confirms, these musical institutions amounted neither to cultural imperialism nor were they rendered ineffective through their creative appropriation by recipients in the countries into which culture was imported. Instead, their proliferation resulted in "expressive isomorphism," which Regev defines as "the process through which expressive cultural uniqueness is constructed by adopting, adapting, adjusting, incorporating, and legitimating creative technologies, stylistic elements, genres, and forms of art derived from world models" (Regev 11). This process can be illustrated with our Amazonian metaphor: At first, the imperialist Fitzcarraldo fails to economically and culturally colonize the natives, as the Indios incorporate his technology seamlessly into their own mythology. But the story does not end with the Indios having the last laugh, because the steamer really does transport them into the future, for better or worse. They arrive in Iquitos, the bridgehead of the Western colonizers, where they look skeptically at the champagne offered to them by a rubber baron. Continuing the fictional story of *Fitzcarraldo* with factual events, the Indios seem to have adapted quickly to their new environment. By 1938, the Peruvian National Symphony Orchestra premiered at the Teatro Municipal de Lima, conducted by the Austrian Theodor Buchwald. The ensemble performed European classics, but also promoted the work of domestic composers, constructing, as Regev put it, "cultural uniqueness with elements from world models." For both Fitzcarraldo and the Indios, stepping on the ship and cutting it loose was fateful. It bound them to the same institutions, making them produce uniqueness and compete in the same tournament.

This view on musical institutionalization implies an answer to the question of musical diplomacy's efficacy. Sociologist Tia DeNora usefully describes music as an "affordance structure" that enables performers and listeners to "get things done" (DeNora 44). In this view, the transformative potency of music is not to be found in "the music itself," but in the framing of its performance. Under certain circumstances, music can afford people to do extraordinary things. In the present chapter, we saw American "matinee girls" using music to expand the boundaries of their social world as they took license to get emotionally carried away. Faux Americans were jazzing the cabarets in early 1920s Germany. Four Liverpuddlians were taking the world by storm. Such deployment of music was made possible by an incongruousness of expectations among performers and audiences that rendered encounters open and unpredictable. The ossification of conventions in the course of music genres' institutionalization made these transformative moments less likely. One could argue that it is this very predictability rather than the transformative potential that made certain music attractive to musical diplomats, whose profession requires them to minimize as much as possible any imponderables when orchestrating international dialogue. But one may also regard it a pity that classical music, jazz, and rock so seldom now lend themselves to taming river demons and reaching a better future.

WORKS CITED

Adelt, Ulrich. "Machines with a Heart: German Identity in the Music of Can and Kraftwerk." *Popular Music and Society* 35.3 (2012): 359-74. Print.

Applegate, Celia. *Bach in Berlin: Nation and Culture in Mendelssohn's Revival of the "St. Matthew Passion."* Ithaca, NY: Cornell UP, 2005. Print.

---. "How German Is It? Nationalism and the Idea of Serious Music in the Early Nineteenth Century." *19th-Century Music* 21.3 (1998): 274-96. Print.

Blanning, Tim. *The Triumph of Music: The Rise of Composers, Musicians and Their Art*. Cambridge, MA: Belknap, 2008. Print.

Boorman, Stanley, Eleanor Selfridge-Field, and Donald W. Kummel. "Printing and Publishing of Music." *New Grove Dictionary of Music and Musicians*. Ed. Stanley Sadie. 2nd ed. vol. 20. London: Macmillan, 2001. 326-81. Print.

Braun, Anna. "Where Was Pop? Die Robert Fraser Gallery zwischen Popmusik und bildender Kunst in 'Swinging London.'" *Popgeschichte: Band 2: Zeithistorische Fallstudien 1958-1988*. Ed. Bodo Mrozek, Alexa Geisthövel, and Jürgen Danyel. Bielefeld: transcript, 2014. 65-88. Print.

Broyles, Michael. "Art Music from 1860 to 1920." *The Cambridge History of American Music*. Ed. David Nicholls. Cambridge: Cambridge UP, 1998. 214-54. Print.

Cohen, H. Robert. "On the Dissemination of Information about Music in Nineteenth-Century Europe: An Introduction to the Session." *Revista de Musicología* 16.3 (1993): 1619-26. Print.

Cooper, Andrew F. *Celebrity Diplomacy*. Boulder: Paradigm, 2008. Print.

Davidson, Mary Wallace. "John Sullivan Dwight and the Harvard Musical Association Orchestra: A Help or a Hindrance?" *American Orchestras in the Nineteenth Century*. Ed. John Spitzer. Chicago, IL: U of Chicago P, 2012. 248-68. Print.

De Grazia, Victoria. *Irresistible Empire: America's Advance through 20th Century Europe*. Cambridge, MA: Harvard UP, 2005. Print.

DeNora, Tia. *After Adorno: Rethinking Music Sociology*. Cambridge: Cambridge UP, 2003. Print.

DeVeaux, Scott. "Who Listens to Jazz?" *Keeping Time: Readings in Jazz History*. Ed. Robert Walser. 2nd ed. New York: Oxford UP, 2015. 313-18. Print.

DiMaggio, Paul J., and Walter Powell. "The iron cage revisited: Institutional Isomorphism and Collective Rationality in Organizational Fields." *American Sociological Review* 48 (1983): 147-60. Print.

Dunkel, Mario. "'Jazz—Made in Germany' and the Transatlantic Beginnings of Jazz Diplomacy." *Music and Diplomacy from the Early Modern Era to the Present*. Ed. Rebekah Ahrendt, Mark Ferraguto, and Damien Mahiet. New York: Palgrave Macmillan, 2014. 147-68. Print.

---. "Marshall Winslow Stearns and the Politics of Jazz Historiography." *American Music* 30.4 (2012): 468-504. Print.

Eschen, Penny M. von. *Satchmo Blows up the World: Jazz Ambassadors Play the Cold War*. Cambridge, MA: Harvard UP, 2004. Print.

Fosler-Lussier, Danielle. *Music in America's Cold War Diplomacy*. Berkeley: U of California P, 2015. Print.

Gienow-Hecht, Jessica C. E. "Sonic History, or Why Music Matters in International History." *Music and International History in the Twentieth Century*. Ed. Jessica C. E. Gienow-Hecht. New York: Berghahn, 2015. 1-30. Print.

---. *Sound Diplomacy: Music and Emotions in Transatlantic Relations, 1850-1920*. Chicago, IL: Chicago UP, 2009. Print.

---. "Trumpeting Down the Walls of Jericho: The Politics of Art, Music and Emotion in German-American Relations, 1870-1920." *Journal of Social History* 3.3 (2003): 585-613. Print.

Gilbert, David. *The Product of Our Souls: Ragtime, Race, and the Birth of the Manhattan Musical Marketplace*. Chapel Hill, NC: U of North Carolina P, 2015. Print.

Hughes, Meirion. *The English Musical Renaissance and the Press 1850-1914: Watchmen of Music*. Aldershot: Ashgate, 2002. Print.

Hurley, Andrew Wright. *The Return of Jazz: Joachim-Ernst Berendt and West German Cultural Change*. New York: Berghahn, 2009. Print.

Jackson, Jeffrey H. *Making Jazz French: Music and Modern Life in Interwar Paris*. Durham, NC: Duke UP, 2003. Print.

Kater, Michael H. *Gewagtes Spiel: Jazz im Nationalsozialismus*. Köln: Kiepenheuer & Witsch, 1995. Print.

Levine, Lawrence W. *Highbrow / Lowbrow: The Emergence of Cultural Hierarchy in America*. Cambridge, MA: Harvard UP, 1988. Print.

Lindberg, Ulf, et al. *Rock-Criticism from the Beginning: Amusers, Bruisers, Cool-Headed Cruisers*. New York: Peter Lang, 2005. Print.

Maase, Kaspar. *BRAVO Amerika: Erkundungen zur Jugendkultur der Bundesrepublik in den fünfziger Jahren*. Hamburg: Junius, 1992. Print.

Magee, Jeffrey. *Irving Berlin's American Musical Theatre*. New York: OUP, 2012. Print.

Malchow, Howard L. *Special Relations: The Americanization of Britain?* Stanford, CA: Stanford UP, 2011. Print.

Miller, Karl Hagstrom. *Segregating Sound: Inventing Folk and Pop Music in the Age of Jim Crow*. Durham, NC: Duke UP, 2010. Print.

Nathaus, Klaus. "Popular Music in Germany, 1900-1930: A Case of Americanisation? Uncovering a European Trajectory of Music Production into the 20th Century." *European Review of History* 20.5 (2013): 755-76. Print.

Newman, Nancy, and John Spitzer. "Gender and the Germanians: 'Art-Loving Ladies' in Nineteenth-Century Concert Life." *American Orchestras in the Nineteenth Century*. Ed. John Spitzer. Chicago, IL: U of Chicago P, 2012. 290-310. Print.

Notaker, Hallvard, Giles Scott-Smith, and David J. Synder. "Introduction: Reasserting America in the 1970s." *Reasserting America in the 1970s: US Public Diplomacy and the Rebuilding of America's Image Abroad*. Ed. Idem. Manchester: Manchester UP, 2016. 1-7. Print.

Ogasapian, John, and N. Lee Orr. *Music of the Gilded Age: American History through Music*. Westport, CN: Greenwood Press, 2007. Print.

Osterhammel, Jürgen. "Globale Horizonte europäischer Kunstmusik, 1860-1930." *Geschichte und Gesellschaft* 38 (2012): 86-132. Print.

Pisani, Michael V. *Imagining Native America in Music*. New Haven: Yale UP, 2005. Print.

Poiger, Uta G. *Jazz, Rock, and Rebels: Cold War Politics and American Culture in a Divided Germany*. Berkeley: U of California P, 2000. Print.

Regev, Motti. *Pop-Rock Music: Aesthetic Cosmopolitanism in Late Modernity*. London: Polity, 2013. Print.

Rumpf, Wolfgang. *Pop & Kritik: Medien und Popkultur. Rock 'n' Roll, Beat, Rock, Punk. Elvis Presley, Beatles/Stones, Queen/Sex Pistols in Spiegel, Stern & Sounds*. Münster: LIT, 2004. Print.

Ryan, John. *The Production of Culture Perspective in the Music Industry: The ASCAP-BMI Controversy*. Lanham: UP of America, 1985. Print.

Scharlau, Ulf, and Petra Witting-Nöthen. *"Wenn die Jazzband spielt...": Von Schlager, Swing und Operette: Zur Geschichte der Leichten Musik im deutschen Rundfunk*. Berlin: Springer, 2006. Print.

Simmeth, Alexander. *Krautrock transnational: Die Neuerfindung der Popmusik in der BRD, 1968-1978*. Bielefeld: transcript, 2016. Print.

Sorba, Carlotta. "Between Cosmopolitanism and Nationhood: Italian Opera in the Early Nineteenth Century." *Modern Italy* 19.1 (2014): 53-67. Print.

Suisman, David. *Selling Sounds: The Commercial Revolution in American Music*. Cambridge, MA: Harvard UP, 2009. Print.

Stradling, Robert, and Meirion Hughes. *The English Musical Renaissance 1860-1940: Construction and Deconstruction*. London: Routledge, 1993. Print.

Wald, Elijah. *How the Beatles Destroyed Rock 'n' Roll: An Alternative History of American Popular Music*. New York: Oxford UP, 2009. Print.

Weber, William. *The Great Transformation of Musical Taste: Concert Programming from Haydn to Brahms*. New York: Cambridge UP, 2008. Print.

Werron, Tobias. "On Public Forms of Competition." *Cultural Studies – Critical Methodologies* 14.1 (2014): 62-76. Print.

Woolcott, Alexander. *The Story of Irving Berlin*. New York: Putnam, 1925. Print.

The Paradoxes of Cultural and Music Diplomacy in a Federal Country
A Case Study from Flanders, Belgium

Alessandro Mazzola

In Belgium, similarly to other federal systems, cultural diplomacy is not only aimed at representing the country in the international arena. It also plays a key role in the cultural, political, and economic relations between subnational entities, as well as between them and the central state (Michelmann). The different shapes and contents of Belgian cultural diplomacy, indeed, can be observed as the result of cooperation and arrangements to ensure the coherence of the country's foreign policy. Nevertheless, cultural diplomacy is also strongly affected by the competition over material resources and over the space for subnational identity representation undertaken by the country's federated communities. In the case of Belgium, in other words, cultural diplomacy reflects the issues and claims involved in the conflict existing between its major language communities, the Flemish Dutch-speaking group in the north, and the French-speaking group in the south.

As a response to the political mobilization of different language groups, Belgium's institutional setting has given a high degree of autonomy to its constituent units. The country's federalization that started in 1970 has established political regions and cultural communities endowed with exclusive jurisdiction over a number of both space- and person-related matters, including the elaboration and implementation of cultural policies. In spite of this, claims for greater sub-national autonomy continue to characterize the country's contemporary politics and, in particular, the political debate in Flanders, the country's Dutch-speaking northern region. In this context, so-called Flemish nationalists articulate a hierarchical representation of the country's regional groups based on a utilitarian vision of the economic achievements, greater development, and institutional efficiency of Flanders (Huysseune). Not surprisingly, the representation of Flanders's wealthier economy and good governance, together with a generalized will for internationalization, are key themes in the ideology and discourse of the Nieuw-Vlaamse Alliantie (N-VA), the Flemish nationalist party that scored its most recent electoral success in the 2014 federal elections, becoming the largest party in the country and reawakening the historical conflict between the French and Flemish language communities (De Wever and Kesteloot).

In such a situation, we can observe several complications for a coherent national-Belgian approach towards cultural diplomacy. The purpose of this chapter is to analyze one example of Flemish cultural diplomacy in the context of federal Belgium, and to highlight its form as a practice that both interacts with the pressures coming from Flemish nationalistic discourses and, at the same time, exists as a direct consequence of the country's federal organization.

The role of culture in the genesis and evolution of the conflict characterizing Belgium has been deeply observed and analyzed in academic literature (Martiniello, "Culturalisation"; Blommaert). Language and ethnicity, in particular, represent key elements in the study of the Belgian case and of its different separatist trends including the forms of Flemish nationalism. Indeed, observers have highlighted strong culturalizations and ethnicizations of the Belgian domestic conflict that, mostly in non-violent form, have involved many different aspects of the sociocultural history and life of the federal state (Martiniello, "Culturalisation"; Blommaert). Nowadays, culture seems to be relegated to a marginal dimension, since political and economic elements have taken priority in the public debate. The aim of this paper is to reconsider the role of culture as an element that, based on a utilitarian vision, has great relevance in the debate as it can evoke ideas, principles, and attitudes involved in the competition and conflict between Belgium's federated entities today.

To this end, I will focus on cultural diplomacy. The specific use of culture made by institutions in a context like Belgium emerges as a means to produce and share forms of competition and the hierarchical representation of the federal state's different political components. More specifically, my hypothesis is that cultural diplomacy in Flanders can be observed as producing discourses on the region's economic development and structural efficiency. My chapter focuses on one specific case of cultural diplomacy concerning music as a cultural form, namely Antwerp's conservatory and international art campus deSingel. More specifically, I will analyze documentary sources pertaining to deSingel's official policy plan *Beleidsplan 2011-2015* (DeSingel Internationale Kunstcampus) which includes detailed information on international activities and networks. The chapter is also based on non-documentary sources including two in-depth interviews. The first interview was conducted with deSingel's general and artistic manager Jerry Aerts. The second interviewee was Jan Peumans, leading member of the nationalist and conservative Flemish party New Flemish Alliance (N-VA) and President of the Flemish Parliament.

It is also important to remark that my analysis will focus on the organizational, structural, and financial aspects of deSingel's music diplomacy rather than on purely musical dimensions, and on the ways these different dimensions are articulated within international and Belgian contexts. It is arguable that the research findings presented here are not only specific to music, and for this reason I will often employ the term cultural diplomacy instead of the more specific music diplomacy. I understand cultural diplomacy as a sector of public interest and policy action that is larger than music diplomacy. Nevertheless, deSingel is mainly recognized as a music institution, and the cases analyzed and examples provided in this chapter concern only cultural diplomacy projects involving music.

There are several reasons for selecting deSingel as a representative case study. First, the institution is one of the most important actors in the country's and Europe's cultural landscape, as well as one of the most strongly supported by public funds in the Flemish community. Secondly, deSingel is located in Antwerp, the largest city in Flanders and contemporary metropolitan stronghold of the Flemish nationalist party Nieuw-Vlaamse Alliantie (N-VA).[1] Last but not less important, deSingel has great symbolic relevance in the language conflict for its history. It is a direct descendant of the Royal Conservatory of Antwerp founded in 1898 as the first full Dutch-language institute for art education in Belgium, an iconic place in the evolution of the historical antagonism between French-speaking elites and Dutch-speaking populations in the country. Nowadays, as I will explain, this institution, perhaps more than any other, meets the guiding principles of integration and internationalization that inform contemporary Flemish cultural policy.

---

[1] Significantly, the leader of N-VA Bart De Wever has also served as mayor of Antwerp since January 2013.

INSTITUTIONAL AND POLICY CONTEXT: CULTURAL DIPLOMACY AS A REGIONAL TASK

Belgium is a federal country whose institutional and policy structures are based on the right of self-determination of the French and Flemish language groups considered to be constitutive elements of the nation (Martiniello, "Sortir" 71). Since the 1970s, a step-by-step process of institutional reform was implemented with the aim of pacifying the long-lasting conflict opposing the political elites of the two major language groups: The francophones in Wallonia and the néderlandophones in Flanders. The Flemish/francophone divide, indeed, is the central axis around which three political regions (Flanders, Wallonia and the Brussels-capital region) and cultural communities (Flemish, French-speaking, and a small German-speaking community, which has no actual role in the conflict) have been established (Jacobs 4). The federal reforms were implemented on the principle of a multicultural state and aimed to delegate powers from the central state to subnational entities defined by language. However, the historical divide (so-called Community Cleavage) and the related claims for greater autonomy characterizing the two largest language communities have not ceased. Rather, in the last decades they have emerged with great strength within the Flemish political landscape in particular. This state of things occurred for essentially two political and economic reasons: The territorialization of national politics (with all the most important party families splitting into Flemish and French-speaking parties) and the emergence of Flanders as one of Europe's richest regions (Blommaert).

The federalization of political-institutional structures has determined a major upheaval in the political representation and governance of Flemish and francophone parties, with all the country's political families—the Christian-Democrat, the Socialist and the Liberal—splitting into Dutch- and French-speaking parties. As a consequence, problems of negotiation, cooperation, political legitimacy and stability come out each time a new executive has to be formed, dramatically shown by the 2010-2011 crisis when cabinet negotiations took a record time of 353 days before a new democratic government could be formed. The split of party families led political analysts to criticize the process of federal reform and to question its effectiveness as a solution for a conflict that, largely in non-violent forms, continues to characterize Belgium to the extent that it can be considered as a "federalism of disunion" (Martiniello, "Immigrant Integration" 120). Furthermore, in the last two decades the Community Cleavage has increasingly featured questions of economic efficiency and good-versus-bad governance. A process of rapid development started after World War II allowed Flanders to take over the center of economic power from the formerly dominant Wallonia's industrial centers (Witte et al.). Nowadays, differences in economic performance, employment rate, and structural efficiency have increased the territorial dualism between the two regions. Flanders and Wallonia are often represented in antagonistic terms in the political debate. Flemish nationalists, in particular, managed to dominate the debate and achieve electoral success from 2007 onwards, during the global financial crisis, claiming for a further separation of socio-economic matters including social benefits, welfare, and the social security system.

It is on these premises that Flemish cultural diplomacy can be regarded as a political instrument which functions beyond the tasks of representing the region in the international arena. Apart from ideological and political conflict, specific organizations and the structures of the federal system itself greatly influence cultural diplomacy. In Belgium, cultural communities have exclusive jurisdiction over so-called 'person-related matters' including public policy-making with regard to art and culture-related activities. They operate within the limits of their own language territory except for the French and Dutch-speaking bilingual region of Brussels in which the Flemish and Francophone communities share jurisdiction. Cultural diplomacy is one of the initiatives in which language communities have a high degree of autonomy. In fact, the federal government does not have competences since the *in foro interno, in foro externo* principle introduced by a constitutional reform in 1988 guarantees the right for sub-state entities to manage the foreign policy concerning those matters for which they are granted domestic autonomy. Significantly, there is no cabinet position responsible for culture-related matters in the federal government (Craenen). Although the communities are invited to cooperate under the coordinating role of the federal government, Belgian foreign policy is not always granted concrete institutional coherence with regard to the directions to take and actions to implement in matters pertaining to cultural diplomacy. Since the federal reform of 1993, the communities have enjoyed self-government with regard to international relations, and cultural policies are governed by the principle of subsidiarity according to which the government's role is limited to general regulations and subsidies to non-governmental associations. Since then, and alongside the principle of democratic access that characterized the public approach towards culture and the arts, a business-oriented approach based on long-term policy planning has emerged in Flanders.

A generalized fascination for a utilitarian vision of culture as a means to promote local development, as well as the specific attention towards its business-related values, are not exclusive characteristics in the Flemish or Belgian contexts. They are common features of the approach towards cultural policies and diplomacy taken by both national and sub-national entities all around Europe. In Belgium, however, the cause-and-effect relationship between the tensions in the federal system and the local, municipal, and regional policy-making level is particularly evident. Economic inequalities are the basis of separatist claims voiced by Flemish nationalists, since pro-federalist positions within this political tradition seem to have been less dominant in the last years than during the era of state reforms. A harsh debate concerns the question of social security transfers between regions and, more generally, the gap between the richer Flanders and the poorer Wallonia. This debate revolves around the regional development paradigm that identifies Europe's wealthiest regions as endowed with particular sociocultural characteristics that foster development (Keating et al.). In Belgium, in both the regional and national public discourses, reference is often made to particular sociocultural specificities and endogenous virtues to explain Flanders's economic success (Huysseune).

In this context, Flemish cultural diplomacy shifts from the principles of cooperation to competition as it goes along with the trends and directions of the sub-national political environment increasingly dominated by Flemish nationalist trends. As a form of soft power aimed at attracting foreign audiences and institutions (Nye), it reflects the region's dominant political imperatives. Nowadays, a particular symbolic geography of a richer and more efficient Flanders versus a poorer and less efficient Wallonia seems to have an influence on the forms and contents of cultural diplomacy in Belgium.

POLITICAL CONTEXT: FLEMISH NATIONALISM

An analysis of the specific development of Flemish nationalism throughout the evolution of Belgian politics would exceed the purpose of this chapter. Nevertheless, it is important to briefly outline the evolution of Flemish nationalism and to highlight its contemporary ideological features as they affect the context and dynamics of the case study presented here. Flemish nationalism has been an established component of Belgian institutional politics since the interwar period. It is grounded in the ideology of the nineteenth-century Flemish Movement that was created to support social and cultural emancipation of non-Francophone populations at a time when Belgium was dominated by French-speaking elites. In the years before and after the Second World War, two forms of Flemish nationalism, one moderate and another more radical, emerged in the Belgian political landscape. These ideological trends have been translated into formal political parties and have influenced institutional politics up to the late 2000s: on one side the moderate-nationalist and pro-federalist party Volksunie (VU) established in 1954; on the other, the far-right and ethno-nationalist party Vlaams Blok/Belang (VB), born from the radical-separatist wing that split from the VU in 1978.

Seen as a direct expression of the traditional language-related struggle, VU was characterized by an idea of culture articulated within the claim for the emancipation of Dutch-speaking people and, by extension, as a means to pursue democratization. In the era of federal reforms from the 1970s to the early 2000s, VU aligned with the pro-federalist and pro-Belgium approach of the rest of the Flemish political groups, an attitude that represented the ground on which legislation concerning local and international cultural policy was thought and implemented. On the other side, the approach of VB was (and still is) framed within the traditional ethno-nationalist desire for congruence within the nation, in this specific case an independent Flemish nation, and a culturally homogeneous people. The making of a Flemish independent community and the protection of this community against external influences, even by rejecting culturally different people, are key issues that direct the party's rhetoric towards racism and xenophobia still today. Interestingly, the party has often prioritized its connection to the Netherlands and other Dutch-speaking countries, while being radically opposed to European integration (for a national and international analysis of VB see Swyngedouw; Jamin).

The bipolar nature of Flemish nationalism entails two completely different approaches towards cultural diplomacy as either an element to represent or share specific political ideas or as a concrete policy tool. Since the constitutional reform of 1993 that ratified the communitarization of foreign relations, the shape of international cultural policy and cultural diplomacy has partially reflected the twofold attitude of Flemish nationalism. In general terms, Belgian communities have been active in promoting a 'Europe of the Regions' and representing local specificities and interests (Massart-Piérard). The language communities of Belgium tended to establish strong relationships with neighboring countries speaking the same language. Flanders, in particular, developed its own policies in the longstanding international network called Nederlandse Taalunie (Dutch Language Union), the union of Dutch-speaking countries that includes Holland as well as Suriname and South Africa (Bursens and Massart-Piérard 96). Besides the principle of language affinity, Flanders's international cultural policy focused on an identity-building project aimed at promoting the region's cultural peculiarities. A series of historical and newly established agencies including cultural organizations, schools and concert halls were presented as cultural ambassadors tasked with implementing cooperative projects with partners worldwide. Special subsidies were granted to international activities in line with this strategy.

In the early 2000s, with the process of federalization being completed, VU fell apart and left space for the separatist extreme-right to represent the main ideological profile of Flemish nationalism. The political representation of VB has been limited, however, as the other Flemish parties agreed not to cooperate with the extreme-right and to contain the party in a so-called *cordon sanitaire* (buffer zone). In the same period, a new Flemish nationalist party emerged in the landscape of Belgian politics: the Nieuw-Vlaamse Alliantie (N-VA). Although the party's main aim is to achieve independence for Flanders, N-VA has reformulated this imperative in a contemporary diplomatic, pragmatic, and pro-European setting as they wish to establish an independent Flemish republic within the European Union and the international political arena. The party has effectively differentiated itself from the radical image of nationalism represented by VB. N-VA describes its goal as a democratic project that has nothing to do with radicalism, but that concerns questions of economic and structural efficiency as well as ethic and civic values (Maly). While VU and VB, for different reasons, never achieved large electoral success, N-VA gradually affirmed itself as a mainstream party with a large electorate, becoming the country's largest party in the 2010 federal elections.

The rise of N-VA in the regional and national political scene, and the generalized support for neoliberal and austerity policies in both language communities, highlighted a pragmatic attitude towards cultural diplomacy in the whole of Belgian politics. Nowadays, N-VA's policy approach aims particularly to the reduction of public spending as well as to the optimization of the institutional and government structure. Concerning the segment of cultural policy, one example of the influence of this institutional pragmatic approach is the so-called Arts Decree implemented in 2004 and amended in 2008. The Arts Decree represents the main instrument for cultural actors to access public funding for both national and international cultural activities. It provides two- and four-year funding for organizations and projects concerning cultural activities, arts education, and culture-related initiatives. Support for international initiatives can be obtained by organizations that propose activities incorporated within larger projects. Concerning the optimization of institutional and policy structures, a set of institutions has been selected and given the status of official cultural institutions of the Flemish Community and have been identified as main international actors. These institutions can rely on greater support from the regional government.

DESINGEL IN FLANDERS AND EUROPE: AN EXAMPLE OF FLEMISH CULTURAL DIPLOMACY IN THE AGE OF N-VA

As outlined above, the Flemish cultural sector is marked by the presence of main cultural actors selected as official institutions of the respective communities. The Antwerp-based international arts campus deSingel acquired the status of official cultural institution in 2004. It integrates a variety of culture-related activities covering different domains such as music, dance, theater, the performing arts, and architecture. It is a major public actor in the Belgian music landscape for activities ranging from music education to production and promotion. In addition, it is one of the country's most renowned venues for chamber, jazz, and experimental music. Established in a large campus in the periphery of Antwerp, deSingel's activities take place in a one-thousand-seat concert hall, an eight-hundred-seat theater, various music and theater studios, an exhibition area, a reading room, and a café.

According to the Arts Decree, deSingel's official recognition as a community institution does not entail, in itself, direct access to public funding. Like any other non-governmental association, institution or actor, deSingel is called to submit its own plans in order to find public support for its activities. However, its large-scale infrastructure, multi-profile activities, and leading position in the Flemish cultural landscape facilitate access to subsidies. In this regard, President of the Flemish Parliament Jan Peumans states:

It is obvious that such a large and active institution, a crown jewel in the Flemish creative and cultural sector, should rely on public subsidies. If you look at all the activities they provide, from education to entertainment, the public investment is no doubt compensated.[2]

Accordingly, deSingel is largely subsidized by the public sector with about seven million Euros from the Flemish Community, plus a few hundred thousand Euros from the Province and the City of Antwerp, to cover almost nine million Euros of annual total costs (see table 1).

---

2 "C'est évident qu'une institution aussi grande et active, un fleuron dans le secteur créatif et culturel flamand, devrait compter sur des subventions publiques. Si vous regardez toutes les activités qu'ils font, de l'éducation au loisir, l'investissement public est sans doute compensé."

Table 1: Overview over DeSingel's Income (2011-2015).

deSingel 2011 income projected onto the years 2012 up to and including 2015 (source: Beleidsplan 2011-2015)

	2011	2012	2013	2014	2015
	€1.024.500	€1.045.000	€1.066.000	€1.087.000	€1.109.000
Flemish Community	€6.910.000	€7.031.000	€7.154.000	€7.279.000	€7.406.000
Province of Antwerp	€200.000	€204.000	€208.000	€212.000	€216.000
City of Antwerp	€150.000	€153.000	€156.000	€159.000	€162.000
Sponsoring	€100.000	€100.000	€100.000	€100.000	€100.000
Other	€530.000	€541.000	€552.000	€563.000	€574.000
	€8.914.500	€9.074.000	€9.236.000	€9.400.000	€9.567.000

Source: Beleidsplan 2011-2015.

As a consequence, a clear commitment to the interests of the region lies at the core of deSingel's official mission to be the beacon of Flemish arts in the international cultural scene. For example, in the official 2011-2015 policy plan, the international dimension of deSingel was clearly highlighted as a fundamental form of contribution to regional development:

for major performing artists from abroad deSingel provides a quality venue of very high standard, and via the arts campus Flemish artists with international potential are sent out to all the most important venues abroad. . . . We are convinced that with this scheme we can make a major contribution to Flanders, which has a lively cultural community that plays an active part in the intense international arts scene. (DeSingel 10)

The idea of arts production as a form of cultural capital to be safeguarded and enriched through contacts and exchanges with local and foreign partners is integral to the intention of acting on an international dimension. The policy plan states: "We shall continue our main task of stimulating and presenting international arts production. In this way we safeguard our capital and remain a leading player on the international art scene" (DeSingel 22).

In fact, deSingel acts on a twofold territorial dimension since it works as a community institution in collaboration with Flemish cultural actors, but also as a main agency in international networks. On one hand, it regularly consults with partners in Flanders and Brussels in order to avoid direct competition, preserving the complementarity of cultural offers and setting up co-productions and joint initiatives. This point is highlighted in the policy plan in the following terms: "in no way is it our intention to compete with other Flemish Community institutions. On the contrary. Together with other institutions, and with an eye to cooperation, we have set up a joint consultative body" (DeSingel 108).

On the other hand, deSingel is one of the country's most active institutions in music diplomacy, collaborating closely with international partners in bordering and neighboring countries such as France, Holland, England, Germany, and Luxembourg. One example of collaboration within and outside the Flemish community is the biennial music festival Opera XXI, coproduced in Flanders by deSingel, the Vlaamse Opera and the Muziektheater Transparant of Antwerp. Characterizing the organization of the event, deSingel's general manager Jerry Aerts asserts:

Working with Flemish institutions is a priority for us. We want to stimulate and inspire other institutions as they represent the same cultural capital that we aim at opening and enriching. Opera XXI is a good occasion for achieving these tasks because it is in this kind of activities that we can bring our experience and structural organization into play. (Aerts)

In addition to Flemish organizations, several institutions from neighboring countries, such as the Dutch Operadagen Rotterdam and the French Centre National de Création Musicale de Lyon GRAME, participate in Opera XXI. The way this itinerant event is exported to third countries and organized in international venues is particularly paradigmatic of the way deSingel understands its representative role in the international arena. In this respect, Aerts discusses the edition hosted by the Italian Teatro Comunale di Bologna in April 2014:

[Opera XXI] is an example of how we do international activities. For instance, lately we have brought the festival to Bologna and produced an amazing play written and directed by Andrea Molino and Giorgio Van Straten, two Italian renowned composers who worked with Flemish professionals for the occasion. It has been a sort of revolution for the Italians as Opera XXI has been thought to bring pop music and styles into the classical frame of the theater. But what we provided, apart from the artistic direction, is structural guidance. We made our structural organization available to local organizers and, of course, we put the money. . . . It was totally impossible for the Theater of Bologna to organize and support the festival on their own. (Aerts)

The purpose of Opera XXI seems not only to be the representation of Flanders through musical and artistic exchange itself, but also to promote the institution's structural and organizational qualities. What this form of music diplomacy seeks to showcase, to Italian audiences in this particular case, are the institutional ideas and mechanisms of the Belgian region's cultural sector, rather than the contents and forms of its art and culture. In other words, the need to attract audiences is pursued through the representation and amplification of a production system rather than of the productions themselves.

If the process of Flemish identity building in the era of federal reforms revolved around the representation of local Flemish art forms and traditional cultural values, today these elements are no longer at the center of international projects. The Flemish community does not support and implement cultural diplomacy initiatives with the sole aim of showcasing its cultural values and identity through the arts and cultural production. Rather, supporting music but also dance, theater or any other art form in the international arena is a means for Flanders to spotlight its level of structural development and organizational capability. This approach can be seen as a reflection of the regional development paradigm that, as mentioned above, dominates the political debate both regionally and nationally. DeSingel director Aerts is explicit in this sense:

A small region in Europe; that is what we are. In the era of globalization we cannot rely on showing our traditional arts or cultural excellence which, certainly, we are proud of. And we are a Dutch-speaking region, not really a widespread language. That is why we prefer to export our know-how, our way to do the things rather than 'the things' themselves. . . . It is undeniable that the education system in our region, for example, is more developed. It simply works well. We have been able to transmit this level of efficiency to music education, and want to show how and why to our partners. That is how we attempt to reinforce the position of Flanders in the international scene. (Aerts)

It is quite clear that this quote reflects a utilitarian vision of the Flemish cultural sector, a vision relying on the idealization of principles such as economic development, system stability, and institutional efficiency. Aerts's words also convey a specific ethnocentric perspective depicting the Flemish way of operating in the cultural industry as a successful model to follow, without questioning the historical circumstances or the structural and economic conditions that led to the region's performance and level of development.

DESINGEL IN BELGIUM AND WALLONIA

As already highlighted, deSingel was recognized as an official institution of the Flemish community in 2004 and, from then on, it has emerged as a main actor in the representation of Flanders in Belgium and beyond. However, its domestic policy is apparently free from any particular obligation to serve exclusive community interests. Interestingly, concerrning deSingel's policies for music education and support, Aerts states:

We have students from everywhere. Of about 580 students attending our courses, forty percent are foreigners. This means something. This means that we are recognized as a place to go for developing your talent. Of course, we are formally asked to support Flemish musicians, but the point is how this definition is regulated institutionally. . . . Flemish musicians are not only those who were born in Flanders, but also those who have been living and studying here. It is not, let's say, an ethnic or a nationalist distinction that we make, not at all. (Aerts)

Aerts affirms to have only a formal commitment with the community interest, in particular with the obligation to support Flemish artists, but also wants to maintain an anti-essentialist approach to the idea of Flemishness. In his view, deSingel's international students represent a tangible example of the way the art center promotes a form of identity whose limits go beyond the geographic territory of Flanders or the Dutch-speaking dimension.

Nevertheless, the logic that informs this kind of agency does not escape from the binary opposition between Flanders and Wallonia in which the Belgian internal conflict and the Flemish nationalist ideology are framed. Indeed, deSingel's activities can be regarded as having both symbolic and structural implications concerning the conflict between the language communities. First, deSingel's structural organization and qualitative standards are likely to be connected to Flanders's generalized prosperity and directly attributed to a form of local ethos, an attitude to business that could be considered an endogenous trait of Flemish people. This argument has great relevance in the political debate and public opinion in Belgium. Jan Peumans affirms:

I am sure that Flemings have a different mentality. This is the reason why we have a different level of efficiency. We are enterprising people and we put transparency first in our institutions. The same cannot be said for the other side of the country. It is a cultural difference that concerns both the people and the political class.[3]

---

3 "Je suis sûr que les flamands ont une mentalité différente. C'est la raison pour laquelle nous avons un différent niveau d'efficacité. Nous sommes des gens entreprenants, et nous mettons d'abord la transparence dans nos institutions. On ne peut pas dire la même chose pour l'autre côté du pays. Il s'agit d'une différence culturelle, qui concerne le peuple et la classe politique."

The hypothesis that deSingel would produce, in a certain sense, the binary cultural opposition between the regions as it is understood by Flemish nationalists is not easy to demonstrate. It is understandably difficult to assess whether the operating institution follows the nationalists' ideas, or if the latter seek to appropriate the former's work and use it as a confirmation of the cultural superiority of Flemings. However, this hypothesis is formally rejected by Aerts only to be reaffirmed shortly after when he describes deSingel as a resource for the whole country:

We operate in a city governed by nationalists; we have nationalists among the members of our board. This does not influence our work. In what we represent, I don't see any instrumentalization from Flemish nationalists. . . . We don't close the door to French-speaking students, musicians, scenographers or technicians. They can come here and take advantage of our structures, program, and policy which are the product of a better organized system. (Aerts)

This quote shows how the position of deSingel as an official community institution is somehow ambivalent. On the one hand, there are not specific obligations or purposes to push forward the Flemish cultural identity, and deSingle represents itself as unconcerned with Flanders. On the other hand, however, its activity and leading position in the cultural sector bring out and reinforce an idea of structural and economic primacy of Flanders in the national context. To summarize, with regard to its functioning as a center for music education and cultural divulgation, the implications of deSingel with political nationalism are likely to be more symbolic than structural.

The symbolic role of deSingel in the Belgian domestic conflict described above is thus enforced as a structural rather than a cultural matter. As such, it can concretely inform policy choices and direct the action of cultural institutions in the national context. In this sense, it is interesting to compare the way deSingel constructs and maintains its international and national inter-community relationships with other partners. Indeed, the art center does not always seem to maintain the same approach. In the international scenario, as explained above, deSingel acts as a support partner when it comes to integrating international projects such as Opera XXI, providing structural and even financial support. The same cannot be said with regard to contacts and exchanges with Belgian French-speaking cultural institutions. As a matter of fact, deSingel is not involved in any interregional project with Wallonia.

In general, the reason for the lack of cooperation between deSingel and French-speaking cultural actors can be connected to the differences in the economic performance between the two regions as well as the imperatives of institutional structural efficiency that dominate the contemporary political debate. According to utilitarian principles, cultural institutions and agencies would not be attractive as potential partners for their Flemish counterparts. When questioned about what French-speaking cultural institutions represent for deSingel, Jerry Aerts replies:

We do not have prejudices against Wallonia; there are very good schools and places for music in the south of Belgium. The point is that it is not convenient for us to make deals with them, or at least it has not been the case so far. . . . For example, some time ago we were in contact with Théâtre de la Place in Liège. This is just to prove that we are not *a priori* opposed to interregional cooperation. I don't know if any form of cooperation will be undertaken in the future, but it is difficult to organize things together in Belgium. There is a difference in the way we work on, organize, and finalize our projects, as well as in the way we use public subsidies. We are just like two separate neighboring countries. (Aerts)

According to Aerts, obstacles to inter-community cooperation seem to be related to Flanders's different and more effective subsidy system, and higher level of organizational efficiency as opposed to the real or presumed lower potential of Wallonia. It is important to remark that, as it has emerged above, differences in economic or structural efficiency are not conceived as an obstacle when deSingel is called to cooperate with economically and structurally weaker international partners, such as in the case of the collaboration on Opera XXI with the theater of Bologna.

This evident contradiction reflects the relationship between the Belgian communities as it is regulated by the country's federal arrangements. One guiding principle to the Belgian system, indeed, is that the governmental institutions that form the federation do not interfere with each other in matters that fall under regional jurisdiction. This is clearly stated by Jan Peumans:

The principle is not to stick your nose in the other's public affairs. If they make what for us is a mistake, we have to respect their choice and not insist on changing or affecting their decisions, their practices. That is how we decided to act as a federal country when we reformed the constitution.[4]

---

4 "Le principe est de ne pas mettre ton nez dans les affaires publiques de l'autre. S'ils font ce que pour nous est une erreur, nous devons respecter leur choix et ne pas insister pour changer ou influencer leurs décisions, leurs pratiques. C'est comme ça que

While Flemish cultural institutions can promote themselves as efficient models on the international arena, they cannot play the same role towards their French-speaking counterparts. Not only does this principle frame the concrete action of a cultural actor such as deSingel, but it also informs the mutual understanding between Flemish and French-speaking public actors. The limits of the Belgian institutional setting are, according to Jerry Aerts, regrettably overlooked:

I still believe that we could have a national-Belgian role, especially because we are not perceived as a Flemish institution by the people. In other words, it is a pity. It is a waste of resources the fact that cooperation with Wallonia is so difficult, but it is one of the negative implications of our divided system. So it is difficult to open a productive debate about that in the country.

Although inter-community relationships are certainly affected by dichotomies, economic hierarchies and discourses about productivity and efficiency, these final quotes are key to understanding how the Belgian situation is also strongly conditioned by the limits of its federal system as it has been thought and implemented in the last decades. It is arguable that Belgium's federal arrangement not only can have serious consequences for sector economies—for the national cultural industry in this specific case—but also it undermines the possibility of developing dialogue and cohesion.

CONCLUSIONS

This chapter has shown that both Belgium's regional political context and the federal institutional structure have an effect on Flemish cultural diplomacy and, more specifically, on the action of a main actor such as Antwerp's arts and music center deSingel. On a national level, deSingel acts as a Flemish institution since it establishes forms of cooperation in local networks and avoids direct competition with other actors in the region. It furthermore plays a symbolic role in the reproduction and promotion of Flanders's cultural capital and helps to transform the Flemish identity towards a modern and cosmopolitan perspective. This transformation echoes the change in the ideological construction of Flemish nationalism that evolved, in the last decade, from a traditional and conservative approach to cultural identity and ethnicity to a discourse based on efficiency,

---

nous avons décidé d'agir en tant que pays fédéral, quand on a réformé la Constitution."

development, and modernity. In other words, there is a linear correspondence between the values represented by deSingel, the utilitarian perspective on culture dominating the institutional-political environment, and also the principles of contemporary Flemish nationalism. This correlation, indeed, is linked to the discourse on the superiority of Flanders in Belgium and the claims for independence as elaborated by nationalists today. The representation of Flanders's structural efficiency, a topic that nationalist movements themselves have produced and popularized, informs international cultural exchanges between the region and foreign countries. DeSingel positions itself as a model organization to be represented and promoted on the European stage, and maintains international relations with the aim of providing structural guidance and organizational help to its partners. Cultural diplomacy serves to represent and share a specific idea of Flanders as it has emerged from its conflicting and antagonistic relationships with Wallonia.

Inter-community cooperation between Flanders and Wallonia is not institutionally granted. The position of Wallonia is, indeed, an ambiguous one since the principles that inspire Flemish extra-regional cultural policies and those which regulate the political contacts between the Communities are in contradiction. On the one hand, the Flemish Community wants to make its own structural efficiency available to non-Flemish actors characterized by weaker structures or lower financial means. On the other hand, it cannot play this role in Wallonia since the Communities cannot interfere in each other's internal affairs. Networking is a priority for deSingel which puts strong emphasis on the internationalization of the cultural capital produced or supported through its structures. Among the local and international partners with which the institution continuously cooperates, Belgian French-speaking actors are not considered as potential partners.

In spite of its institutional role, deSingel does not want to be perceived as framed within a strong Flemish identity, or at least it does not want to be associated with any of its nationalistic or ethnocentric understandings. The cultural center welcomes students, musicians and other artists from everywhere, including Wallonia, to join the music school as well as to perform and collaborate with local colleagues. They can develop their talent while enriching the local cultural scene; likewise, they can be presented as a product of the Flemish cultural sector. However, the exchange that exists between deSingel and its European and international partners, with thousands of artists and students being both sent to and received from partner institutions in foreign countries, cannot exist with French-speaking institutions in Belgium. While it is clearly affirmed that deSingel identifies cooperation as a main dynamic in its functioning—and non-competition is agreed upon with other Flemish cultural institutions—the approach to Wallonia seems to be forcibly oriented towards competition or, better, towards a kind of unilateral relationship.

Music is among the most powerful elements through which the good of a nation, its values and achievements, can be showcased. In different contexts, projects of cultural diplomacy concerning music can be articulated within the perspective of a competition for national prestige (see Nathaus in this volume). In the example presented in this chapter, music has been scrutinized in its organizational, structural, and financial rather than strictly musical dimensions, including the allocation of public funding, the coordination of activities such as production, events, and education as well as the implementation of projects. The case of deSingel demonstrates that it is through these constellations that music can function in Flanders as a means to represent the region's prestige in the international arena. Flemish cultural identity, in the case of deSingel, is not conveyed by the music itself, but rather by the different structures and institutional actors through which it is produced, supported, and shared with audiences. Such utilitarian vision of culture is articulated within the dynamics of competition between language communities in Belgium. Although limited to one specific case study, the findings discussed in this chapter can open a specific perspective to observe the social and political role of music and culture in contemporary European societies, particularly in ethnically, culturally, and politically fragmented contexts. This perspective entails that the relationship between culture, language, and identity can go far beyond cultural forms themselves.

WORKS CITED

Aerts, Jerry. Personal interview. 29 Sept. 2014.

Blommaert, Jan. "The Long Language-Ideological Debate in Belgium." *Journal of Multicultural Discourses* 6.3 (2011): 241-56. Print.

Bursens, Peter, and François Massart-Piérard. "Kingdom of Belgium." *Foreign Relations in Federal Countries*. Ed. Hans Michelman. London: McGill-Queen's UP, 2009. 91-113. Print.

Craenen, Godelieve. "België en de Europese Unie." *La Participation de la Belgique à l'élaboration et à la Mise en oeuvre du droit Européen*. Ed. Yves Lejeune. Brussels: Bruylant, 1999. 39-72. Print.

DeSingel. *DeSingel Internationale Kunstcampus: Over Grandeur en het Boomhutgevoel. Kapitaal en Innovatie in de Kunsten*. Beleidsplan 2011-2015. Antwerp: 2011. Print.

De Wever, Bruno, and Chantal Kesteloot. "When was the End of Belgium? Explanations of the Past." *Journal of Belgian History* 42.4 (2012): 218-28. Print.

Huysseune, Michel, ed. *Contemporary Centrifugal Regionalism: Comparing Flanders and Northern Italy*. Brussels: KVAB, 2009. Print.

Jacobs, Dirk. "Alive and Kicking? Multiculturalism in Flanders." *International Journal on Multicultural Societies*, 6.2 (2004): 280-99. Print.

Jamin, Jerôme. "Extreme-Right Discourse in Belgium: A Comparative Approach." *Mapping the Extreme Right in Contemporary Europe: From Local to Transnational*. Ed. Andrea Mammone, Emmanuel Godin and Brian Jenkins. New York: Routledge, 2012. 62-77. Print.

Keating, Michael, John Laughlin and Kris Deschouwer. *Culture, Institutions and Economic Development: A Study of Eight European Regions*. Cheltenham, Northampton: Edward Elgar, 2003. Print.

Maly, Ico. *N-VA: Analyse van een Politieke Ideologie*. Berchem: EPO, 2012. Print.

Martiniello, Marco. "Culturalisation des Différences, Différenciation des Cultures dans la Politique Belge." *Les Cahiers du CERI* 20 (1998): 1-41. Print.

---. "Immigrant Integration and Multiculturalism in Belgium." *Challenging Multiculturalism: European Models of Diversity*. Ed. Raymond Taras. Edinburgh: Edinburgh UP, 2013. 120-37. Print.

---. *Sortir des Ghettos Culturels*. Paris: Presses de Sciences Po, 1997. Print.

Massart-Piérard, F. "Les Entités Fédérées de Belgique, Acteur Décisionnels au sein de l'Union Européenne." *Politique et Société* 18.1 (1999): 3-40. Print.

Michelmann, Hans, ed. *Foreign Relations in Federal Countries*. London: McGill-Queen's UP, 2009. Print.

Nye, Joseph. *Soft Power: The Means to Success in World Politics*. New York: Public Affairs, 2004. Print.

Peumans, Jan. Personal interview. 9 June 2016.

Swyngedouw, Marc. "The Extreme Right in Belgium: Of a Non-Existing Front National and an Omnipresent Vlaams Blok." *New Party Politics of the Right: Neo-Populist Parties and Movements in Established Democracies*. Ed. Hans-Georg Betz and Stefan Immerfall. Basingstoke: Macmillan, 1998. 59-75. Print.

Witte, Els, Jan Craeybeck and Alain Meynen. *Political History of Belgium from 1830 Onwards*. Brussels: Vrije Universiteit Brussel UP, 2000. Print.

Dervish on the Eurovision Stage
Popular Music and the Heterogeneity of Power Interests in Contemporary Turkey

Nevin Şahin

Turkey's journey of the Eurovision Song Contest (ESC), dominated by nationalistic identity claims, started in 1975, culminated in the country's victory in 2003, and abruptly came to an end in 2012 in Baku. Turkey's four decades of ESC participation illuminated conflicting power interests from the selection process of the songs to the decision process of the stage performances. The debates peaked in the 2004 final ESC night in İstanbul regarding the representation of whirling dervishes. Different stakeholders, including the tourist industry, the national broadcast channel Türkiye Radyo ve Televizyon Kurumu (TRT), the Ministry of Culture and Tourism, Sufi circles, and the singer and winner of the 2003 ESC Sertab Erener, influenced the participation of whirling dervishes in the 2004 round of the ESC. In doing so, they created a web of contesting power dynamics, which can be theorized in the context of public diplomacy.

Historian Jessica Gienow-Hecht emphasizes the heterogeneity in the structure of agency in cultural diplomacy (10). In a parallel manner, this chapter argues that there are heterogeneous power interests of different agents in the context of popular music and diplomacy in Turkey. How does the performance of "Turkishness," emblematized by whirling dervishes on the ESC stage, reflect the competition and collaboration of actors in the cultural domain? In an effort to highlight power dynamics behind Turkey's ESC performance, this chapter first focuses on Turkey's ESC history. It then moves towards the competitive staging of whirling dervishes in other public events, followed by a Bourdieusian analysis of power and music diplomacy.

TURKEY AT THE EUROVISION SONG CONTEST: A SHORT HISTORY

Turkey's participation in the ESC has been a source of national pride and shame from the very beginning that can be compared to the Turkish reception of international soccer matches. Turkish soccer fans have treated matches between Turkish and non-Turkish teams like a war for many years. The experienced technical director and soccer celebrity Yılmaz Vural, for instance, did not hesitate to call the Ukrainian team Dynamo Kyiv "crusaders" in late 2016 (HaberTürk). Similarly, the ESC turned into a "war zone" for the Turkish nation after the country's debut in 1975 when the journalist Burhan Felek referred to the first ever contestant of Turkey, Semiha Yankı, as a "fedai" (warrior) (Şıvgın 201). Every year, the contest was treated as another war to be won over Europe and became a spectacle of nationalism (Şıvgın 205), raising debates related to the contest and finding resonance in wider popular culture. In the debuting year, for instance, two winners came out in the national final and the jury selected Semiha Yankı's "Seninle Bir Dakika" (One Moment with You) to represent Turkey in Stockholm, where ABBA's epic victory had brought the contest to. The other winner, Cici Kızlar's "Delisin" (You Are Insane), meanwhile, became the soundtrack of the namesake movie starring Tarık Akan, the most famous actor in Turkey at that time, and gained nationwide reputation just like the former.

Although the jury of experts sought to represent Turkish national culture, they selected entries that followed popular music trends in Europe. For the ESC in 1982, Tahir Nejat Özyılmazel's (Neco) disco-pop song "Hani?" (Where?) was selected as the Turkish contribution to the ESC. The title was deemed appealing since it sounded like the English word "honey" (Dilmener 294). In a similar effort, Çetin Alp and Kısa Dalga Vokal Grubu were selected to represent Turkey at the 1983 ESC with their song "Opera." The lyrics of the song involved names of opera composers such as Wagner, Puccini, and Verdi, and referenced well-known European operas like Tosca, Carmen, and La Traviata. The band performed on the ESC stage with the English translation of their name (The Short Waves) and although the song was in Turkish, the naming of composers and operas made it sound "more European" as in the case of Neco's song (Dilmener 295). This also led to comments on social media that the song echoed the title of the runner up in the 1980 ESC, "Theater," by German singer Katja Ebstein.

Besides artistic concerns, such global issues as the 1979 Oil Crisis also found entrance in Turkey's representation at Eurovision. In 1980, the Turkish celebrity singer Ajda Pekkan represented the country with a song named "Pet'r Oil." With lyrics like "Artık dizginlerim senin elinde petrol" (Oil, you now bridle me), the song equated the inevitable demand for oil during the embargo of Arab countries with the need for a lover's affection. That song was special in that TRT decided that year to directly select composers of the ESC song, rather than allowing national selection. In addition, the song was recorded in three different versions, Turkish, English, and French, and included "oriental" elements like the peculiar düyek beat in contrast to previous songs which had tried to adapt to the aesthetics of European popular music (Meriç 295-96). Despite the new strategies for better ranking, the song received 23 points and placed fifteenth (out of 19), ending up only slightly better than Semiha Yankı's debut entry, which had come in last (Akın 125). In 1983, Çetin Alp's "Opera" would stand for another episode of failure as it became the second Turkish contribution to the ESC to place last in the contest, and the first ever to receive zero points (Kuyucu 21).

Similar to the preparations for an international soccer match, Turkey prepared for the ESC with nationalistic enthusiasm and an updated strategy as a response to the failure of the previous years. But still there came another failure. By blaming "defeat" on the jealousy of Europeans ("Fortress Europe"), Turkish journalists and critics negotiated the fact that the Turkish contributions tended to do poorly in the ESC, forming antagonisms between East and West, and Christians and Muslims (Şıvgın 202-03). Up until Şebnem Paker's third place in the 1997 ESC in Dublin, the results almost always evoked the same feelings of disappointment among the Turkish audience. The long-awaited victory came only in 2003 with Sertab Erener's contribution to the ESC, but this success was followed by criticism.

Sertab's performance of the winning song "Everyway that I Can" was criticized by Turkish audiences, particularly with regard to her intonation, which was frequently off on the ESC final in Riga, as well as her narrow victory over Belgium's entry by only two points. Most of all, journalists and commentators focused on criticizing the language preference in the song, emphasizing that the song was the first ever Turkish entry performed solely in English. The use of English lyrics had become possible after the ESC changed its language rule in 1999, which had tied the songs of participating countries to their official languages (Schacht and Swann). As an English-language song, "Everyway that I Can" challenged Turkey's linguistic nationalism. The disappointment of previous contests therefore took a different form at the 2003 ESC: critics claimed that Turkey was allowed to win only because it had given up its linguistic sovereignty by embracing a Western European language (Kuyucu 29). Despite the Europeanization efforts of the preceding entries and the use of English lyrics, Sertab's song and performance included many neo-Ottoman elements, such as an oriental beat performed with goblet drums and the seraglio-themed music video as figure 1 shows, which thereby promoted "ethnic" styles in the ESC (Solomon 147).

Fig. 1: A Screenshot of Sertab Erener's "Everyway that I Can" featuring neo-Ottoman mis-en-scène.

Source: Courtesy of *YouTube*.

This trend was followed by the Ukrainian singer Ruslana in 2004, who performed with dancers that evoked the Hutsul people of Ukraine, and by the Greek singer Helena Paparizou in 2005, whose song included traditional Greek instruments and a local "ethnic" sound (Baker 174). Despite these controversies, Sertab's success made İstanbul the host city of the 2004 ESC.

THE VICTORY AND THE DEBATES ON PERFORMANCE: THE ESC IN İSTANBUL 2004

Sertab's 2003 ESC victory provided the country with abundant opportunities for cultural tourism. Similar to the victory the previous year, however, the 2004 ESC in İstanbul triggered controversies. The Ministry of Culture and Tourism put great effort in representing the country's cultural and tourism features, thus seeking to cater to the "tourist gaze" (Urry 1-2) of European audiences. The Ministry organized a reception for the contesting countries in the Dolmabahçe

Palace, delivered presents and souvenirs to the delegates of these countries, and filmed 46 "postcards" (video clips displayed before a country's performance to entertain spectators during the preparation of the stage and the installment of props) with images of different parts of Turkey instead of receiving the videos from delegations of participating countries (Selcuk). The concern for the "tourist gaze" was an issue throughout the performances of the contest. Anatolian Fire, a modern dance group based on local themes and figures from Anatolian folk dances, for instance, performed before the moderators announced the voting results (Üstünel), thus musically promoting the regions of Anatolia as a tourist destination.

Besides promoting tourism to Turkey, Sertab's personal effort regarding her opening performance was significant for the evening. She prepared a medley including her 2003 winning song and the more operatic ballad "Leave," an adaptation of her earlier song "Aşk" (Love), which had been released in 1999. Similar to Sertab's 2003 ESC performance in Riga, the first part of the medley was accompanied by belly dancers. For the second part, she insisted on the accompaniment of male and female whirling dervishes. Musicologist Victor Vicente found this performance design meaningful as he identified Sufi connotations in the ballad (234-35). Nevertheless, Sertab's preference for, and insistence on, female whirling dervishes led to a broad-scale debate due to the largely accepted gender segregation in Mevlevi practices, in which men and women were not allowed to whirl together, and women were prohibited from whirling in public. The general coordinator of the contest, Bülent Osma, argued that the organization committee did not favor the use of female whirling dervishes as it was not in line with the tradition, but they eventually decided to have both male and female dervishes, considering that it was only a show, not a religious ritual, and that Sertab found it unmodern to question the participation of women in stage performances (Altuntaş).

Although the debate concerning the ESC opening performance had cooled down, the debate between non-governmental organizations of Mevlevi Sufism (Mevlevi NGOs) did not cease. The vice president of the International Mevlana Foundation and descendant of the thirteenth-century Sufi poet Mevlana Jalal ad-Din Rumi, Esin Çelebi, said Sertab knew that women can also whirl, but that it was not appropriate for men and women to whirl together. According to Çelebi, Sertab's insistence on a mixed gender whirling performance was regrettable (Gülmez). Another member of the foundation, Işın Çelebi, once more emphasized that whirling is not a show but a ritual. She said the famous Turkish singer Zeki Müren and "queen of pop" Madonna had consulted the foundation years ago on including female whirling dervishes with colorful dresses in their performances. According to Çelebi, both Madonna and Zeki Müren dropped the idea of whirling in their stage shows after the foundation had informed them about the religious meaning of the whirling ceremony (Haber Vitrini).

The debates on female whirling dervishes were over before the ESC final, and Sertab managed to share the stage with half-naked male belly dancers, which is unusual in the Turkish context, and mixed gender whirling dervishes, as can be seen in figure 2, which is also not common in the Turkish context.

Fig. 2: A screenshot from the ESC 2004 opening ceremony in İstanbul, 15 May 2004.

Source: Courtesy of *YouTube*.

As her 2004 performance was not further criticized by mainstream media concerning whirling dervishes, she continued her successful stage performances, sharing the stage with the people she met during the ESC.

WHIRLING DERVISHES BETWEEN RITUAL AND ENTERTAINMENT

The whirling dervish controversy, despite dominating her ESC experience, did not recur in Sertab's career afterwards. However, the whirling dervish started to occupy the national agenda especially after the debate concerning the ESC in İstanbul. Sertab has performed and collaborated internationally since the late 1990s. Long before performing at the ESC, she released singles together with international musicians. In 1999, for instance, she recorded a maxi single with the a cappella group Voice Male, and the following year she performed in a Turkish adaptation of Ricky Martin's cover song "Private Emotion" (originally recorded by The Hooters), which he first released featuring the Swedish singer Meja. The same year, she covered her operatic ballad "Aşk" with Greek singer Mando, with half of the lyrics in Greek partly sung by herself. After their successful collaboration on the single "Φως/Aşk" (Love), Mando and Sertab coincidentally competed against each other in Riga in 2003. Probably as a result of her victory at the 2003 ESC, Sertab hit the top of the Greek charts with her singles "Here I Am" and the competing song "Everyway that I Can" ("Greece Top 20").

Sertab's international collaborations with musicians not only resulted in commercial success but also led to improvements in musical and cultural relations between Greece and Turkey. Despite the countries' shared history, which is filled with wars and conflicts since the Ottoman period (including the war between Turkish and Greek armies in 1922 and the Cyprus Operation in 1974), Sertab continued to work for peace and friendship on the stage with other Greek artists. After the ESC final in İstanbul, she gave a concert with the Greek popstar Sakis Rouvas, whose ESC entry ended up in third place in 2004. Co-organized by the Ministries of Culture of both countries, the concert took place before a large audience in Sultanahmet, a historical region of central İstanbul (Vatmanidis). The main theme of the concert was friendship and peace, underlined by Sertab and Rouvas's shared performance of John Lennon's signature song for a peaceful world, "Imagine."

Nevertheless, the collaboration was not always peaceful. Rouvas had previously collaborated with another Turkish pop singer, Burak Kut. As he was also cast for the Turkish voice in the Walt Disney animation film *The Hunchback of Notre Dame* in 1996, Kut recorded the soundtrack of the movie with Rouvas in 1997. This collaboration led to a peace concert at Ledra Palace on the Green Line in Cyprus, which separated the Turkish and Greek Cypriots after the war in 1974. Unfortunately, both Greek and Turkish Cypriots protested the concert, and Rouvas interpreted this protest as a demonstration of the fact that the two nations were not ready for peaceful diplomacy (Akbaş). Compared to Kut's effort, Sertab's collaboration with Rouvas can be regarded as a diplomatic success in that this collaboration attracted a peaceful audience in contrast to the protests in 1997.

Keeping the collaboration of pop singers and Ministries of Culture in mind, we can return to the whirling dervishes to see if there is a similar path of diplomatic collaboration. Even though the debate was mainly on gender during the ESC, the actual issue related to whirling dervishes became their increasing visibility, to which the ESC night inevitably contributed. Whirling dervishes emerged in the Turkish context several centuries ago, when, following Rumi's death on 17 December 1273 in Konya, Mevlevi Sufism became an order. Ever since, devotees of this order have performed whirling in their special white gowns, accompanied by a special music performed in the background as part of the ritual called the Sema ceremony. Although the order became illegal by the implementation of law No. 677 in 1925 by the Turkish Republic, whirling gradually gained cultural heritage value and Sema ceremonies became part of the tourism in Turkey. The yearly Şeb-i Arus (Wedding Night) festivals held in December in Konya in order to commemorate Rumi, who interpreted death as reunion with "the Beloved" like a wedding, attract thousands of people to the city.

2004 was significant not only for the ESC in İstanbul but also because it was the year the Mevlana Cultural Center in Konya opened during the Şeb-i Arus Festival. In terms of size, staging, and spectacle, the opening event resembled the ESC. Before the opening of the Mevlana Cultural Center, the Şeb-i Arus festivals had taken place in sports halls. Both the Turkish state and Mevlevi NGOs criticized the relegation of this important ritual to such an irrelevant place as a sports hall. As a consequence, the Turkish government funded the construction of the Mevlana Cultural Center, which was especially built for whirling ceremonies and also included smaller halls for other events. The opening ceremony of the cultural center took place on Sunday, 12 December, with fireworks and an excessive crowd comparable to the actual Şeb-i Arus celebrations on 17 December. The Prime Minister at the time, Recep Tayyip Erdoğan, was present to honor the opening ceremony, and the audience applauded when he crossed the stage where the whirling ceremony was to take place. When Vicente attended this ceremony during his fieldwork in Turkey, he was shocked by what he described as the Erdoğan's "inappropriate behavior to cross the whirling ground in a linear way" (159). The whirling ground was considered a holy place for the whirling ritual and only the *postnişin*, the dervish representing Rumi in the ritual, was traditionally allowed to walk straight across the whirling ground. Vicente was also astounded that the emcees warned the audience to respect the sacred ritual, asking them to turn off their cell phones and to refrain from using their cameras, applauding, and leaving their seats so as to preserve the tranquility of the ceremony (160). His bewilderment by the political leader's disrespectful behavior and the emcees' reminder implied what was emphasized in Osma's declaration concerning the appearance of whirling dervishes on the Eurovision stage: the whirling ceremony was treated both by the Prime Minister and the audience more like a show than a ritual.

Sertab's desire to see female whirling dervishes on the ESC stage was based on a secularized image of whirling dervishes detached from their ritualistic context. This detachment was so far-reaching that even in the original, ritualistic context of the Sema ceremony, the emcees felt the necessity to remind the audience that, in contrast to the ESC, the ceremony was not a show, but a ritual—a sacred event. All of a sudden, the whirling ground of the Mevlana Cultural Center built especially for a religious Sufi ritual turned into a mere performance hall where people needed to be asked to leave behind their secular attitudes towards the stage, which contributed to Vicente's disappointment. The changing meaning of the whirling ground in the experiences of different actors signaled the heterogeneity of interests.

The event in 2004 revealed the shared interest of Mevlevi NGOs and the government to promote whirling dervishes, leading to their collaboration in cultural heritage management. Representatives of the Ministry of Culture and Tourism and the International Mevlana Foundation prepared a comprehensive application to UNESCO on the cultural heritage status of Mevlevi Sufism (Yılmaz). In 2005, UNESCO proclaimed the Mevlevi Sema Ceremony an Intangible Cultural Heritage of Humanity, officially inscribing the ceremony on its Representative List in 2008. Meanwhile, the Ministry of Culture and Tourism, the International Mevlana Foundation, and UNESCO jointly celebrated the 800th anniversary of Rumi's birth in 2007 as the so-called Mevlana Year. This level of international recognition inevitably provided abundant opportunities for cultural and national representation, similar to the visibility afforded by the ESC.

Following Sertab's performance at the 2004 ESC, the second most significant name to bring whirling dervishes to the stage was Sami Savni Özer, a popular performer of religious music and an alleged member of a Sufi order, the Cerrahis. A pioneer of Islamic pop in Turkey, he started releasing albums in the 2000s in which he sang hymns with a more secular, pop sound. His main success came with his 2006 album *İnliyoruz Hasretinle* (We Are Yearning for You). He recorded a video for the eighth track "Demedim Mi" (Didn't I Say) with whirling dervishes as figure 3 shows, and he appeared on mainstream pop music channels with his video in Turkey.

Fig. 3: Screenshot from the video of Sami Savni Özer's "Demedim Mi."

Source: Courtesy of *YouTube*.

The piece was a hymn of the Bektashi order, another Sufi order different from Mevlevi Sufism. Although the piece has a Sufi message that would also fit Mevlevi Sufism, it is not a Mevlevi piece of music. The hymn became very popular when it was released in 2006. Although Özer became famous across Turkey for his soundtracks of Cem Yılmaz's movies, he continued performing the Bektashi hymn "Demedim Mi."

The success of this hymn associated with whirling dervishes gave rise to more appearances of whirling dervishes on music TV channels as well as in movies. For instance, director Doruk Somunkıran's 2009 TV project *Sufi Klipler* (Sufi Videos) made "Demedim Mi" popular once more. According to conservative critics, TV representations of religious music could not be combined with mundane images of daily life, but rather had to be accompanied by "natural" images, such as flowers and the sun (Somunkıran). In contrast with this conservative approach, Somunkıran nonetheless decided to put religious music into the context of everyday life. In addition to including the streets and city walls of İstanbul in his videos, Somunkıran concentrated on whirling dervishes. "Demedim Mi" was part of the project and it was sung by Hayko Cepkin, a rock musician with Armenian origins. Besides his ethnic and religious difference compared to the majority of the country, his combination of Muslim Sufi music with a Mohawk, blue hair, and a hard rock sound were also unusual. Next to all the new and alternative images integrated into the scene, Hayko, with the accompaniment of whirling dervishes, whirled around as if he were another whirling dervish in the video. This unusual appearance of a rock singer with whirling dervishes in the Bektashi hymn was just one indicator for the hymn's popularity. "Demedim Mi" was performed in almost every occasion possible, frequently with the accompaniment of whirling dervishes as reflected in the video, shown in figure 4. That the hymn was parodied in Selçuk Aydemir's 2011 movie *Çalgı Çengi* (Musician and Dancer) testifies to its great popularity.

Fig. 4: A screenshot from the Hayko Cepkin episode of the Sufi Klipler *project.*

Source: Courtesy of *YouTube*.

Nancy Snow emphasizes the importance of reciprocity and multi-directionality of public diplomacy: "While dialogue between cultures is an admirable goal, it begins with dialogue between individuals, whether they are representatives of governments or private citizens" (17). Nothing can illustrate this better than Turkish public diplomacy on the level of micro-cultures regarding the adaptations of this Bektashi hymn. Besides the range of styles in random performances, this hymn also accompanied the dialogue between politics and the wider public in Şeb-i Arus İstanbul 2013, the second largest whirling event following the one in Konya.

A collaboration of the metropolitan municipality, private entrepreneurs, and several other sponsors, Şeb-i Arus İstanbul 2013 commemorated Rumi on 13 December that year. The intended audience were İstanbul residents, who could not travel to Konya for the annual Şeb-i Arus festivals. The event imitated the aforementioned Konya festivals, in which a concert of religious music precedes the Sema ceremony. The concert at the 2013 event in İstanbul starred Sami Savni Özer, the singer who had first popularized the hymn, and two pop-arabesque singers, Serkan Burak Tektaş (Alişan) and Ahmet Kutsi Karadoğan

(Kutsi), who had never been associated with religious music in their careers. With ticket prices ranging from 25 to 235 TRY (app. €9 to €85 at that time), the event had a diverse audience from every district of the city, with people from different economic backgrounds and political orientations in attendance. The invited politicians sat in the front rows as they had in Konya, and Prime Minister Erdoğan was invited on stage first to salute the audience. Despite the prime minister's short salutation, which had a mere message of love and tolerance related to Rumi, his speech was protested by the audience—a response to the Gezi uprising which had taken place the same year, and which witnessed Ziya Azazi whirling in Taksim square while wearing a gas mask, shown in figure 5.

Fig. 5: Ziya Azazi whirling in Gezi Park, in toxic green whirling gown and with gas mask, June 2013.

Photo: Arda Bengü.

Supporters of the prime minister countered the booing and whistling with applause ("Başbakan"), turning the event into a "protestival," a portmanteau of the words protest and festival (St John 130, 133). Sami Savni Özer afterwards held the microphone towards Erdoğan so that he could sing along to the Bektashi hymn "Demedim Mi." After the concert, the whirling dervishes appeared on stage in order to perform the ritual, but neither the Sema ceremony nor the

Bektashi hymn could outshine the protests of the audience. The audience inevitably associated whirling dervishes with this competition between popular figures and political messages.

This contextual connection between Eurovision and the whirling dervish, embodied in a popularized and politicized hymn, signals the relationship between music and power, in which dialogue and protest can be observed alongside images of whirling dervishes. The debate on the appearance of whirling dervishes on the ESC stage, the collaboration of different actors in promoting the cultural heritage value of the Sufi ritual of whirling dervishes, and the sharing of the stage with pop-arabesque singers and politicians with dervish performers point to the heterogeneity of power interests that intersect in the domain of music. A theoretical glimpse at this relationship and identification of different actors claiming power over Mevlevi Sufism can offer new perspectives in understanding the intersecting cultural agendas involved in the country's musical diplomacy.

PERFORMERS AND AUDIENCES AS AGENTS IN THE STRUGGLE FOR REPRESENTATION

The gender, national, religious, and political controversies related to the performance of whirling dervishes revolve around issues of cultural heritage and national representation. Different religious, political, and cultural actors appropriate whirling for their own benefits, especially when their interests intersect with one another, utilize different strategies within the struggle to dominate the whirling ground.

As mentioned above, the inscription of the Mevlevi Sema Ceremony on UNESCO's Representative List of Intangible Cultural Heritage of Humanity resulted from the collaboration between the Turkish Ministry of Culture and Tourism and a Mevlevi NGO. This collaboration between two actors with different structures and agendas brought diplomatic success on an international level. But it should be kept in mind that this "heritagification" of Sufi practices privileges institutions over communities. At the 2008 UNESCO convention, governments were encouraged to put effort in making decisions and implementing policies on intangible cultural heritage, while taking precautions to preserve potential heritage, which led to an extensive demonstration of the nationalist interests of governments in cultural heritage management (Aykan 2). The convention implied that heritage does not have inherent value, but that it acquires cultural value through the socio-political construction of heritage (Byrne

229). According to Jean During, this led to a situation in which state authorities "skillfully appropriate the cultural heritage, turn it into an instrument of power and use it to their own advantage" (144).

The "heritagification" of Mevlevi Sufism in Turkey was not solely in the hands of state authorities, but it began as a collaboration between the state and NGOs. In truth, however, the state authorities and representatives of Mevlevi foundations did not always collaborate. Despite their common success in the recognition of the Mevlevi Sema Ceremony as cultural heritage, they conflicted with each other in the debate on the visibility of whirling dervishes in Sertab's opening performance for the 2004 ESC. Whereas the International Mevlana Foundation was completely opposed to the appearance of whirling dervishes on the Eurovision stage, TRT, together with the Ministry of Culture and Tourism, supported the idea to some extent. The conflict was resolved by state authorities who eventually claimed that the performance of whirling dervishes was not part of the religious ritual but only an element of a secular stage show. Four years after the ESC in İstanbul, however, the Ministry delivered a notice which contradicted the earlier decision. According to the notice, the ritualistic structure of the Mevlevi Sema Ceremony was confirmed holistically as cultural heritage and all events involving whirling dervishes other than the ceremony itself were condemned and imposed with sanctions so as to stop the corruption of the ritual ("Mevlevilik ve Semâ"). In a sense, the ministry was now condemning the Eurovision performance that had officially been approved. The recently gained and internationally recognized cultural heritage status of the whirling dervishes provided new opportunities for the country to appeal to the "tourist gaze," on the one hand, but made the state authorities discard long benefitted opportunities of this gaze on the other. The lack of mutual agreement on how to interpret dervish performances resulted in upcoming notices by the ministry reaffirming the sanctity of whirling dervishes.

During my fieldwork on contemporary experiences of Mevlevi Sufism in 2013, I observed the commemoration ceremonies for Rumi in December. The official ceremony was held in Konya. Organized annually by the Ministry of Culture and Tourism, this 10-day event attracted an international audience, turning the month of December into Konya's peak tourist season. The opening of the 2013 celebrations started with a candle lighting ceremony in central Konya on a symbolic location where Rumi and his spiritual mentor, Shams Tabrizi, allegedly met. The lighting ceremony was followed by the March of Love and Tolerance towards the Mevlana Cultural Center, which had been opened a few months after the 2004 ESC with a ceremony of similar glamor. The ceremony at the Mevlana Cultural Center went on in two sessions every day until 17 December, with each session including a concert of religious music, readings from the *Masnavi* poetry collection, and a Sema ceremony as figure 6 shows. The whirling dervishes were for the event's conclusion, prolonging the evening ceremony until around 11 pm. The schedule was tiring both for the performers and the audience. Parallel to the candle lighting ceremony, representatives of the state and Mevlevi NGOs gave speeches in the evening ceremonies of the first and the last days of the festival. After their speech on the candle lighting ceremony on 7 December, guest politicians started the March of Love and Tolerance, which ended with a concert of military music provided by a state ensemble named after Mehter, the military band of the Ottoman Empire, in front of the governorate building. The members of the ensemble were dressed like Ottoman soldiers, and they performed traditional pieces on period instruments.

Fig. 6: Whirling dervishes during the Sema ceremony in the opening day of the Şeb-i Arus Festival at the Mevlana Cultural Center in Konya, 7 December 2013.

Photo: Nevin Şahin.

In the early republican period, advocates of the founding father Mustafa Kemal Atatürk's ideology, Kemalists, legitimized their policies by rejecting all Ottoman values for the sake of creating a national identity. This included closing all dervish lodges in the country and pushing whirling dervishes underground (Ayas 45, 66). Conversely, the conservative government of the twenty first century embraced these once rejected values in an effort to create a neo-Ottoman identity against the Kemalist identity of the early republican period. Bearing in mind the conservative government's policies of promoting values and symbols related to the Ottoman Empire, I interpret the appearance of a military band in the official ceremony before the performance of the whirling dervishes in two ways. First, it served the government's conservative claim that it is embracing Ottoman values, thus making visible the dichotomy between Kemalist and neo-Ottoman policies. Second, the military band "self-exoticized" (Volcic 168) the traditional images belonging to the Ottoman period in order to appeal to the VIP audience and the "tourist gaze." In a way, this self-exoticizing strategy was similar to the approach that had allowed Sertab to win the ESC with "oriental" tunes and Ottoman themes in 2003. The whirling dervish as an image of cultural heritage thus served the conservative interests of the state in the Konya ceremonies. The whirling ceremony ended with a prayer of the *postnişin*, including a salutation to the contemporary government. Hence, the whirling dervish on the stage was also involved in the power struggle to establish the neo-Ottoman identity via the *postnişin*'s collaboration with the state in his prayer.

In contrast to the celebrations in Konya, yet another ceremony was organized in Ankara by the Mevlana Culture and Art Foundation, another Mevlevi NGO based in the capital city, which holds looser ties with the state compared to the International Mevlana Foundation. The event took place in a concert hall constructed by a music foundation devoted to Kemalist ideology. The venue carried messages related to this ideological stance as pictures and sayings of Atatürk. Support from the state for this event was minor in that the ensemble on the stage involved a few musicians employed in state ensembles, who had been assigned duties in the Konya festival by the Ministry and who had received official permission to participate in the 2013 event in Ankara. Held on 13 December, the ceremony consisted of a short opening speech by the vice president of the foundation, Gülden Arbaş, a candle lighting ceremony, and the Sema ceremony, shown in figure 7.

Fig. 7: Celebration of Mevlana Culture and Art Foundation in Ankara. State musicians among the ensemble on the right, Mustafa Kemal Atatürk's signature on top and his photo next to the banner of the foundation, 13 December 2013.

Photo: Nevin Şahin.

There were no other formal speeches, no *Masnavi* talks, no music other than that of the Sema ceremony, and no prolonged prayers. In her short speech, Arbaş criticized "those conservatives" who claimed to conserve the ritual but who, in essence, destroyed the humbleness, naivety, and integrity of the ritual in the name of preservation (Şahin). She referred both to the state institutions that organized the Konya event and to the private entrepreneurs who were condemned by the 2008 notice of the Ministry of Culture and Tourism. In her speech, she affirmed the NGO's claim of preserving the simplicity and humbleness of the ritual. In line with her speech, the performance was simple and short, lasting only until 9 pm. Arbaş claimed that the ceremony organized by their NGO adhered to the authentic ritual more closely than the state's, and the performance afterwards affirmed her claim. This competition between one NGO and the state did not resemble the collaboration that brought the ritual the status of intangible cultural heritage.

The protests against the prime minister right before the Sema ceremony in İstanbul and the contrasting celebrations in Konya and Ankara mentioned above showed that, in addition to the state and Mevlevi foundations, the performers, and even the audience, can become actors claiming power of representation in the context of whirling dervishes. Influenced by Wittgenstein's language-game in his theory on "obeying a rule" (*In Other Words* 9), Pierre Bourdieu focuses on the fields of struggle for power (*Practical Reason* 58, 59) and compares power relations in the field to a card game. Just as joining a card game necessitates the pre-acceptance of the rules, the agents entering the field tacitly accept the legitimated forms of struggle, putting power in the center of cultural life. Loïc Wacquant, in addition, compares this card game analogy to a "battlefield" (268), where bases of identity and hierarchy are constantly disputed. The fluidity of power relations in the field challenging hierarchies corroborates Gienow-Hecht's notion of a heterogeneity of power interests in music diplomacy. The context of Mevlevi Sufism in twenty-first-century Turkey exemplifies this heterogeneity where multiple actors struggle for power over the image of the whirling dervish and constantly change roles, compete one day and collaborate another day, seeking to realize identity claims and achieve recognition beyond national borders. The war analogy of the Turkish audience in the contexts of soccer mentioned at the beginning, thus, not only applies to the competition for victory and collaboration for representation in the ESC, but also to the heterogeneous struggles for representing the values and meanings attached to whirling ceremonies on national and international levels.

CONCLUSIONS: DERVISH CEREMONIES AS "BATTLEFIELDS" OF CULTURAL IDENTITY

Turkey's Eurovision history, on the one hand, and recent developments in the representation of whirling ceremonies as cultural heritage on the other, shed light on the heterogeneity of strategies of similar actors in the context of cultural diplomacy. As the most significant figure of Turkey's ESC history, Sertab Erener has been a cultural ambassador of a modern and historically connected Turkey on a European stage. Not only did she mediate between competing cultures and nations, but she also combined tradition with modernity, associating the ritual of whirling dervishes with modern popular music. This effort, besides arousing debates between institutions on the representation of whirling dervishes, helped the whirling dervish image gain recognition beyond the religious domain and national borders, resulting in processes of cultural heritage management, popularization, and politicization.

Since then, the whirling dervish both as image and practice has been appropriated by a variety of actors ranging from directors to artists, tourism companies, and political institutions. The ESC winner wants to include whirling dervishes in her performance on the opening ceremony of the contest, challenging the ritualistic meaning with a secularized stage show. The Mevlevi NGO and the Ministry collaborate for international recognition of the whirling ceremony as cultural heritage. The dancer whirls in a special whirling gown with a gas mask on his face as a way of protesting the government at Gezi Park. The dervish salutes the government at the end of the Sema ceremony in Konya. The state-employed musicians apply for official permission to perform in the NGO-organized Sema ceremony in Ankara instead of the state-organized Sema ceremony in Konya. The audience mark the Sema ceremony with protest by whistling and applauding in İstanbul. These actors all contribute to the struggle for power over the image and use of the whirling dervish. Debates over the representation of whirling ceremonies show that collaboration can lead to international recognition, as in the inscription of the Mevlevi Sema Ceremony on UNESCO's Representative List of Intangible Cultural Heritage of Humanity, which resulted from a shared initiative of the Ministry of Culture and Tourism and the International Mevlana Foundation. At the same time, competition among actors can lead to a "protestival" spectacle, as in the case of Şeb-i Arus İstanbul 2013. In conclusion, Mevlevi Sufism has an expansive area of influence both at the national and international levels. In twenty-first-century Turkey, performances of whirling dervishes involve complex interplays of power, and heterogeneous interests struggling for the power of representation lie beneath the tranquility of whirling ceremonies.

WORKS CITED

Akbaş, Arzu. "Barış Kıvılcımını Burak Kut'la Attık." *Hürriyet Kelebek* 7 July 2004. Web. 11 Mar. 2015. <www.hurriyet.com.tr>.
Akın, Altuğ. "'Eurovision Şarkı Yarışması' Üzerine Monografik Bir İnceleme." *İletişim Araştırmaları* 8.2 (2010): 115-132. Print.
Alp, Çetin and The Short Waves. "Opera." Eurovision Song Contest 1983. *YouTube*, Web. 30 Oct. 2015. <https://youtu.be/dq64xw9tE2M>.
Altuntaş, Deniz. "Semazen Krizi Bitti." *Milliyet* 15 May 2004. Web. 16 Feb. 2015. <http://www.milliyet.com.tr/2004/05/15/ magazin/amag.html>.
Ayas, Güneş. *Mûsiki İnkılâbı'nın Sosyolojisi: Klasik Türk Müziği Geleneğinde Süreklilik ve Değişim.* İstanbul: Doğu Kitabevi, 2014. Print.
Aykan, Bahar. "Intangible Heritage's Uncertain Political Outcomes: Nationalism and the Remaking of Marginalized Cultural Practices in Turkey." Diss. City U of New York, 2012. Print.

Baker, Catherine. "Wild Dances and Dying Wolves: Simulation, Essentialization and National Identity at the Eurovision Song Contest." *Popular Communication* 6.3 (2008): 173-89. Print.

"Başbakan Erdoğan'a Şeb-i Arus'ta Protesto." *Radikal* 14 Dec. 2013. Web. 1 Feb. 2014. <http://www.radikal.com.tr/politika/basbakan-erdogana-seb-i-arusta-protesto-1166189/>.

Bourdieu, Pierre. *In Other Words*. Cambridge: Polity, 1990. Print.

---. *Practical Reason: On the Theory of Action*. Oxford: Blackwell Publishing, 1998. Print.

Byrne, Denis. "A Critique of Unfeeling Heritage." *Intangible Heritage*. Ed. Laurajane Smith and Natsuko Akawaga. New York: Routledge, 2009. 229-52. Print.

Çalgı Çengi. Dir. Aydemir, Selçuk, Fida Film, 2011. Film.

Cepkin, Hayko. "Demedim Mi." *Sufi Videoclips*, 2009. Web. 30 Oct. 2015. <https://youtu.be/ncjQsM1F1aY>.

Cici Kızlar. *Delisin*. Arzu Film, 1975. Web. 8 July 2016. <https://youtu.be/3OnqQrQLHp8>.

Delisin. Dir. Engin Orbey, Perf. Tarık Akan. Arzu Film, 1975.

Dilmener, Naim. *Bak Bir Varmış Bir Yokmuş: Hafif Türk Pop Tarihi*. İstanbul: İletişim, 2006. Print.

During, Jean. "Authority and Music in the Cultures of Inner Asia." *Ethnomusicology Forum* 14. 2 (2005): 143-64. Print.

Ebstein, Katja. "Theater." Eurovision Song Contest 1980. *YouTube*, Web. 8 July 2016. <https://www.youtube.com/watch?v=9_RDzyncNgU>.

Erener, Sertab. "Everyway that I Can." Eurovision Song Contest 2003. *YouTube*, Web. 30 Oct. 2015. <https://www.youtube.com/watch?v=axJt-Rw2Urg>.

---. "Φως/Aşk." Feat. Mando. *YouTube*, 2000. Web. 30 Oct. 2015. <https://www.youtube.com/watch?v=T4hJF-W2cdc>.

---. "Leave." Opening Performance, Eurovision Song Contest 2004. *YouTube*, Web. 30 Oct. 2015 <https://youtu.be/VwERBeWsBkI>.

---. "Zor Kadın." feat. Voice Male. Sony, 1999. CD.

---. and Rouvas, Sakis. "Imagine." Joint concert. *YouTube*, 7 July 2004. Web. 30 Oct. 2015 <https://youtu.be/MaKwitFkXHY>.

Gienow-Hecht, Jessica C. E. "What are We Searching for? Culture, Diplomacy, Agency and the State." *Searching for a Cultural Diplomacy*. Ed. Jessica C. E. Gienow-Hecht and Mark C. Donfried. New York: Berghahn, 2010. 3-12. Print.

"Greece Top 20." 31 Aug. 2003. Web. 10 Oct. 2015. <www.top40-charts.com>.

Gülmez, İlknur. "Kadın ve Erkek Sema Yapamaz." *Milliyet*. 15 May 2004. Web. 16 Feb. 2015. <http://www.milliyet.com.tr/2004/05/15/magazin/amag.html>.

HaberTürk. "Yılmaz Vural: 'Craig Thompson'u Döverdim.'" 7 Dec. 2016. Web. 28 June 2017. <http://www.haberturk.com/spor/futbol/haber/1333755-yilmaz-vural-craig-thomsoni-doverdim>.

Haber Vitrini. "Mevlana'nın 22. Kuşaktan Torunu Eski Bakan Çelebi: Biz Madonna'ya Bile İzin Vermedik." 15 May 2004. Web. 17 Feb. 2015. <http://www.habervitrini.com/gundem/mevlananin-22-kusaktan-torunu-eski-bakan-celebi-biz-madonnaya-bile-izin-vermedik-130344/>.

Her Şey Çok Güzel Olacak. Dir. Ömer Vargı. Perf. Cem Yılmaz. Filma-Cass, 1998. DVD.

International Mevlana Foundation. Web. 13 Nov. 2014. <http://mevlanafoundation.com/about_en.html>.

Kural, Ahmet and Murat Cemcir. *Demedim Mi*. Selçuk Aydemir, dir. *Çalgı Çengi*, Fida Film, 2011. Web. 30 Oct. 2015. <https://youtu.be/ov_5HuAFIn0>.

Kuyucu, Mihalis. "Medya Sanat ve Dil Üçgeni: Türkiye'nin Eurovision Şarkı Yarışmasında Kullandığı Şarkı Dili Üzerine Bir İnceleme." *İdil* 2.8 (2013): 14-38. Print.

Martin, Ricky. *Private Emotion*, feat. Sertab Erener. Columbia, 2000. CD.

Meriç, Murat. *Pop Dedik: Türkçe Sözlü Hafif Batı Müziği*. İstanbul: İletişim, 2006. Print.

"Mevlevi Sema Ceremony." *UNESCO Intangible Heritage Lists*. Web. 2 Oct. 2015. <http://www.unesco.org/culture/ich/en/RL/mevlevi-sema-ceremony-00100>.

"Mevlevilik ve Semâ Törenleri Hakkında Genelge." *Notice* 22 Oct. 2008. Web. 19 Apr. 2016. <http://teftis.kulturturizm.gov.tr/TR,14823/mevlevilik-ve-sema-torenleri-hakkinda-genelge.html>.

Neco. "Hani." Eurovision Song Contest 1982. *YouTube*, Web. 29 June 2017. <https://youtu.be/sU67JnNuqSA>.

Özer, Sami Savni. *İnliyoruz Hasretinle*. Beyza Müzik, 2006. CD.

---. "Demedim Mi." *YouTube*, 2006. Web. 30 Oct. 2015. <https://www.youtube.com/watch?v=h3QRjJs9d40>.

---. "Demedim Mi." Şeb-i Arus İstanbul 2013. *YouTube*, Web. 30 Oct. 2015 <https://www.youtube.com/watch?v=5PjYKD8KTiE>.

Paker, Şebnem and Grup Etnik. „Dinle." Eurovision Song Contest 1997. *YouTube*, Web. 30 Oct. 2015. <https://youtu.be/LAyNvKpwp1M>.

Pekkan, Ajda. "Pet'r Oil." Eurovision Song Contest 1980. *YouTube*, 24 Feb. 2012. Web. 30 Oct. 2015. <https://youtu.be/6Fu7K1hwXDc>.

Rouvas, Sakis and Burak Kut. *Someday/Bir Gün*. Soundtrack of *The Hunchback of Notre Dame*, 1997. YouTube, 22 Apr. 2007. Web. 8 July 2016. <https://youtu.be/hfaDpbl7cF0>.

Şahin, Nevin. Fieldnotes. 13 Dec. 2013. Print.

Schacht, Kira and Glenn Swann. "How English is the Eurovision Song Contest?" *The Guardian* 13 May 2017. Web. 20 Sept. 2017. <https://www.theguardian.com/tv-and-radio/datablog/2017/may/13/how-english-is-the-eurovision-song-contest>.

Selcuk. "Bakanlıktan Eurovision Finalinde Tanıtım Stratejisi." *Wow Turkey* 20 Mar. 2004. Web. 16 Feb. 2015. <http://wowturkey.com/forum/viewtopic.php?t=5034&start=60>.

Solomon, Thomas. "Articulating the Historical Moment: Turkey, Europe and Eurovision 2003." *A Song for Europe: Popular Music and Politics in the Eurovision Song Contest*. Ed. Robert Deam Tobin and Ivan Raykoff. Aldershot: Ashgate, 2007. 135-45. Print.

Somunkıran, Doruk. "'Sufi Klipler' Yayına Girdi." 25 Aug. 2009. Web. 1 May 2012. <http://doruksomunkiran.com/sufi-klipler-yayina-girdi/>.

St John, Graham. "Protestival: Global Days of Action and Carnivalized Politics at the Turn of the Millenium." *The Pop Festival: History, Music, Media, Culture*. Ed. George McKay. New York: Bloomsbury, 2015. 129-47. Print.

Şıvgın, Zeynep Merve. "Rethinking Eurovision Song Contest as a Clash of Cultures." *Journal of Gazi Academic View* 9.17 (2015): 193-213. Print.

The Hunchback of Notre Dame. Dir. Gary Trousdale and Kirk Wise. Walt Disney Pictures, 1996. DVD.

United Nations Educational, Scientific and Cultural Organization (UNESCO). *Convention for the Safeguarding of the Intangible Cultural Heritage: Basic Texts*. Paris: UNESCO, 2008. Print.

Urry, John. *The Tourist Gaze: Leisure and Travel in Contemporary Societies*. 2nd ed. London: Sage, 2002. Print.

Üstünel, Aydın. "Eurovision Organizasyonu Göz Doldurdu." *Deutsche Welle* 17 May 2004. Web. 17 Feb. 2015. <http://www.dw.com/tr/eurovision-organizasyonug%C3%B6z-doldurdu/a-2524540>.

Vatmanidis, Theo. "Sertab and Sakis in Concert in İstanbul." *ESC Today* 6 July 2004. Web 1 Apr. 2015. <www.esctoday.com>.

Vicente, Victor A. "The Aesthetics of Motion in Musics for the Mevlana Celal ed-Din Rumi." Diss. U of Maryland, 2007. Web. 30 June 2018. <https://drum.lib.umd.edu/handle/1903/7198>.

Volčič, Zala. "The Notion of 'The West' in the Serbian National Imaginary." *European Journal of Cultural Studies* 8.2 (2005): 155-75. Print.

Wacquant, Loïc. "Pierre Bourdieu." *Key Sociological Thinkers*. Ed. Rob Stones. Hampshire and New York: Palgrave Macmillan, 2008. 261-76. Print.

Yankı, Semiha. "Seninle Bir Dakika." Eurovision Song Contest 1975. *YouTube*, Web. 30 Oct. 2015. <https://www.youtube.com/ watch?v=7Ln18ergNHE>.

Yılmaz, Zeki. Personal Interview. 20 Aug. 2013.

Part II:
Infiltration and Appropriation

Between Propaganda and Public Diplomacy
Jazz in the Cold War

Rüdiger Ritter

Recent research demonstrates that jazz had an important function not only in the conception of United States foreign policy, but also of the State Socialist countries in Eastern Europe. In describing the US conception as a whole, public diplomacy plays an important role (Cull, *The Cold War*; Critchlow; Bayles). Focusing on music and jazz, we find terms like cultural diplomacy (Fosler-Lussier, "Music Pushed"), sound diplomacy (Gienow-Hecht, *Sound Diplomacy*), or jazz diplomacy (Davenport, *Jazz Diplomacy*). The variety of terms used by Western scholars describing the US efforts to use music—and specifically, jazz—in their foreign policy contrasts the Western lack of terms describing the conception of their State Socialist counterparts, which is labeled as propaganda. Although the term was also used in State Socialist scholarship (Lukin; Mazurek), there is a telling subtext in the use of the term in the Western academic circles. During the Cold War, a dichotomous notion separating "us" (meaning "The West") from "them" (meaning "The East") was in use in the countries of the Western world. Democratic countries of the West, often referred to as "us," implement public diplomacy, whereas non-democratic countries, such as Nazi Germany during World War II or the Soviet Union and her satellites during the Cold War, simply spread propaganda (Colucci). This use of language had to do with the fact that Nazi Germany and State Socialist countries both used the term officially, for instance in official denominations. Joseph Goebbels's ministry was officially called *Reichsministerium für Volksaufklärung und Propaganda* (Reich Ministry of Public Enlightenment and Propaganda) and State Socialist governments used the term as well. For example, in the Soviet Union, the term Agitprop, a combination of the words "agitation" and "propaganda" was used as denomination of the main persuasion strategy since the beginning of this state.

According to this logic, the "free" countries of the West implemented "good" public diplomacy, and the "unfree" countries of the East implemented "evil" propaganda. This implies the idea that only the West has an elaborated concept of using culture as a means to promote its values abroad, but not the East, which only relied on propaganda and agitation without deeper ideological considerations. However, both US public diplomacy and Soviet propaganda were theoretically founded in academic discourses. In the Western world, political scientists and opinion researchers like Paul Lazarsfeld and Jacques Ellul started this discourse, whereas the State Socialist discourse was rooted in the foundational works of Marxist-Leninist theory. In the latter, and in stark contrast to how the term is understood in Western circles, propaganda is positive as it refers to the way governments communicate political goals to the people and, thus, transport basic ideological values to people (Bussemer; Kamiński; Kenez). In the Soviet Union, there was a solid academic discourse on the theory of propaganda. During the Brezhnev era in the 1960s and 1970s, an article from the *Bol'shaya Sovetskaya Ėntsiklopediya* presents an overview of concepts in Soviet politics and culture (95). Is the Western depiction of Eastern "propaganda" simply nothing more than a stereotypical construction projected onto the "East" through a seemingly "objective" West, recalling the process of Orientalism criticized by Edward Said? Is not the Cold War period one of the best examples that the US and their allies in the West engaged in propaganda as well by spending enormous sums of money and implementing a large bundle of measures designed to transport their basic ideologies of freedom and democracy? While the English term public diplomacy does not sound as harsh as the seemingly evil word, is it not simply a euphemism? In this context it is telling that the term had a positive connotation in the US during the 1950s. The early jazz tours were discussed in US middlebrow magazines as "good propaganda" (Stearns). Would it not therefore be more honest to speak of propaganda actions of the Cold War superpowers rather than juxtaposing public diplomacy and propaganda?

Instead of using the terms public diplomacy (implemented by the US government) or propaganda (implemented by the State Socialist countries of the former Eastern Bloc), the aim of this paper is to compare what I will call, following Werner Wirth, strategies of persuasion with jazz (Wirth and Kühne). I will particularly focus on the Soviet Union and Poland, because these countries had a special position among the Eastern Bloc countries: The Soviet Union was the "homeland" of Socialist ideology and Poland was the country in the Eastern Bloc whose jazz scene was seen as a kind of "window to the West." Rejecting generalized notions of US and State Socialist cultural politics with regard to jazz as a whole, I will compare the use of jazz as a vehicle for the persuasion of the people in Eastern Europe. Specifically, I am interested in how US foreign and State Socialist domestic policies were implemented in the Soviet Union and Poland. Convincing the local populations was the shared goal of both the US and the State Socialist administrations; therefore, the measures taken are to a certain extent comparable as both governments used jazz as a means of persuasion. In how far were what we call public diplomacy on the US side and propaganda on the State Socialist side similar?

THE US JAZZ STRATEGY AT THE BEGINNING OF THE COLD WAR

At the beginning of the Cold War, the US government intended to use classical music as a vehicle of persuasion rather than jazz due to the fact that until the end of the 1940s jazz was regarded as a music of lower value, and the US government thought they could only convince "Old Europe" with its traditions of high culture by exporting music from the high cultural sphere. As a result, the US mainly financed orchestra tours of representative ensembles such as the Boston Symphony Orchestra (Gienow-Hecht, "World"). However, the US government soon realized that jazz had a far greater persuasive potential than classical music in Europe. When Charles E. Bohlen, US Ambassador to Moscow in the early 1950s, informed the US government that the Soviet youth was hungry for jazz, he provided a powerful argument for the official promotion of this musical genre (Ritter, "Broadcasting"). Exploiting the appeal of jazz to politically destabilize the USSR, if not the whole Eastern Bloc, seemed to be an almost logical consequence.

This became possible because at the beginning of the 1950s, jazz began to be accepted as an official musical form in the US as initiatives like Norman Grantz's "Jazz at the Philharmonic" concerts and other similar activities increasingly promoted jazz in American society. A new meaning of jazz evolved as it was no longer envisioned as a primitive form of music by an unloved minority but as a symbol for American core values including freedom, equality, and democracy. It was this ideology the US government wanted to promote by spreading US jazz abroad.

The government's idea was not to entertain some scattered jazz aficionados, but to create a serious basis for a revolution through the promotion of jazz music, which reached a wider audience than diplomatic speeches and political rhetoric. Scholars such as Penny von Eschen and Danielle Fosler-Lussier have demonstrated that US administrations made intensive efforts in this regard (Eschen,

Satchmo; Fosler-Lussier, *Music*). Financed by the US State Department, numerous musicians and ensembles were brought into the Eastern Bloc to perform jazz (Davenport, *Jazz Diplomacy*).

In 1955, the US-financed radio station Voice of America (VOA) started a daily jazz program which was moderated by Willis Conover and could be listened to via shortwave in various Eastern European capitals, including Moscow (Ripmaster; Ritter, "Broadcasting"). The propagation of jazz was intended to demonstrate that the US did not only produce a better music and culture, but that it also had a superior political and economic system. Jazz music was supposed to accomplish what aggressive rhetorical strategies seemingly could not achieve: to win the hearts of the youth, to alienate them from communism, and to encourage them to actively oppose the Soviet Union.

THE STATE SOCIALIST JAZZ STRATEGY DURING LATE STALINISM

The end of World War II in Moscow was celebrated with Soviet jazz. On 9 May 1945, Eddie Rosner's Belarus SSR Jazz Orchestra performed at Red Square as part of the end of war celebrations (Starr). Like their US colleagues, Soviet cultural policy makers were aware of the great popularity of jazz among young people in the Eastern Bloc countries. Since Socialist education of young people was one of the crucial tasks of the political intelligentsia, the negotiation of jazz turned out to be one of the most important tasks for them. But when the US changed from a World War II ally to the main enemy at the beginning of the Cold War, performing jazz in public was increasingly restricted.

As jazz began to be an accepted and even became an official form of culture in the US, the cultural politics of Josef Stalin and his culture minister Andrei Alexandrovich Zhdanov sought to remove jazz, the music of the new enemy, from public life in the Soviet Union. Jazz was depicted as having a minor quality and was viewed as a threat to the political promotion of communism (Gorodinskij; Šneerson). Musicians were deprived of their official status and, in some cases, were even sent to the gulag, such as Eddie Rosner (Pickhan and Preisler). Great efforts were made to implement counterpropaganda measures among the youth to prevent jazz's corruptive influence. For instance, officials attempted to promote various forms of Soviet popular music to replace jazz. With his at the same time conformist and popular song compositions, sometimes including "harmless" jazzy elements, Soviet composer Isaak Dunayevskii played an important role here (Stadelmann), and the government sought to implement shifting policies towards jazz in the other State Socialist countries accordingly (see Ignácz in this volume).

FAILURE OF US AND SOVIET GOALS

As we have seen so far, in the first decade after World War II the political function of jazz changed fundamentally on both sides of the Iron Curtain. For the US government, jazz became the most important musical genre to persuade Eastern Bloc inhabitants of US values, and for the Stalinist rulers jazz was regarded as dangerous. Despite these differences, both political administrations regarded jazz as a crucial means in the competition to convince people in the Eastern Bloc of their system's superiority.

At the beginning of the Cold War, the strategies implemented by both counterparts were antagonistic: the US administration started to promote jazz whereas the Soviet administration started to limit people's access to this music. Both sides formulated ambitious goals: while the US administration intended to use jazz in order to spread the political message of freedom, equality, and democracy, the Soviet administration wanted to cut off their population from any Western influences. Regarding these aims, both counterparts failed, as they soon had to realize that neither was the jazz propagation of the US the beginning of a strong movement demanding American freedom and democracy in the Eastern Bloc, nor did the governments of the USSR and their satellites succeed in totally preventing the public's contact with jazz.

Beginning with the post-Stalinist thaw in the mid-1950s, Soviet cultural policy makers realized their failure and implemented more elaborated policies regarding jazz. A bit later, their US colleagues realized their failure to implement their goals as well and adapted their policies accordingly. Setting aside their initial goals, from the 1960s onwards the USA and the USSR developed new, more differentiated methods of persuasion with jazz. These more elaborated strategies will be described below.

ROCK PUSHES JAZZ ASIDE IN THE LATE 1950S

One of the reasons for the change of strategies was the changing social and cultural function of jazz starting at the end of the 1950s. The years of the first important East-West encounters in jazz, such as the Dave Brubeck tour to Poland in 1958 (Hatschek) and the Willis Conover tour in 1959 (Ritter, "Broadcasting"), marked the beginning of a world-wide fascination of young music listeners with a new musical style, starting with the sensational success of Bill Haley's song "Rock Around the Clock."

From then on, a new pop music genre called rock 'n' roll not only occupied the hearts of young people, it also pushed jazz aside. Rock 'n' roll and the musical styles developing from its roots became the music of the youth, whereas jazz slowly transformed into a kind of art music, received less by younger audiences than by middle-aged people (Wicke). This development had important consequences for the use of jazz as means of a persuasion strategy in the East and West. Convincing the youth with jazz proved to be increasingly difficult because this was not the music they wanted to hear anymore. From the 1960s onwards, diplomatic efforts in the East and West switched from jazz to rock 'n' roll and rock.

Jazz, however, did not entirely lose its importance as a means of persuasion. From the 1960s onwards jazz listeners in the Eastern Bloc tended to be educated middle-class and middle-aged people with considerable social status and influence. Convincing them was an important purpose under the new conditions. Cultural politicy makers developed convincing strategies for the youth using mainly rock 'n' roll and rock, and for older people using jazz. It is also because of this development that the generic goals of political leaders who relied on cultural forms such as jazz in East and West were replaced by rather differentiated models.

NEW JAZZ STRATEGIES IN THE EASTERN BLOC COUNTRIES AND IN THE US

In the Eastern Bloc countries, the death of Stalin marked a starting point for more liberal jazz politics. In Poland, where the erosion of the Stalinist system started very early, the composer Henryk Czyż had already demanded the need for an idiosyncratic Polish jazz tradition in 1954 at a conference of the Polish Composer's Union (Tompkins). During the next decade, this idea was formulated also in other State Socialist countries. In the Soviet Union this idea officially occurred relatively late, and was discussed at a greater scale in a meeting of the Composers' Union of 1962 (Gaut; Abeßer). Here, composer Dmitri Shostakovich demanded in a forceful speech the composition of jazz music by local composers in order to offer young listeners alternatives to the music of the capitalist class enemy (Ritter, "Negotiated"). Every State Socialist country developed its own model of implementing this new strategy. In general, restrictions against jazz were loosened, and composers were asked to develop stylistic ideas on how to create genuine forms in their own country.

Again it was Poland where a second element of this new jazz strategy was implemented for the first time (Friszke). The Polish regime started collaborating with the jazz scene and opened the path for the first large-scale jazz festivals. State institutions not only approved but also financed the first public jazz festival in Sopot near Gdańsk in 1956, and the most important Polish jazz ensemble of this festival, the Sekstet Komedy, received an official government grant (Brodacki). Until the second half of the 1960s, the most important countries of the Eastern Bloc launched their own jazz festivals. Among them were the Jazz Jamboree in Warsaw, which has been held since 1958, the Prague Jazz Days, beginning in 1964 (Zaddach), and the festivals in Moscow starting in 1962 (Ritter, "Negotiated"). All of these festivals were financially and logistically sponsored by their respective governments. Local jazz musicians were encouraged to present their compositions in order to demonstrate to the public that the State Socialist world was a promising field for fruitful jazz development. In order to emphasize that, open competition with US jazz at these festivals was created. In Poland, musicians from the US and other Western countries had been performing at the first public jazz events since the late 1950s.

1956 marked a turning point for US public diplomacy (Stöver). Not only had the Hungarian Revolution that same year failed, but the US strategy of aggressively encouraging an uprising in the near future, as it did in a Radio Free Europe (RFE) broadcast cast the US administration in a bad light. US officials had to learn that it would be counterproductive to demand an open fight for freedom and democracy because they themselves could not guarantee substantial help. As a consequence, the US State Department stopped the strategy of promoting jazz openly in order to create an oppositional milieu. Instead, officials continued to use jazz as a kind of advertisement for their own country. Sending jazz musicians to the Eastern Bloc from that point onward had the primary aim to create a climate that was friendly to the United States, which corresponded to the new political line of peaceful coexistence (Mania). What did the implementation of these new persuasion strategies by both sides mean for the development of jazz music and the jazz milieus in Eastern Bloc countries? The following glimpses into several aspects show that, in effect, these new strategies created rather favorable conditions for jazz because of unintended and coincidental incidents.

INSTITUTIONS AND JAZZ PERSUASION STRATEGIES

The use of jazz as a component of state-organized persuasion strategies entailed the creation of new institutions or the reuse of existing institutions as places where the implementation of concrete measures of the persuasion strategy was planned. In 1956, the US created an Advisory Committee of the Arts as a sub-organization of the Office of Cultural Presentations, situated at the State Department's Bureau of Educational and Cultural Affairs. Likewise, a Jazz and Folk subcommittee were set up in 1964. Here, cultural policy makers were advised by leading radio journalists and jazz experts on the necessity or uselessness to send jazz ensembles abroad (Campbell; Ansari). In Eastern Bloc countries, public diplomacy strategies were conceptualized in state-organized Composers Unions (Tomoff). Resulting from the Marxist-Leninist understanding of culture as an important means for education (which was supervised under party and political power structures), every cultural activist including jazz performers and composers had to enroll in special arts unions. While it was illegal for any practitioner of cultural activities not to be a member of such an organization, approved membership meant official acceptance of one's cultural work and financial safety.

The discussion structure in both the US advisory panels and the State Socialist Composers' Unions was very similar: members of the government dialogued with composers, musicians, and media experts on how to cope with jazz and which measures were to be taken. Here, controversial discussions took place before final decisions were made. In both cases, the proceedings became classified, remained unpublished, and were distributed to commission members only for internal use.

Radio broadcasting is an additional example of how the implementation of state-organized persuasion strategies led to the creation or the strengthening of state-controlled institutions (Badenoch, Fickers, and Heinrich-Franke). Radio stations in Eastern Europe and other European countries were quasi-monopolistic institutions. In the US, by contrast, radio was a commercial field not controlled by the government (Hilmes). The founding of Voice of America as a government-financed station meant a break with this tradition (Heil) as the government spent considerable amounts of money in order to create a strong presentation of US government politics on shortwave radio (Johnson). State Socialist governments, on their hand, strengthened the quality of their stations in order not to lose the monopoly on information in the ether (Mikkonen). In the emerging "radio battles," jazz music broadcasts had their place (Ritter, "Kontrollwahn"). State Socialist radio promoters faced the problem of coping with the influence of Western shortwave stations (Roth-Ey). On the State Socialist side, the State-controlled radio stations began focusing on agents of cultural politics and their institutions for the transmission of information. In terms of jazz-based persuasion strategies, hosts of music and jazz programs were included to create effective strategies. The counterparts of America's Willis Conover were the Soviet radio broadcaster Arkadij Petrov, the Polish moderator Adam Jaroszewski, the Hungarian host Janos Gonda, and others.

East-West meetings in the jazz community were regarded as important by both sides so that journalists but also members of the secret service or other internal organizations related these events in detail. Perhaps the best example for this is the jazz festival in Tallinn of 1967, where American musician Charles Lloyd performed with his band while Willis Conover was present (Ritter, "Broadcasting"; see Feustle in this volume). After his return to the US, Lloyd described his simultaneous feelings of optimism and fear, whereas the key Soviet article on the festival praised the birth and international acceptance of a genuine Soviet jazz culture. US ambassador William E. Thompson ordered a detailed report of the event in order to judge its impact on US jazz persuasion strategies, concluding that Lloyd's and Conover's presence had been a great success for American aims (Thompson).

But for the Soviets, the Tallinn festival marked a breakpoint. On the one hand, the presentation of Soviet jazz was regarded as a success by Soviet cultural policy makers; on the other hand, communist party officers realized that with this festival they had begun to lose control over the cultural sphere, which they could not accept under any circumstances. Estonian organizers had invited Lloyd and Conover without being authorized by the Moscow leading party organizations to do so. As a result, the Estonian organizers of the festival were offended by their Moscow colleagues for having acted independently and without their permission, as an internal document of communist party control organs stated (*Materialy*). As a result, the organizers of the festival were expelled from their positions, and the already planned next edition for the following year could not take place. Even if Moscow's political cultural actors regarded the festival as a success for the emerging Soviet jazz scene, they stopped its further development, instead aiming for the unconditional control of all jazz events in their country.

JAZZ FESTIVAL STRUCTURES IN EASTERN EUROPE: A WIN-WIN-SITUATION FOR THE COMMUNITY

After new jazz festivals had been set up in various Eastern Bloc countries since 1958, they soon became a working place for cultural policy makers from both sides (Applegate). Eastern European politicians supported these festivals logistically and financially because they wanted to demonstrate the modernity and openness of their own cultural sphere with regard to current and modern forms of music in accordance with the new Soviet jazz strategy. They also had a second aim: By fulfilling the wishes of their own national jazz scenes, they hoped to prevent them from developing anti-state oriented political actions. As jazz seemed to be relatively harmless after the rise of rock, political cultural agents in Eastern Bloc countries decided to cope with possible risks. Their colleagues from the West were willing to support these festivals, too. By sending jazz musicians or ensembles to these events, they intended to create or consolidate an America-friendly climate. Both political administrations thus shared an interest in continuing this festival structure.

As a result, a festival organizing mechanism evolved which was supported by activists from both sides. The jazz community of a given Eastern Bloc country created festival organizing boards that undertook concrete preparations for events. For logistic and financial support, the State Socialist governments provided help. If the festival board wanted to invite guests from the West, they contacted the US government either via US ambassadors in their countries or through personal contacts. VOA host Willis Conover played an important role in this as he could draw from a large network in Eastern Europe. After the festival, both sides celebrated the event as a success of their own strategies. Consequently, the organization of the following edition of the festival one or two years later was an almost logical step.

The best example for this mechanism is the Warsaw Jazz Jamboree which was held annually since 1958 throughout the whole Cold War period, only with a short interruption in the time of Polish martial law at the beginning of the 1980s. Here, the shared allocation of money by Polish and US or Western governments resulted in the performances of first-class jazz musicians in Warsaw being all but an exception. Likewise, the Debrecen Jazz Days festival in Hungary continued for decades. Other festivals were less long-lasting. The Prague Jazz Days, for instance, did not survive the end of the Prague Spring in 1968. But even in this case festival organization created a network of musicians, government employees, and media (especially radio) employees who used the infrastructure of US public diplomacy and the public diplomacy of the Eastern Bloc countries for their own purposes.

EMERGING TRANSNATIONAL JAZZ SCENES IN THE EASTERN BLOC: A CONSEQUENCE OF COLD WAR COMPETITION?

As a result of the new jazz policy, the Soviet Union encouraged the rise of a indigenized azz scene: jazz ensembles were officially registered, and musicians could compose, perform, and submit their compositions to radio stations. In addition, the government opened special public venues such as bars or cafes that catered to the new jazz scene (Ritter, "Negotiated"). In their efforts to create their own jazz culture, both the government and the jazz community referred to musical traditions in the Soviet Union. In fact, composers of the 1950s and 1960s could harken to the works of such early Soviet jazz musicians as Leonid Utyosov (Akimov), Aleksandr Tsfasman, or the German-Russian Eddie Rosner (Pickhan and Preisler), who were famous in the Soviet Union but almost totally unknown outside the Soviet world. Jazz and jazz education were included in Soviet institutions of higher musical education, and soon the Soviet jazz scene included musicians and composers like Oleg Lundstrem, Vadim Lyudvikovskiy, German Luk'yanov, and many others. Additionally, the Soviet government used the community to demonstrate the high quality of jazz music in the USSR.

Similar to the US State department tours, Soviet jazz ensembles had been sent on tours abroad since the mid-1960s. First, they toured other State Socialist countries, such as the Czech Republic (Prague Jazz Days) or Poland (Warsaw Jazz Jamboree). Beginning in the 1970s, they also travelled to the West, as in the case of the famous Ganelin-Trio, which performed in the US in 1988 (Ritter, "Radio"). The development of local jazz scenes in Eastern Bloc countries was supported by the US government as well. For American politicians, the members of these scenes were important progenitors of a pro-American orientation and as such had great value with regard to their persuasive power.

One of the most important US-American supporters of Eastern European jazz scenes of that time was VOA radio host Willis Conover. His radio show earned him such a great reputation in the Eastern Bloc countries that festival organizers invited him to their initial festivals at the beginning of the 1960s. Conover provided logistical help through the shipping of records, organizational help by establishing contacts to American jazz musicians and jazz institutions in the US, and personal help by inviting individual musicians with grants to the US, as for instance to the Berklee College of Music, and even sponsoring them. Although Conover continued to declare his engagement as purely private, he could not deny that his aims and the aim of US political-cultural agents were the same (see Feustle in this volume).

Perhaps the strongest consolidation of a national jazz scene in a country in the Eastern Bloc occurred in Poland (Brodacki). Starting with musicians like Krzysztof Komeda (Batura), and later with Zbigniew Namysłowski, Adam Makowicz or Tomasz Stańko, to mention only a few, Polish jazz became its own brand (Ciesielski). Soon Polish jazz gained a high reputation not only within the Eastern Bloc countries but also in the West, especially in the US. Besides being highly original, the Polish jazz scene managed to present an image of itself as politically independent, if not dissident to the political regime while at the same time benefiting from collaboration with the Polish government. Polish musicians as well as their Soviet colleagues were honored with medals by their governments. Adam Makowicz even received a medal of honor from the US. This demonstrates that both sides understood the consolidation of local jazz scenes in State Socialist countries as a success of their own respective persuasion strategies (Fosler-Lussier, "Music Pushed"; Hatschek).

LEARNING FROM EACH OTHER: CULTURAL COMPETITION AS INNOVATION TRIGGER

Comparing the internal papers of cultural promotion officers on both sides of the Iron Curtain, one finds processes of constant mutual observation and learning (Aust and Schönpflug). A good example is the mutual observation of the use of jazz in American and Eastern European radio stations. The most famous jazz program of the US was Willis Conover's *Music USA-Jazz Hour*, which was broadcast via shortwave every night throughout the entire Eastern Bloc. Since this program had a wide audience, Soviet cultural policy makers attached a certain political significance to it. Conover's program as well as VOA as a whole was listened to and criticized not only by ordinary citizens, but by the Soviet government. They analyzed these programs in order to adapt their own persuasion strategies and their radio programs.

State-owned publishers issued books and articles in scholarly journals in order to differentiate the ostensibly higher quality of their own broadcasting programs from the "harmful" activities of the US (Kurčatov). In reality, however, they provided detailed analyses of US-broadcasting practices, aiming to adapt these methods to their own broadcasts. From the mid-1960s on, the Soviet radio station Junost' launched a jazz program called *Radioklub Metronom*, for which Conover's show served as a blueprint (Kiseleva). Here, jazz from the Soviet Union, from other Eastern Bloc countries, and even from the US was presented in order to offer the audience an *ersatz* to Conover's program. In the concrete example of the observation of Conover's broadcast, this process of mutual observation was continued on the other side of the Iron Curtain. From the research department of VOA, Conover obtained copies of these Eastern Bloc publications which had concrete mentions of his broadcast so that he could respond to any attacks made on his show.[1]

CHALLENGES OF SOVIET PERSUASION STRATEGIES: AMBIVALENT CONTACTS TO THE WEST

The crucial idea for cultural policy makers in all Eastern Bloc countries was the strong effort to maintain control over all phenomena of cultural life at any time. This was not only a consequence of the basic positions in the role of culture in Marxist-Leninist ideology, but also a question of concretely maintaining political power. In their attempt to implement persuasion strategies with jazz, however, this idea limited State Socialist options.

As a consequence, any attempts to open Soviet and State Socialist cultural life towards forms of culture coming from abroad automatically entailed an ideological threat (Gould-Davies). Tensions occurred between promoters of cultural opening, on the one hand, and defenders of state control, on the other. The history of jazz in the Eastern Bloc is therefore a history of rapid changes between acceptance and restriction of that music with sharp and abrupt changes of diametrically opposed positions, often within short periods of time, without the option of a clear long-term perspective. In many cases, the personal sympathy or antipathy of an individual state politician decided the policy regarding jazz in any given town and even throughout the entire country. In contrast to the German NS regime with its openly racist approach to jazz, State Socialist countries never officially prohibited jazz. Even under Stalinism, when jazz was excluded from the public sphere and heavily restricted, no formal act of prohibition was made.

---

1   See copies of Jurij A Lukin's papers in the Willis Conover Collection (WCC) at the University of North Texas. Conover's assistant Efim Druker marked sentences related to VOA and Conover's broadcast.

The more the cultural policy makers in any Eastern European Bloc country followed an ideology and believed in the need for strict control, the more their interpretation of a persuasion strategy with jazz caused problems for them. Among the Eastern Bloc countries, great differences in practical realization occurred. While states like Poland or Hungary allowed their own jazz musicians access to some tours in restricted ways in the West, for Soviet political-cultural actors even a tour of a Soviet jazz ensemble into other State Socialist countries proved to be a problem. For instance, when a Soviet jazz band performed at the Prague Jazz Days in 1965, they were accompanied not only by high-ranking cultural policy makers like the president of the Composers Union, but also by secret service agents (Ritter, "Broadcasting"). This strong fear of foreign influence also explains why State Socialist political-cultural actors accepted tours of Western jazz ensembles. For them, this was the smaller evil: it was better to have US jazz musicians touring around the Eastern Bloc than to allow their own people to travel abroad. In the former, control over the public was possible; in the latter, it was not. During the existence of the Soviet Union and the Eastern Bloc, this strong idea of control limited the general options of Soviet and State Socialist persuasion strategies with jazz.

CHALLENGES OF US PERSUASION STRATEGIES: JAZZ AND RACE

A constant problem of the US administration with their implementation of persuasion strategies with jazz was the need to deal with discrimination against African American citizens confronted by the Civil Rights Movement. US officials as well as their ideological enemies in the East knew perfectly well that racial inequality in the US was one of the main problems in propagating jazz as a model for American values and democracy (Davenport, "Jazz and the Cold War"; Dudziak; Eschen). Therefore, an important question was how to cope with this inevitable issue. Speaking of jazz automatically meant that racial inequalities had to be brought up, which could disturb the proper image of America as a country of personal freedom and equal rights. Documents from US administrations suggest a sharp contradiction between the restricted awareness of racial inequality in the state apparatus, on the one hand, and the fabrication of an overwhelmingly positive image for the world on the other (*Racial Issues*). Conover himself, who had actively fought for desegregation in Washington after World War II (and who was offended by a branch of the Civil Rights Movement calling themselves *Black nationalists*) (Kofsky, my emphasis), did not speak on this issue in his broadcasts. If, in any case, racial inequality was spoken of in official media, it was amplified by the Civil Rights Movement, and was thus framed as a soon-to-be cured symptom in an overall democratic system.

Jazz fans in Eastern Bloc countries had an entirely different approach to this issue than their US-American colleagues. Among fan cultures in the East, American jazz musicians were usually highly valued, and this value tended to be even higher if the musicians were black. In his book *Black Music, White Freedom*, which was first published unofficially in the Soviet *samizdat* in 1977, the Russian writer Efim Barban connected this idea to the Négritude Movement, thus giving it a theoretical conception (Barban). As jazz was considered an Afrodiasporic musical tradition, fan cultures in the Eastern Bloc projected onto black musicians the highest degree of authenticity and originality. The State Socialist government tried to benefit from this preference for black musicians. They installed their own ideological narrative as the real defenders of human values exemplified by their treatment of black people who could, according to them, live in peace only in Socialist countries, whereas they were oppressed and persecuted in the capitalist West. Soviet officials supported this argument by pointing to African American intellectuals and musicians who had embraced socialism such as W.E.B. Du Bois and Paul Robeson (Baldwin).

This official façade of interracial friendship and comradeship, however, obscured a variety of racist stereotypes and prejudices. Poland is a particularly telling example: positive opinions towards black people were found most of all in the small jazz community whereas resentments against them were widespread in other parts of society (Antoszek; Ząbek). For instance, so-called guest workers from sub-Saharan African countries experienced the silent but powerful everyday racism that existed under Socialism (Moskalewicz; Fereira). Racial discrimination in the Soviet Union was spoken of in no single way during the entire Socialist period, nor was it addressed in the oppositional movements in Socialist countries. Thus, US officials did not speak about race because of the existing inequalities in American society, while USSR officials stressed this point in order to activate anti-American sentiments.

CONCLUSION

Both the US and State Socialist countries used jazz as a persuasion strategy in the Eastern Bloc for their ideological purposes. Yet, the basic conditions of its implementation by US actors differed with regard to the Eastern Bloc countries. This resulted in consequences for the argumentation on both sides. Especially at the beginning of the Cold War, jazz was perceived as American music not only in the US, but also in Europe, if not in the whole world. Even after the consolidation of national jazz scenes in Eastern Europe, this perception remained. This meant that US political-cultural agents could spread their own music, albeit sometimes a bit naïvely, and their State Socialist counterparts had to accept it. In the words of Fosler-Lussier, jazz was the "music pushed" from the point of view of the US whereas it was "music pulled" from the view of the East ("Music Pushed"). The crucial problem of State Socialist cultural-political actors was that they were forced to use a "foreign" music as a means to persuade their own population of the supremacy of their own cultural and ideological model which, according to Marxist-Leninist ideology, per definition could not be the case. It was a demanding task to bring ideology and reality together, which proved to be a constant problem for State Socialism.

The US administration had a similar inconsistency problem with their ideology of democracy and freedom as they promoted Afrodiasporic popular music at a time when the question of racial equality remained unsolved. Even if these ideological inconsistencies could not be hidden totally from the public, the US government's use of jazz as a crucial persuasion strategy in Eastern Europe worked out because Eastern Europeans knew little about segregation while the attraction of jazz music performed by black artists was extraordinarily high.

Looking at the implementation of persuasion strategies with regard to jazz itself, we clearly see parallels. After the failure of their initial actions during the 1950s, both counterparts explored differentiated models, but we find similarities in the institutional implementation of persuasion strategies. Both sides organized or reused think tanks to develop concrete measures. Radio was used by both sides as an important means for jazz transmissions. Tours by key musicians were regarded as important political endeavors which had to be organized and financed by the state. Thus, government-sponsored initiatives gave the jazz community a variety of options which, without the Cold War, might not have existed. It is telling that most of the Eastern European jazz festivals, having been so powerful over a number of decades, came into serious financial problems after the Cold War. Thus, jazz milieus benefited from this cultural competition. In a way, the Cold War did not so much disturb jazz's development but rather proved to be an important stimulus. In this sense, the Cold War created its own cultural model, making the situation of constant threat in certain ways productive for musical developments (Gienow-Hecht, "Cold War Culture"; Langenkamp).

WORKS CITED

Abeßer, Michel. "Between Cultural Opening, Nostalgia and Isolation. Soviet Debates on Jazz between 1953 and 1964." *Jazz Behind the Iron Curtain.* Ed. Gertrud Pickhan and Rüdiger Ritter. Frankfurt am Main: Peter Lang, 2010. 99-116. Print.

Akimov, Vladimir Vladimirovich. *Leonid Utësov.* Moscow: Olimp, 1999. Print.

Aksenov, Vasilij. "Prostak v mire dzhaza, ili ballada o tridcati begemotach." *Junost'* May 1967. Web. 5 July 2011. <http://readr.ru/vasiliy-aksenov-prostak-v-mire-dghaza-ili-ballada-o-tridcati-begemotah-html>.

Ansari, Emily Abrams. "Shaping the Policies of Cold War Musical Diplomacy: An Epistemic Community of America Composers." *Diplomatic History* 36.1 (2012): 41-52. Print.

Antoszek, Andrzej. "Cultural (Mis)-Representations: African American Culture and its Local, (East-Central) European Appropriations." *International Conference on Migration, Citizenship and Intercultural Relations.* 19-20 November 2012. Deakin University, Australia. Web. 14 August 2016. <http://www.conferencealerts.com/show-event?id=ca1mhsmm>.

Applegate, Celia. "Music at the Fairs: A Paradigm of Cultural Internationalism?" *Crosscurrents. American and European Music in Interaction, 1900-2000.* Ed. Felix Meyer, Carol Oja, Wolfgang Rathert, and Anne Shreffler. Basel: Boydell Press, 2014. 59-71. Print.

Aust, Martin, and Daniel Schönpflug. "Vom Gegner lernen: Einführende Überlegungen zu einer Interpretationsfigur der Geschichte Europas im 19. und 20. Jahrhundert." *Vom Gegner lernen: Feindschaften und Kulturtransfers im Europa des 19. und 20. Jahrhunderts.* Ed. Martin Aust and Daniel Schönpflug. Frankfurt am Main: Campus, 2007. 9-35. Print.

Badenoch, Alexander, Andreas Fickers, and Christian Henrich-Franke, eds. *Airy Curtains in the European Ether: Broadcasting and the Cold War.* Baden-Baden: Nomos, 2013. Print.

Baldwin, Kate A. *Beyond the Color Line and the Iron Curtain: Reading Encounters between Black and Red, 1922-1963.* Durham: Duke UP, 2002. Print.

Barban, Efim. *Chernaya Muzyka, Belaya Svoboda: Muzyka i Vospriyatie Avangardnogo Dzhaza.* Saint Petersburg: Kompozitor, 2007. Print.

Batura, Emilia. *Komeda. Księżycowy chłopiec: O Krzysztofie Komedzie-Trzcińskim.* Poznań: Dom Wydawniczy Rebis, 2010. Print.

Bayles, Martha. *Through a Screen Darkly: Popular Culture, Public Diplomacy, and America's Image Abroad.* New Haven, Connecticut: Yale UP, 2014. Print.

Brodacki, Krystian. *Historia Jazzu w Polsce*. Kraków: PWM, 2010. Print.

Bussemer, Thymian. *Propaganda: Konzepte und Theorien*. 2nd ed. Wiesbaden: Verlag für Sozialwissenschaften, 2008. Print.

Campbell, Jennifer L. "Creating Something Out of Nothing: The Office of Inter-American Affairs Music Committee (1940-1941) and the Inception of a Policy for Musical Diplomacy." *Diplomatic History* 36.1 (January 2012): 29-39. Print.

Ciesielski, Rafał. "'Jazz in Poland' or 'Polish Jazz'?" *Jazz w Kulturze polskiej*. Vol 1. Ed. Rafał Ciesielski. Zielona Góra: Oficyna Wydawnicza Uniwersytetu Zielonogórskiego, 2014. 39-45. Print.

Colucci, Giuseppe. "The Subtle Distinction between Cultural Diplomacy and Propaganda." 28 March 2011. Web. 29 July 2018. <http://giuseppecolucci.wordpress.com/2011/03/28/the-subtle-distinction-between-cultural-diplomacy-and-propaganda/>.

Critchlow, James. "Public Diplomacy During the Cold War: The Record and its Implications." *Journal of Cold War Studies* 6.1 (2004): 75-89. Print.

Cull, Nicholas J. "'Public Diplomacy' Before Gullion: The Evolution of a Phrase." 18 April 2006. Web. 8 July 2018. <http://uscpublicdiplomacy.org/blog/public-diplomacy-gullion-evolution-phrase>.

---. *The Cold War and the United States Information Agency: American Propaganda and Public Diplomacy, 1945-1989*. Cambridge: Cambridge UP, 2008. Print.

Davenport, Lisa E. "Jazz and the Cold War: Black Culture as an Instrument of American Foreign Policy." *Crossing Boundaries: Comparative History of Black People in Diaspora*. Ed. Darlene Clark Hine and Jacqueline McLeod. Bloomington: Indiana UP, 2001. 281-315. Print.

---. *Jazz Diplomacy: Promoting America in the Cold War Era*. Jackson: UP of Mississippi, 2009. Print.

Dudziak, Mary. *Cold War Civil Rights: Race and the Image of American Democracy*. Princeton: Princeton UP, 2000. Print.

Ellul, Jacques. *Propagandes*. Paris: A. Colin, 1962. Print.

Eschen, Penny M. von. *Race Against Empire: Black Americans and Anticolonialism, 1937-1957*. Ithaca: Cornell UP, 1997. Print.

---. *Satchmo Blows Up the World: Jazz Ambassadors Play the Cold War*. Cambridge: Harvard UP, 2004. Print.

Fereira, Rui C. "Historia i ewolucja słowa 'Murzyn' w świecie na tle Polskiego Społeczeństwa." *Afryka, Azja, Ameryka Łacińska: Wyzwania Społeczno-gospodarcze w XXI Wieku: Praca Zbiorowa*. Ed. Mamadou Wague. Warsaw: Wydawn. i Druk, 2002. Print.

Fosler-Lussier, Danielle. *Music in America's Cold War Diplomacy*. Oakland: U of California P, 2015. Print.

---. "Music Pushed, Music Pulled. Cultural Diplomacy, Globalization, and Imperialism." *Diplomatic History* 36.1 (January 2012): 53-64. Print.

Friszke, Andrzej. "Kultura czy ideologia? Polityka Kulturalna Kierownictwa PZPR w Latach 1957-1963." *Władza a Społeczeństwo w PRL: Studia Historyczne*. Ed. Andrzej Friszke. Warsaw: Instytut Studiów Polityczny, 2003. Print.

Gaut, Greg. "Soviet Jazz: Transforming American Music." *Jazz in Mind*. Ed. Reginald T. Buckner and Steven Weiland. Detroit: Wayne State UP, 1991. 60-82. Print.

Gienow-Hecht, Jessica. "Cold War Culture." *The Cambridge Companion to Jazz*. Ed. Mervyn Cooke and David Horn. Cambridge: Cambridge UP, 2010. 332-46. Print.

---. *Sound Diplomacy: Music and Emotions in Transatlantic Relations. 1850-1920*. Chicago: U of Chicago P, 2009. Print.

---. "The World Is Ready to Listen: Symphony Orchestras and the Global Performance of America." *Diplomatic History* 36.1 (January 2012): 17-28. Print.

Gitler, Ira. "Charles Lloyd in Russia: Ovations and Frustrations." *Down Beat* 13 July 1967: 15. July 1967. Web. 8 July 2018. <http://www.geocities.ws/rstubenrauch/Lloyd/downbeat/rojac_lloyd_db_jul1367.html >.

Gorodinskij, Vladimir. *Muzyka duchovoi nishchety*. Moscow: Muzgiz, 1950. Print.

Gould-Davies, Nigel. "The Logic of Soviet Cultural Diplomacy." *Diplomatic History* 27.2 (2003): 193-214. Print.

Hatschek, Keith. "The Impact of American Jazz Diplomacy in Poland During the Cold War Era." *Jazz Perspectives* 4.3 (2010): 253-300. Print.

Heil, Alan J. *Voice of America: A History*. New York: Columbia UP, 2003. Print.

Hilmes, Michele. "The Origins of Commercial Broadcasting in the United States." *Die Idee des Radios: Von den Anfängen in Europa und den USA bis 1933*. Ed. Edgar Lersch and Helmut Schanze. Konstanz: UVK, 2004. 73-81. Print.

Johnson, A. Ross, and R. Eugene Parta, eds. *Cold War Broadcasting: Impact on the Soviet Union and Eastern Europe: A Collection of Studies and Documents*. Budapest: CEU Press, 2010. Print.

Kamiński, Łukasz. "Struktury Propagandy w PRL." *Propaganda PRL: Wybrane Problemy*. Ed. Piotr Semków. Gdańsk: IPN, 2003. 10-13. Print.

Kenez, Peter. *The Birth of the Propaganda State: Soviet Methods of Mass Mobilization, 1917-1929*. Cambridge: Cambridge UP, 1985. Print.

Kiseleva, Natal'ja, and Maksim Kusurgašev. *Dvaždy dvadcat', ili 40 Sčastlivych Let: Radiostancija Junost*. Moscow: Radiostancija Junost, 2002. Print.

Kofsky, Frank. *Black Nationalism and the Revolution in Music*. New York: Pathfinder, 1970. Print.

Kurčatov, A. "Amerikanskoe Radioveshchanie: Propaganda i Shpionazh." *Mezhdunarodnaya Zhizn'* (September 1971): 103-10. Print.

Langenkamp, Harm. "(Dis)Connecting Cultures, Creating Dreamworlds: Musical 'East-West' Diplomacy in the Cold War and the War on Terror." *Divided Dreamworlds? The Cultural Cold War in East and West*. Ed. Peter Romijn, Giles Scott-Smith, and Joes Segal. Amsterdam: Amsterdam UP, 2012. 217-34. Print.

Lazarsfeld, Paul, Bernard Berelson, and Hazel Gaudet. *The People's Choice: How the Voter Makes Up his Mind in a Presidential Campaign*. New York: Columbia UP, 1948. Print.

Lukin, Jurij A. et al. *Iskusstvo i Ideologicheskaya Zhizn' Partii*. Moscow: Mysl', 1976. Print.

Mania, Andrzej. *Bridge Building: Polityka USA wobec Europy Wschodniej w Latach 1961-1968*. Kraków: Uniwersytet Jagielloński, 1996. Print.

Materialy dzhaz-festivalja "Tallin-67" i polozhenie o Vsesojuznom festivale molodezhnych dzhazovych ansamblei, May 1967. Rossiiskii Gosudarstvennyi Archiv Sotsialno-Politicheskoi Istorii – Molodezh (RGASPI-M), Fond M-1 34.146. [Archive of Social and Political History, Moscow]

Mazurek, Józef. *Zteorii Propagandy Socjalistycznej*. Warsaw: Książka i Wiedza, 1974. Print.

Mikkonen, Simo. "Stealing the Monopoly of Knowledge? Soviet Reactions to US Cold War Broadcasting." *Kritika* 11.4 (Autumn 2010): 771-805. Print.

Moskalewicz, Marcin. "'Murzynek Bambo-czarny, wesoły...': Próba Postkolonialnej Interpretacji Tekstu." *Teksty Drugie* 1-2 (2005): 259-270. Print.

Pickhan, Gertrud, and Maximilian Preisler. *Von Hitler vertrieben, von Stalin verfolgt: Der Jazzmusiker Eddie Rosner*, Berlin: be.bra, 2010. Print.

"Propaganda." *Bol'šaja Sovetskaja Ènciklopedia*. Vol. 21. 3rd ed. Moscow: 1975. 95-6. Print.

Racial Issues in the US: Some Policy and Program Indications of Research. NARA Washington DC, RG 306, Entry 1009, Box 22, Folder S-3-66. 3 April 1964: 1. Print.

Ripmaster, Terence. *Willis Conover: Broadcasting Jazz to the World*. New York: iUniverse, 2007. Print.

Ritter, Rüdiger. "Der Kontrollwahn und die Kunst: Die Macht, das Ganelin-Trio und der Jazz." *Osteuropa* 11 (2010): 223-34. Print.

---. "Broadcasting Jazz into the Eastern Bloc: Cold War Weapon or Cultural Exchange? The Example of Willis Conover". *Jazz Perspectives* 7.2 (2013): 111-131. Web. 8 July 2018. <http://dx.doi.org/10.1080/17494060.2014.885641>.

---. "Negotiated Spaces: Jazz in Moscow after the Thaw." *Meanings of Jazz in State Socialism*. Ed. Gertrud Pickhan and Rüdiger Ritter. Frankfurt am Main: Peter Lang, 2016. 171-192. Print.

---. "The Radio: A Jazz Instrument of its Own." *Jazz Behind the Iron Curtain*. Ed. Gertrud Pickhan and Rüdiger Ritter. Berlin: Peter Lang, 2010. 35-56. Print.

Roth-Ey, Kristin. *Moscow Prime Time: How the Soviet Union Built the Media Empire that Lost the Cold War*. Ithaca: Cornell UP, 2011. Print.

Stadelmann, Matthias. *Isaak Dunaevskij—Sänger des Volkes: Eine Karriere unter Stalin*. Köln: Böhlau, 2003. Print.

Starr, S. Frederick. *Red and Hot: The Fate of Jazz in the Soviet Union 1917-1980*. New York: Oxford UP, 1983. Print.

Stearns, Marshall W. "Is Jazz Good Propaganda." *The Saturday Review* 14 July 1956. Web. 8 July 2018. <http://www.unz.com/print/SaturdayRev-1956jul14-00028/>.

Stöver, Bernd. "Das Veto der Bombe: Amerikanische Liberation Policy im Jahr 1956: Das Beispiel Radio Freies Europa." *Kommunismus in der Krise: Die Entstalinisierung 1956 und die Folgen*. Ed. Roger Engelmann, Thomas Großbölting and Hermann Wentker. Göttingen: Vandenhoeck & Ruprecht, 2008. 201-218. Print.

Thompson, William E. *Review of 1967 Tallin [sic] Festival by Vassiliy Aksyonov*. Department of State Airgram: NARA Washington DC, American Embassy Moscow. 26 May 1967. Print.

Tomoff, Kiril. *Creative Union: The Professional Organisation of Soviet Composers, 1939-1945*, Ithaca: Cornell UP, 2006. Print.

Tompkins, David G. *Composing the Party Line: Music and Politics in Early Cold War Poland and East Germany*. West Lafayette: Purdue UP, 2013. Print.

Wicke, Peter. "Music, Dissidence, Revolution, and Commerce: Youth Culture between Mainstream and Subculture." *Between Marx and Coca-Cola: Youth Cultures in Changing European Societies, 1960-1980*. Ed. Axel Schildt and Detlef Siegfried. New York: Berghahn, 2006. Print.

Wirth, Werner, and Rinaldo Kühne. "Grundlagen der Persuasionsforschung: Konzepte, Theorien und zentrale Einflussfaktoren." *Handbuch Medienwirkungsforschung*. Ed. Wolfgang Schweiger and Andreas Fahr. Wiesbaden: Springer, 2013. 313-23. Print.

Ząbek, Maciej. *Biali i Czarni: Postawy Polaków wobec Afryki i Afrykanów*. Warsaw: Wydawnictwo DiG, 2007. Print.

Zaddach, Wolf-Georg. "Jazz is not just Music: It is the Love of Youth: Zur tschechoslowakischen Jazz-Szene der 1950er und 1960er Jahre." *Jugend in der Tschechoslowakei. Konzepte und Lebenswelten (1918-1989)*. Ed. Christiane Brenner, Karl Braun, and Tomáš Kasper. Munich: Collegium Carolinum, 2016. 437-458. Print.

"Liberated from Serfdom"
Willis Conover and the Tallinn Jazz Festival of 1967

Maristella Feustle

The events of the 1967 Tallinn Jazz Festival were the culmination of years of American public diplomacy through jazz, the longest and most sustained example of which was Willis Conover's radio program *Music USA* on the Voice of America (VOA). *Music USA* began at the end of 1954 as one hour of light popular music, followed by an hour of jazz. Both hours were later shortened to 45 minutes of music with news breaks interspersed, but Conover's regular announcement that it was "time for jazz" in the second hour became a fixture in the lives of fans and musicians around the world. In the nations of the Warsaw Pact, the program was a reliable source of the latest developments in jazz amid limited access to Western commercial recordings. While the program started on a provisional basis with uncertain plans for the future, Conover's commitment to quality, his personal network with major jazz musicians, and his prior experience as a leading jazz broadcaster in Washington DC increased the odds of success in public diplomacy using jazz, even as jazz and politics sometimes mixed like oil and water.

Conover's own words and actions paint a picture of a man who loved jazz and wanted to share it, boundaries notwithstanding. As he had earlier assisted in the racial integration of the Washington DC club scene during the late 1940s (Conover, *CD 1*, Track 2), he showed a lifelong disdain for arbitrary conditions that separated people with a common passion for music, whether it be the color of one's skin or geopolitical situations. This decision was at once principled and pragmatic, from the earliest days of his career, through his years at the VOA, and through struggles over his participation with the National Endowment for the Arts and the John F. Kennedy Center for the Performing Arts (Breckenridge 124). Conover recognized that he existed in a lifelong catch-22 situation, because the perception of his actions depended upon the politics behind the eye of the beholder, whether on Capitol Hill, in Moscow, or in the office politics of the VOA. If he talked about politics, there would be trouble. If he did not talk about politics, there would be trouble. Through a political lens, his every word and act could be taken with the assumption of bad faith, so it made sense to keep the focus on the music, when music was his purpose in the first place.

Conover's *via media* proved effective, both for his continued employment, and for the success of jazz in the musical diplomacy of the VOA. This chapter will present the Charles Lloyd Quartet's performance at the 1967 Tallinn Jazz Festival, which broke the "stagecraft" of prior jazz diplomacy with the Soviet Union, and proceeded despite numerous official attempts to derail it, as a case study in the effectiveness of Conover's approach over the twelve years since his VOA program began in 1955.

CONOVER'S BACKGROUND AND JAZZ MUSIC AS PUBLIC DIPLOMACY

Before *Music USA* began, several precedents worked in favor of jazz as an instrument of diplomacy. First, jazz already had a small, but dedicated audience in Central and Eastern Europe before the onset of the Cold War and even before and during World War II. Even in the Soviet Union itself, critic S. Frederick Starr describes a "Red Jazz Age" between 1932 and 1936 in which jazz especially flourished (107-10). The *New York Times* noted that "Each of the big hotels in Moscow has its own jazz band and dancing floor ... [Many] Russians go there, especially on 'Red Saturday,' the night before their free day. Foreigners on these nights are decidedly in the minority ... Jazz is staging a remarkable comeback in Soviet Russia after years of virtual prohibition" (qtd. in Starr 110-11). One American diplomat who was there to witness the popularity of jazz was Charles Bohlen, who later proposed what eventually became Willis Conover's *Music USA* (Starr 109-10).

While not officially banned, jazz was conditionally tolerated in the Soviet orbit insofar as it could be leveraged ideologically. Anthropologist Alexei Yurchak explains that

[C]ultural forms at times could be considered proletarian and at other times bourgeois, [and] they were not necessarily defined by class ... therefore, if jazz was clearly an example of bourgeois culture in some contexts, it did not have to be so in all contexts. This is why jazz was criticized but also tolerated. (166-67)

However, as Starr notes, the period of toleration that began in 1932 ended by 1936 amid other political developments in the USSR (163). Nevertheless, when the United States government decided to use jazz in public diplomacy, it did so out of a desire to continue cultivating an existing point of cultural contact.

Secondly, while Conover's *Music USA* was the most famous example of jazz in American diplomacy, it was neither VOA's nor Conover's first attempt. A *Washington Post* profile of Conover notes in 1951 that the radio host produced jazz programs for the VOA several years before the beginning of *Music USA* (Stein "Jockey" B11). One such example from 1949 survives on a broadcast transcription disc in the Willis Conover Collection (WCC) at the University of North Texas. Titled *American Jazz*, the program features Conover discussing and playing the music of Duke Ellington in English, with a parallel translation in Swedish following Conover's spoken segments (Conover, "American Jazz #1").

The US National Archives chronicle other jazz programs which came and went in the early 1950s. An early success came with Leonard Feather's *Jazz Club USA*, which ran from 1950 through 1952. The content of Feather's programs focused mainly on traditional and swing jazz, though a few programs also focused on more progressive sounds from Stan Kenton and Woody Herman, and Charlie Parker and Bud Powell do appear in the playlist. Still, the program summaries notably show a lack of emphasis on bebop, which was the most transformative force in modern jazz at the time. In addition, Feather's programs, and indeed Conover's *American Jazz*, contained no overt political content, which set a precedent for *Music USA*. Thus, Bohlen's proposed jazz program built on existing precursors in American public diplomacy for instrumentalizing jazz as a tool for public diplomacy. Bohlen knew there was a pre-existing audience in the USSR, where he understood jazz to be undergoing a renaissance after the death of Stalin.

Therefore, the Voice of America set about looking for a broadcaster. Their first choice was not Willis Conover, but a congenial sportscaster named Ray Michael. He was a competent broadcaster who went on to have a successful career in the region, but his specialty was not jazz. The long-term product of Michael's broadcast was likely to be serviceable, but unremarkable. Or, as Conover put it, "My feeling was, since I am not an expert in sports, that I would do a sports program about as well as he would do a jazz program, since my interest was not in sports and his was not in jazz" (qtd. by Groce 3).

However, Willis Conover had found out by chance that the VOA was looking for a jazz broadcaster at a point in his career where he would welcome a change. He had recently lost $12,000 (over $100,000 in the present day) through an unsuccessful concert promotion. Worse yet, his contract at WWDC radio was not renewed after he lost his sponsor, Ballantine Ale. Conover's correspondence in 1954 hints at his dissatisfaction with the commercialism of WEAM radio and his struggles to play music he believed worthy of airplay. But WEAM was good for one development: It was there that he heard that the VOA had a program in need of a host (Conover, *CD 1*, Track 3).

Conover's career in the preceding 16 years had prepared him well for the position at the Voice of America. In 1939, Conover left college after one year at Salisbury State Teachers College in Maryland to work as an announcer at WTBO radio station in Western Maryland after winning an announcer's contest. It was during his time at WTBO that he discovered jazz via Charlie Barnet's recording of Billy May's arrangement of "Cherokee," and Billy May's arranging style led him to discover Duke Ellington (Conover, *CD 1*, Track 1). Conover was drafted in September of 1942, and served until February of 1946. His experience interviewing people on radio helped secure him a position as a classification specialist at Fort Meade in Maryland, keeping him close to Washington DC.

Conover's career in the capital city began when he saw an opportunity at the Stage Door Canteen in Washington, during a party where the selected music was not holding the crowd's interest. Selecting a better set of music, Conover caught the attention of the wife of a local broadcaster at WWDC (Conover, *CD 1*, Track 3). From there, Conover worked weekends at WWDC when on leave from the Army base, and hit the ground running as a full-time employee at WWDC when he completed his military service (Stein, "That Fatal" S8). In short order, Conover was interviewing major artists such as Duke Ellington, Peggy Lee, Stan Kenton, and others, building a network of contacts he later drew upon in arranging interviews for his VOA broadcast. Most of the guests he interviewed for the Voice of America were musicians he had interviewed or otherwise crossed paths with as a broadcaster or concert promoter, including Ellington, Lee, Kenton, Billie Holiday, Louis Armstrong, Billy Taylor, and Dizzy Gillespie (Feustle).

Conover's personal network and encyclopedic knowledge of jazz were unique assets he could offer the VOA, and which consequently set the show apart. His was not a mere token jazz program from the VOA, but one as good as any that one might hear on American radio. While musicians rightfully receive much of the attention as proof of Conover's impact, listening is not a passive act that leaves the hearer unaffected. In proposing the term "musicking," musicologist Christopher Small observed that listeners are intentional participants in the making of music. Indeed, they are participants in "musicking," either listening to a live ensemble or a recorded broadcast (Small). As Paddy Scannell notes, the success or failure of a program depends greatly on how it engages listeners as participants, not as passive targets. Due to the immediacy of the human voice and its unique tone color in every individual, radio can be an intensely personal medium if used intentionally and sincerely. Scannell used as his main example Kate Smith's success in raising millions of dollars in War Bonds over the radio. Smith's sincerity made the message personal, and listeners were moved to contribute (Scannell).

The features identified by Small and Scannell resonate well with Conover's approach years earlier. Through his spoken word style, and in his approach to programming music, Conover engaged listeners as participants. In addition to the resonant, baritone timbre of his voice, Conover took care to remain intelligible amid linguistic and technological barriers. He spoke slowly and simply for the benefit of speakers of English as a second or third language. Conover's approach likely held the listeners' attention amid static and other interference on shortwave radio bands.

Musically, Conover also took particular care to include a balance of what he called "traditional, middle, and contemporary" jazz in planning the *Jazz Hour*, so that the program itself had a balanced presentation of jazz styles. In browsing Conover's early playlists, one may accordingly find "T, M, and C" in the margins as he ensured that all were represented (WCC, Series 1, Sub-Series 1, Box 1). Such attention to detail was in response to the polarization of jazz audiences in the 1940s between traditionalism and modernism, concurrent with the revival of early New Orleans jazz styles and the advent of bebop. A dedicated disciple of Duke Ellington (Stein, "The Jockey's" B11), whose music spanned the 1920s onward, Conover was more disposed to see jazz from a perspective of continuity than rupture. As one who made his living broadcasting jazz, he also had an interest in not being pigeonholed as an advocate of any one subgenre to the exclusion of another. Conover also took care to craft a program with a holistic sense of progression to a climactic point, demonstrating that the broadcaster's curation of the program was an essential aspect of a quality program (*CD 1*, Track 3).

Regardless of other circumstances, the greatest chance *Music USA* had for success was that it was done well, and Conover was able to ensure that. At *Music USA*'s inception, no one could have imagined that it would continue for 41 years to outlive the Soviet Union. Nor could anyone be sure what "success" would look like. Conover's initial contract was for 80 programs—a number someone decided would be sufficient for the VOA to see how the show was received so VOA could cut its losses if the show were unsuccessful (WCC, Series 3, Sub-Series 1, Box 7). Initially, Conover's programs were broadcast on the weekend while Ray Michael had the weekdays, but by the middle of 1955, the roles had reversed and Conover was the lead host. Different weekend hosts continued through 1961.

In addition to his handling of the music and spoken portions of the program, Conover had a further asset in his independence as a contractor. The number of programs per contract and the amount of compensation changed, but Conover remained an independent contractor with the Voice of America for the rest of his life. That relationship arose from the initial wait-and-see approach to the program: the VOA position started out as a side job for Conover, who continued to toil at WEAM for most of 1955. At the outset, *Music USA* had no indication of becoming the lifelong vocation it ultimately became. Though Conover was in his mid-30s when *Music USA* began, he decided for years to come that the benefits of being a contractor outweighed the obligations and liabilities of being a full-time employee of the US government. He was entirely in control of his time and pursuits, without concern for dual employment issues, and continued to pursue numerous other non-VOA projects throughout his career. Those projects, which survive in Conover's personal archive at the University of North Texas, included concert promotion, writing for newspapers and magazines, preparing liner notes, hosting concerts and television shows, narrating films, and working for other broadcasters, as he did in the early 1960s at WCBS, the flagship station of the Columbia Broadcasting System in New York City. Recording schedules show that Conover generally pre-recorded several programs in a span of one or two days at the VOA, leaving the rest of his time free to commute between Washington DC and his residence in New York City (WCC).

More importantly, remaining a contractor gave Conover maximum control over the content and nature of his programs for the Voice of America. Sacrificing a federal employee pension, and government-provided health care, Conover protected the integrity of his program. It was his program, and he could walk away with it. His independence provided a degree of separation from governmental involvement. As the dialogue at the end of this chapter demonstrates, he could always maintain that *Music USA* was not Uncle Sam telling people what to listen to and what to think about it, but, as with Leonard Feather's *Jazz Club USA*, it was an actual jazz expert brought in specifically to run a music broadcast as he saw fit.

With Conover's quality, independence, and sincere enthusiasm, *Music USA* gained improbable momentum. The program was initially aimed at the Soviet Union and its satellite nations, but radio waves do not stop at national borders. Rather, they travel impressive and surprising distances after dark, depending on atmospheric conditions. Therefore, early positive responses via listener mail came from Yugoslavia and Poland, Denmark, Norway, Trinidad, Guatemala, India, and Australia (WCC, Series 3, Sub-Series 1, Box 7).

A memo from the VOA's John Wiggin to both Conover and Ray Michael in early 1956 instructs:

> Please plug on every program for two weeks that: *Music USA* is getting a lot of mail. We are very pleased with these letters and we will try to answer any questions on the program without identifying the sender. (WCC, Series 3, Sub-Series 1, Box 7)

Consequently, by the spring of 1956, *Music USA* was expanded to worldwide coverage ("Voice's Jazz Program" 1). Signs of success continued in the Warsaw Pact nations as well. In 1956, Ernest Nagy, the General Consul of the United States Embassy in Budapest recognized the difficulties jazz musicians faced in Hungary and rented the Hungarian Record Company's studio for a recording session of a group of Hungarian jazz musicians. According to the Embassy:

> At the time the Communist government had banned jazz. It could only be heard by secretly listening to the Voice of America's *Jazz Hour* program hosted by Mr. Willis Conover. Two employees of the Embassy smuggled the record to Mr. Conover … This recording of that 'Jazz From Hungary' program is one of the remaining links to Hungary's underground jazz scene of the 1950s. (*Revolutionary Jazz*)

Such a response points to the importance of Conover in particular, and not just any broadcaster, as an authoritative source of jazz, and it speaks to the personal connection Conover had made with his listeners.

The University of North Texas Music Library holds the only currently known complete recording (Conover, "Hungarian Jazz Guests"). The program's introductory material and playlist show that it was hurried into production after the violent suppression of the 1956 Hungarian Revolution. In a rare acknowledgement of political circumstances, Conover presented it as a symbol of solidarity with the anti-Soviet "freedom fighters" of Hungary. At the time, it was unknown how the musicians had fared after the uprising, i.e. if they were alive, imprisoned, or in hiding. It only emerged in late 2016 that they had been able to hear themselves on VOA and regarded it as a great achievement (Gorondi).

Still, just two years later, relations between the US and the Soviet Union had improved to a point that the two nations signed a cultural exchange agreement in 1958, paving the way for a sponsored tour of the Soviet Union by Benny Goodman in 1962 and numerous other events. When this window of opportunity opened, Conover and the Voice of America were not only ready to cover the events, but they had helped prepare the ground by continuously cultivating audiences for jazz wherever the broadcasts were accessible. While some were casual fans, others developed a lifelong passion. Danielle Fosler-Lussier observes that "[t]he existence of these expert fans was likely due to another US propaganda effort: the broadcasting of American music on Voice of America radio, especially Willis Conover's *Music USA*" (87-88).

Crucially, however, *Music USA* did not facilitate a one-way conversation, but rather a two-way exchange. Beginning with his visit to Poland in 1959, Conover began broadcasting large segments of live jazz performances by overseas bands ("Recording Schedule", 1962-1973). This decision served to encourage the musicians, expose their work to a global audience wherever the VOA's signals reached, and demonstrate with evidence that a successful cultural exchange was taking place. From the series of *Music USA* broadcasts in Poland in 1959, highly skilled musicians were taking what they heard on Conover's program and making new music with it, participating in an exchange of jazz made increasingly global by Conover's propagation of international jazz artists on his program.

As jazz festivals such as Poland's Jazz Jamborees and the Prague Jazz Festival proliferated in Eastern Europe, Conover broadcast excerpts on his program, and reported back to American audiences on the festivals in magazines like *Down Beat*. He continued to devote multiple programs to events including the Warsaw Jazz Festivals of 1965 and 1966, Prague Jazz Festivals of 1965-1967, and the Bled, Yugoslavia, Barcelona, and Moscow jazz festivals of 1966 ("Recording Schedule", 1962-1973).

PUBLIC DIPLOMACY AT THE TALLINN JAZZ FESTIVAL

In 1967, Conover accompanied the Charles Lloyd Quartet[1] in their travels to the Soviet Union (Yurchak 181). According to *Down Beat* magazine, the Tallinn Jazz Festival was also the first time "live modern American jazz"—that is, post-bop jazz—had come to the Soviet Union through the inclusion of the quartet. From the outset, the quartet's invitation to the Soviet Union was fraught with uncertainty. A letter from Alexei Batashev to Conover dated 25 February 1967 shows that Lloyd was under consideration as a performer several months in advance, belying the impression that authorities' figuring out what to do with him was an *ad hoc* affair (WCC, Series 3, Sub-Series 1, Box 9b). Rather, the

---

1 Charles Lloyd (sax), Keith Jarrett (p), Ron McClure (b), and Jack DeJohnette (d) (Gitler 15).

officially-unofficial nature of Lloyd's trip had the practical effect of maintaining authorities' leverage in the transaction by keeping every decision conditional and subject to change.

Lloyd was technically welcome to attend as a tourist. It was a proverbial foot in the door, and a first step toward possibly being able to play. When Lloyd's manager, George Avakian, was told ten days before the departure date that no foreigners would be allowed to perform, he was ready to call off the trip. Then, they received official confirmation that they would be welcome, presumably as performers. An unnamed Soviet diplomat in New York claimed to Avakian that the group would not be welcome, and that the Soviet people "don't really like American jazz," but they received their visas and traveled anyway (Gitler 15).

Upon landing in Estonia, the group continued to experience what Ira Gitler called an "on again, off again routine, replete with bureaucratic excuses, and cries of scheduling difficulties" (15). Lloyd was asked to do a clinic or workshop, but insisted that he be allowed to play for people. The group was requested to do a TV show, but in an empty studio. On 12 May, the group was pulled off the program five minutes before they were scheduled to perform. While the official news organ *Izvestia* had announced the performance, the KGB prevailed, forcing organizers to reassert that Lloyd's group was to be there strictly as spectators (Starr 287), suddenly claiming they had "no official sanction" to let the group perform. Avakian was told that an eleven-man committee had called off the concert (Gitler 15). In a subsequent oral history, George Avakian adds that Willis Conover himself interceded to help make the performance happen (Avakian, Side F, Track 2).

Finally, on 14 May, the group performed and received an eight-minute and twenty-second ovation—from people who allegedly did not really like American jazz—to the horror of festival officials who admonished, "We are not children. Please sit down!" (Gitler 15). This loss of control had consequences. The festival's chief organizer, Heinrich Schultz (misspelled as "Henry Shults" in the cover notes to the album *Charles Lloyd in the Soviet Union*), saw his career grind to a sudden halt when he was removed from his position (Vermenich). Jazz writer William Minor notes that the festival was "a mark of Estonia's independence that they could hold such an event without official approval, but as a result, many of the city leaders were sacked, and [as of 1995] such a festival never occurred there again" (109).

Despite the consequences for the local leadership, the 1967 Tallinn Jazz Festival had achieved a lasting effect through the inclusion of what was then cutting-edge jazz to a live audience in spite of the authorities who tried in various ways to derail the Charles Lloyd Quartet's performance. *Down Beat* quoted

Avakian: "I had a strong sense of history. My feeling was involved with the young people of the audience. This was the music the young people wanted, not just a tour arranged by officials. My biggest hope is that we've opened a door that will stay open" (Gitler 15).

Avakian was not alone in this assessment. One may assess the Tallinn festival as a turning point for the musicians because they said so themselves: Fellow Soviet saxophonist Boris Ludmer went so far as to say that "[t]he Tallinn Festival liberated us [the musicians] from serfdom. We played one hundred percent differently after Tallinn" (Starr 286). It is not insignificant that the musicians saw the event as being so momentous: They were the most obvious and public participants in the music, and would feel the most impact of the negative reception of their music. Moreover, the reference to liberation from serfdom points to more than aesthetic liberation, but a social and psychological change.

TALLINN'S IMPACT IN THE EAST AND THE WEST

S. Frederick Starr elaborates on the turning point that Tallinn represented, noting that a full exchange of jazz culture with the Soviet Union had been lacking thus far: Official trips by Benny Goodman and Earl Hines were very isolated occasions, happening four years apart (1962 and 1966). There was also a disconnection between the USSR and other Warsaw Pact nations with American and European artists going quite freely to jazz festivals in Eastern and Central Europe, but only a few European artists going to the USSR. Therefore, with the Charles Lloyd Quartet, "the possibility of achieving in Tallinn what had not been accomplished through the official cultural exchanges was most appealing" (286). Since this exchange was not driven by governments, but by jazz musicians and fans, a milestone in cultural exchange occurred as the connection between musicians and listeners had taken on a momentum of its own. Through its persistence, the Charles Lloyd Quartet had broken the stagecraft of prior jazz diplomacy described by Starr, in which jazz was carefully managed for social acceptability and older forms of jazz, such as that of Benny Goodman, were favored.

Years of Conover's music-first approach made this breakthrough possible. He had said on numerous occasions that he did regard jazz as a microcosm of American society, and regarded it as an ideal cultural medium for that reason; to him, it spoke louder than words. He made similar statements over the years that were variations on a theme; in 1958, he told *High-Fidelity* magazine:

Jazz . . . is a reflection of our national life. Americans can't see that fact: we're too close to it. To me, and I think to most people, democracy is a pattern of laws and customs by which we agree voluntarily to abide: within this fixed and clearly defined framework we have freedom. . . . People in other countries, in other political situations, detect this element of freedom in jazz. (Randal 88)

Similarly, he told *Time* in late 1966: "Jazz tells more about America than any American can realize. It bespeaks vitality, strength, social mobility; it's a free music with its own discipline, but not an imposed, inhibiting discipline" ("Nation: Swinging Voice"). Still, Conover always strove to compartmentalize politics, writ large, from his work. In addition to excluding overt political content from his programs, he remained secretive about his political leanings, working equally well with the Johnson, Nixon, Ford, and Carter administrations. In a 1994 oral history with Billy Taylor, the interviewer, by noting Conover's precarious health and lack of coverage, tried to goad Conover into discussing the political battle over healthcare as it was being debated during Bill Clinton's first administration. Conover stopped Taylor outright, saying, "Dr. Taylor, never discuss politics or religion" (*CD 2*, Track 8).

Of course, Conover's *via media* also met resistance. To paraphrase author Allen Furst (himself paraphrasing Trotsky), "you may not be interested in politics, but politics are interested in you" ("Leon Trotzky"). In a discussion with a Soviet gentleman he refers to as "V", Conover's desire to avoid politics was accordingly challenged on his trip to Tallinn, which aptly summarizes the intersection of Cold War politics and jazz (WCC, Series 3, Sub-Series 1, Box 15). In the same interview, Conover explained why he was in Tallinn: "To see the Soviet people I met in Prague again, and to listen to your music, and to write friendly words about your musicians whenever I can honestly do so." V brought up Vietnam as a stumbling block between American and Soviet relations. In this private exchange, Conover was frank: "Well, if your government would take steps to solve its end of Vietnam, our government's end would automatically go away." He later added: "Anyway, I don't want to talk about Vietnam. It's not that I can't talk about it, but I didn't come here for that reason." An extended portion from the interview is particularly revealing:

V.: "Why did you come here?"
Conover: "I told you. To say hello and listen to your music. You think I'm here for political reasons?"
V.: "Everything is political."
Conover: "Do you think I'm here for political reasons?"

V.: "Everything is politics."
Conover: "What do you mean? Are you saying that when Soviet dance troupes and concert pianists come to America, they've been sent by Russia for political reasons?"
V.: "Everything is politics."
Conover: "Then you believe that I've been sent here for politics."
V.: "I believe you are here for the reasons you say, but I still say that in effect your presence is political."
He later adds: "the fact that your music program is broadcast on the Voice of America makes it a political program."
Conover: "Would you be happier if I quit broadcasting *Music USA*?"
V. "No, but if only you were not broadcasting it on the Voice of America."
Conover (*sarcastically*): "Where do you want to hear it, on Radio Free Europe?"
Conover: "Seriously, what would you rather I did? I'm doing a pure music show. There isn't a political word in it. What can I do to make it 'less political' for you? The Voice of America decided to do a jazz program 13 years ago, partly because they knew there were people in other countries who would like to hear jazz and partly because jazz began as an American music and so the Voice of America should broadcast jazz to show something of what our people do. Because I was in domestic radio and because jazz was my hobby, I wound up doing a jazz radio program for the Voice of America." ... "What should I say to them: 'No, I won't do a music program because somebody in Russia would think it's political?" (WCC, Series 3, Sub-series 1, Box 15)

It is unclear if V. is serious or needling Conover for a reaction, as V. goes on to maintain that Conover surely could have broadcast jazz on Radio Moscow thirteen years prior, but only for a month.

Nevertheless, Conover made a valid point: He was subject to criticism and scrutiny no matter what he did, but it was not about to stop him from doing the radio program he wanted to do. In the same archival box as Conover's transcribed dialogue with "V," there is another scrap of writing—one of many on which he jotted down random thoughts and observations as he found the words to express them. It is a generalized summary of his reaction to the personal and professional costs of persevering in what he believed to be the right course of action: Even if he did not "win" in attaining the approval of others and any esteem or material benefit that might follow, he remained true to himself. It is fitting in light of the foregoing dialogue with "V.":

You can't win their way.
You can't win negatively: doing what won't offend them.
That way, you can't win.

So, do it the best of your way:
You may not win your way,
But you may win ... Anyway, your way you have a 50/50 chance of winning; their way, you can't win. Do it your way, wholeheartedly. (WCC, Series 3, sub-series 1, Box 15)

Conover indeed did it his way, wholeheartedly, and it was his approach, his authority as a jazz broadcaster, and even his own intercession in Tallinn (Avakian, Side F, Track 2) that set the stage for the Charles Lloyd Quartet's groundbreaking performance at the Tallinn Jazz Festival of 1967. The festival thus marked years of Conover's work as an ambassador for jazz coming to fruition.

WORKS CITED

Avakian, George. Interview by Olivia Mattis. *Oral History of American Music: Yale University Library*. Tape Recording.

Breckenridge, Mark A. "'Sounds for Adventurous Listeners': Willis Conover, the Voice of America, and the International Reception of Avant-Garde Jazz in the 1960s." Diss. University of North Texas, 2012. Print.

Conover, Willis. "American Jazz #1." *Voice of America*. 23 Aug. 1949. *UNT Digital Library*. Web. 1 Aug. 2017. <https://digital.library.unt.edu/ark:/67531/metadc861664/>.

---. *CD 1 and 2. Series 3: CD Reference Copies 2000-2012*. Box 10. Smithsonian Jazz Oral History Program Collection. CD.

---. "Hungarian Jazz Guests." *Music USA* #856-B, *Voice of America*. 23 Nov. 1956. Web. 1 Aug. 2017. <https://digital.library.unt.edu/ark:/67531/metadc790677/>.

---. Interview by Clifford Groce. *The Association for Diplomatic Studies and Training: Foreign Affairs Oral History Project Information Series*. 8 Aug. 1989. Web. 31 July 2017. <https://www.adst.org/OH%20TOCs/Conover,%20Willis.TOC.pdf>.

---. The Willis Conover Collection (WCC), UNT Music Library.

Feustle, Maristella. "Willis Conover's Washington." *Current Research in Jazz* 8. Web. 31 July 2017. <http://www.crj-online.org/v8/CRJ-Conover.php>.

Fosler-Lussier, Danielle. *Music in America's Cold War Diplomacy*. Berkeley: U of California P, 2015. Print.

Gitler, Ira. "Charles Lloyd in Russia: Ovations and Frustrations." *Down Beat*. 13 July 1967: 15. Print.

Gorondi, Pablo. "Hungarian Musicians Recall Secret Jazz Recordings from 1956." *Associated Press*. 28 Oct. 2016. Web. 31 July 2017. <http://www.businessinsider.com/ap-hungarian-musicians-recall-secret-jazz-recordings-from-1956-2016-10>.

"Jazz Club USA – Tracklist.pdf." *Old Time Radio Researchers Library*. Web. 31 July 2017. <http://otrrlibrary.org/OTRRLib/Library%20Files/J%20Series/Jazz%20Club%20USA/Jazz%20Club%20USA%20-%20Tracklist.pdf>.

"Jazz Gains in Popularity as Soviet Lifts Ban." *New York Times*. 17 May 1933: 15. Web. 31 July 2017. <https://timesmachine.nytimes.com/timesmachine/1933/05/17/119091492.html?pageNumber=15>.

"Leon Trotsky. 2. Misattributed." *Wikiquote*. <https://en.wikiquote.org/wiki/Leon_Trotsky#Misattributed>. Web. 19 June 2018.

Minor, William. *Unzipped Souls: A Jazz Journey Through the Soviet Union*. Philadelphia: Temple UP, 1995. Print.

"Nation: Swinging Voice." *Time Magazine*. 9 Dec. 1966. Print.

Randal, Edward L. "The Voice of American Jazz." *High Fidelity*. Aug. 1958: 88. Print.

"Recording Schedule, 1962-1973." Willis Conover Collection. *UNT Digital Library*. Web. 31 July 2017 <https://digital.library.unt.edu/ark:/67531/metadc95/m1/112/>.

Revolutionary Jazz / Forradalmi Jazz. United States Embassy in Budapest, 2016. Liner notes accompanying compact disc containing Willis Conover's 1956 "Hungarian Jazz Guests" program for guests at an embassy reception. Print. Available at <https://iii.library.unt.edu/record=b6026336~S12>.

Scannell, Paddy. "Preservation of Archival Audio." Keynote address at Radio Preservation Task Force conference. *Library of Congress, Washington DC*. 26 Febr. 2016. Web. 31 July 2017. <https://www.c-span.org/video/?405381-2/preservation-archival-audio>.

Small, Christopher. *Musicking: The Meanings of Performing and Listening*. Middletown: Wesleyan UP, 1998. Print.

Starr, S. Frederick. *Red and Hot: The Fate of Jazz in the Soviet Union 1917-1991*. New York: Limelight, 1994. Print.

Stein, Sonia. "That Fatal 'Slip of a Lip' Can Sink an Announcer, Too." *Washington Post*. 10 Mar. 1946: S8. Print.

---. "The Jockey's Got to Know His Steed." *Washington Post*. 27 Jan. 1951: B11. Print.

Vermenich, Yuri. "Moi Druzya: Dzhazfeny." Web. 31 July 2017 <http://www.jazz.ru/books/vermenich/5.htm>.

"'Voice's' Jazz Program Soon to Be World Wide." *The Hartford Courant*. 2 Apr. 1956: 1. Print.

Yurchak, Alexei. *Everything Was Forever, Until It Was No More: The Last Soviet Generation*. Princeton: Princeton UP, 2006. Print.

A Musical Inquisition?

Soviet 'Deputies' of Musical Entertainment in Hungary during the Early 1950s

Ádám Ignácz

At the beginning of 1948, the Soviet government began to intervene in the internal affairs of musical life in the Soviet Union. The major party ideologist Andrei Zhdanov outlined the new aesthetic principles in two speeches during the convention of Soviet musical experts in the Central Committee of the Communist Party of the Soviet Union (CPSU) in which he incited his audience to struggle against formalism and cosmopolitanism. When on 10 February 1948, his words became party decree (Zhdanov), the process of creating socialist realist aesthetics of music, based on the idea that musical aesthetics had to correspond to communist values defined by the CPSU, appeared to be accomplished. From then on, Zhdanov's speeches (and the decree in the wake of them) were looked upon as unquestionable measures for every kind of music in the Soviet Union and the rapidly Sovietized satellite states in Eastern Europe. Especially from 1949 on, the Soviet policy of adopting socialist realist aesthetics was also emulated in Hungary. The local communist government identified this policy as the only model for Hungarian musical politics and ideology. It can already be documented, however, that nobody gave exact orders or analyzed in what manner this model should properly be followed. In my chapter I argue that the so-called musical revolution and the transformation of musical life according to Zhdanovian socialist realist principles was a rather arbitrary and improvised initiative, in which Hungarian policy makers and musical experts often used the Soviet ideas and prescriptions only as pretexts for Sovietizing the music scene according to their own personal plans.

In fact, local experts and musicians tended to have only a superficial knowledge of musical socialist realism and Soviet music due to language difficulties, especially the genres of the so-called *bitovaya muzyka* (everyday or popular music).¹ The intentions of Soviet musical advisors and guests, who visited Hungary, were primarily to hammer into Hungarian heads the basic Zhdanovian demands about eliminating the gaps between art music and popular music or finding folk musical origins in all kinds of musical compositions. In their lectures and presentations given in Hungary, however, the Soviets very rarely referred to the theoretical background of socialist realism or detailed descriptions of how to manage this transformation process. Notwithstanding these circumstances, music diplomacy played an important role in the Sovietization of both art and entertainment music in Hungary. By examining the Soviet-Hungarian intercultural and musical relations during the High Stalinist period (1949-1953), I will inquire about the extent of Soviet influence in the Sovietized Hungarian popular musical arena.

SOVIET FOREIGN POLICY AND HUNGARY

Historians of Soviet foreign policy and Soviet-Hungarian bilateral relations all agree that Hungary was geopolitically marginal within the Soviet sphere of influence before 1953/54 (Borhi; Borsody; Hajdú; Baráth, *Kreml Árnyékában*). It is obvious, however, that the Soviet Union influenced both foreign and domestic policies in Hungary already from the very end of World War II. Still, the USSR paid little attention to popularizing the communist worldview or the Soviet-type social system and lifestyle before the aggravation of the Cold War in 1948.

The turning point in international relations took place in 1949 when the so-called system of political vassalage reached its developed form. Political vassalage describes the process by which Eastern European governments, including the Hungarian one, became subordinated to the Kremlin. Anxious to gain the favor of Stalin, party leader Mátyás Rákosi repeatedly tried to surpass Soviet expectations (Rainer 91-100). The Soviets relied on the help of their satellites in both

---

1 In my paper, I systematically avoid using the widely used but normative term 'light music' (*könnyűzene* in Hungarian) while maintaining the distinction between the concepts of pop music and popular music. The former is generally used to refer to the musical lineage originating in the rock and roll of the second half of the 1950s, including the many trends of beat and rock music. Popular music, however, similar to the Russian term, *bitovaya muzyka*, is to be understood as a much wider, dynamic, socially, historically, and politically invested category which includes a large number of traditions and genres ranging from operetta to jazz, dance, and folk music.

economic and military terms. The Sovietization of Hungarian society and culture, however, was generally not reckoned among the most perennial topics of Soviet foreign policy. Cultural Sovietization was more in the interest of the Hungarian communist party than in Moscow's.

According to the evidence collected by the historian Magdolna Baráth ("Testvéri"; "T. et.-nak átadva"), one of the major consequences of the vassalage was the involvement of Soviet *advisors* (usually party officials, diplomats, soldiers, members of secret policy, or experts) in various fields of everyday life in Hungary. That the control of economic, military and intelligence activities enjoyed priority is indicated by the fact that the first advisors from 1948 worked mainly in these domains. Their growing presence in Hungary's cultural and civil life, however, could be observed only after 1950 (Baráth, *Kreml Árnyékában*).

One should emphasize that these advisors, who held greater power than Hungarian officials, acted on Soviet orders, even though they had always been formally invited by the host countries. Officers in the Hungarian ministries and institutions often sought the help of their Soviet colleagues who initially only provided assistance in the tasks required by Moscow or the Hungarian government, but later on they also worked for both the Soviet and Hungarian secret services. Theoretically, advisors did not have the authority to give direct instructions to local institutions. Notwithstanding, their words were often received as commands. Their communication has not been exposed to careful historical examination due to the nature (or even absence) of evidence as Soviet advisors preferred private conversations over public statements in order to avoid publicity.

SOVIET-HUNGARIAN CULTURAL RELATIONS IN THE 1940S AND 1950S

Cultural relations between the Soviet Union and Hungary were formally coordinated by the state-funded Hungarian-Soviet (Friendship) Society (Magyar-Szovjet [Baráti] Társaság) which was established in Budapest shortly after World War II in June 1945. In its first few years, the Society tried to recruit those who were interested in Soviet culture and obtained the support of prominent intellectuals such as Albert Szent-Györgyi, Zoltán Kodály, or Gyula Illyés. Initially the creation of a mass organization of "millions of people" and the

Cultural Sovietization of Hungary were not on the agenda until 1948/49.² Radical changes concerning the reorganization of Hungary's cultural life started only from 1949 on. Scholars point towards different events which may have encouraged the Hungarian Communist Party to initiate the so-called Cultural Revolution, the transformation of Hungarian culture according to Stalinist principles. Some emphasize the importance of the visit of Soviet composer Mihail Chulaki in February 1949 (Standeisky 164-66), while others focus on the role of a ministerial deputy (Vladimir Baikov) who was not satisfied with the efficiency of the Hungarian ideological struggle against American influences (Baráth, "A Szovjetunióról" 66).

In May 1949, Mátyás Rákosi, General Secretary of the Hungarian Communist Party and Stalin supporter, issued a call for the Cultural Revolution after winning the one-party elections. The so-called Agitation and Propaganda College of the Hungarian Working People's Party (HWPP) decided on immediate measures concerning the promotion of the Soviet Union already in June 1949. For that purpose, the College expressed the completely unrealistic demand of setting up a group responsible for the propagation of the Soviet way of life within a mere few weeks. The College wanted to establish literary, theatrical, and musical committees in order to realize "the drastic overhaul of the cultural front, regarding the basic principles of Soviet culture."³

József Révai, the Party's major Stalinist ideologist and Minister of Public Education, supplemented these objectives in his programmatic article entitled "Let Us Learn from Soviet Culture" ("Tanuljunk a szovjet kultúrából") which was published in the newly released journal *Szovjet Kultúra* (Soviet Culture):

We have not yet met the requirements of getting acquainted with Soviet culture. An occasional acquaintance with this culture ... is important, but insufficient. We need to get acquainted with it *continuously* in order to facilitate its integral and constant influence on our new, improving culture. (Révai "Szovjet Kultúra" 1, emphasis in original, all translations are my own)⁴

---

2 MNL OL P2148, 1. d. Cited according to the Hungarian archival citation system. D. refers to *doboz* (box).

3 MNL OL M-KS 276 f. 54/32. ő.e. (f. refers to fonds, ő.e. is an abbreviation of *őrzési egység*, a smaller unit such as a folder within a fonds).

4 "a szovjet kultúra komoly megismerése érdekében eddig nem tettünk eleget. Az alkalmi ismerkedés ezzel a kultúrával . . . fontos, de nem elegendő. Arra van szükség, hogy *folyamatosan* ismerkedjünk ezzel a kultúrával, hogy lehetővé tegyük szerves és *állandó* hatását, a mi születő, új kultúránkra."

From then on, the party propagated the Soviet Union as a *utopian* state, re-narrating Soviet-Hungarian cultural relationships and subordinating them to the myth of an interstate friendship.⁵ Drawing attention to the advantages of friendship between the two nations, Révai wrote: "the Soviet Union gives us more than we give and can give to her ... In establishing a socialist state, society, economy and culture, the Soviet Union is far more experienced than our nation" ("Szovjet Kultúra" 3).⁶ Révai still emphasized the importance of remaining loyal to the Soviets in his speech which he delivered at the second congress of the Hungarian-Soviet Society in February 1953 ("Révai József" 3-4). Ferenc Erdei, Excecutive Director of the Society, tried to surpass him by expressing appreciation for the Soviet artists and scientist who "helped us generously" and who "lent wings to the workers of Hungarian culture with their art and education" (MNL OL P2148 1. d.).⁷

THE REPRESENTATIVE PUBLIC SPHERE

Hungarian ministries and institutions tried to introduce Soviet cultural products and methods in many different ways. One might stress the importance of written documents (such as the translation of Soviet fiction, philosophy, media coverage, academic books and articles), visual culture (such as paintings and photographs) and music (such as records), or the presence of the above-mentioned advisors. The role of official Soviet *deputies and guests*, however, seems to have been even more important from my point of interest. These guests (usually artists, writers, and scholars) usually visited the satellite states on ceremonial or festive occasions, and they were instructed to represent the current official position of the Soviet government in the limelight of publicity while advisors often remained incognito.

The so-called Friendship Months, which became one of the major symbols of interstate cultural relations, were among the most significant public events which

---

5   On the ideological background of the term Great Friendship, and the Polish and Eastern-German comparison see Behrends.

6   "A Szovjetunió többet ad nekünk, mint amennyit mi adunk és adhatunk neki . . . A Szovjetunió tapasztalatai mérhetetlenül nagyobbak a mi tapasztalatainknál, . . . a szocialista állam és társadalom, gazdaság és kultúra felépítésében."

7   "önzetlenül segítve . . . művészetükkel és tanításaikkal szárnyat adtak a magyar kultúra dolgozóinak."

the Soviet guests attended. Hundreds of thousands of people were forcefully mobilized to attend these events, and a huge machinery was responsible for the organization, including the staff of the Ministry of Public Education, the Institute of Cultural Relations, the All-Hungarian Association of Trade Unions, the Hungarian-Soviet Society, the State Security Office and, of course, the Central Committee of the Party (MNL OL P2148 5. d.). The local government never had much of a choice in selecting the guests, although it could make suggestions. Since only official contacts were permitted between Hungarians and Soviets during the period of High Stalinism in the early 1950s, the Soviet deputies never came to Budapest spontaneously and voluntarily, but only as representatives of the Soviet regime.

If vassalage is an appropriate term to define the political relations, one can use another feudal term in connection with guests and delegates: representative publicity. This Habermasian concept describes the blurring of boundaries between private and public spheres (Habermas 58-68). Applied to Eastern Europe after 1949, representative publicity refers to the establishment of a distorted communication framework in which Soviet participants aimed at representing the splendor of the Soviet Union while Hungarians were expected to show great admiration for all Soviet presentations and instructions. Therefore, it may seem that the Soviets manually controlled all domestic decisions and administrative measures in Hungarian domestic politics. As mentioned above, some evidence, however, raises doubts about this picture.

SOVIET GUESTS IN HUNGARY AND THEIR ROLE IN THE SOVIETIZATION OF MUSICAL ENTERTAINMENT

Considering that the cultural delegations were often led by musicians, music certainly played an important role in public diplomacy. Soviet musicians (composers, performers) and musicologists frequently visited Hungary from 1949 onwards in order to play concerts, give presentations, or participate in local discussions, symposiums, and public debates. According to public speeches of such Soviet composers as Michail Chulaki, Kirill Molchanov, Vladimir Zacharov or Jury Milyutin, the Sovietization (i.e. the Zhadovian transformation) of classical musical life always took priority over musical entertainment and popular musical genres. However, since socialist realist musical aesthetics insisted on abandoning the 'bourgeois' distinction between 'serious' and 'light' music, Stalinist cultural policy was committed to the demarcation between politically 'useful' and 'useless' (or hostile) rather than 'higher' and 'lower' spheres of art. Soviet composers, whose compositions usually exemplified the relatedness of the two musical spheres, had to handle, at least in their verbal manifestations, those spheres simultaneously.[8] As we shall see below, however, the topic of popular music and classical music received unequal treatment in Soviet-Hungarian public diplomacy in the Stalinist period. Popular music was usually judged by the criteria of (socialist) high culture, and only very few Hungarian documents bear witness to an actual and properly Soviet interest in popular music.

Of those Soviet musical delegates who visited Hungary during the Stalinist period, the General Secretary of the Association of Soviet Composers, Mihail Chulaki probably made the first observation on Hungarian musical entertainment. The Hungarian musicological journal *Zenei Szemle* (Musical Review) considered Chulaki's visit in early 1949 as one of the most important musical events of post-war Hungary. Edited by committed communist musicologists after late 1948, the journal expressed great appreciation for members of the Soviet delegation who "represented the musical life of the Soviet Union, and its humanistic magnificence" ("Szovjet Kultúra Hónapja" 1).[9]

However, as the article added, "we are indebted even more [to Chulaki] for spending most of his time with us, in order to discuss all the issues of our musical life. As a result, our tasks have become so obvious and conscious that the only thing left is to act" ("Szovjet Kultúra Hónapja" 1).[10]

On 24 February 1949, Chulaki gave a talk at the Hungarian Academy of Music on post-war Soviet music. According to a public report published in the journal *Új Világ* (New World), the audience was encouraged to ask him questions. One of those questions from the audience inquired about the relationship between classical and popular music in the Soviet Union, giving Chulaki the opportunity to define the official Soviet position:

In the West, it is impossible to overcome the differences between 'serious' and 'light' [music]. Light music degenerated and became an instrument of the most inferior type of entertainment. It adapted itself to the unhealthy erotic atmosphere of pubs, night clubs and

---

8   See, for instance, the oeuvre of Milyutin or Alexander Novikov. The latter was also invited to Budapest to introduce his mass musical compositions in 1951.

9   "a Szovjetunió zenekultúráját, ennek a zenekultúrának a mindenkihez szóló humanista nagyszerűségét reprezentálták."

10 "[Csulakinak azonban] főleg sokat köszönhetünk, aki csaknem minden idejét velünk töltötte, átbeszélve, átvitázva zeneéletünk minden problémáját. Ezután oly világossá és tudatossá váltak feladataink, hogy most már csak meg kell oldanunk őket."

dance clubs. Moreover, serious music remained the privilege of those few who had the upper hand over the masses by their superior existential and social status.

(The reporter comments on Chulaki's statement): Contrary to this, there is no gap between light and serious music in the Soviet Union. Both of them embody the emotional experiences of people, both of them communicate intellectual contents toward great masses of people, both of them are rooted in rich folk music traditions, and they both take their nutrimental juices from these traditions. (Chulaki qtd. in Új Világ 7)[11]

This direction, however objective it may have seemed, provided little help for the practical realization of socialist realist musical entertainment. The Hungarian Working People's Party understood that they had to undertake general measures before a more comprehensive Zhdanovian program could be implemented. It is no accident that *Zenei Szemle*, which highly praised Chulaki's remarks, focused on what the Soviet deputy said about "severe and straightforward"[12] criticism and self-criticism (Chulaki 1) and a fully centralized institutional framework which would guarantee a major transformation of the Hungarian musical landscape into a version of the Soviet Union.

Besides Chulaki's visit there was another important event in 1949, namely the Budapest concerts of the Osipov Folk Ensemble, a folk orchestra that was considered to be one of the important export products of Stalinist Soviet Culture. According to contemporary reviews, Hungarian audiences enthusiastically welcomed this Soviet group at all of their concerts (Kadosa 39). Following the tour, the musicology department of the Hungarian Association of Musicians dedicated a complete review session to the visit of the Osipovs. Participants agreed that contrary to the "sloppy" performance styles of dance music and jazz musicians, the real artists of the Soviet group had the ability to raise popular

---

11 "Nyugaton a könnyű és komoly közötti különbség áthidalhatatlan. A könnyűzene lesüllyedt a legalacsonyabb fokú szórakozás eszközévé. Lokálok, bárok, dancingok beteg erótikus [(sic!)] világához idomult, a komolyzene pedig azoknak a kevésszámúaknak a privilégiuma lett, akiket anyagi és társadalmi helyzetük a tömeg felé emelt. (A riporter válasza): Ezzel szemben a Szovjetunióban a könnyű és komoly zene közötti szakadék ma már ismeretlen, mindkettő a nép érzésvilágát szólaltatja meg, mindkettő magas eszmei tartalmak közvetítője a széles néptömegek felé és mindkettő a gazdag népzenei hagyományok talajában gyökeredzik, és onnan szívja tápláló nedveit."

12 "őszinte, nyílt kritika."

music to the level of symphonic music, and therefore their performances served the "noble" amusement of the working people (MNL OL P2146.).

A year later in 1950, the tour of the Pyatnitsky Choir received an even warmer response by some Hungarian music critics. The ensemble was accompanied by a dance group and an orchestra of Russian folk instruments. Members of the Pyatnitsky Choir were recruited from all over the Soviet Union, representing the 'equality' and 'friendship' of the Soviet nations. As Viktor Lányi, reporter of the journal *Új Világ* stated, the audience of one of the Budapest concerts "was holding its breath" during the famous song "Steppe Only Steppe," while "it fully felt the essence of the new way of music" (Lányi 20).[13]

The international tour of Pyatnitsky indicated already a modified definition of popular music in Hungary. An article entitled "The Effect of Soviet Music," written for the Hungarian-Soviet Society, reported about commercially successful Western (i.e. American) music in the past tense and praised the proliferation of Soviet entertainment and folk music (MNL OL P2148 5. d.). Simultaneously, the Association of Hungarian Musicians invited Vladimir Zacharov, the leader and chief composer of the Pyatnitski Choir, to speak about his group's inspirations and artistic approaches at a plenary session. Responding to questions following his talk, Zacharov pointed out that the Soviet youth had been successfully weaned away from listening and dancing to jazz and Western dance music as a result of the successful propagation of folk and certain ballroom dances (MNL OL P2146 62. d.).

The Pyatnitsky Choir was also one of the important role models for musicologist Iván Vitányi. In his article "On the New Hungarian Social Dance Culture," Vitányi demanded the domestication of newly designed folk dances which could help to shape the "new socialist man" and to develop the socialist consciousness of the people (16). As he pointed out, American social dances had already been successfully suppressed in the Soviet Union, but not yet in Hungary (16-17).

Vitányi found one of his positive examples in the ball scene of the Soviet film *Kubanskie Kazaki* (Cossacks of the Kuban, 1950) while he was searching for models for new Hungarian social dances. To Vitányi's mind, the scene demonstrated the collective spirit of the people, and it expressed the joviality and happiness characterizing new social dances of the future. Vitányi emphasized the

---

13 Since, beginning in 1949, publishing anything that deviated from the official line was not permitted anymore, we should not attempt to infer how ideologically committed journalists were at that time. This commitment can only be clearly proven by the quantity of somebody's writings and by the nature of their verbal communication during non-public debates in the committees and departments.

importance of the already existing Hungarian dance musical initiatives which tried to imitate Soviet examples. That is why he mentioned the new state-supported Dance with Us movement, which introduced two czardas-type Hungarian dances, the so-called karikázó (round dance) and farkastánc (wolf's dance). Vitányi was not the only one in favor of these endeavors. The popular music department of the Hungarian Association of Musicians and the Association of Dancers launched a monumental joint initiative to create the choreography and accompanying tunes of these dances which were supposed to replace tango and swing in Hungary (MNL OL P2146 62. d.).

The diatribes against jazz and Western dance music initially seemed to be successful. A series of propagandistic articles from 1950 and 1952 reported that the bourgeois jazz music and partner dances were expected to cause protest and indignation among socialist people. The new audience apparently already denied "the bad taste and pornographic songs and lyrics of nonsense of English and American jazz titles": "Our youth ... loves dancing, but it is fed up with the raving, worrying ... dances" ("Szünjék" 9).[14] According to the official media, swing and samba were systematically popularized by the US and socialist countries had to be alert in order to prevent being infiltrated by the "poison of cosmopolitanism" ("Szünjék" 9).

In 1951, the Hungarian Working People's Party called upon every jazz and dance musician of the country to join the "musical revolution" (MNL OL XIX-I-3-n 1. d.). In the same year, the All-Hungarian Association of Trade Unions organized a music competition which aimed at struggling against cosmopolitanism ("Tánczenekaraink" 1). The Association primarily invited local bands which had participated in the World Festival of Youth and Students (WFY) in East Berlin a few months earlier. The aim was to eliminate the "artful sounds," the "cacophonic jazz-harmonies" or "distorted rhythms" (Tamássy 37-38) and to acquire the severe performing style that stays loyal to the musical message and intellectual content. The twelve bands which entered the competition, among them the groups led by Mihály Tabányi, Lajos Martony, and Péter Hajdú, were forced to compile a colorful program reflecting the "optimistic atmosphere" of the third WFY, "expressing the youthful impetus and desire for peace characteristic of young people" ("Tánczenekaraink" 1).[15] The program turned out to be

---

14 "Ez az új közönség . . . visszautasítja az ízléstelen, pornográf kuplékat, az angol, amerikai értelmetlen jazz-számokat." "Ifjúságunk . . . szeret táncolni, de felháborodnak az ízléstelen, testet-lelket elgyötrő . . . táncokon."

15 "fejezzék ki az ifjúság békevágyát, fiatalos lendületét, a III. VIT . . . optimista hangulatát."

colorful indeed. Contemporary Hungarian stars such as Tabányi and Martony played covers of Soviet hits, presented a cover of the official March of the World Federation of Democratic Youth, and even a version of Alexander Alexandrov's famous "Cantata about Stalin" ("Tánczenekaraink" 1).

The most important element, however, was missing, namely socialist realist-inspired Hungarian popular songs produced and performed by Hungarian musicians. Socialist realist musical discourses revealed and named only the allegedly wrong, hostile, and inadequate elements and attributes of works of art, and made only vague and contradictory references to the criteria of ideal composition. The accessibility to the broadest masses or the simplicity and clarity of form were definitely included in the list of those criteria. The requirements of ideological commitment and national/popular spirit were among the most frequent ones, too (Heller). Besides, composers and musicologists continuously proclaimed the need for the primacy of the melody since they believed that music has to imitate the intelligent and expressive human speech. As a result, they demanded linear melodies that are easy to sing and memorize. Simultaneously, they launched a campaign to promote thinking in clear and easy harmonic structures in order to avoid the "formalist cacophony" of jazz music and to create a jolly and optimistic musical atmosphere. Opinions differed regarding the implementation of new Hungarian social dances: while some composers and musicologists wanted to keep the traditional dance-rhythms (such as slow fox, waltz, polka, etc.) and integrate them into the new musical material, others advocated the design of completely new rhythms based on the peculiarities of Hungarian folk songs (MNL OL P2146 61. d.; 62. d.; 66. d.; Ignácz, "Hungarian in Form").

Similar to the lyrics of classical compositions, the ones of popular music pieces had to depict the new socialist way of life in Hungary. As the director of Hungarian Radio, István Szirmai stated at a debate session in 1950, "our youth is growing, the factory is producing, and a new type of socialist man is growing up in the factories who is dancing, loving or having fun. Therefore, dance songs have to portray the humor and playfulness of this new man" (MNL OL P2146, d. 62).[16] At the beginning, patriotic and folkish, rural topics were also welcomed. The topic of love, however, was considered dangerous and risky, as it was connected with sexuality, melancholy, or resignation. According to a 1954 press debate, these lyrics "allow for no glimmer of hope, and passion for life and

---

16 "nő az ifjúság, termel a gyár, a gyárban egy új típusú szocialista ember nő fel, aki táncol, szeret, szórakozik, a táncdalok az ő életétének humorát, játékát adják vissza."

work." Instead "they are training for cynicism, laxity of morals, and extravagance, as if everyone were living only in the here and now" (G. Horváth 8)."[17]

Although there was supposed to be a tacit agreement as to what "socialist content" should mean in the field of popular music, members of the Association of Musicians assumed very different viewpoints regarding the primacy of lyrics or sound. Many argued that good music depends on the preexistence of good lyrics. According to the politically most influential composer, Ferenc Szabó, ideologically committed dance music has to be based on the rhythmic, intellectual, and emotional message of the lyrics. Some of his colleagues claimed that the message and structure of music could enrich the fantasy of librettists. However, nobody doubted the view that only those popular songs could be successful in which sound and lyrics are inseparable from one another other. It is no accident that in the first years of communist rule the idea of instrumental dance music was hardly discussed.

HUNGARIAN DANCE MUSIC COMES TO TRIAL: THE CRITIQUE OF KIRILL MOLCHANOV

Beginning in late 1950, a few efforts were launched to implement communist musical ideals. The first serious test of Hungarian-produced socialist realist dance songs was an evening of the First Hungarian Musical Week on 20 November 1951 where Ilona Hollós, László Kazal and other famous singers of the time performed 25 songs accompanied by the State Radio Dance Orchestra. A few days later, on 24 November, higher local officials and foreign guests were invited to evaluate the event at a review session hosted by the Budapest Academy of Music (MNL OL P2146 61.d.). The Soviet delegation was led by Tikhon Khrennikov, President of the Association of Soviet Composers, who otherwise was known in his country not only as an ardent supporter of socialist realism (Tomoff; Heikinheimo), but also as the main censor of jazz and American dance music (Starr 180). However, Khrennikov's talk in Budapest focused exclusively on such general aspects as the dangers of formalism and cosmopolitanism, refraining from analyzing the popular musical compositions of the Hungarian Musical Week. Khrennikov appointed Kirill Molchanov in his stead to critically evaluate the conditions of socialist realist dance music in Hungary.

---

17 "akire hatnak, abból kiölik a jövőbe vetett hitet, az életkedvet, munkakedvet, a nemes emberi érzelmek megbecsülését és tiszteletben tartását. Cinizmusra, erkölcsi lazaságra nevelnek, szertelenségre, azon az alapon, hogy ki tudja, mi lesz holnap."

Molchanov, General Secretary of the Soviet Association, downplayed the importance of popular music in favor of program music and opera. He said, however, that supporters of socialist realism all have to be concerned with popular music, because the global hegemonic aspirations of the US and the destructive effects of cosmopolitanism are embodied in the "bourgeois" popular music of recent years (MNL OL P2146 61.d.). The Soviet deputy expressed fierce criticism about the pieces he had heard a few days before, calling them mentally empty and in want of ideas. According to him, songs which attempted to force "sensible" lyrics related to the new contemporary life into jazz schemes were even worse than their musical models (MNL OL P2146 61.d.), that is, the original jazz compositions. Molchanov inquired why Hungarian composers of popular music were not making more use of the wealth of Hungarian folk music. He reminded the audience that the Hungarian people had already created their songs and dances. In order to reflect the spirit of the people in popular music, one would only need to call Hungarian folk songs and dances in mind (MNL OL P2146 61.d.).

It is difficult to assess the impact of Molchanov's speech, again, since he echoed only the widely known basic Zhdanovian demands, without going into any theoretical or practical details. Following his exhortations, however, beginning in early 1952, the state increasingly controlled the composition and distribution of dance music in Hungary. State control manifested in regular consultation sessions about popular music and the establishment of a state-funded dance music composing course. In this course (called *tánczeneszerzői tanfolyam* in Hungarian), enthusiastic novices studied the theory of socialist realism, the history of folk music, and technical aspects of composing. At the end of the course, they had the opportunity to discuss their works with a delegated working group of the Association of Hungarian Musicians which then assisted the publishing and recording of the most valued pieces.

The politically influential composer Endre Székely first drew attention to the necessity of those consultations in Hungary. Székely regularly enjoyed the hospitality of his Soviet colleagues and had first-hand experience on how dance music composition courses were organized in the Soviet Union. He delivered his remarks at a review session on 25 January 1952, an event which was incidentally dedicated to the "morals of the Hungarian Musical Week." Several participants of the meeting agreed that Molchanov's perspicacity was disturbed by the bad amplifying and the lack of translations of the texts. Zdenkó Tamássy, the former leader of the popular music department of the Association of Hungarian Musicians, also expressed his sincere surprise about the complete lack of Soviet help (MNL OL P2146 62.d.).

Thus, Soviet instructions eventually proved futile. With very few exceptions, the "Hungarian-style" popular songs composed under the supervision of censors did not become popular. The concept of folk music-based national dance music obviously had undergone a crisis by the spring of 1953. Examining the tracklists of radio programs, live shows, and music festivals shows that the imaginary "jazz-free" new popular music scene suffered from a severe shortage of musical material to be aired. Since communists were constantly lagging behind in designing the new style, the topic of what to play and listen to at the "stage of transition" (which the communists referred to as "the interregnum"), was permanently on the agenda (MNL OL P2146 62.d.). To many, the adaptation of popular Soviet songs, such as the ones of Isaak Dunayevsky or Jury Milyutin, and their "Magyarization" seemed to be the best solution to remedy this deficiency. There were frequent clashes, however, concerning the extent to which jazz, foxtrot or tango covers of Soviet hits could serve the purposes of socialist entertainment. Pianist László Turán, member of the Radio Dance Orchestra, complained already at a conference held on 30 September 1950 that his band had been criticized by a few participants for as slight a modification as accelerating the original tempos and trying to make the converted Soviet compositions more dance-able using dotted rhythms and syncopations (MNL OL P2146 62.d.).

SOVIET DANCE MUSIC IN HUNGARY BEYOND 1953

It was under these circumstances that Jury Milyutin visited Budapest. The Stalin-prize-winning composer of operettas, dance music, and soundtracks drew attention to the ideological message of dance music compositions and the importance of intonation in his talks held at the Academy of Music in February and March 1953 ("Miljutyin" 7). It is noteworthy that Milyutin showed compliance towards those high-quality pieces which remained perfect in their socialist intellectual content, but were less nationalistic in their intonation. Still, he finally urged his Hungarian colleagues to turn their attention to the "most noble and most complicated task" of composing popular songs national in both form and content ("Miljutyin" 7).

The musicologist János Maróthy, who later became an initiator and major figure of the local political and aesthetic discussions concerning popular music, considered Milyutin's talks a fundamental inspiration. In his article "Urgent Tasks," published immediately after the visit of the Soviet delegation, Maróthy discussed what is probably the last large-scale concept of national dance music (Ignácz, "Music"), but his contribution added little that was new to the musical discourse of social realism. The point under discussion was once more, like in the earlier Stalinist years, the importance of the so-called "Hungarian-style school," which Maróthy described as the most progressive socialist realist dance music endeavor in the country (Ignácz, "Music").

It seemed inconceivable, even in early 1953, that there could be any transformation in the Stalinist artistic approach or in the rigid system of censorship seeking to prevent cultural infiltration. Stalin's death in 1953, however, caused a dramatic political and social change in each country of the Eastern European satellite states. As a consequence, the Hungarian-Soviet Society was forced to admit its former faults, including the way in which they had idealized the Soviet Union, thus making Soviet culture virtually inaccessible to a broader audience (MNL OL P2148 4.d.).

Soviet-Hungarian relations also underwent a change because of the détente. The communication became less ritualized, and more functional with the result that questions of popular genres in public diplomacy lost relevance. The same trend was indicated by the report entitled *Proposal for the Reinforcement of Interstate Relations* (Javaslat a Nemzetközi Kapcsolatok Erősítésére) issued by the Ministry of Public Education in May 1954. The document contained important critical remarks about Soviet-Hungarian relations in the field of popular music. It observed that popular music is the only musical field where the "exchange of experiences" between Eastern European countries is still absent. The Ministry encouraged the cultural policy makers to organize a pan-European estrade festival in co-operation with Czech, Bulgarian, East German, French, Italian, Polish, and Soviet bands. This festival, however, was never realized. This document appears to be the only one questioning Soviet responsibility for the failure of renewing Hungarian popular music. None of the presentations and performances of the above-mentioned Soviet deputies were deemed to be relevant aspects of cultural exchange (MNL OL XIX-i-3-o.).

CONCLUSION

This contribution argued that political leaders and cultural elites in Hungary tried to transform popular culture by using elusive Soviet models and examples. It seems that, contrary to other fields of public life, Soviet deputies of popular music were not in all instances instruments of a "manual control" of Hungarian cultural life and musical production. They did not always manage to directly influence the popular music scene in Hungary. Therefore, their speeches need to be treated with the utmost caution when reconstructing the history of Hungarian popular music of the early 1950s.

Even though the main intention of Chulaki, Zacharov, Molchanov or Milyutin was to hammer the Zhdanovian artistic approach into Hungarian heads, policy makers and musicians used their ideas as pretexts for Sovietizing the popular music scene on their own account and according to their own methods and plans. The reason for the relative independence of Hungarian cultural policy in this field was most probably the relative insignificance of popular music in Soviet public diplomacy. If Stalin and his comrades had declared the transformation of Hungarian popular culture a priority, Hungarian communists would have had no alternative but to be entirely at their disposal and to strictly follow Soviet instructions.

During the Stalinist period of the late 1940s and early 1950s, the Sovietization of popular music, everyday culture, and leisure time in Hungary was less important than that of the economy and state machinery. The significance of Soviet interventions in Hungarian cultural policy was, however, enlarged by the Hungarian government's efforts to surpass Soviet expectations in many fields of everyday life. The very reforms in Hungarian cultural life and Soviet-Hungarian relations took place only after Soviet pressure had forced the Hungarian government to admit some of its former mistakes in June 1953. At that time, a new period of different competing conceptions began. The 'dogmatic' approach and Zhdanov's principles did not completely retreat, but the emphasis slowly shifted from technical and compositional questions to the aesthetic education of musicians and audiences as well as institutional positions and circumstances of production and distribution.

At a meeting held on 27 February 1954, lyricist József Romhányi and composer Béla Tardos spoke quite openly about the paralyzing effects of state control over the process of composing. They already considered all administrative measures or direct interventions, even the Soviet ones, risky and admitted that socialist realist musical entertainment does not gain anything from restrictions of artistic freedom anymore. From then on, the Association of Musicians and the Ministry of Public Education tried to outline only the general ideological framework, and it was the artists' and theoreticians' personal responsibility to comply with the guidelines of socialist realism in their own individual ways (MNL OL P2146 62.d.).

At the same time, the regime began to gather more information about the needs and expectations of the audience. This new direction—which brought public procurement contracts—was not much different from the cultural policy established after the Hungarian Revolution of 1956. The creed of this policy was from the very beginning decent and classy entertainment and aesthetic education of the youth. It seems that these changes in Hungary brought about a collapse of the idea of *aesthetic totalitarianism*.[18]

WORKS CITED

"A Szovjet Kultúra Hónapja Után." *Zenei Szemle* 1 (1949): 1. Print.
"A Zeneszerzők és Zenekritikusok prágai Kongresszusának Határozatai." *Zenei Szemle* 6 (1948): 293-96. Print.
Baráth, Magdolna. *A Kreml Árnyékában: Tanulmányok Magyarország és a Szovjetunió Kapcsolatainak Történetéhez, 1944-1990*. Budapest: Gondolat, 2014. Print.
---. "A Szovjetunióról Kialakult és Kialakított kép Változásai." *A Kreml Árnyékában. Tanulmányok Magyarország és a Szovjetunió kapcsolatainak történetéhez, 1944-1990*. Ed. Baráth, Magdolna. Budapest: Gondolat, 2014. Print.
---. "Testvéri Segítségnyújtás.' Szovjet Tanácsadók és Szakértők Magyarországon." *Történelmi Szemle* 3 (2010): 357-86. Print.
---. "'T. et.-nak Átadva': Szőnyei Tamás Interjúja Baráth Magdolnával." *Magyar Narancs* 3 (2012). Web. 3 Aug. 2018. <http://magyarnarancs.hu/belpol/t-et-nak-atadva-78331/>.
Behrends, Jan C. *Die erfundene Freundschaft. Propaganda für die Sowjetunion in Polen und in der DDR (1944-1957)*. Köln: Böhlau, 2005. Print.
"Beszélgetés Miljutyin Elvtárssal." *Új Zenei Szemle* 3 (1953): 8-10. Print.
Borhi, László. *A Vasfüggöny Mögött: Magyarország Nagyhatalmi Erőtérben, 1945-1968*. Budapest: Ister, 2010. Print.
Borsody, István. "A Szovjetunió Közép- és Kelet-Európa-politikája és Magyarország, 1941-1947." *Magyarország és a Nagyhatalmak a 20. Században*. Ed. Romsics Ignác. Budapest: Teleki László Alapítvány, 1995. 163-69. Print.
Chulaki, Mihail. "A Szovjet zene Időszerű Kérdései: Mihail Csulaki Előadása a Zeneakadémián 1949. február 24-én." *Zenei Szemle* 1 (1949): 28-36. Print.
"Csulaki, Oborin és Vlaszov a Zeneakadémia növendékei között." *Új Világ*. 26 Feb. 1949: 7. Print.
Horváth, Zoltán G. „Néhány Megjegyzés Tánczenénkről." *Új Zenei Szemle* 5 (1954): 8. Print.

---

18 Research for this chapter was supported by the Hungarian National Research, Development and Innovation Office (NKFIH, PD 115373).

Habermas, Jürgen. *Strukturwandel der Öffentlichkeit*. Berlin: Suhrkamp, 1999. Print.

Hajdú, Tibor. "Szovjet Diplomácia Magyarországon Sztálin Halála Előtt és Után." *Magyarország és a Nagyhatalmak a 20. Században*. Ed. Romsics Ignác. Budapest: Teleki László Alapítvány, 1995. 195-201. Print.

Heikinheimo, Seppo. "Tikhon Khrennikov in Interview." *Tempo* 173 (1990): 18-20. Print.

Ignácz, Ádám. "'Hungarian in Form, Socialist in Content': The Concept of National Dance Music in Stalinist Hungary (1949-1956)." *Made in Hungary. Studies in Popular Music*. Ed. Emilia Emilia and Tamás Tófalvy. New York: Routledge, 2017. 69-76. Print.

Ignácz, Ádám. "'Music for Millions': János Maróthy and Academic Research on Popular Music in Socialist Hungary." *Muzikologija* 23 (2017): 117-25. Print.

Kadosa, Pál. "Az Oszipov népi Zenekar Magyarországi Vendégszereplése és Annak Tanulságai." *Szovjet Kultúra* 1 (1950): 39. Print.

Lányi, Viktor. "A Magyar-Szovjet Barátság Hónapjának zenei Eseményei." *Szovjet Kultúra* 3 (1950): 20. Print.

Maróthy, János. "Tánczenénk Fejlesztésének Néhány Sürgető Feladata." *Új Zenei Szemle* 5 (1953): 1-6. Print.

"Miljutyin Elvtárs a Szórakoztató Zenéről." *Művészeti Dolgozók Lapja* 19. Mar. (1953): 3. Print.

MNL OL P2148. Documents of the Hungarian-Soviet Society. National Archives of Hungary, Budapest. Print.

MNL OL P2146. Documents of the Association of Hungarian Musicians. National Archives of Hungary, Budapest. Print.

MNL OL MNL OL M-KS 276. Documents of the Hungarian Working People's Party. National Archives of Hungary, Budapest. Print.

MNL OL MNL OL XIX-i-3-n. Documents of the Ministry of Public Education. National Archives of Hungary, Budapest. Print.

MNL OL XIX-i-3-o. Documents of the Ministry of Public Education. National Archives of Hungary, Budapest. Print.

Rainer, János M. "Sztálin és Rákosi, Sztálin és Magyarország, 1949-1953." *Sztálin és Európa, 1944-1953. Magyarország és a Kreml, 1949-1965: Dokumentumok*. Ed. Litván György. Budapest, 1998: 91-100. Print.

Révai, József. "A 'Szovjet Kultúra' Megjelenéséhez." *Szovjet Kultúra* 1 (1949): 1. Print.

---. "Révai József Elvtárs Beszéde: Mindvégig ki Fogunk Tartani a Magyar-Szovjet Barátság nagy ügye Mellett." *Új Világ* 19 Feb. 1953: 3-4. Print.

Standeisky, Éva. "A Kígyó Bore: Ideológia és Politika." *A Fordulat Évei, 1947- 1949: Politika, Képzőművészet, Építészet*. Ed. Éva Standeisky. Budapest, 1998. 164-66. Print.

Starr, S. Frederick. *Red and Hot: Jazz in Russland 1917-1990*. Vienna: Hannibal, 1990. Print.

"Szűnjék meg az Imperializmus Propagandája a Könnyűzenében." *Művészeti Dolgozók Lapja* 15 Aug. 1950: 9. Print.

"Tánczenekaraink VIT versenye a Kozmopolitizmus Elleni harc Jegyében." *Művészeti Dolgozók Lapja* 31 Aug. 1951: 1. Print.

Tamássy, Zdenkó. "A Magyar Tánczene Kérdései." *Új Zenei Szemle* 6-7 (1950): 37-8. Print.

Tomoff, Kirill. "'Most Respected Comrade...': Patrons, Clients, Brokers and Unofficial Networks in the Stalinist Music World." *Contemporary European History* 1 (2002): 33-65. Print.

Vitányi, Iván. "Az új Magyar Társasági Tánckultúráról." *Művelt Nép* 8 (1950): 16-17. Print.

Zhdanov, Andrei A. [A.A. Zsdanov]. *A művészet és filozófia kérdései*. Budapest: Szikra, 1949. Print.

Part III:
Education and Promotion

Dancing in Chains
Why Music Can't Keep the World Free

Martha Bayles

My title comes from Friedrich Nietzsche (247), but currently it is being quoted by Chinese writers, artists, scholars, and journalists as a way of describing the experience of working under the growing repressions of President Xi Jinping. There are, of course, many Western scholars and journalists who make similar complaints about various formal and informal pressures to "self-censor."[1] So in that broad sense, we are all dancing in chains.

But there are chains and there are chains. The political liberty and freedom of expression enjoyed by those of us who live and work in the West are not perfect. But they are a lot better than the authoritarian alternative.

There was a time, half a century ago, when American popular music was seen as a beacon of political liberty and free speech and expression. As such, it played an important role in making liberal democracy attractive to millions of people living under fascist or communist domination. That time spanned World War II and the Cold War, and while the story was never a simple morality tale, neither was it false.

The thesis of this essay is that the relationship between American popular music and US public diplomacy has changed drastically. Not only has popular music ceased to be a beacon of liberal democracy, it has also, at times, propagated a negative image of Western freedoms that repels ordinary people and strengthens tyranny.

---

[1] There are countless examples of this view, but one very prominent statement came from the novelist Salman Rushdie, who stated before an audience at the University of Vermont on 15. Jan. 2015, "the moment somebody says, 'I believe in free speech, but,' I stop listening" (Associated Press).

This essay has four parts: 1) an overview of how popular music (first jazz then rock) enhanced American prestige during the crucial period of World War II and the Cold War; 2) a brief summary of the drastic changes that have occurred since the Berlin Wall fell in 1989; 3) some examples of how today's popular music does and does not support freedom in the world; and 4) a warning that if Americans—and Europeans—are to develop a renewed public diplomacy for the twenty-first-century, we will have to draw more cogent lessons from this history than we have so far drawn.

FROM GOLDEN GLOW TO PLASTIC PEOPLE

Europeans and Russians discovered jazz around 1917, when Sidney Bechet accompanied the composer-conductor Will Marion Cook on a European tour. Then, during World War II, the jazz programs of the US Armed Forces Network provided respite, not only to US servicemen, but also to ordinary Europeans. Building on this popularity, the Voice of America (VOA) began in 1955 to beam "the music of freedom," as host Willis Conover called it, to a regular audience of 100 million worldwide, including 30 million behind the Iron Curtain (Thomas). Then in the early 1960s, the State Department sponsored tours by such jazz masters as Sidney Bechet, Louis Armstrong, Duke Ellington, Dave Brubeck, Benny Goodman, and Dizzy Gillespie.

The appeal of the VOA broadcasts is well documented. To the Russian novelist Vassily Aksyonov, they were "America's secret weapon number one . . . a kind of golden glow over the horizon" (Richmond 207). To a young Russian fan, Conover's program was "a source of strength when I am overwhelmed by pessimism" (Lester). Looking back on his years as an underground jazz musician in Czechoslovakia, novelist Josef Škvorecký writes that "our sweet, wild music was a sharp thorn in the side of the power-hungry men, from Hitler to Brezhnev, who successively ruled in my native land" (83).

The tours were more challenging, in part because key decision makers at the State Department were less interested in the music than in using African American jazz masters to blunt Soviet criticism of American racism. Historian Penny von Eschen notes that there was "a glaring contradiction" in using "black artists as goodwill ambassadors . . . when America was still a Jim Crow nation" (9). This is true. But as von Eschen also notes, the tours succeeded in large part because the musicians were allowed to speak freely about racial discrimination. Even Gillespie, whose acerbic comments on the topic upset his State Department sponsors, admitted that "our interracial group was powerfully effective against Red propaganda" (Gillespie qtd. in Eschen 17).

And the music transcended politics. During the darkest years of the twentieth century, millions of people around the world came to see jazz as proof that freedom and democracy can co-exist with a highly cultivated artistic sensibility. It would be nice to think that artistic cultivation is a necessary condition for successful musical diplomacy, but to judge by what happened next, it is not. As the Cold War unfolded, the official export of jazz mattered less than the unofficial export of a vigorous but much less refined genre of music: rock.

Rock music, or rock 'n' roll as it was called then, first gained a following in the Soviet Union in the 1950s, via smuggled 45s, audiotapes made from foreign radio broadcasts, and (my personal favorite) the *roentgenizdat*—an ingenious method of transferring the grooves on a vinyl record to discarded X-ray plates. This "music on ribs" became a booming underground industry, with a distribution network that at one point reached as far as Siberia (Ryback 32-3). By the mid-1960s, VOA had caught up with the craze and was broadcasting the various styles of rock (and soul) popular at the time.

But rock's greatest moment came later, during the 1970s and 1980s, when growing communication and travel facilitated a steady eastward flow of American and British popular music, from commercially successful rock, soul, and folk acts to more underground groups, such as Frank Zappa's the Mothers of Invention and the Velvet Underground. With their dark lyrics and discordant sounds, the latter two would never have passed muster with VOA. But given the rebellious mood of their fans in Eastern Europe and the Soviet Union, their unofficial status only added to their impact (Bayles, "Struggle").

The best example of this impact is the Plastic People of the Universe, a Czech band modeled after the Velvet Underground. Formed in 1968, shortly after Russian tanks crushed the Prague Spring, the Plastic People's music was neither refined nor especially crowd-pleasing—indeed, their 1970s performances were more like avant-garde "happenings" than rock concerts. But over time, the band's stubborn defiance of the communist authorities attracted a following. In 1976, when its members were subjected to a Kafkaesque trial, Václav Havel spoke out in their defense, and the trial became a rallying point for the Czech movement of resistance to Soviet domination (Vaughan).

Thus did the American counterculture, intended to subvert authority at home, become even more subversive overseas. The process continued through the 1980s, as American and British popular music became second nature to a generation of Russians and East Europeans. Then came the collapse of the Berlin Wall, followed by the 1990s—a transformative decade whose definitive history has yet to be written, perhaps because our present world is still reeling from the transformations it brought.

POST-COLD-WAR TRANSFORMATIONS

We now turn to three of those transformations: a steep decline in US public diplomacy efforts; an upsurge in the export of US popular culture; and the rise—in Russia, China, and many other countries—of a new kind of authoritarianism, in which social and economic freedoms are expanded, at least for a while, while political liberty remains as restricted as ever.

The first transformation occurred between 1993 and 2001: funding for US cultural and educational exchanges was cut by one third, from $349 million to $232 million (Curb Center 18). Overseas this meant closing many American libraries and cultural centers that had long served as meeting places and free-speech zones. Finally, in 1999, the US Information Agency (known overseas as USIS), which had conducted public diplomacy since 1953, was dismantled, and its activities scattered throughout the State Department. This meant a drastic loss of independence, not only in terms of budget, but also in terms of public diplomats' ability to operate in the field.[2]

The second transformation was the opening of new media markets around the world, as state-controlled terrestrial channels gave way to new, privately owned satellite services. Hungry for content, these services acquired a huge number of US feature films, TV programs, and popular music, at a time when many of the most successful individuals in Hollywood were busy pushing the envelope of violence and vulgarity. The result was a sudden flood of American entertainment into parts of the non-Western world where the vast majority of people had no real exposure to, or knowledge of, life in the United States.

Did anyone in the US government worry where this might lead? In most cases, no. But there were some notable exceptions. For example, in 1998, when the USIS was about to be closed, its director, Joseph Duffey, warned against leaving "the portrayal of American culture . . . exclusively to the mainstream media." With remarkable prescience, Duffey continued:

---

2   This statement, like many others made in this essay, is based on the many interviews the author conducted with former public diplomats and foreign service officers (see *Through a Screen Darkly*).

While the United States enjoys a dominant position in the production and exportation of entertainment products, it remains debatable whether these products best serve America's broader interests and ultimately democracy itself. . . . If morally questionable programming is viewed as destructive to the moral fiber of American citizens, then what can be said of such programming when it is given wider airing on the international stage? On the one hand, it can have the same corrosive effect in countries that embrace American entertainment. . . . On the other hand, in countries that are repelled by American and Western values, such as those in the Pacific Rim, espousing a new "neo-Confucianism," or Islamic countries that reject Western secularism, such programming only confirms the worst suspicions that the West, and America in particular, is morally corrupt and intellectually devoid. (13)

The third transformation was even more worrisome: the rise of a new type of authoritarian rule, which, rather than control every aspect of people's lives, seeks only to control political thought and behavior. At the heart of this new approach are the media. With the exception of North Korea, the world has moved beyond the age of stultifying state propaganda. Instead, the media in Russia, China, and other authoritarian states have spent the last two decades copying Western entertainment and "infotainment," while at the same time strictly forbidding anything resembling Western political reporting—or press freedom more generally (Diamond et al.).

As Duffey suggests, these same regimes have also learned how to turn some of the West's popular culture against it, citing crude and sensationalist films, TV shows, and popular music as evidence that Europe and (especially) America are "immoral," "decadent," and "gay" (13). This provides these regimes with an excuse to crack down on Western cultural imports—a form of censorship that upsets Westernized elites but is often supported by the majority of the population. The next step, seen first in Putin's Russia and now in Xi's China, is to broaden the crackdown to include dissidents, artists, writers, scholars, activists, bloggers, and everyone else who dares to raise their voice against the government (see Diamond et al.; see Ostrovsky; Arutunyan for Russia; for China see Brady; Stockmann).

A different but equally worrisome dynamic is at work in the online recruitment efforts of violent Islamist extremist groups such as ISIS, Al Qaeda, and Boko Haram. These groups also denounce the immorality and decadence of Western media, but when staging and filming their own acts of brutality and murder, they, too, borrow from those media. In particular, they borrow the style and imagery of American action films, videogames, reality shows, even pornography (Cottee, "Pornography"; "Challenge"; "Jihad"). The result is a horrific form of entertainment-propaganda that attracts young men (and some women) in both the Middle East and the West by appealing to their craving for excitement and adventure—not to mention freedom from the constraints of life in traditional Islamic families and communities (Fernandez).

These new threats are every bit as complex as those the West faced during the early years of the Cold War. But disturbingly, we do not seem to be grasping them as quickly.

HOW POPULAR MUSIC DOES—AND DOES NOT—SUPPORT FREEDOM

Back in 1917, President Woodrow Wilson described the new medium of film as "a universal language [that] lends itself importantly to the presentation of America's plans and purposes" (qtd. in de Grazia 299). Since then, Washington has consistently labored to boost the export of Hollywood's products. On occasion, these efforts have alienated other governments, as when Washington used coercive measures to pry open resistant foreign markets. But boosting the export of popular culture has never alienated Americans, in part because it imposes no burden on the taxpayer. On the contrary, it makes a hefty profit and helps to right the balance of trade.

Add the tributes to jazz and rock music that emerged from the former Soviet sphere after the end of the Cold War, and you have a sufficient explanation of why the export of popular culture in general, popular music in particular, has long been considered good business and good public diplomacy. But is this still true?

The export of popular music is still good business. Global revenue for the US music industry (including concerts and touring) has held steady at $15 billion since in 2012 (Media and Entertainment Spotlight). This figure is declining because of competition from European and Asian markets and, of course, the digital revolution. But America is still home to the "big three" record companies—Universal Music Group, Sony Music Entertainment, and Warner Music Group—as well as a strong indie sector. And it still dominates the global performance-rights market, as well as earning half of all "synch revenue," or fees paid for the use of music in other media, such as films and videogames (Media and Entertainment Spotlight).

But the evidence suggests that, with regard to communicating America's most cherished ideals of political liberty and freedom of expression, there is good news and bad news. Some of today's exports are effective in communicating these ideals; others are not.

First, the good news. In nearly every country, there is a localized version of the TV format pioneered as *Pop Idol* in Britain, *American Idol* in the United States. These shows are referred to as "reality shows," because they feature ordinary people, as opposed to professional performers. But there are two kinds of reality shows: the *exhibitionist* kind, where naïve, deluded people compete on the basis of foolishness and shamelessness; and the *talent-based* kind, where singers, dancers, chefs, and other ambitious amateurs compete on the basis of effort and skill. The pop-idol show is talent-based, and the values it displays—hard work, playing by the rules, and accepting the outcome of a fair contest—are everywhere associated with democracy.

Perhaps the most striking case occurred in China. For the observer of popular culture, there have been few more fascinating spectacles in recent years than Beijing's efforts to create what might be called "Youth Culture with Chinese Characteristics." During the 1990s and 2000s, these efforts were part of a system of carefully calibrated censorship, in which mass-market newspapers and films enjoyed very little latitude; but small-circulation newspapers, the fine arts, and English-language scholarship enjoyed a lot more. It all depended on the size and potential influence of the audience. But in television the pattern was different: the degree of control depended less on the size of the audience than on the content. TV news, especially political news, was tightly controlled, but TV entertainment was given relatively free rein.

Thus, in 2004 a regional TV channel, Hunan Satellite TV, came up with a pop-idol show called *The Mongolian Cow Sour Yogurt Super Girl Contest* (after its main sponsor). Better known as *Super Girl*, the show became a local hit, and when the channel got permission to broadcast it via satellite, it sparked a national craze. Auditions in Hunan, Guangdong, Henan, Zhejiang, and Sichuan provinces drew over 120,000 contestants. Fans held mass demonstrations in streets and shopping malls, prompting the official state newspaper, *China Daily*, to comment that millions of Chinese were being "swept . . . into a euphoria of voting that [was] a testament to a society opening up" (Zhou Dake qtd. in Zhou). And the season finale attracted 400 million viewers and 8 million texted votes (a number that would doubtless have been higher if texting did not cost money).

The winner, a 21-year-old music student from Sichuan named Li Yuchun, was a charismatic figure who defied convention by dressing in jeans and loose shirts, wearing no makeup, and performing songs ordinarily sung by men. Tall and slim with spiky hair, Li's appearance would not have raised an eyebrow in the West. But in China, the victory of this apparent tomboy set off a huge public debate—especially after the Hong Kong edition of *Time* magazine asked, "*Super Girl*—experiment in democracy?"

The show's popularity made it hard for the Central Propaganda Department to cancel it outright. But according to an official in the Central Committee Global Communications Office whom I interviewed in Beijing, *Super Girl* prompted "an urgent debate in the higher circles of government" (Bayles, *Through a Screen Darkly* 104). Eventually, the propaganda department decided to do what it does best, launching a campaign to "guide" public opinion back in the right direction. This happened in stages: first, *China Daily* asked: "How come an imitation democratic system ends up selecting the singer who has the least ability to carry a tune?" (Zhou 52). Second, a rumor was planted about Li's sexual orientation. Third, an official opinion poll (predictably) found high levels of public disapproval of *Super Girl* (Bayles, *Through a Screen Darkly* 101-6).

With this justification, *Super Girl* was canceled just in time for the 2008 Olympics in Beijing. The following year it was revived, but it was no longer the same. Indeed, it was no longer a bona fide pop-idol show, because instead of being chosen through a process of viewer voting, the winner was now selected by a panel of "experts." Even the normally compliant *China Daily* seemed disappointed. Griped one editorial, "the public voting system was dropped in favor of professional musicians and star-makers from entertainment companies acting as judges. It was the least interesting competition of the three years, because we all knew the answer" (Tian).

But here we see a crucial difference between past and present: Li Yuchun was not sent to re-education camp or prison, as would certainly have been the case in Maoist times. On the contrary, she was made into a Party-approved superstar. In 2008, she released an album called *Youth of China*, billed as a "gift blessing" to the Beijing Olympics. Today, her music is exported under the Anglicized name of Chris Lee; she is in demand as a celebrity model for designers like Jean Paul Gaultier, Donatella Versace, and Karl Lagerfeld; and she makes commercials for Coca-Cola and L'Oréal Paris ("Li Yuchun").

Far be it from me to begrudge Li her success. But I do wonder why, in the frothy cloud of international celebrity that now surrounds her, there is never any mention of the tomboy from Sichuan whose independent spirit and disruptive power to win votes made her threatening enough to provoke a government crackdown.

Now for the bad news. Against this backdrop of authoritarian entertainment-propaganda, it is painful to see American and European pop stars, a group who despite certain constraints enjoy more freedom of expression than almost any artists in history, enriching themselves by lending their glamour to kleptocrats and dictators. In May 2014 the American R&B singer Erykah Badu gave a concert in Swaziland celebrating the birthday of King Mswati III. When human rights organizations raised an outcry, Badu's response was: "I can't be held responsible . . . I signed up as an artist, not as a political activist" (Brown). To another critic who pointed out that Swaziland has not had a free election in 27 years, Badu's response was: "I think that's how kingdoms twerk" (Brown).

The reference to twerking was no accident. As defined by the *Oxford English Dictionary*, to twerk means to dance "in a sexually provocative manner involving thrusting hip movements and a low, squatting stance." Performers like Badu are so accustomed to defending their right to free expression with regard to sexual content, they can be deaf to other kinds of criticism—including criticism based on something they claim to care about, such as the rights of ordinary people not to be starved and oppressed.

Badu is not alone in having poor political judgment. The list of other musical luminaries who have received lavish payment for concerts and serenaded tyrants includes the following:

- Kanye West was paid €2.7 million in 2013 by President Nursultan Nazarbayev of Kazakhstan, who presides over a deadly gulag worthy of Stalinist Russia.
- Jennifer Lopez was paid €1.3 million in 2013 by President Gurbanguly Berdymukhamedov of Turkmenistan. Berdymukhamedov, who insists on being called "The Protector," is known for having brutally crushed the "personality cult" of his predecessor, only to erect a 21-meter-high gilded statue of himself on horseback. Turkmenistan is consistently found on Freedom House's "Worst of the Worst" list.
- Sting was paid €2.1 million in 2010 by President Islam Karimov of Uzbekistan, who is known to have forced large numbers of children into slave labor.
- Mariah Carey was paid €900,000 in 2011 by Libyan President Muammar al-Gaddafi. Despite claiming later that she felt "horrible and embarrassed" about this, Carey went on in 2013 to accept €1.4 million to perform for Isabel dos Santos, the daughter of Angola's deeply corrupt dictator, José Eduardo dos Santos.

Of the performers on this list, the only one to offer a convincing apology was Jennifer Lopez. The rest settled for variations on this inane comment from Erykah Badu: "In the end, I love everyone, and I see freedom ahead for those enslaved *and* the slave masters" (Brown, emphasis in original).

Troubling as it is, this habit of performing for dictators is hardly the sum total of America's twenty-first-century musical outreach. More significant are the changes American music has undergone since the days when jazz constituted the "music of freedom," in Willis Conover's memorable phrase. American music still commands the world stage, and not always to ill effect. But there is no denying that for millions of people around the world, US musical exports are no longer about freedom in the positive sense meant by Conover. Instead, a great many of those exports are narrowly, obsessively, about sex.

Popular music has always been about romance, eroticism, and good times. But only recently has it verged on soft-core pornography. Significantly, this is not true of the pop-idol TV show. Perhaps this is because pop-idol shows are watched (and voted on) by families. Or perhaps it is because the contestants understand that they are not in a market where singing matters less than bumping and grinding for the camera. Whatever the reason, the pop-idol show offers living proof that musical entertainment can attract large audiences without succumbing to nonstop vulgarity.

Tune in to a commercial radio channel on any continent and you will hear popular music that does not quite sound American, often because it utilizes non-American instruments and vocal styles, but that nonetheless conforms to an American template. That is to say, the music is melodically catchy, rhythmically infectious, and structured into three-minute songs. To describe this music as derivative of American pop is to annoy those who champion "world music" as pushback against the US cultural hegemon. But except for the rare case when an unaltered folk style makes its way into the mainstream, the music referred to as "world music" is a hybrid, and its hybridity is deeply American.

Or more accurately, *Afro-American*. I borrow this term from the eminent critic Henry Pleasants, who used it to describe the dominant musical idiom of the United States. *Afro-American* no longer refers to the ethnicity of the musicians involved, because today these come from every part of the globe. Instead, it refers to a range of musical practices introduced into the Americas by enslaved Africans and their descendants. As used here, the term encompasses a broad range of musical styles, from ragtime to rap, that share certain distinctive characteristics, among them rhythmic complexity and the ability to absorb musical influences from very diverse sources (Pleasants, *Serious Music*; Pleasants, *Great American Popular Singers*).

The two genres of Afro-American music that have proved most globally absorptive in the late twentieth and early twenty-first-centuries are the pop style associated with Michael Jackson; and hip-hop, also known as rap.[3]

---

3   Hip-hop is the more inclusive term of the culture, used to describe both musical and nonmusical aspects, such as music, clothing, dance, graffiti, and education. Rap origi-

With the advent of MTV in the 1980s and the "concert spectacular" pioneered by Michael Jackson, American pop music shifted its priority from pleasing the ear to dazzling the eye. This created a problem, because musical talent does not always correlate with physical appeal. The Indian film industry, which relies heavily on music, solved this problem years ago by having "playback singers" with beautiful voices provide the soundtrack for actors with beautiful faces. This solution has not caught on in America, where lip-syncing is considered cheating. Instead, the American solution, adopted in the heyday of MTV, has been to crank up the sexual heat.

According to one study, the percentage of American music videos containing sexual content rose from 47 to 73 percent between 1985 and 2005 (Turner 160). Most of this content was not explicit, but it was relentless: an unending stream of female bodies (the point of view was relentlessly male), writhing and gyrating in outfits that grew ever tighter and scantier. The highest concentration of these images appeared in videos by black performers, including rappers and pop singers—a fact that has not gone unremarked, either in African American communities or overseas.

A similar pattern is evident in hip-hop. By the mid-2000s many African Americans who had grown up embracing hip-hop as a grassroots, multimedia art form began objecting to the way commercial rap videos were depicting black women as gold-digging "bitches" and "ho's." The same videos also depicted black men as foul-mouthed pimps and gangbangers, but that was less remarked upon. In 2005 the black women's magazine *Essence* launched an online debate about the topic ("Take Back the Music"). And as editor in chief Diane Weathers told me, there were quite a few comments from African readers expressing "disgust at what their African-American brothers and sisters are doing in entertainment. They wonder if we've lost our minds" (Weathers).

This is not to suggest that Africans dislike hip-hop. On the contrary, its less offensive forms are popular throughout the continent. This is hardly surprising, given that the original rappers were West African *griots*: oral historians who could recite clan histories, offer praise songs, and practice the fine art of ritual insult. In the Caribbean, where enslaved Africans were cut off from their clan histories and had few occasions for praise, the *griot* tradition became focused on

---

nally referred only to the rhyming verses spoken by a rapper working with an emcee, or deejay. But later it came to be used interchangeably with hip-hop. These are not formal definitions, but it seems that in contemporary American English, rap connotes the more vulgar, commercialized type of music, while hip-hop connotes grassroots, often political, expression.

insult. Over time, this gave rise to two broad tendencies: bragging about oneself while bad-mouthing one's rivals; and, in straitened political circumstances, giving voice to the voiceless.

In North American hip-hop, which was created in the 1970s largely by Afro-Americans and Afro-Caribbean immigrants to New York, the first tendency dominated, as rappers and emcees vied for gigs. But during the 1980s and 1990s, when rap caught on with the larger and more lucrative white audience, the danger arose that, like nearly most previous genres of Afro-American music, it would be appropriated by white performers. One way to "keep it black" was to "keep it ghetto." First this meant gangsta rap, which began with a political message but soon devolved into lurid tales of gang violence. Next came party rap, with its many references to hard drinking, striptease, and lap dancing.

Gangsta and party rap have made a lot of money, both in America and overseas. But they have also tarnished hip-hop's reputation. Throughout the world, rappers continue to speak out against injustice and tyranny. But their reach is limited, because as noted by journalist Robin Wright, serious political rappers in places like the Arab Middle East must struggle to distance themselves from "the materialism, misogyny, vulgarity, and 'gangsta' violence' of 'Western hip-hop'" (121).

DOES POPULAR MUSIC HAVE A PLACE IN A RENEWED AMERICAN PUBLIC DIPLOMACY?

After the attacks of September 11, 2001, Washington scrambled to revive public diplomacy in the Arab Middle East. One highly visible effort was Radio Sawa, a government-sponsored radio channel playing a commercial-style mix of American and Arab pop music. There have been many criticisms of Radio Sawa, beginning with the fact that it replaced VOA's Arabic service, which at the time was lobbying for funds to expand its programming. VOA's Arabic service never received those funds—indeed, that service was terminated, in large part because, only a few days after the attacks of 9/11, its news editors had attempted to broadcast an interview with Taliban leader Mullah Omar (Bayles, *Through a Screen Darkly* 165-66).

A more important criticism, expressed by many Americans who know the region well, was that a radio channel playing pop music is a pitifully inadequate response to the violent radicalization of Arab Muslim youth. Underlying this criticism is the obvious but little noted fact that, unlike Eastern Europeans yearning to breathe free, most Arabs did not see the United States as a beacon of hope for political change. On the contrary, they understood all too well that Washington had long supported many of the region's most repressive governments.

Still other critics (including this one) argued that, unlike VOA, which followed the public diplomacy strategy of reaching out to a carefully targeted audience of thinkers, movers, and shakers, Radio Sawa followed the commercial strategy of trying to attract a large, undifferentiated youth audience. Because entertaining the masses is not considered part of public diplomacy, these critics concluded that Radio Sawa was not the best use of resources.

Does this mean popular music can no longer be used in US public diplomacy? Yes and no.

Let us begin with hip-hop. The first wave of hip-hop diplomacy occurred in the mid-2000s, when the State Department began sending "hip-hop envoys" to North Africa and the Middle East, as well as to Pakistan, Mongolia, and Indonesia. The idea was to draw disaffected Muslim youth away from violent extremism by connecting with young Americans who personified their nation's racial and religious diversity, as well as its freedom of expression. In 2006 a similar program was started in Muslim immigrant neighborhoods in Britain, the Netherlands, and France, to the discomfiture of some British, Dutch, and French officials (Aidi).

In one respect, this effort was strikingly on target. According to Toni Blackman, the first and most celebrated hip-hop envoy, a key message of the program was that not everyone in hip-hop "behaves like a juvenile delinquent on MTV." Indeed, Blackman has repeatedly emphasized that the vulgar, offensive rap that "mainstream radio and television represent . . . Lil Wayne, or Jay-Z or 50 Cent, . . . is not what we're talking about" ("Hip-Hop Diplomacy").

Blackman has also described her own performances as an attempt to "reach across generations" with expressions of "spirituality, religion, feelings and emotions, love songs, celebration of one's parents . . . true stories from the heart" ("Hip-Hop Diplomacy"). To judge by the reaction of one Moroccan participant, the message got across—and the message was not just about hip-hop, it was also about America: "I went around saying to a lot of rappers, men and women, it's not what you see in TV and movies," this participant said. "People in America, they are not so vulgar, they are just talking like us, about real topics" ("Hip-Hop Diplomacy").

"Real topics" can pose a challenge, however. Hip-hop is a form of music that emphasizes speech and rhythm over melody and harmony. And like all speech, the supercharged lyrics of hip-hop can be turned to any purpose. For example, during the Arab Spring, hip-hop was used to express a variety of views: anti-regime, pro-regime, anti-democracy, pro-democracy, and religious sectarian—even radical Islamist. In such a context, it is tricky for an American hip-hop envoy to connect with a particular audience without inadvertently taking sides in a local conflict (Aidi).

This challenge is reflected in the second wave of hip-hop diplomacy, a State Department program called Next Level, which in recent years has reached out to hip-hop performers in Bangladesh, Bosnia and Herzegovina, El Salvador, Honduras, India, Montenegro, Senegal, Serbia, Tanzania, Thailand, Uganda, and Zimbabwe. As stated on its Facebook page, this program's aims are "to promote cultural exchange, entrepreneurship, and conflict prevention" ("About Next Level"). Suzi Analogue, an American participant who traveled to Uganda with the program, has a loftier view. Testifying on the program's website, she claimed that its purpose is "to promote peace and understanding worldwide." Then, perhaps feeling the need to say something more down to earth, she added, "in hip-hop music globally, the beat itself serves as the backbone for people to come together and share ideas and self-expression" ("Uganda").

These claims recall Conover's Cold War statement that jazz is "the music of freedom." To support that claim, Conover sometimes compared the interplay of soloist and ensemble in a jazz performance to that of individual and community in American democratic society. In other words, Conover's claim tried to connect jazz with something important about America—namely, its system of political liberty and protection of individual rights. By contrast, the claims being made on behalf of hip-hop diplomacy seem hopelessly vague, perhaps because the program is trying to *avoid* the genre's connection with politics?

Let me close with a less visible use of musical public diplomacy: a series of presentations on the highly commercial genre of country music identified with Nashville, Tennessee, held by a former diplomat from Austin, Texas named David Firestein. Firestein did not grow up listening to country music (Austin being a long way, geographically and culturally, from Nashville). But after serving several years in Russia and China, Firestein came to believe that the State Department was too "jazz and hip-hop oriented" for socially conservative audiences overseas (Firestein, Event). So he used his fluent Mandarin and Russian to introduce foreign audiences to a more socially conservative form of American popular music.

Firestein's country music diplomacy struck a responsive chord. As he explained to me, "the Chinese and the Russians really liked the strong vocals and the melodies. They also liked the lyrics, because they emphasized a different side of America, a side they could relate to better: hard work, family, and learning the difference between right and wrong" (Firestein, personal interview).

When the Chinese presentation was broadcast on the Mandarin service of Radio Free Asia (RFA), there were many calls asking for more. One caller exclaimed, "'Make Firestein ambassador!'" (Southerland).

In Washington I observed one of Firestein's presentations before an audience of 55 secondary-school teachers visiting from Muslim-majority countries (Event). He captured their attention through the simple device of handing out the lyrics of several hit songs, playing the songs, and discussing their themes: small-town life ("Boondocks," by Little Big Town); pride in humble origins ("Redneck Woman," by Gretchen Wilson); the work ethic ("Hardworking Man," by Brooks & Dunn); family ("Watching You," by Rodney Atkins); and faith ("Jesus, Take the Wheel," by Carrie Underwood). About the last song, Firestein declared, "You don't have to be Christian to appreciate this song. I'm not Christian, I'm Jewish, but I get goose bumps whenever I listen to it." The reaction was sustained applause (Firestein, Event).

Today VOA plays country music, and the domestic audience for the genre is actually becoming younger and more diverse (Rau). But in its wisdom, the State Department never followed up on Firestein's idea, and country music diplomacy ended when he took early retirement. Would the world be a better place if the State Department had scaled up his idea, perhaps even sending "country music envoys" to places where they would be appreciated?[4] It would be nice to think so, but given the hostility felt towards America in many parts of the world, it seems unlikely that even the most carefully crafted musical diplomacy would help very much.

But silence is not an option. Against the attacks being directed against liberal democracy, America and Europe need a renewed public diplomacy capable of defending liberal democracy as the only form of government that, in Abraham Lincoln's words, speaks to "the better angels of our nature" (Lincoln). This does not mean PR, "counter-narratives," or the type of manipulative "messaging" that tries to put a positive spin on real problems. Rather it means candid and open

---

4   There is one subgenre of country music, broadly defined, which the US government has sponsored overseas, and that is bluegrass. Created in the 1940s by the Kentucky musician Bill Monroe, bluegrass survives today as a "roots" style performed with creative variations by groups such as the Stash Wyslouch String Band, a group that has toured with the State Department's American Music Abroad program. However, a few moments of listening will reveal pronounced differences between bluegrass and Nashville country as exemplified by Hank Williams, George Jones, Loretta Lynn, Johnny Cash, Dolly Parton, Merle Haggard, Willie Nelson, and the like. Rarely, if ever, have these Nashville performers been invited to serve as "musical ambassadors."

discussion of those problems, to show that democracy is better than dictatorship at facing hard facts and devising solutions that do not oppress the powerless. Such a renewed public diplomacy would be effective precisely because so many people around the world are forbidden to speak their minds on any topic of public significance. And it would be even more effective if accompanied by the right music!

WORKS CITED

"About Next Level." *Facebook*. Next Level USA, 1 Aug. 2016. Web. Aug. 2016. <https://www.facebook.com/NextLevelUSA/info/?entry_point=page_nav_about_item&tab=page_info>.

Analogue, Suzi. "Uganda On The Beat: Suzi Analogue's Beatmaking Notes From Kampala." *USC Center on Public Diplomacy* 24 June 2015. Web. 1 Nov. 2015. <https://uscpublicdiplomacy.org/tags/next-level-0>.

Arutunyan, Anna. *The Putin Mystique*. Newbold on Stour: Skyscraper Publications, 2014. Print.

Associated Press. "Rushdie Defends Charlie Hebdo, Free Speech." *YouTube*, 15 Jan. 2015. Web. 24 July 2017. <https://youtu.be/q9cYuQonbXs>.

Atkins, Rodney. "Watching You." *If You're Going Through Hell.* Curb, 2006. CD.

Bayles, Martha. "The Struggle for Hearts and Minds: America's Culture War and the Decline of US Public Diplomacy." *The Hedgehog Review* 16.1 (2014): Web. 16 Aug. 2016. <https://iasc-culture.org/THR/THR_article_2014_Spring_Bayles.php>.

---. *Through a Screen Darkly: Popular Culture, Public Diplomacy, and America's Image Abroad.* New Haven: Yale UP, 2014. Print.

Brady, Anne-Marie. *Marketing Dictatorship: Propaganda and Thought Work in Contemporary China.* Lanham: Rowman & Littlefield, 2009. Print.

Brooks & Dunn. "Hardworkin' Man." *Hardworkin' Man.* Arista, 1993. CD.

Brown, August. "Erykah Badu on Performing for a Dictator." *Los Angeles Times*, 1 May 2014. Web. 16 Aug. 2016. <http://www.latimes.com/entertainment/music/posts/la-et-ms-erykah-badu-on-performing-for-dictator-thats-how-kingdoms-twerk-20140501-story.html>.

Cottee, Simon. "The Challenge of Jihadi Cool." *The Atlantic*, 24 Dec. 2015. Web. 16 Aug. 2016. <https://www.theatlantic.com/international/archive/2015/12/isis-jihadi-cool/421776/>.

---. "The Jihad Will Be Televised." *The Atlantic*, 28 June 2016. Web. 16 Aug. 2016. <https://www.theatlantic.com/international/archive/2016/06/terrorism-execution-film/489152/>.

---. "The Pornography of Jihadism." *The Atlantic*, 12 Sept. 2014. Web. 16 Aug. 2016. <https://www.theatlantic.com/international/archive/2014/09/isis-jihadist-propaganda-videos-porn/380117/>.

"Cultural Diplomacy and the National Interest: In Search of a 21st-Century Perspective." *Report for Curb Center for the Arts, Enterprise, and Public Policy*. Vanderbilt University, 2005. PDF file.

de Grazia, Victoria. *Irresistible Empire: America's Advance Through Twentieth-Century Europe*. Cambridge: Harvard UP, 2005. Print.

Diamond, Larry, et al. *Authoritarianism Goes Global: The Challenge to Democracy*. Baltimore: Johns Hopkins UP, 2016. Print.

Duffey, Joseph. "Hollywood Disinformation." Interview in *New Perspectives Quarterly* 15.5 (1998): 13-17. Print.

Eschen, Penny M. von. *Satchmo Blows Up the World: Jazz Ambassadors Play the Cold War*. Cambridge: Harvard UP, 2006. Print.

Fernandez, Alberto M. "Countering the Islamic State's Message." *Journal of International Security Affairs* 30 (2016). Web. 16 Aug. 2016.

Firestein, David. Event hosted by the International Educators Program (IEP). Gallaudet University, Washington DC, 19 June 2007.

---. Personal interview. 5 May 2007.

"Hip-Hop Diplomacy." *YouTube*, 24 Apr. 2012. Web. 16 Aug. 2016. <https://www.youtube.com/watch?v=ud7VsICdqQw>.

Hisham, Aidi. "The Grand (Hip-Hop) Chessboard." *Middle East Report* (2011): 25-39. 5 May 2016. Web. 24 Aug. 2018. <http://www.tennessean.com/story/money/industries/music/2016/05/05/country-music-sees-growth-millennials-hispanic-fans/83963618/>.

Lester, James. "Willis of Oz: A Profile of Famed Voice of America Broadcaster Willis Conover." *Central European Review* 1.5 (1999): Web. 16 Aug. 2016.

Lincoln, Abraham. "First Inaugural Address of Abraham Lincoln." *The Avalon Project*. Yale Law School, 2008. Web. 16 Aug. 2016. <http://avalon.law.yale.edu/19th_century/lincoln1.asp>.

Little Big Town. "Boondocks." *The Road to Here*. Equity, 2005. CD.

"Li Yuchun." *Business of Fashion*. Web. 16 Aug. 2016. <https://www.businessoffashion.com/community/people/li-yuchun>.

"Media and Entertainment Spotlight: The Media and Entertainment Industry in the United States." *SelectUSA*. International Trade Administration, US Department of Commerce, Web. 16 Aug. 2016. <https://www.selectusa.gov/media-entertainment-industry-united-states>.

"Next Level." US Department of State. Web. 1 Nov. 2015. <https://www.nextlevel-usa.org/about/>.

Nietzsche, Friedrich. "Human, All-Too-Human, Part II, section 140." *Project Gutenberg*. 24 Oct. 2011 Web. 16 Aug. 2016. E-Book. <http://www.gutenberg.org/files/37841/37841-h/37841-h.html>.

Ostrovsky, Arkady. *The Invention of Russia*. New York: Penguin, 2017. Print.

Pleasants, Henry. *Serious Music—and All That Jazz: An Adventure in Music Criticism*. New York: Simon & Schuster, 1969. Print.

Pleasants, Henry. *The Great American Popular Singers*. New York: Simon & Schuster, 1974. Print.

Rau, Nate. "Country Music Sees Growth with Millennials, Hispanic Fans." *The Tennessean*. 5. May 2016. Web. 16 Aug. 2016.

Richmond, Yale. *Cultural Exchange and the Cold War: Raising the Iron Curtain*. University Park: Pennsylvania State UP, 2003. Print.

Ryback, Timothy. *Rock Around the Bloc: A History of Rock Music in Eastern Europe and the Soviet Union*. New York: Oxford UP, 1990. Print.

Škvorecký, Josef. *Talkin' Moscow Blues*. New York: Ecco Press, 1990. Print.

Southerland, Dan. Personal interview. 6 May 2007.

Stockmann, Daniela. *Media Commercialization and Authoritarian Rule in China*. Cambridge: Cambridge UP, 2012. Print.

"Take Back the Music Campaign: Mission Statement." *Essence*. 8 Nov. 2005. Web. 3 Aug. 2018. <http://www.essence.com/essence>.

Tian, Gan. "Not Everybody Happy with TV Singing Sensation." *China Daily*, 8 Sept. 2009. Web. 2014.

Turner, Jacob S. "An Examination of Sexual Content in Music Videos." Master's thesis. University of Delaware, 2005. Print.

"twerk." *Oxford English Dictionary Online*. 2016. Web. 16 Aug. 2016. <https://en.oxforddictionaries.com/definition/twerk>.

Underwood, Carrie. "Jesus, Take the Wheel." Some Hearts. Arista, 2005. CD.

Vaughan, David. "Vaclav Havel." *Český Rozhlas 7, Radio Praha*. 2008. Web. 16 Aug. 2016. <http://old.radio.cz/en/article/36022>.

Weathers, Diane. Telephone interview. Apr. 2005.

Wilson, Gretchen. "Redneck Woman." *Redneck Woman*. Epic, 2004. CD.

Wright, Robin. *Rock the Casbah: Rage and Rebellion Across the Islamic World*. New York: Simon and Schuster, 2011. Print.

Zhou, Raymond. "Setting Record Straight." *China Daily*, 15 Oct. 2005. Web. 7 Sept. 2018. <http://www.chinadaily.com.cn/opinion/2005-10/15/content_536982.htm>.

Becoming a Blue-Collar Musical Diplomat
Billy Joel and Bridging the US-Soviet Divide in 1987

Nicholas Alexander Brown

Songwriter and performer Billy Joel holds an exalted status in the upper echelon of popular artists in the United States. His accomplishments include over 150 million record sales, thirty-three "Top 40" singles, and six GRAMMY awards among twenty-three GRAMMY nominations. Joel is a Songwriters Hall of Fame inductee and has been awarded a Kennedy Center Honor and the Library of Congress Gershwin Prize for Popular Song (Joel, "Billy Joel Biography"). Beyond these major financial and musical successes, Joel's greatest achievement has been the popular appeal of his songs and lyrics, which are informed by his background as a child of the working class in the golden era of American prosperity. His desire to "play my music from my experience" (Schruers 242) created an oeuvre that pinpoints integral aspects of the human condition, from love and youthful rebellion to depression, addiction, and suicide. Joel created a platform via his music from which he has the power to influence political and cultural issues.

Joel's July and August 1987 tour of the Soviet Union, which included three concerts each in Moscow and Leningrad with an excursion to Georgia, is an example of his assuming the global stage with a fiery self-made and self-marketed brand of blue-collar diplomacy. Now, over thirty years since the tour, Joel acknowledges that he and his band "were literally offering a musical bridge to our cultures, and we knew that was important" (Gamboa). In establishing an image as a blue-collar or working-class musician, Joel successfully marketed himself as a cultural ambassador who could transcend the elitism of the political and diplomatic sphere by aligning himself with the general populace in both the United States and Soviet Union. This served to ease Cold War tensions on a citizen-to-citizen level and was driven by several motivations; Joel's genuine interest in grassroots political engagement, personal legacy building, his role as a self-appointed celebrity diplomat, and prospective commercial benefits. Joel has a record of taking advantage of his status as a public figure to champion social, political, and cultural causes. He is pictured here attending a gala at the Metropolitan Opera in 2009, representing his support of classical music throughout his career (see fig. 8).

Fig. 8: Billy Joel at the Metropolitan Opera.

Photo: David Shankbone/Creative Commons, 2009.

JOEL'S POLITICAL ENGAGEMENT

Billy Joel's life story is filled with conditions that inform his political engagement. Joel's father Howard was of German-Jewish origin and his family escaped Nazi persecution by emigrating to the United States via Cuba in 1942. Howard was drafted into service with the US Army shortly thereafter and participated in the liberation of Dachau. Rosalind, Joel's mother, was native to Brooklyn and the descendant of a Russian-Jewish and English family. Joel was born in the Bronx in 1949 and his parents quickly relocated to the working-class suburb of Hicksville on Long Island, where "the American work ethic was in full bloom" (McKenzie 4-5). Both of Joel's parents were amateur musicians and they encouraged their son to learn classical music, beginning with piano lessons at the age of four.

In 1956 Howard and Rosalind divorced, leaving Rosalind in Hicksville with Joel and his sister Judy. Howard relocated to Vienna, Austria and eventually started a new family. Joel was impacted by the separation of his parents and recounts the hostile treatment he received from neighbors and classmates who did not view him as their equal: The Joel family was the only single-parent and culturally Jewish household in a majority Catholic neighborhood. Joel was baptized Protestant and enjoyed going to various Christian church services with friends in childhood (Bielen 5). On top of these social conditions, Joel's mother struggled to make ends meet and worked multiple jobs. The experience of growing up in this family environment was formative in developing Joel's personality and thick skin. He recounts this period by commenting: "We were blue-collar poor people...not poor poor people. You don't go to the welfare line when you're blue-collar poor, you find work, somehow. You never ask for a handout—you would die first!" (Bielen 5-6). Joel began working as a musician during his youth and developed a strong work ethic that was rooted in his working class upbringing, which has served him throughout his career, no matter the professional or personal difficulties. He climbed his way from the bottom of the music industry, as a local nightclub musician, to the very top echelon, as the longest running resident act in the history of Madison Square Garden (Buehrer).

In the early 1970s Joel struggled to find his niche in the commercial music industry in the United States. The turning point came when he gave up "trying to make it as a rock star" and pursued autobiographical narratives in his songwriting; Joel describes this shift as an attempt to "do what I always wanted to do—write my own experiences and chuck the commercial influences" (McKenzie 27). Joel states that his "[s]ongs mean something. They mark different periods of my life, whether I was happy or sad. It's the same for everyone" (DeCurtis 143). He champions the voice of the working class in his lyrics, offering a glimpse of the life experiences and challenges that many Americans face in everyday life. Joel's portrayal of the American experience contradicts the fabricated utopian vision of the lifestyle modeled by the Cleaver family in the 1950s television show *Leave it to Beaver*.

The story of the working class emerges in Joel's lyrics, which combine with a distinct musical idiom that is influenced by a wide cross-section of popular artists and styles, including classical music, Elvis, the Beatles, R&B, James Brown, and Ray Charles. His lyrics resonate with a wide range of people across generations in the United States, because they address issues that pervade society. Listeners can relate personally to the topics and emotions contained in his songs, therefore making relatability a key ingredient in understanding the popular appeal of his music. Joel himself has struggled with depression, alcoholism, suicide, failed relationships, and disastrous financial dealings. In a song like "Captain Jack," for example, Joel describes witnessing suburb dwellers buying drugs from the inner-city public housing projects across from his one-time apartment. Bill DeMain refers to this type of narrative as a "look out the window" song, representing someone watching what takes place in the world immediately around them (117).

Beyond his music, Joel has a long track record of being engaged in political advocacy. His ideology can be described as liberal nationalism, and is captured in his own words: "I'm very chauvinistic. Not in a political sense, but in a national sense. I love my country. I don't think any government really represents the people, but I do know that there are a lot of nice people in this country and that's about as chauvinistic as I can get" (qtd. in Myers 88). In the 1970s Joel was vocal about global events, separately from his music. He particularly took issue with vitriolic and anti-American international responses to the Iranian hostage crisis that were insensitive to the differences between the American political apparatus and the average citizens who have little or no say in foreign policy. Later on, Joel took a stance in opposition to President Carter's request that the US Olympic Committee boycott the 1980 Olympics in Moscow, which was a protest of the Soviet invasion of Afghanistan. He felt that American athletes should have the opportunity to compete, regardless of the political conditions of the Cold War (Myers 86-88). This opposition to President Carter indicates that Joel's politics are not consistently aligned with the values of the Democratic Party. Joel's public political positions are most representative of the moderate independent political ideology in the US, in which individuals are known to support positions or politicians of both major political parties and are not devout party loyalists.

Joel's attentiveness to American foreign policy continues to the present. His 2007 song, "Christmas in Fallujah," criticizes the Iraq and Afghanistan wars, while simultaneously shedding light on the plight of the American soldier, who follows orders, is "tired" and "cold," and realizes that "no one gives a damn." Troops are stuck in war-torn Iraq where there is "a sea of blood" (Schruers 293-94). This type of vivid imagery in Joel's lyrics conveys his interpretation of the human experience via an artistic form that aims to resonate with people of diverse cultural backgrounds. Joel can always be found on the side of the everyman or everywoman, a representation of his own humble upbringing and empathy for citizens who are taken advantage of by their political leaders.

Since the early 2000s, Joel has frequently participated in liberal presidential campaigns, headlining fundraisers like "Change Rocks" in 2008 to support then-Senator Barack Obama's campaign. This fundraiser generated approximately $8 million in campaign contributions (Schruers 291). During the tumultuous 2016 presidential campaign in the United States Joel garnered Twitter and popular press coverage for a quip made during his May 27 concert at Madison Square Garden. Joel facetiously dedicated his song "The Entertainer" to Donald Trump (Polus), mocking Trump and minimizing the legitimacy of his standing as a presidential candidate. When asked in an interview with Boston's public radio station WGBH if he would be willing to perform at Trump's inauguration in January 2017, Joel stated "No. I won't be anywhere near the place" (Boston Public Radio Staff). While Joel attended Trump's 2005 wedding to Melania Knauss, his recent comments indicate disdain for the forty-fifth president's politics (Firozi).[1]

MARKETING BILLY JOEL AS A MUSICAL AMBASSADOR

Joel's tour to the Soviet Union was the greatest example of his self-driven insertion into political affairs, but it was not the first instance in which he performed in communist nations. Prior to the Soviet tour, Joel performed in Fidel Castro's Cuba in March of 1979 at the Karl Marx Theater (of all places). The appearance was part of Havana Jam, a major three-day music festival that featured American and Cuban artists. The American contingent was the first

---

[1] In the first two years of the Trump presidency Joel has been very vocal about his disdain for the administration's policies towards refugees and immigrants. In the days following the 11-12 August 2017 white supremacy riots in Charlottesville, VA, Joel wore a "Star of David" patch on his suit during his monthly Madison Square Garden concert in protest of the rise of neo-Nazism and the administration's weak response (Respers France).

sanctioned delegation of US musical acts to perform in Cuba in over twenty years (Bego 147-50). As always with Joel, this appearance had a personal motivation beyond the desire to make a political statement on US-Cuba relations. "My father had lived in Cuba, so I was interested for that reason," stated Joel in a biography by Hank Bordowitz (107). Howard Joel spent time in Cuba while in transit to the United States as a refugee from Germany (Bego 148). The Cuba performance afforded Joel the opportunity to symbolically connect with a period of his estranged father's life by experiencing Havana and the Cuban people.

    John Rockwell of the *New York Times* came away from the festival impressed with Joel's role, commenting: "in the right context rock-and-roll still has the power to be subversive" (Rockwell). Given that Joel's songs and lyrics come from a place of acknowledging and empowering the underappreciated working class, he uses his art to take a stand on the world stage by ideologically unshackling the body politic through his music. Other international appearances, like Joel's shows in Israel, drew fire from elements of the American political establishment, particularly during the period of the Camp David Accords. This 1979 peace treaty between Israel and Egypt (brokered by American President Jimmy Carter, Egyptian president Anwar Sadat, and Prime Minister Menachem Begin of Israel) called for Israel's withdrawal from the Sinai Peninsula and the development of Palestine's independent government. To Joel, there was no fathomable reason to avoid preaching his musical gospel in nations filled with strife. He eloquently summarizes his approach as follows: "I played in Israel for the same reason I played in Cuba—to play for the people. We wanted to see what the people in Israel were like instead of listening to the propaganda we get in [the United States]" (Bego 151-152). But even his historic appearances in Cuba and Israel were not enough to satisfy Joel's zeal for stepping into the middle of contentious diplomatic situations. Despite Joel's stated motivations for bridging cultural divides, it is entirely plausible that his pursuit of a performance in Cuba could have been a strategic move to expand his commercial viability and appeal among audiences in communist countries. He positioned himself as a self-made musical ambassador whose popular appeal could transcend negative attitudes towards American foreign policy or politicians, evidenced by a warm reception from the concert audience in Havana. In retrospect, the Havana Jam appearance proved to be an early step in a series of efforts by Joel to deliver his music—through live performances—to international markets. An undercurrent to Joel's own commercial ambitions was the capacity of his performances—as a form of soft diplomacy—to ease the tensions of the Cold War.

In 1985 the US and the Soviet Union advanced a new agreement for cultural exchange immediately following a period of icy relations. The easing of cultural relations on the Soviet side stemmed from their promotion of the *glasnost* policy that stood for greater openness and publicity (Cameron and Lebor). This caused a noticeable shift in how flexible Soviet citizens could be with relative freedom of speech. As a result, it was possible for an artist like Billy Joel to realistically conceive the first full-fledged tour of the Soviet Union by an American rock musician. According to author Mark Bego, "The very idea of being able to be the first Western rock star to play a full-out series of rock concerts in the Soviet Union became a quest of Billy Joel's" (231-232).

The US had a history of major cultural exchanges with the Soviet Union between the 1950s and 1970s. Many of the early exchanges were restricted to high art forms like orchestral music, jazz, ballet, and musical theater, including a landmark 1955-1956 tour to Leningrad and Moscow of *Porgy and Bess* by George and Ira Gershwin that featured an African American cast (Bego 231). The overall intention of these exchanges from the American perspective, as outlined by Theodore Cuyler Streibert, director of the US Information Agency in 1955, and summarized by Lisa Davenport, was to increase international recognition for American "cultural achievements," "refute communist propaganda," and use culture to ease political and diplomatic tensions (39). Davenport describes the gradual decline in cultural exchanges between the US and USSR in the 1970s as a result from American involvement in Vietnam (145), as the USSR and China were involved in supporting the North Vietnamese communist regime in opposition to the US (Suri). Additionally, American jazz tours to the USSR were halted in 1979 upon the USSR's invasion of Afghanistan (Davenport 148).

Joel's 1987 tour reflects a shift in emphasis of the cultural exchanges towards popular culture. Shortly before Joel's tour launched in late July of 1987 there was a major series of concerts in the USSR called the July Fourth Disarmament Festival. Soviet and American artists performed, most notably James Taylor, Bonnie Raitt, the Doobie Brothers, and Carlos Santana (Bego 232). While press accounts of Joel's tour position his appearances as unique forays into the Soviet Union by an American artist, the fact is that others had come before him. Where Joel's tour stands apart from the July Fourth Disarmament Festival is that his shows featured him and his band, and not a lineup of multiple headliners performing short sets. Despite the earlier appearances by American artists in 1987, the narrative Joel provides about his tour suggests he leverages the experience to benefit his legacy. He has effectively curated extensive promotion of his tour's impact on cultural affairs for almost three decades.

In the mid-1980s Joel was engaged in bitter legal and financial disputes with Frank Weber (his longtime manager and former brother-in-law), which put a great strain on Joel's finances and ultimately cost him millions in income, due to poor investments and other deceptive business practices (Schruers 206). In 1989 Joel filed a lawsuit against Weber, accusing him of unauthorized expenditures in the range of $30 million (Dougherty). This ongoing turmoil may have contributed to Joel's desire to launch the 1987 tour, which he viewed in part as a commercial opportunity that could lead to the stabilization of his finances. The tour required an extensive financial investment on Joel's part, of $2 million for the basic expenses of running the trip (Bego 233), which could only be effectively recouped through the sale of tour-related recordings, merchandise, and broadcasts. Beyond his personal financial motivations, the tour was officially made possible when a formal invitation was extended by the USSR's Ministry of Culture (*Billy Joel – A Matter of Trust Deluxe Edition*). In order to get to this point, it is likely that both US and Soviet diplomats were engaged in off-the-record negotiations.[2]

THE PEOPLE'S MUSICIAN

The primary platform from which Joel was able to establish a bond with the Soviet people was the concert stage. The tour schedule, which featured six concerts (see table 2), indicates that Joel had high expectations for ticket sales; 100,000 people were projected to attend performances during the tour (Peasley G3). Communist officials reported that 22,000 tickets were sold for the first Leningrad show (Barringer C15) and the *New York Times* reported that the Moscow shows were sold out (Associated Press). If those reports are accurate, Joel's advance audience estimate was on target and likely even surpassed. Joel

---

2   The author's Freedom of Information Act request to the US Department of State for any records related to Joel's Soviet Tour yielded no declassified pertinent information. The documents do prove that the US Embassy in the USSR was at minimum aware of the tour. If any documentation exists outlining a formal US government role in planning the tour it remains in classified files. The National Archives and Records Administration and the affiliated Ronald Reagan Presidential Library in Simi Valley, California report that their collections do not contain any accessible records about the tour (Langbart; Ross).

also performed an "unscheduled concert" during his visit to Tbilisi in the week before his public shows in Moscow, though the exact date of this appearance is not recorded in the existing accounts of the tour (Bego 232).

Table 2: Billy Joel 1987 Soviet tour concert dates.

Venue	Date
Olympic Sports Complex, Moscow	26 July 1987 27 July 1987 29 July 1987
Lenin Sports & Concert Complex, Leningrad	2 August 1987 3 August 1987 5 August 1987

Source: "Jumpy in Moscow."

Joel's carefully chosen set list maximized the opportunities for the Soviet audiences to connect with the American working class experience, as represented by Joel. The concerts opened with "Prelude/Angry Young Man" from Joel's 1976 album *Turnstiles*. His brash lyrics capture the universal plight of the young working class man, who is in a constant struggle to survive in a world that seems to be against him:

There's a place in the world for the angry young man
With his working class ties and his radical plans
He refuses to bend he refuses to crawl
And he's always at home with his back to the wall
And he's proud of his scars and the battles he's lost
And struggles and bleeds as he hangs on his cross
And likes to be known as the angry young man ("Prelude/Angry Young Man")

The representation of the working class in these lyrics was relatable to many in the general USSR populace, as the Central Committee of the Communist Party began to publicly recognize citizens' need to express their frustration with "civic and employment-related problems" (Buchanan 9). Joel's lyrics in "Prelude/Angry Young Man" can be interpreted as empowering the voices of the disenfranchised youth, especially men who have made symbolic sacrifices and received "scars" from fighting in "battles." While Joel is not addressing specific movements of resistance or dissent among the USSR's citizenry in these lyrics, he makes a case for the value of struggle and sacrifice for improving individuals' socio-economic or personal status. He even references Christian theology in the song, by stating how the narrator "bleeds as he hangs on his cross," implying that sacrifices listeners make of their own well-being can serve the greater good.

As Joel performed "Prelude/Angry Young Man" on the first formal show of the tour in Leningrad he was met with the proverbial sound of crickets in the audience. The front rows of the arena were filled with Soviet party officials, which was to be expected given that government officials (regardless of the country) frequently attend cultural diplomacy events that they are sponsoring, hosting, or monitoring. Their icy response to Joel's act led the singer to think that he was "going right down the tubes" (Bielen 109). Realizing that his actual fans—referred to as "young true bloods" in Richard Scott's biography on Joel (59)—were seated behind the officials, Joel had his staff move young people from the back to the front to liven-up the crowd once the regime's senior representatives departed mid-show. The fans were understandably timid about reacting positively towards Joel, given the presence of the ominous Soviet regime, but his encouragement and moving them forward had a profound effect on altering the audience dynamic (Bielen 110). Prior to Joel's live performances in the USSR, some music fans there would have become familiar with his recordings through the bootleg market, as American rock albums were banned from sale for much of the communist era. State television stations managed to broadcast several of Joel's music videos in the lead up to his concerts (Scott 58). The reality was that many in the audiences had not heard Joel's music prior to his appearances in Leningrad and Moscow, but they responded favorably to what one Soviet audience member perceived as the "forbidden" quality of his songs and performance, given that rock music had been previously officially banned by the communist party (*Billy Joel – A Matter of Trust Deluxe Edition*).

"Prelude/Angry Young Man," and effectively the entire tour set list, served to give voice to common struggles faced by young people of the working class in both the Soviet Union and the United States, highlighting the frequent disconnect between the political classes and the body politic. The Soviet shows included "The Ballad of Billy the Kid," "Allentown," "Goodnight Saigon," "The Longest Time," "Only the Good Die Young," "Sometimes a Fantasy," and "Uptown Girl." Two of these songs were particularly poignant for the blue-collar outreach: "Allentown" and "Goodnight Saigon" touched upon two of the most contentious issues in the American working class during the 1980s, economic collapse and processing the lingering effect of the Vietnam War. Both songs appeared on the 1982 album for Columbia Records, *The Nylon Curtain*, which Walter Everett describes as a representation of "the plastic (i.e., forced artificial) and tranquilizing quality of American, chiefly suburban, life...an American counterpart to the Soviet Union iron curtain" (Everett 116). "Allentown" tells of the difficulties of economic hardships and unemployment faced by the children of the baby-boomers. The collapse of the Bethlehem Steel Corporation specifically provided material for Joel's creative depiction of the disappearing opportunities in working-class America, as "they're closing all the factories down" (Schruers 153). Joel tells of "waiting here in Allentown / For the Pennsylvania we never found / For the promises our teachers gave / If we worked hard / If we behaved." The working-class dream seems to be beyond the grasp of the average blue-collar worker, a depressing realization that conflicts with the traditional American expectation of vertical class mobility through hard work. Joel's audiences in Leningrad and Moscow would have recognized a parallel with the narrative in "Allentown" and the economic situation under their political leaders, whose policies failed to deliver the common prosperity promised by communist ideologies (Ball and Dagger). Instead, by 1985 the regime was in search of viable remedies to address economic stagnation, production failures, and "shortages of goods" (Buchanan 9). Americans were reacting to similar financial crises and Joel managed to channel those sentiments into his lyrics. During the tour, Joel introduced "Allentown" with the help of his translator, recounting the plight of Americans living in the city and asking the audience, "Maybe that sounds familiar?" (*Billy Joel – A Matter of Trust Deluxe Edition*).

"Goodnight Saigon," Joel's commentary on the Vietnam War, outlines the radical shift towards a dark pessimism in American society after President John F. Kennedy's 1963 assassination, colored by the economic struggles of the working class. This song describes the transformation of men from basic training in the Marine Corps, of being "so gung ho / To lay down our lives," to the horrors of combat, when "we would all go down together." In the recent Schruers biography on Joel, the songwriter cites having been motivated to compose "Goodnight Saigon" by the experiences of his Vietnam veteran friends. Joel had long questioned the American interventionist policy of attempting to shape the internal affairs of foreign nations. One poignant saying he recalls from the period is "Vietnam is sending the black man to kill the yellow man for the white man who stole the land from the red man" (qtd. in Schruers 154). This comment is a harsh summation and condemnation of American foreign policy and race relations. Similar debates raged in the USSR as to the burden of the Soviet participation in the Afghan War of 1979-1992, which was met with high levels of dissatisfaction among the Soviet people due to high financial and human resource drains (Office of Soviet Analysis iii).

The positive reception Joel received for his original songs throughout the Soviet Union served as proof that these themes resonate from Moscow to Long Island. Joel was ultimately met with "cheering enthusiasm," but not without making his tour staff anxious about being chastised or even punished for his riling up the crowds (Bego 232). The tour manager purportedly hid in a bathroom after one of the Moscow shows, in fear of reprisal from angry representatives of the Soviet Central Committee who were in attendance (Bordowitz 161). Columbia Records president Walter Yetnikoff, who was part of the tour entourage, commented that Joel "rocked harder than the Soviets wanted him to rock" and that "American rock 'n' roll ripped up the Iron Curtain" (Bego 233). Felicity Barringer reported in the *New York Times* that Billy Joel "won the souls of those in a stony Soviet audience, leaving them cheering, dancing on chairs and looking around in fearful wonder as they followed the music and not the rules" (C15). During these synergistic moments in the concerts, music successfully created a bond between Joel, his band, and the local audiences that helped Joel see past the political differences between the US and USSR. He described this change in his perception of the Soviet Union in a *Rolling Stone* interview by stating, "The Cold War ended at a lot sooner for me than it has for everyone else" (Wild), suggesting that the warm reception his music received during the 1987 tour had a major impact on Joel's personal beliefs.

The shows also included a cover of the Beatles' "Back in the USSR," which hinted at Joel's respect for the revered British band, but more importantly served to show honest appreciation for the citizens of the country. In a video documentary of the tour, American flags can be seen being waved enthusiastically by Soviet men and women throughout the audience. Joel, with help from his translator, concluded the night by saying "Don't take any shit from anybody" (*Billy Joel – A Matter of Trust Deluxe Edition*), a rallying cry that had enormous appeal to the generally repressed Soviets. The second cover that Joel included in the shows was Bob Dylan's "The Times Are A-Changin'," a powerful protest song that directly calls out American government officials as needing to "Please heed the call / Don't stand in the doorway / Don't block up the hall," for a social and political revolution was emerging that would change the course of history. Beyond the themes of global unrest, war and economic disillusionment, the songs on Joel's tour sought to bridge cultural boundaries by touching upon such common themes as love, unemployment, family, war, and death.

In addition to sharing the rabble-rouser spirit of his protest songs, some of Joel's onstage behavior showed his bucking of establishment expectations and thinking, at least symbolically. Joel electrified the audiences by delivering a genuine rock show. He climbed on his piano, crowd surfed, and danced around with his microphone stand. One of the band members, Mark Rivera, recently recounted how the general concert attendees completely overran the front VIP section at the arena in Moscow after the Soviet officials departed in the middle of the show. He remarked, "It wasn't a protest. It was just the guys jumping up and down on the chairs because they were having so much fun" (Gamboa). Joel's music and performance moved them to unleash their inner excitement and feelings.

During the second show in Moscow, Joel had a famous explosion against the video crew that was capturing the show for the future cable television and video specials. The most shocking aspect of this was that public outbursts were not generally tolerated in Soviet society. Joel, who believed the video crew was interfering with the live audience's enjoyment of the performance by shining bright lights on them (and tapping into their inhibitions about being seen to enjoy American rock music by authorities), had a violent outburst that involved flipping over an electric piano and swinging a music stand over his head (Bego 233). The international press quickly picked up on this moment and headlines read "Billy Joel Has a Tantrum," though the Associated Press reported that "the audience seemed unsure if the temper tantrum was part of the show" (Associated Press). In video footage of the incident, the audience immediately surrounding stage did not skip a beat of rocking out to the music. Joel recounts that young audience members came up to him after the concert and told him "they really liked it" (*Billy Joel – A Matter of Trust Deluxe Edition*). For better or worse, these antics increased the Western press attention for the tour and implied that Joel was a man of the people for adamantly protecting the audiences' best interests, even to the detriment of his own documentary production.

Several of the powerful instances of cultural exchange on Joel's tour took place away from the concert stage. He gained mass attention through publicity stunts like being the first American to appear on the Soviet music television program *Muzykalnyj Ring*, or *The Music Ring*. Additionally, the final concert on the tour was the first live rock concert to be broadcast simultaneously to the US and Soviet Union. The truly special moments were always based on interactions with common everyday Soviet citizens, for whom Joel felt a kindred spirit. He fondly recalls giving his leather jacket to "the hippie guy," Oleg Smirnoff, Joel's translator; Smirnoff never wore the jacket and displayed it on his wall. Joel retrospectively acknowledged that "the importance of the relationship we had with the people there is still hanging on people's walls" (Scott 61-62). Joel clearly had a profound impact on individual citizens, irrespective of whether or not his tour enhanced overall US-USSR cultural relations. Many of the personal interactions between Joel and locals are captured in *A Matter of Trust*, showing his gifting a personal St. Christopher medal to an aspiring musician (O'Connor, "Review/Television" C30). He is also depicted wandering through traditional markets and being physically embraced by locals, which prompted many beaming smiles on Joel's part (*Billy Joel – A Matter of Trust Deluxe Edition*).

After attending a performance by local musicians in Tbilisi, Georgia, Joel was inspired to include the traditional Georgian folk song "Odoya" on his live tour recording *Kohuept*. In the context of US music diplomacy during the twentieth century, Joel's inclusion of local artists performing a folk work functioned as a form of "musical flattery," a principle outlined by Danielle Fosler-Lussier (78) that observes American musicians paying homage to local cultures during international exchanges by performing and recording native music. Mario Dunkel (149-50) emphasizes the prevalence of this practice during tours to the Eastern Bloc by American jazz artists in the 1950s.

Joel had a moving experience at the grave of musician and poet Vladimir Vysotsky, who died in 1980 while publication of his poems and songs was restricted by the communist regime. Vysotsky's work conveyed the spirit of the Soviet people, much to the chagrin of the political elites, and commented on the struggles of life under communist rule in the same way that Joel's songs represent the American working class experience. Joel, his then-wife Christie Brinkley, and their daughter Alexa went on to visit Vysotsky's mother. All of this memorialization of Vysotsky served as a gesture of respect for the artist and the people who saw him as their voice against the deprivation forced upon them by their government (Bielen 110).

DUAL PROPAGANDA ROLES

A *Quid pro quo* scenario is at the root of most diplomatic negotiations or exchanges, including in music diplomacy. Exploring Joel's Soviet tour inherently requires a consideration of what may have motivated the US and Soviet governments to allow the tour to occur. Putting aside Joel's personal intellectual, musical, and commercial motivations, there were tangible diplomatic benefits to this tour for both governments. The Soviets, with their tolerance of Joel's riling up of their young citizens, could point to the freedom to get wild at the concerts and the leeway Joel had to interact with the populace as proof of their seriousness about the *glasnost* policy. The regime's acceptance of visible and public dissension, albeit in a contained concert setting, was undoubtedly a meaningful and surprising gesture to many Soviets.

Writing in *The Washington Post*, Alex Heard explains that one of the communist regime's motivations for authorizing Joel's tour was to learn more about American rock 'n' roll and to copy it as a means for matching the global dominance of American pop and rock music. Oleg Smoliensky, director of the USSR cultural enterprise Goskonzert (госконцерт) during the time of Joel's tour, is quoted as saying "Soviet officials are pleased...We did not make a mistake in choosing [Joel]. You have achieved a lot in this field. Our cultural exchange will help us catch you" (Heard W7). This sense of gamesmanship is also seen in the competition to win the medal count at Olympic games. Whether this endorsement of Joel's tour was intended to drive perception of the communist party's promotion of rock music or not, it is indicative of complex political aims being at the core of why the officials did not block Joel's tour. They manipulated it to their own ends, while revealing how they were uncomfortably making strides towards greater openness in Soviet society.

The American government side of the exchange was equally nuanced. On the surface, the tour served as an example of global American dominance of popular music and culture. Here was Joel, a blue-collar American guy, filling arenas in the Soviet Union with catchy pop music that was decidedly connected to the American working class experience, which has always been a point of similarity in cultural exchanges. Allowing Joel to adopt the role of unsanctioned musical ambassador can be interpreted as having several benefits to American propaganda efforts during the Cold War. Joel, in speaking his mind in his lyrics—including against policies of the US government, such as the Vietnam War—was a symbol of American freedom of expression. By sanctioning this, the Regan administration projected a model of democratic open society that would have a positive influence on Soviet citizens who might intensify their demands for the same type of freedoms, especially given the parallels between the contemporary Soviet engagement in Afghanistan and the Vietnam conflict.

Western English-language press coverage of Joel's tour conveyed a striking narrative of his overwhelming effect on young people in his audiences, one of reaching the hearts and minds of youth in a rabble-rousing American way, complete with instances of bucking authority. Reports of 200 chairs being broken at one of the Leningrad concerts, a result of fans rushing to the foot of the stage ("Jumpy in Moscow"), give a visual symbol of breaking down what was perceived as the forced neutral decorum expected by the Soviets. Among the headlines were "Pop Weekend: From Moscow to LA: Soviets Warm Up to Billy Joel" (*Los Angeles Times*), "In Moscow, a New Era? Protest and Rock Fete are

Tests of Glasnost" (*New York Times*), and "Billy Joel parts the Iron Curtain" (*Globe and Mail*). The North American press largely portrayed Joel's tour as having the effect of unnerving the Soviet regime: "Considering his effect on seats, can you wonder the Kremlin is nervous?" ("Jumpy in Moscow"). In reality, the local audience benefitted from Joel's engagement with concert-goers in this fashion. Communist goals of promoting *glasnost* via the tour were met concurrently with the American perception of the tour as a penetration of Soviet society with American values and freedom of expression. As such, Joel and his tour functioned as propaganda for both the USSR and the United States, a careful balancing act that fulfills the expectation of music diplomacy satisfying aims for all parties engaged.

The successes of Joel's Soviet tour enabled him to partner with Mikhail Gorbachev, the General Secretary of the Communist Party in the Soviet Union from 1985 to 1991 and the official ultimately responsible for *glasnost*, for a charity concert entitled "Together for Our Children—Musicians Unite with Stars to Immunize Children." The event took place after the disintegration of the Soviet Union in 1993 in Los Angeles and was broadcast globally (Harring 19). This symbolic partnership would not have been possible if Joel's previous tour of the USSR had compromised his ability to work with Moscow's political leaders.

CONCLUSION: COMMERCIAL LEGACY BUILDING

Since 1987, Joel's engagement with the memory of his Soviet tour has exceeded what was accomplished personally or for international relations over the course of the trip to Leningrad, Moscow, and Tbilisi. Several initiatives that directly relate to the tour indicate Joel's long-term vision for developing the legacy of the tour commercially. In the almost thirty years since the actual tour, Joel has been involved in the release of several audio and video recordings that intend to sell the success of the Soviet trip to the history books, bolstering Joel's place in the pantheon of civically engaged popular and rock musicians from the United States.

An immediate and visible product of the tour was the release of a documentary in 1987 called *Billy Joel from Leningrad, USSR* as part of the *HBO World Stage* series, which gives a curated visual and musical snapshot of Joel's energetic engagement with his audiences throughout the tour. The one-hour film was conceived by Robert Dalrymple and Rick London, and commemorates the tour as ". . . a nonstop celebration—of togetherness, of rock music, and, of course,

Billy Joel" (O'Connor, "TV Reviews" C22). Columbia Records released the album *Kohuept* in late 1987, which included live and studio recordings from the Soviet tour. Curiously, this recording was Joel's first in ten years not to reach gold level sales of 500,000 albums sold, and as such it was not perceived as a clear commercial success (Bego 237). A second film, *Billy Joel – A Matter of Trust: The Bridge to Russia* Dalrymple in 1987 and aired on ABC in 1988 under the title *A Matter of Trust: Billy Joel in the USSR*. In 2014, Joel was involved in releasing a "deluxe edition" of *Billy Joel – A Matter of Trust: The Bridge to Russia*, which includes the first DVD/Blu-ray versions of the 1987 Soviet concerts to be released, a two-CD recording of Soviet tour performances, and a new documentary film produced by Showtime and directed by Jim Brown.[3]

These various recordings, television documentaries, and video releases have served three purposes: to generate additional revenue from the tour, to promote the perceived impact of Joel's tour in the history of US-Soviet relations during the waning years of the Cold War, and to raise Joel's visibility as an artist of purpose on the commercial marketplace. By marketing the story and music through films and sound recordings, the 1987 tour is revisited by longstanding Joel fans and is used to reach new audiences that may not be otherwise drawn to the singer's brand of music. While the continued commercial potential of the Soviet appearances continues to receive attention from Joel in the second decade of the twenty-first century, the cultural exchange nonetheless proved to be a meaningful experience for him personally while drawing attention to the capacity of an American artist to make public relations splash behind the Iron Curtain.

As Russia and the United States are again in a period of icy relations, albeit under different circumstances, both countries would be wise to engage in music diplomacy as they did through Billy Joel's tour. Music diplomacy offers opportunities for societies to engage informally, connect through similar social tropes, and work towards a better understanding of cultural and political differences. Joel saw an opportunity to advance his political activism by engaging in Cold War music diplomacy. He marketed himself as an "Ambassador of Rock" (Kent A38) with his 1979 appearance in Cuba, the 1987 tour to the USSR, and in the decades since. Joel's foray into the musical scenes of communist countries was launched in part to positively influence US-USSR relations at a grassroots level and cement Joel's legacy as an American celebrity who could connect with the working class based on his personal background.

---

3 Sales figures for the various commercially released documentaries of the 1987 tour are not available at the time of publication.

Joel's bottom-up initiative and courage in guiding the direction of the Soviet exchange at all levels revitalized the potential to bridge differences, no matter how intense the divisions, by sharing the story of working-class America with the populace of the USSR.

WORKS CITED

A Matter of Trust: Billy Joel in the USSR. Perf. Billy Joel. Dir. Martin Bell and Wayne Isham. Prod. Robert Dalrymple and Rick London. ABC, 18 Jun. 1988. Television.

Associated Press. "Billy Joel Has a Tantrum." *New York Times* 28 Jul. 1987: C11. *ProQuest*. Web. 26 May 2015. <https://www.nytimes.com/1987/07/28/arts/billy-joel-has-a-tantrum.html>.

Ball, Terrence, and Richard Dagger. "Communism." *Encyclopædia Britannica* 08 Jun. 2008. Encyclopædia Britannica, Inc. Web. 17 Jan. 2017. <https://www.britannica.com/topic/communism>.

Barringer, Felicity. "A Rocking Billy Joel Breaks Through Soviet Reserve." *New York Times* 27 Jul. 1987: C15. *ProQuest*. Web. 6 Oct. 2015. <https://www.nytimes.com/1987/07/27/arts/a-rocking-billy-joel-breaks-through-soviet-reserve.html>.

Bego, Mark. *Billy Joel: The Biography*. New York: Thunder's Mouth Press, 2007. Print.

Bielen, Ken. *The Words and Music of Billy Joel*. Santa Barbara, California: Praeger, 2011. Print.

Billy Joel – A Matter of Trust: The Bridge to Russia. Dir. Wayne Isham. Perf. Billy Joel. Legacy, 1987. VHS.

Billy Joel – A Matter of Trust: The Bridge to Russia Deluxe Edition. Dir. Jim Brown. Perf. Billy Joel. Legacy, 2014. DVD.

"Billy Joel from Leningrad, USSR." *HBO World Stage*. HBO, 27 Oct. 1987. Television.

Bordowitz, Hank. *Billy Joel: The Life & Times of an Angry Young Man*. New York: Billboard Books, 2006. Print.

Boston Public Radio Staff. "Piano Man Billy Joel On: Dropping Out of School, the 'Physicality' of Performance, and Playing Fenway." *WGBH News* 15 Aug. 2016. Web. 14 Jan. 2017. <https://www.wgbh.org/news/2016/08/15/boston-public-radio-podcast/piano-man-billy-joel-dropping-Sout-school-physicality>.

"Briefly: Billy Joel Parts the Iron Curtain." *Globe and Mail* 4 May 1987. Lexis-Nexis. Web. 26 May 2015. <https://advance-lexis-com.libproxy.mit.edu/api/document?collection=news&id=urn:contentItem:4M9N-1PS0-TXJ2-N0VN-00000-00&context=1516831>.

Buchanan, Donna A. *Performing Democracy: Bulgarian Music and Musicians in Transition*. Chicago: U of Chicago P, 2006. Print.

Buehrer, Jack. "Billy Joel's Record-Breaking Madison Square Garden Run Conquers the Haters." *Village Voice* 2 July 2015. Web. 24 Jan. 2016. <https://www.villagevoice.com/2015/07/02/billy-joels-record-breaking-madison-square-garden-run-conquers-the-haters/>.

Cameron, Jane, and Adam Lebor. "Young Guardian: Glasnost Generation—Inside the Soviet Union." *The Guardian* 26 Aug. 1987. LexisNexis. Web. 26 May 2015.

Davenport, Lisa E. *Jazz Diplomacy: Promoting America in the Cold War Era*. Jackson, Mississippi: UP of Mississippi, 2009. Print.

DeCurtis, Anthony. *In Other Words: Artists Talk About Life and Work*. Milwaukee, Wisconsin: Hal Leonard, 2005. Print.

DeMain, Bill. *In Their Own Words: Songwriters Talk About the Creative Process*. Westport, CN: Praeger, 2004. Print.

Dougherty, Steve. "A $90 Million Matter of Distrust Pits Billy Joel Against his Ex-Manager." *People* 9 Oct. 1989. Web. 14 Jul. 2016. <https://people.com/archive/a-90-million-matter-of-distrust-pits-billy-joel-against-his-ex-manager-vol-32-no-15/>.

Dunkel, Mario. "'Jazz—Made in Germany' and the Transatlantic Beginnings of Jazz Diplomacy." *Music and Diplomacy from the Early Modern Era to the Present*. Ed. Damien Mahiet, Mark Ferraguto, and Rebekah Ahrendt. New York: Palgrave Macmillan, 2014. 147-168. Print.

Dylan, Bob. "The Times They Are a-Changin'." 1964. *The Times They Are a-Changin'*. Perf. Bob Dylan. Columbia Records, 1964. Vinyl.

Eaton, William. "Pop Weekend: From Moscow to L.A: Soviets Warm up to Billy Joel." *Los Angeles Times* 27 Jun. 1987. Web. 26 May 2015. <http://articles.latimes.com/1987-07-27/entertainment/ca-4094_1_billy-joel>.

Everett, Walter. "The Learned vs. the Vernacular in the Songs of Billy Joel." *Contemporary Music Review* 18.4 (1999): 105-129. EBSCOhost. Web. 21 Aug. 2015. <https://www.tandfonline.com/doi/abs/10.1080/07494460000640051?journalCode=gcmr20>.

Firozi, Paulina. "Billy Joel on a Trump Inauguration: 'I won't be anywhere near that place.'" *The Hill* 16 Aug. 2016. Web. 14 Jan 2017. <https://thehill.com/

blogs/ballot-box/presidential-races/291673-billy-joel-on-a-trump-inauguration-i-wont-be-anywhere>.

Fosler-Lussier, Danielle. "Cultural Diplomacy as Cultural Globalization: The University of Michigan Jazz Band in Latin America." *Journal of the Society for American Music* 4.1 (2010): 59-93. Web. 15 Jan. 2017. <https://doi.org/10.1017/S1752196309990848>.

Gamboa, Glenn. "Recalling Billy Joel's '87 Tour of Russia." *Newsday* 16 May 2014. Web. 26 May 2015. <https://www.newsday.com/entertainment/music/recalling-billy-joel-s-87-tour-of-russia-1.8045125>.

Harring, Bruce. "Gorbachev, Joel Team up for Charity." *Daily Variety* 21 Apr. 1993: News; 19. *LexisNexis.* Web. 26 May 2015. <https://advance-lexis-com.libproxy.mit.edu/api/document?collection=news&id=urn:contentItem:3S3M-FPB0-0006-00WK-00000-00&context=1516831>.

Heard, Alex. "Rock Diplomacy." *The Washington Post Magazine* 6 Sept. 1987: W7. Web. 26 May 2015. <https://advance-lexis-com.libproxy.mit.edu/api/document?collection=news&id=urn:contentItem:3S8G-NS70-000B-1405-00000-00&context=1516831>.

Joel, Billy. "Allentown" lyrics. *BillyJoel.com*. BillyJoel.com Web. 6 Oct. 2015. <https://www.billyjoel.com/song/allentown-12/>.

---. "Billy Joel '*A Matter of Trust—The Bridge to Russia*' to be released on 2CD live album, DVD/Blu-Ray concert film & deluxe edition." *BillyJoel.com*. BillyJoel.com 25 Feb. 2014. Web. 10 Jul. 2016. <https://www.billyjoel.com/news/billy-joel-matter-trust-bridge-russia-be-released-2cd-live-album-dvdblu-ray-concert-film-deluxe/>.

---. "Billy Joel Biography." *BillyJoel.com*. BillyJoel.com Web. 14 Jul. 2016. <https://www.billyjoel.com/biography/>.

---. *Kohuept*. Perf. Billy Joel. Columbia Records, 1987. CD.

---. "Prelude/Angry Young Man" lyrics. *BillyJoel.com*. BillyJoel.com Web. 6 Oct. 2015. <https://www.billyjoel.com/song/preludeangry-young-man/>.

---. *The Nylon Curtain*. Perf. Billy Joel. Columbia Records, 1982. CD.

---. *Turnstiles*. Perf. Billy Joel. Columbia Records, 1976. CD.

"Jumpy in Moscow." *Globe and Mail* 8 Aug 1987. *LexisNexis*. Web. 26 May 2015. <https://advance-lexis-com.libproxy.mit.edu/api/document?collection=news&id=urn:contentItem:4M9R-R9X0-TXJ2-N194-00000-00&context=1516831>.

Kent, George. "Letter to the Editor: Ambassador of Rock Visits Leningrad." *New York Times* 13 Nov. 1987 late city final ed.: A38. *LexisNexis*. Web. 26 May 2015. <https://advance-lexis-com.libproxy.mit.edu/api/document?collec

tion=news&id=urn:contentItem:3SJD-NDT0-0017-52NV-00000-00&context=1516831>.

Langbart, David. Inquiry to the National Archives. Message to Nicholas A. Brown. 15 Sep. 2015. E-mail.

Lennon, John, and Paul McCartney. "Back in the USSR." 1968. *The White Album*. Apple, 1968. Vinyl.

McKenzie, Michael. *Everything You Want to Know About Billy Joel*. New York: Ballantine, 1984. Print.

Myers, Donald M. *Headliners: Billy Joel*. New York: Tempo, 1981. Print.

O'Connor, John J. "Review/Television: Documentary Chronicles Billy Joel's Soviet Tour." *New York Times* 15 Jun 1988: C30. *ProQuest*. Web. 26 May 2015. <https://www.nytimes.com/1988/06/15/movies/review-television-documentary-chronicles-billy-joel-s-soviet-tour.html>.

---. "TV Reviews: Billy Joel in Soviet on HBO." *New York Times* 27 Oct. 1987: C22 late city final ed. *LexisNexis*. Web. 26 May 2015. <https://www.nytimes.com/1987/10/27/arts/tv-reviews-billy-joel-in-soviet-on-hbo.html>.

Office of Soviet Analysis, Central Intelligence Agency. "USSR Domestic Fallout from the Afghan War." Feb. 1988. Web. 17 Jan. 2017. <https://www.cia.gov/library/readingroom/docs/DOC_0000500659.pdf>.

Peasley, Sarah. "Billy Joel's Soviet Concerts." *The Washington Post* 2 May 1987. Web. 26 May 2015. <https://advance-lexis-com.libproxy.mit.edu/api/document?collection=news&id=urn:contentItem:3SJD-NDT0-0017-52NV-00000-00&context=1516831>.

Polus, Sarah. "Reliable Source: Did Billy Joel Just Diss Donald Trump? Probably." *The Washington Post* 31 May 2016. Web. 10 Jul. 2016. <https://www.washingtonpost.com/news/reliable-source/wp/2016/05/31/did-billy-joel-just-diss-donald-trump-probably/?noredirect=on&utm_term=.1a73f6ac2652>.

Potter, Lee Ann. "Teachable Moments Inspired by the Gershwin Prize." *Celebrating the Music of Billy Joel* [Program Booklet]. Washington DC: Library of Congress, 2014. Print.

Respers France, Leah. "Billy Joel Dons Jewish Star Against Neo-Nazis." *CNN.com* 22 Aug. 2017. Web. 21 Sep. 2018. <https://edition.cnn.com/2017/08/22/entertainment/billy-joel-yellow-star/index.html>.

Rockwell, John. "Pop: Billy Joel Brings Cuban Crowd to its Feet." *New York Times* 6 Mar. 1979: C11. Web. 9 Jul. 2016. <https://www.nytimes.com/1979/03/06/archives/pop-billy-joel-brings-cuban-crowd-to-its-feet.html>.

Ross, Whitney. Re: Research Inquiry [Billy Joel USSR Tour]. Message to Nicholas A. Brown. 3 Mar. 2016. E-mail.

Schruers, Fred. *Billy Joel: The Definitive Biography*. New York: Random House, 2014. Print.

Scott, Richard. *Billy Joel: All About Soul*. New York: Vintage Press, 2000. Print.

Suri, Jeremi. "China, the Soviet Union, and the Vietnam War." *Encyclopedia of the Vietnam War*. Ed. Stanley I. Kutler. New York: Charles Scribner's Sons, 2006. *US History in Context*. Web. 15 Jan. 2017.

Taubman, Philip. "In Moscow, a New Era? Protest and Rock Fete are Tests of Glasnost." *New York Times* 29 Jun. 1987 late city final ed.: A1. Web. 26 May 2015. <https://www.nytimes.com/1987/07/29/world/in-moscow-a-new-era-protest-and-rock-fete-are-tests-of-glasnost.html>.

Wild, David. "On Fire Again: Billy Joel." *Rolling Stone* 25 Jan. 1990. Web. 26 May 2015. <https://www.rollingstone.com/music/music-news/billy-joel-on-fire-again-the-rolling-stone-interview-79266/>.

Music Trade in the Slipstream of Cultural Diplomacy
Western Rock and Pop in a Fenced-In Record Market

Sven Kube

Western cultural diplomacy significantly influenced the musical preferences and listening habits of music fans in Eastern Bloc countries. Throughout the Cold War era, policy-makers in the capitalist democracies of the West used the popular appeal of genuinely Western genres from jazz and blues to rock, pop, and disco for the purpose of disseminating Western values and ideals in Bloc societies. In the early decades of the East-West power struggle, American authorities including the Department of State and the United States Information Agency (USIS) cooperated with private sponsors to send distinguished jazz and gospel performers on live concert tours through adversarial countries (Davenport; Eschen; Fosler-Lussier). To the excitement of young music listeners in particular, radio stations of countries including the United States, Great Britain, and West Germany transmitted the latest in contemporary hit music deep into Bloc territory (Nelson; Cummings; Schlosser). This chapter looks beyond the direct agency of Western policymakers, showing that the performance of Western sounds on stages and their omnipresence on the ether impacted the production of records and consumption of music in the Eastern Bloc.[1]

Although the state-owned music industries of communist countries had a mandate to promote ideologically unproblematic popular music performed by domestic artists, the familiarity of large audiences with Western pop shaped the repertoire of those record companies. Because of the country's close proximity

---

1   This paper is based on a presentation that summarized a dissertation in progress during the research phase. Contemporary witnesses who contributed oral histories to the dissertation research will remain unnamed in this article.

to Western cultural production in geographical and linguistic terms, music fans in the German Democratic Republic (GDR) benefited from this circumstance more than their peers in most other Soviet satellite states. As the GDR music industry sought to profit from the extremely high demand for popular music from Western countries, East Germans depended less and less on Western cultural diplomacy to access recorded content as the Cold War progressed. As its political authorities continued to denounce Western genres as subversive propaganda of cultural imperialists, the GDR's record industry made a habit of acquiring licenses from record companies in the capitalist hemisphere to domestically produce and mass-distribute the works of international star performers. Circulating commercially on disks pressed in East Berlin, Anglo-American rock and pop came to represent a popular cultural commodity among the people and, at the same time, an immensely profitable catalog component for the state-owned industry. This article clarifies that the dissemination of Western music in Eastern Bloc societies did not solely depend on the undertakings of Western cultural diplomats. It reveals that cooperation between record companies in East and West resulted in the familiarization of communist consumers with hit records of the capitalist entertainment industry. By examining the influx of Western pop music into the GDR's walled-in marketplace, it underscores a facet of Cold War contestation that all Bloc states faced in similar ways: Isolationist policies did not succeed in insulating domestic audiences from the appeal of popular Western cultural commodities.

BUILDING AN EAST GERMAN MUSIC INDUSTRY

World War II left Germany's entertainment industry in rubble. In contrast to the Allied zones, where prewar recording companies like Deutsche Grammophon and Electrola resumed production soon after the Third Reich's surrender in May 1945, Germany's East entered the postwar period without a music production infrastructure of its own. Moreover, while the American occupiers enlisted recording labels to disseminate their distinct brand of popular culture in the West, Soviet presence did not trigger any form of cultural Russianization or Sovietization in the Eastern part (see Ignácz in this volume). The administrators of the Soviet occupied zone valued German high-brow culture and swiftly reopened renowned sites of classical music performance in Dresden, Leipzig, and Berlin. They also granted a license to press records to Ernst Busch, a staunchly communist folk singer and stage performer who had worked at Radio Moscow during the Third Reich era. Enjoying comprehensive Soviet support,

Busch became the founding father of the East German music industry. The catalogue of his Lied der Zeit (Song of the Times) enterprise blended political content with light entertainment. Yet in the course of the new state's efforts to consolidate and nationalize all industrial operations, tensions arose between Lied der Zeit's entrepreneur and Sozialistische Einheitspartei Deutschlands (SED, the GDR's Socialist Unity Party). To acquire full control over the country's record production, the political élite opted to disown Busch. In April 1953, Lied der Zeit became a nationally owned enterprise ("Lied der Zeit").

As a state-owned monopolist, the record company evolved into a major player on East Germany's cultural circuit. In 1955, when the GDR's Ministerium für Kultur (MfK, Ministry of Culture) replaced the Ministerium für Leichtindustrie (Ministry of Light Industries) as the supervising body, Lied der Zeit became Deutsche Schallplatten (DS, German Records). At the same time, Harri Költzsch, a twenty-seven year-old mid-level supervisor at the MfK with an academic background in Economics, took the general manager position at DS (Register der Volkseigenen Wirtschaft). Mandated to transform the firm into a profitable venture whose musical output would meet the cultural demands of the people, Költzsch remained at the helm for the next thirty-three years and oversaw DS's development in the fashion of a Western tycoon. Under his auspices, DS developed into a flagship enterprise. It maintained five recording studios, operated two manufacturing plants, and employed a labor force of about 750. Its annual industrial output skyrocketed from roughly four million sound carriers in 1960 to seven million by 1970 and reached twenty million by the mid-1980s (Schindler 73). When Költzsch eventually stepped down as General Director in 1988, he did so realizing that "his" company, much like the Eastern Bloc as a whole, had exhausted its potential for economic growth. The development of Deutsche Schallplatten between 1955 and 1988, however, bears testimony to his qualities as a successful manager in an economy of scarcity.

Despite its status as a state-owned monopolist, DS remained surprisingly independent from the GDR's policymakers for a variety of reasons. First, the MfK applied a comparably liberal approach to political supervision. Traditionally a junction for state representatives and intellectuals, the ministry always acted as one of the lesser conformist authorities. The other two producers of recorded music, radio and television, by contrast, reported to committees at the Council of Ministers, which were staffed with SED hardliners. Moreover, DS's General Director succeeded in containing the influence of the party. With the exception of top-level supervisory positions like Director of Artistic Production, the company's employees felt no political pressure. Költzsch's approach of staffing elevated positions with party members provided him sufficient freedom to emphasize talent and expertise when hiring music producers, sound engineers, and other personnel with professional responsibilities. Most importantly, perhaps, DS flourished economically. The music enterprise was one of very few cultural producers in the GDR that did not permanently depend on state subsidies. In fact, for many years DS represented a significant contributor to the national budget: The earnings that it transferred to the state grew from less than ten million East German marks in 1955 to about eighty million by 1975 and approached the two-hundred million mark in 1989 (Schindler 74). Additionally, DS earned substantial amounts in hard currencies, which the GDR required desperately. Scant surviving evidence suggests that by the 1980s, DS had about two million in freely convertible valuta (predominantly American dollars, British pounds, and West German marks) at its disposal while it likely earned up to three million for the state every year (Ministerium für Kultur, "Staatliche Auflagen"). Költzsch's ability to satisfy his political superiors, his emphasis on qualifications and know-how in hiring, and the company's outstanding economic performance under his management guaranteed DS a degree of autonomy that was rare, if not unique, in the GDR's cultural sphere.

The record company's successful course of development was not predetermined. After Költzsch took office, he spent much time lobbying for increased investment to modernize the outdated manufacturing facilities. In 1957, Költzsch called for six-figure valuta investments in order to establish the production of long-playing records. In order to deflect the manager's demand for record presses that needed to be bought for hard currencies, representatives of the state authorities even proposed to stall all modernization efforts and simply outsource the production of albums to the Czech Republic (Ministerium für Kultur, "Fragen"). State authorities provided the means for DS to keep up with the general technological developments in the music industry such as longplay production and stereophony during the 1960s, yet the closing of new development gaps remained the General Director's top priority. By the early 1970s, the GDR mobilized unprecedented funds to comprehensively modernize its music monopolist. In 1973, the Council of Ministers approved a plan to ensure the "increased satisfaction of the citizens' cultural demands with recording disks and music cassettes" (Ministerrat der DDR). It allotted millions in domestic and hard currencies for DS to double its annual output of records from eight to sixteen million in only three years, and increase the manufacturing of cassettes twentyfold in the same period. While buying materials and labor from amounts in domestic currency, DS spent valuta on technological equipment for the recording of music and the manufacturing of sound carriers. Depending exclusively on microphones, mixing desks, vinyl presses, and other facilities made in capitalist countries, DS resembled an imported industry. Profitability was the key condition for the existence of such a construct, and in order to guarantee it DS required complete control over the home market and free hand to cooperate with partners in the capitalist world.

Its capacity to generate highly sought-after valuta is crucial to conceptualizing the dual nature of DS as a communist corporation. On the one hand, it represented a monopolist that controlled the GDR's strictly isolated marketplace for recorded music. Apart from occasional joint ventures with fellow monopolists in communist brother states, DS supplied all sound carriers that East German money could buy. Költzsch never tired of calling on his contacts in the MfK to rigorously suppress even the slightest ambitions of unaffiliated music producers to distribute recordings independently. These efforts became frequent when music cassettes enabled musicians and other actors to disseminate their creations commercially in small editions (Meyer). On the other hand, DS was a recording company with a profoundly international orientation and a wide network of partner firms in the capitalist world. These relations had formed during the postwar era, when Lied der Zeit turned to firms in Germany's West to purchase materials like pvc granulate, paper labels, and record sleeves. Even after the GDR had walled in its domestic market in 1961, DS intensified relations with its capitalist partners to be prepared for material shortages that may have stalled the production flow. As these business relations across the Iron Curtain blossomed regardless of the frosty geopolitical climate, Western companies developed an interest in something DS had to offer to them: classical music.

CLASSICAL MUSIC AND CULTURAL PRESTIGE

In the aftermath of World War II, East Germany developed into a stronghold of classical music. After the Soviets had promoted Germany's classical heritage in their attempts to create diversions during the immediate postwar period, the GDR's cultural policymakers continued on that trajectory. The MfK poured enormous sums into world-renowned classical music institutions such as Staatskapelle Dresden and Gewandhausorchester Leipzig. Presenting itself as the patron of the German nation's high-brow heritage, the GDR hoped to gain prestige in cultural and diplomatic circles. Cautious of progressive genres like jazz and outright anxious about the challenges that rock music posed to social norms in Western societies, GDR cultural planners decided to heavily promote classical music on the home front as well. Werner Rackwitz, who chaired the musical division at the MfK, insisted that "historical continuity from the heydays in human civilization" was indispensable for the development of the GDR's "musical life and the socialist national culture" to fend off the "destructive aberrances [and] impoverishment" that contemporary Western styles represented (Rackwitz 1-2). As modern socialist approaches to contemporary song and dance failed to strike a chord with the public, cultural officials resorted to acting as the true guardians of Germany's musical heritage. Naturally, East Germany's recording industry became a main beneficiary of state support for classical music. The MfK insisted that DS's classical music division, Eterna, received priority access to talent, funds, and technology to represent the GDR in the international market for recorded high-brow content.

Eterna was the undisputed flagship of Deutsche Schallplatten. The classical music department employed the largest workforce among DS's labels, maintained recording studios in two churches, and enjoyed priority access to imported machines and materials. "Over the entire course of my career at Deutsche Schallplatten," a former sound engineer for Eterna recalled, "I never had to use domestically produced recording tape just once. Anything that had relevance for the sound was imported from the West."[2] Beginning in 1984, the MfK allocated four million East German marks to DS for the purpose of building new production facilities that enabled Eterna to create stereophonic recordings digitally while the GDR was many years away from making digital playback devices available (Stadtrat Mitte). Imported technology incurred additional valuta expenditure. Yet these efforts served a clear purpose: Eterna produced recordings of classical works with world-renowned artists and orchestras that could be licensed to record companies in capitalist countries. In order to make those recordings appealing to Western firms, the quality standards had to be on par with what consumers in the Cold War West had grown accustomed to. The GDR invested heavily in Eterna to enable DS to earn valuta by either co-producing classical recordings with Western partners in the GDR, or by simply exporting finished tapes under licensing agreements. DS prioritized co-productions and licensed exports as the GDR economy grew increasingly dependent on hard currency investments during the second half of the Cold War. Between 1978 and 1988, the share of co-productions among Eterna's album projects grew from less than two-thirds to about ninety percent (Ministerium für Kultur, *Produktionspläne*). Re-cord companies from West Germany, Great Britain, the Netherlands, Japan, and elsewhere were keen to cooperate with DS because the partner-

---

2   "In meiner gesamten Zeit im Betrieb [Deutsche Schallplatten] hab ich nicht ein einziges Mal mit [einer] DDR-Band arbeiten müssen. Alles das, was Einfluss auf den Klang hatte, kam aus dem Westen" (former Eterna sound engineer).

ship gained them state-of-the-art classical music at very affordable prices in Western currencies.

PURCHASING POWER AND POPULAR MUSIC

The second-largest division of DS was Amiga, the GDR's only label for popular music. Amiga remained a necessity in the perception of cultural planners from the earliest days of DS, when music producers and political officials clashed over questions of whether music styles like jazz and beat should feature at all in East Germany's music market, to the second half of the Cold War, when the nation's recording artists struggled to compete with stars from capitalist countries. Amiga released about two-thousand albums, contributing slightly more than a quarter of all albums available in the GDR. These releases, however, accounted for at least half of all album sales in the national market, a circumstance that bore testimony to the high demand for popular content (Rauhut and Rauhut 8). Amiga's commercial relevance fueled suspicions on the part of the party that the label may risk instilling the wrong ideas in young socialist minds. To ensure ideological transparency, all native performers of popular music had to sing in German, and their lyrics had to be submitted long in advance of the scheduled production dates. An allotment key prescribed genre quotas for Amiga's musical output as an additional means to curtail the influence of Western styles. Releases in contemporary pop, rock, and dance music—contemporary genres that had evolved under the creative leadership of Anglo-American artists—could not exceed twenty-five percent of catalog numbers in the annual repertoire. For balancing purposes, the same share was reserved for schlager, a distinctly German blend of upbeat music with sentimental lyrics. The remaining half of release slots required the production of albums with jazz and blues, song and folk, musicals and operettas, children's entertainment, and other content (Leitner 182). While pop music labels in the West specialized in particular genres, striving to create recognizable label identity, Amiga for its monopoly position had to operate in the fashion of a one-stop shop.

The hottest items in Amiga's store were albums that contained contemporary rock and pop music and, to a lesser extent, some releases in the schlager column. The GDR music scene produced a few rock bands and disco outfits that more or less expertly emulated the style and sound of their Western role models. Bands such as Puhdys, Karat, and Stern Meissen represented the most prolific domestic rock bands while artists including Silly, Peter & Paul, and Inka epitomized East Germany's pop sound. With performers like Hauff & Henkler, Frank Schöbel, and Wolfgang Ziegler, the GDR also managed to establish a few homegrown vocalists of the more sedate schlager genre in opposition to the supremely popular West German and Austrian stars. The concentration of power over the production of pop records in the Amiga offices and the lack of state-of-the-art recording equipment for productions outside classical music, however, hampered the appeal of domestic artists in comparison with their Western counterparts. Aware of the citizens' access to Western radio signals, and perhaps also hoping to retain some minimal control over the musical intake of younger generations, cultural policymakers and repertoire managers at DS opted for an approach that blended cultural liberalization with economic profitability. Catering to widespread demand, the GDR's music monopolist integrated the original productions of predominantly American, British, and West German artists into Amiga's catalogue.

Licensed records—albums and singles that contained original recordings by Western artists but were pressed by DS in East Berlin—gradually became a staple position in Amiga's catalog. As far as contemporary pop and rock music were concerned, licensed records accounted for about forty percent of albums and twenty percent of singles released in that category between 1964 and 1990 (Rauhut). As licensed releases were strictly limited in the number of units made, they became a much sought-after commodity. Contemporary music purchasers remember waiting in line much longer than usual when licensed albums were rumored to go on sale. "To us," one GDR record collector recalled, "buying licensed records felt like acquiring material tokens of the big, wide world that was beyond our reach."[3] For consumers of popular culture, Amiga's expanding program of licensed records metaphorically resembled a widening crack in the Wall.

Licensed Amiga disks premiered in 1964. When Beatlemania had just begun to sweep America, young music fans in the GDR were able to purchase early Fab Four singles as "Ain't She Sweet" even before their peers in some Western European countries gained the opportunity (The Beatles). In the second half of the 1960s, DS began releasing the first albums by artists from the United States. For the time being, the two groups who qualified for admission into the communist marketplace were representatives of the urban leftist folk milieu (such as Bob Dylan, Pete Seeger, and Joan Baez) as well as famous African American jazz performers (including Louis Armstrong, Ella Fitzgerald, and Duke Elling-

---

3   "Für uns fühlte sich das [Kaufen von Lizenzplatten] an, als würden wir materielle Dinge aus einer Welt kaufen können, zu der wir keinen Zugang hatten" (GDR record collector).

ton). At least at the beginning, Western artists had to be outspoken adversaries of capitalism or members of disenfranchised minorities to have records released in East Germany. In the following decades, however, Amiga constantly expanded and diversified its Western licensed album program. After the enormous investment offensive of the mid-1970s, DS released hit albums by a large variety of iconic artists that included classic superstars such as Elvis Presley, counterculture icons of Jimi Hendrix's caliber, and disco pioneers like ABBA. In the 1980s, DS fully embraced the Western musical mainstream and offered GDR consumers top sellers by Madonna, Whitney Houston, Michael Jackson, and ZZ Top. Choosing from an album repertoire that captured the corporate music culture of Reagan America, East German record buyers were among the first to enjoy the effects of ideological and political liberalization when the Cold War began to wind down.

Naturally, music albums by Western artists needed to be approved before they could appear as licensed albums on the Amiga label. The review process, however, was a surprisingly laissez-faire matter. Amiga music producers recommended Western releases to their editor-in-chief; once he had signed off, obtaining consent from DS's top-level creative supervisors and economic managers constituted a mere formality. Although translated lyrics for every song had to be forwarded to all DS affiliates involved in the approval process, the projects that Amiga's music producers proposed at their discretion usually made it into stores. Rather than adhering to specific directives of a supervising body, the producers based their decisions on what they considered common sense. "We were aware and did not need to be told that no song could promote drug use, instigate violence, or criticize the great accomplishments of the Soviet Union," one of the producers recalled.[4] Minor adjustments to the original Western releases, however, became necessary every now and then. When Amiga released ABBA's album *Arrival* renamed as *Dancing Queen*, for example, the record's biggest hit was absent. ABBA's iconic single "Money, Money, Money," a tongue-in-cheek celebration of affluence and the good life, could not be considered funny in the self-proclaimed "workers' and farmers' republic," and so Amiga substituted the band's mega hit with an older and obscure flipside (ABBA).

---

4 "Wir wussten schon—und brauchten auch nicht erinnert zu werden—dass die Lieder nicht Drogen verherrlichen konnten, oder zu Gewalt aufrufen konnen, oder Kritik an den großen Errungenschaften der Sowjetunion äußern konnten" (former Amiga editor).

Amiga encountered little interference from state authorities regarding its licensing program. The label remained largely autonomous in its repertoire development and did not have to obtain consent for its Western releases from the corridors of political power. DS's Director of Artistic Production emphasized that the enterprise neither had to arm-wrestle cultural policymakers nor adhere to formal criteria in the process of producing licensed Western records. "It was known," Hansjürgen Schaefer stated in his last interview, "that Deutsche Schallplatten was bolder than broadcasting, especially when it came to lyrics" (Wicke and Müller 117). As licenses had to be paid in hard currencies, and since the company's valuta budget was always tight, DS preferred to buy Western pop music from the same companies that were buying classical music from them: EMI in London provided licenses for the pressing of the Beatles and Queen, the American giant CBS contributed recordings by Supertramp and Johnny Cash, and the West German Deutsche Grammophon supplied tapes by Cream and The Police. Eventually, DS found itself spending much of the hard currencies it was earning from the export of classical recordings on acquiring licenses for the large-scale import of contemporary popular content.

CONCLUSION

The evolution of Amiga's Western licensed music program illustrates a cultural dilemma that virtually all Eastern Bloc countries faced in similar ways. Much like its communist brother states, the GDR failed not only politically and economically but also culturally. Opposed to Western innovations in popular music and unwilling to free cultural production from state monitoring and interference, the country's policy-makers promoted high-brow traditions from bygone centuries that failed to strike a chord with the general public. Cultural authorities came to realize that the popular appeal of Western popular genres was difficult to challenge with state-commissioned counterproposals off the communist drawing board.

Particularly in the GDR, where a vast majority of citizens routinely accessed Western radio and television programs with relative ease, young music fans turned their ears and eyes to the West for modern and exciting sounds. Deutsche Schallplatten responded to the preferences of East German citizens by importing hit music from the United States, Great Britain, West Germany, and other countries west of the Wall. In this sense, Amiga's Western licensed album program represented the admission of lacking competitiveness from a state-owned monopolist that depended on attractive product to exhaust domestic purchasing power. Yet the GDR's music trade with Cold War adversaries also illuminated the remarkable permeability of the Iron Curtain in both economic and cultural regards: It remained at all times penetrable for Western capital, and it was always too porous to keep Western music out. As a result, music trade across the East-West divide manifested in the slipstream of Western cultural-diplomatic endeavors because communist music markets could not defy the cultural and economic hegemony of the capitalist music industry.

WORKS CITED

ABBA. *Dancing Queen.* VEB Deutsche Schallplatten, 1978. LP.

Cummings, Richard H. *Cold War Radio: The Dangerous History of American Broadcasting in Europe, 1950-1989.* Jefferson: McFarland, 2009. Print.

Davenport, Lisa E. *Jazz Diplomacy: Promoting America in the Cold War Era.* Jackson: UP of Mississippi, 2009. Print.

Eschen, Penny M. von. *Satchmo Blows Up the World: Jazz Ambassadors Play the Cold War.* Cambridge: Harvard UP, 2004. Print.

Former Amiga editor. Personal interview. 13 Apr. 2015.

Former Eterna producer. Personal interview. 29 May 2015.

Former Eterna sound engineer. Personal interview. 21 May 2015.

Fosler-Lussier, Danielle. *Music in America's Cold War Diplomacy.* Oakland: U of California P, 2015. Print.

GDR record collector. Personal interview. 13 Nov. 2014.

Leitner, Olaf. *Rockszene DDR: Aspekte einer Massenkultur im Sozialismus.* Reinbek: Rowohlt, 1983. Print.

Lied der Zeit. *Letter to Rat des Stadtbezirks Mitte.* 10 June 1953. C Rep. 304 Nr. 53786. Handelsregister Teil B. Landesarchiv Berlin. 28 May 2015. Print.

Meyer, Martin. *Letter to Rat des Bezirkes Leipzig.* 6 Feb. 1988. DR 1 15091. AWA-Korrespondenz. Bundesarchiv. 2 Apr. 2015. Print.

Ministerium für Kultur. "Fragen der Langspielplatten-Produktion." 1957. DR 1 257. Hauptabteilung Musik. Bundesarchiv. 21 Apr. 2015. Print.

Ministerium für Kultur. *Produktionspläne Eterna.* DR 1 15088. Fachbereich Musik, Ablieferungsverzeichnis. Bundesarchiv. 9 Apr. 2015. Print.

Ministerium für Kultur. "Staatliche Auflagen des Valutaplanes." 21 Dec. 1979. DR 1 10671. Korrespondenz 1978-1981. Bundesarchiv. 10 Apr. 2015. Print.

Ministerrat der DDR. "Beschlußprotokoll der 44. Sitzung des Ministerrates." 10 Jan. 1973. DC20/I-4 2789. Sitzungen des Präsidiums des Ministerrates. Bundesarchiv. 5 May 2015. Print.

Nelson, Michael. *War of the Black Heavens: The Battles of Western Broadcasting in the Cold War*. Syracuse: Syracuse UP, 1997. Print.

Rackwitz, Werner. "Probleme der Prognostik des Musiklebens." Mar. 1968. DR 1 9858. Protokoll des zentralen Seminars der Führungskader des sozialistischen Kulturlebens. Bundesarchiv. 30 Apr. 2015.

Rauhut, Birgit and Michael Rauhut. *AMIGA: Die Diskographie aller Rock- und Pop-Produktionen 1964-1990*. Berlin: Schwarzkopf und Schwarzkopf, 1999. Print.

Register der Volkseigenen Wirtschaft. *HRC 373*. 1953-1963. C Rep. 304 Nr. 55324. Handelsregister Teil C. Landesarchiv Berlin. 28 May 2015. Print.

Schindler, Alexander. *Chronik der DSB Deutsche Schallplatten GmbH Berlin*. 1995. Typescript.

Schlosser, Nicholas J. *Cold War on the Airwaves: The Radio Propaganda War against East Germany*. Champaign: U of Illinois P, 2015. Print.

Stadtrat Mitte. "Standortgenehmigung." 25 July 1984. C Rep. 110-01 Nr. 2524. Städtebauliche Genehmigungsverfahren. Landesarchiv Berlin. 28 May 2015. Print.

The Beatles. "Ain't She Sweet / Cry for a Shadow." VEB Deutsche Schallplatten. 1964. Single.

Wicke, Peter and Lothar Müller, eds. *Rockmusik und Politik: Analysen, Interviews und Dokumente*. Berlin: Ch. Links, 1996. Print.

National Flamencoism

Flamenco as an Instrument of Spanish Public Diplomacy in Franco's Regime (1939-1975)

Carlos Sanz Díaz and José Manuel Morales Tamaral

In December 1963, the flamenco dancer and choreographer Guillermina Martínez Cabrejas, known under her stage name of Mariemma, addressed the Spanish Minister of Information and Tourism, Manuel Fraga, with a long letter of complaint (Martínez Cabrejas). Her point was clear: Because she had been lending a great service to the image of Spain and to the prestige of the authentic "Spanish Dance" worldwide since the 1940s, she deserved some financial compensation after a last-minute cancellation of some scheduled performances by the Ministry. Hence, Mariemma remembered her successful performance in the Comic Opera in Paris "despite the campaign directed against me inside and outside the theater, for I had been declared a 'Francoist' at a time when the public opinion worldwide was resolutely counter to Spain" (Martínez Cabrejas). Not by chance did Mariemma include in her letter the words uttered in 1948 by the highest representative of the Spanish government in Washington DC, the diplomat Jose Félix de Lequerica, who expressed himself after Mariemma's performance in New York in the following terms: "After a long time finding in the international press nothing but a litany of insults against Spain, it is rewarding and soul-stirring to read finally some compliments about something Spanish" (Martínez Cabrejas).[1] That "something Spanish" was flamenco music and dance.

---

1 "A pesar de la campaña desarrollada contra mí dentro y fuera del teatro, por haber sido declarada 'franquista' en momentos en que la opinión mundial se manifestaba resueltamente contra España . . . Después de tiempo que llevamos no encontrando en la prensa más que verdaderas letanías de insultos contra España, es consolador y alegra el alma leer al fin elogios sobre algo español." All translations into English our own.

Strictly speaking, flamenco is a popular Romani-Andalusian musical genre which emerged in its present form in the eighteenth century from the fusion of ancient Moorish, Romani, Castilian and Jewish roots. It is traditionally characterized by a strong passionate and emotional expression displayed on stage in different manifestations—singing (*cante*), musicianship (*toque*), and dancing (*baile*).

The identification of flamenco as a semi-state music and theatrical genre dates back to the origins of the dictatorship of General Franco (1939-1975). Nevertheless, it took some time for flamenco to prevail over other styles and to become an instrument of Francoist public diplomacy, thus giving rise to the phenomenon of "National Flamencoism" (in Spanish, *nacionalflamenquismo*). We define it as the identification of flamenco with the essence of Spanish culture. According to Theresa Goldbach, "a conflation of flamenco with other Spanish national genres, an exaggeration of flamenco costuming, and an overly commercialized interpretation of the genre all marked the style of *nacionalflamenquismo*" (1).[2] National Flamencoism emerged in cultural studies by analogy with National Catholicism (*nacionalcatolicismo*), which refers to the idea that the Roman Catholic religion is the basis for the Spanish national identity (Álvarez Bolado; Botti; Payne 171-91). In both cases, a particular cultural trait is forcibly expanded to impose a common identity to the whole of Spanish society. In both cases, the concept has an homogenizing effect: A variety of cultural identities and values, sometimes in conflict—as happened amongst the regional cultural traditions of the Basque, Catalan, Galician, Castilian, and Andalusian people—were subsumed into something greater, amalgamated in the case of flamenco in a musical genre with popular roots.

This chapter aims to explain how the dictatorship of General Franco created an institutional framework in order to instrumentalize flamenco, thereby putting it at the service of Spain's international agenda. We intend to show the motivations, mechanisms, and some of the initiatives through which the dictatorship seized the cultural wealth of flamenco and its international acclaim, and incorporated it into its foreign propaganda. Our approach intends to go beyond contributions of flamencology and cultural studies, which have underlined the political and identity links between flamenco and the Franco regime primarily from an aesthetic and performative point of view (Washabaugh). Based on unique source material from the Spanish administration, we contend that the political use of flamenco by the dictatorship can be located in a broader context of the diplomat-

---

2   For other cultural approaches to this phenomenon, see Álvarez Caballero, Hayes, and Washabaugh.

ic use of music by governments during the Cold War (Ahrendt; Gienow-Hecht; Tompkins). Despite Spain's relative isolation under the dictatorship, "flamenco diplomacy"—namely, the political instrumentalization of flamenco in the international arena—can be regarded as a local expression amidst a global struggle for prestige and political legitimacy fought with cultural weapons since the 1950s, in which Spain clearly took part.

FLAMENCO MUSIC AND THE FRANCOIST MUSIC DIPLOMACY

Since the late nineteenth century, the social and identity background of flamenco music has generated a debate on the nature of this style. Is flamenco a traditional, pure, and essentially ethnic musical genre (cante jondo), or is it rather a hybrid, popular genre, a commercial and globalized kind of music in a continual process of aesthetic adaptation to different performance practices (Folch; Orozco; Pantaleoni)? At the beginning of the Franco dictatorship, the discussion was reformulated as an opposition between two phenomena. On the one hand, a kind of respectable flamenco music and dance, a regional variant of the authentic Andalusian folklore, could be supported by the state under the formula of "Choirs and Dances" (Coros y Danzas).[3] On the other hand, a commercial and market-oriented variety called género folclórico ("folk genre"), consisting of an amalgam of clichés and stereotypes rooted in distinctive Andalusian particularities, was rejected by the state on the grounds that it allegedly caricatured the real musical Spanish character.

This opposition linked with a wider contemporary debate on the role of popular music in the propaganda and cultural diplomacy of Francoist Spain. Two stages can be distinguished in this regard. In a first phase (1939 to the mid-1950s) Spain was culturally oriented towards the European fascist powers and, gradually after 1945, to Western anticommunist states. Notwithstanding their rivalry, Falange (FET y de las JONS), the sole legal party of the Spanish dicta-

---

3 "Coros y Danzas de la Sección Femenina" (Choirs and Dances of the Womens' Section) was a dancing and singing company created in 1939 and extinguished in 1977 that belonged to the "Falange Española", the Spanish fascist party. According to the Falangist writer Mercedes Formica, the idea of its foundation came from Pilar Primo de Rivera, sister of Falange founder José Antonio Primo de Rivera and founder herself of the Women's Section, the only single mass organization of feminine character that existed during the dictatorship (Richmond 152).

torship created in 1937 from the union of the fascist Spanish Falange and traditionalist groups, and the Catholic Church marshaled cultural affairs.[4] In these years, the Spanish regime advocated creating a "Spanish music," a fusion of several folk music traditions from the regions of Spain, an endeavor which Falange and the Comisaría General de Música (General Music Office) undertook in 1940 through the Ministry of National Education. Their efforts soon exceled.

At the level of "serious music," the government laid the foundations of an idealized Spanish classical music based on the repertoire of world-famous composers, such as Juan Crisóstomo de Arriaga, Isaac Albéniz, Enrique Granados, Manuel de Falla, and Joaquín Turina. Their music was believed to share an unmistakable Spanish air, which was difficult to define beyond the invocation of a certain "soul," "genius," or Spanish "essence" (Moreda Rodriguez, "Folklore and Gender" 637). The Spanish government displayed widely this sort of music in a series of German-Spanish Festivals held jointly with the Nazi government between July 1941 and August 1942 in Bad Elster (Saxony), Madrid, and Bilbao (Moreda Rodriguez, "Hispanic-German"). At the same time, a National Orchestra of Spain and a National Chamber Orchestra were created in 1940, both depending eventually on the Ministry of National Education as the department directly involved in the promotion of classical music throughout Spain. Over time, the dictatorship diversified the initiatives on this issue, launching in 1952 an International Festival of Music and Dance in Granada, which included a session devoted to flamenco singing—specifically pure cante jondo—and in the sixties and seventies both an Opera and a Ballet Festival in Madrid and Barcelona.[5]

In the realm of popular music, the Governement created a National Institute of Musicology and launched the so-called Misiones Folclóricas (Folk Missions) which between 1941 and 1961 collected and transcribed folk material in different regions of Spain, with the aim of creating and publishing a corpus of Spanish folk music. Within this framework, Coros y Danzas emerged as the best musical Spanish trademark abroad, going on an initial international tour through Latin

---

4   The acronym "FET y de las JONS" corresponds to the oficial name of the party, "Falange Española Tradicionalista y de las Juntas de Ofensiva Nacional Sindicalista" (Traditionalist Spanish Phalanx of the Committees of the National Syndicalist Offensive).

5   On the International Music and Dance Festival of Granada and the Opera and Ballet Festival of Madrid and Barcelona, see Archivo General de la Administración (AGA), Alcalá de Henares (Madrid, Spain), Sección de Cultura, (3) 52.15, Boxes 73579 and 88419.

America in 1948 and continuing to visit the US, several European countries, and the Middle East in the following years. This ensemble arrogated the role of representing genuine Spanish musical folklore, which according to Falange was popular, anonymous, choral, and underpinned by the so-called baile suelto, a dance without physical contact between men and women, thus acceptable for strict Catholic sexual morality. By doing so, they subsumed regional particularities under a common national identity which was epitomized in the representation of Castile as the forger of the unity of Spain. Therefore, flamenco found little place in Coros y Danzas performances, where conversely different variants of Andalusian regional dancing were well represented (Stehrenberger). As a genre that concentrates primarily on the individual, flamenco carried too many connotations of anarchy and rebellion. In addition, it was psychologically associated with sexual exuberance and a certain orientalism. In a nutshell, flamenco collided with the cultural roots of National Catholicism.

Despite this first mismatch, a certain type of commercial music of Andalusian and flamenco flavor became very well-accepted beyond Spanish borders, setting the path for a shift in official Francoist cultural policy with regards to music diplomacy. In fact, the backgrounds of a marketable flamenco variant are historically to be found in the late nineteenth century at the *cafés cantantes* (flamenco cafés), and already in the interwar period at the *óperas flamencas* (flamenco operas). The latter consisted of a kind of variety show mixing flamenco and *copla* or *canción española* (Spanish song), which allowed cante jondo to be performed out of its small Romani nucleus for the first time (Cruces Roldán). Between 1933 and 1945 many film productions exemplified this specific usage of flamenco, while some of them were co-productions with the German film industry, such as *Carmen de Triana* (1938), with Imperio Argentina or *Suspiros de España* (1939), with Estrellita Castro (Jarvinen and Peredo-Castro; Paz and Montero 222-23). Likewise, during the 1940s and 1950s some private flamenco groups, like the ones led by Luis Pérez Dávila "Luisillo," Carmen Amaya, and Antonio Ruiz Soler "Antonio," succeeded in their long tours around Europe, Latin America, and the US. They were promoted by such big impresarios as the Frenchman Fernand Lumbroso—who later participated in the Spanish government's musical diplomacy, as we will see below—or the American Sol Hurok (Robinson), with whom Carmen Amaya recorded *Original Gypsy Dances* in 1941 (Arce; Madridejos). *Copla* singers like Lola Flores and Concha Piquer were also prominent figures in flamenco show business.

Against this backdrop, Spanish music diplomacy entered a second phase in the mid-1950s. Spain was opening to the world economy at that time, pursuing international recognition through a strategic alignment with the Western bloc—

for example, the Spanish-US military agreement in 1953 marked a milestone in this regard (Delgado Gómez-Escalonilla et al.; García Delgado and Jiménez 125-49; Viñas 45-332). The country underwent fast and steady economic growth, along with the development of tourism as the first national industry and the rise of a mass consumption of cultural products (Cazorla 133-71; Pack 83-104). Meanwhile, the waning power of Falange amidst the governmental elites and the rise of technocrats and a pragmatic policy called *desarrollismo* (developmentalism) had enormous leverage on Francoist musical concerns. Castile was no longer privileged as the epitome of the Spanish nation, and it was displaced instead by Andalusia as the region that could best represent Spain abroad. Very timely, Andalusia lacked nationalist tensions, and was the ancestral home of a numerous Roma community without political organization (Orozco)—not to mention the sun, joy, and quaintness that millions of tourists were looking for. Andalusia was also the home of flamenco music in its most popular variant, a cultural export easily recognizable worldwide. It was then the reorientation of the Spanish cultural core that lies at the emergence of what we might call flamenco diplomacy—that is, the use of commercial flamenco by the state as a tool for Spain's self-representation abroad.

Since its creation in 1951, the Ministry of Information and Tourism (MIT) joined the Ministry of Foreign Affairs (MFA) as a key official actor in the realm of cultural diplomacy (Delgado Gómez Escalonilla; Jevenois and Romero de Terreros), assuming a critical role in the touristic diffusion of Spain through every kind of instrument, including the promotion of popular culture inside and outside Spain. MIT's most important cultural enterprise in this sense was the Planes Nacionales de Festivales de España (National Plans of the Spanish Festivals). Launched in 1954, they consisted of annual three or four-month campaigns running approximately from May to September and including various dance, music, and theatrical shows performed by significant domestic and international ensembles in theaters, urban gardens, and monumental complexes or natural venues. Building on previous experiences, namely the Granada Festival and the new International Festival of Santander created in 1952, the Festivales de España (FE) turned into the main accomplishment of the high-level state music policy under Francoism (Ferrer Cayón). They enjoyed the highest official support (both in terms of funding and political endorsement), the widest domestic and international propaganda, and, at least according to official Spanish sources, the greatest success.

Decisive support to the FE came when Manuel Fraga was appointed Minister of Information and Tourism in 1962;[6] shortly thereafter he began to work closely with two collaborators, his brother-in-law Carlos Robles Piquer—General Director of Information (1962-67) and General Director of Popular Culture and Entertainment (1967-69)—and Enrique de la Hoz—Deputy General Director of Popular Culture (1962-69). Their networking resulted in a significant increase of the FE from the point of view of their frequency, their quality level, and their funding. As an example, 45 FE and almost 800 different shows took place in 1963, while their number amounted to 83 in 1969 (MIT, Report 1964; Robles Piquer, *Memoria* 264-69). At the same time, the budgets of the Festivals shot up from 4-5 million pesetas per year in the 1950s to 100 million per year in the 1960s.[7] In addition, the MIT and the MFA improved their coordination, permeating—albeit at a lower intensity—the Ministry of National Education.

The FE under Fraga's office had two major targets. Domestically, the FE sought to bring so-called educated art forms to the lower strata of Spanish society, as was the case with other contemporary European dictatorships (Buch et al.). In doing so, they supported "the rise of the cultural and artistic level of the Spanish population, the creation of a refined taste for aesthetic manifestations among the masses, and the human dignity by providing easy access to the highest forms of intellectual creation" (MIT, Report 1964).[8]

At an international level, and reflecting the turn in Spanish foreign policy, the government intended to promote Spain as a tourist destination abroad and to contribute to the international acceptance of the dictatorship through the FE's policy (Sanz and Morales Tamaral). As a result, the MIT enhanced coordination with private travel agencies vis-à-vis the international dissemination of FE since the beginning of the 1960s—for instance, a travel guide from 1965 advertised Madrid as "the capital of good food, joy and flamenco" (MIT, Notes on Advertising). Even the Library of Congress showed an evident interest in these musical shows, asking the MIT for booklets of the FE in October 1964 (Library of Congress).

---

6   For an insider's account of the many activities developed by the MIT in the subsequent decade, see the memories of the Minister Fraga between 1962 and 1969 (*Memoria Breve* 33-255).

7   The evolution of the FE's budgets can be reconstructed in the annual reports located at the AGA, (3) 49.12, Boxes 44166, 44265, and 44267.

8   "... elevación del nivel cultural y artístico de la población española, creación de una autentica afición por las manifestaciones estéticas en las masas populares, dignificación del hombre por su acceso a las formas superiores de la creación espiritual."

Robles Piquer inspired the MIT's master guidelines for the popular culture policy, as well as devised its adaptation to the public relations of the dictatorship. His was the idea of the state as the best mediator among public and private actors behind cultural diplomacy implementation, extolling Spain's unique position between the characteristic abstentionism in cultural matters of liberal states and the excessive interventionism imposed by totalitarian ones (Robles Piquer, *Puntos* 4-9). Robles Piquer had also a notion of what a *ballet español* (Spanish ballet) should mean. Not exclusively identified with flamenco though almost monopolized by it, *ballet español* meant in his view "a cultivated product rooted in popular tradition, traditional dances and clothing, and the experience of its typical values" (Robles Piquer, Letter to Moreno).[9] The dance troupes led by Luisillo, María Rosa, Rafael de Córdoba, Antonio Gades, Vicente Escudero, and Antonio Pavón, all of them renowned flamenco dancers, were labeled by this category.

Nevertheless, Spanish ballet and the social pedagogy behind MIT's cultural businesses clashed with the burst of enthusiasm triggered by trendy Western pop and rock 'n' roll music. Particularly popular among young people, events like the Festival de Benidorm were not role models in the eyes of the Ministry, "for they tend[ed] to distort the audience's taste, create bad taste, or decrease rather than increase the artistic culture of the Spanish people" (MIT, Confidential Report).[10] The criterion was to be "modern but Spanish," as the title of a song recorded in 1970 by the popular Spanish singer Manolo Escobar stated ("Moderno pero Español").[11] Characteristically, the concert by the Beatles in Madrid in July 1965 was boycotted by the Spanish government through a massive police presence. The four British pop stars received a bullfighter's hat as a welcome gift upon their arrival at Madrid's airport, and they were later shown by the media among flamenco dancers on a visit to a sherry wine cellar, both signs of

---

9 "procedimiento de elaboración culto, efectivamente, del acervo popular, las danzas y vestiduras más autóctonas y la vivencia de sus valores típicos."

10 "propenden a deformar el gusto del público, o a crear el mal gusto y a que el nivel de la cultura artística de los españoles descienda antes que aumente."

11 The song was part of the original soundtrack of the film *En un lugar de La Manga* (dir. Mariano Ozores, 1970). This is a commercial comedy typical of the touristic Spain of the 1960s, in which the conflict between tradition and modernity is exemplified by the main character's refusal to sell his property, located on the Mediterranean Coast, to a real estate developer. For a long-term perspective on the dialectics between modernity and tradition in the use of Spanish popular music as a tool of musical diplomacy see Marc.

the dictatorship's unease with foreign popular music, as well as symptoms of the government's desire to *españolizar*—in other words, to adapt any kind of cultural expression to Spanish standards (Luqui 97-112). The Spanish government sought ultimately to avoid an explicit prohibition of modern music trends, thus adapting them to acceptable art forms for the dictatorship's values and, at the same time, diminishing its subversive and unsettling potential (Gracia García and Ruiz Carnicer).

FLAMENCO MISSIONS TO GERMANY AND THE SOVIET UNION

Two dance exchanges with Germany and the USSR better elucidate the actors, motivations, and outcomes that played an important role in the implementation of flamenco diplomacy within the institutional framework of the FE. The first state-guided flamenco mission concurred with the 25th anniversary of the end of the Spanish Civil War (1936-39), which was lavishly celebrated by the dictatorship in 1964 under the slogan "25 Years of Peace" ("XXV Años de Paz"). For this occasion, the MIT encouraged an ambitious cultural program inspired by pedagogic and political motivations, including popular contests, documentaries, exhibitions, and all kinds of musical concerts. The aforementioned Opera Festival, together with the Spanish-Latin American Music Festival, were launched in Madrid for the occasion. The official commemoration's goals were twofold. Firstly, it sought to assert the essentially conservative, nationalist, and authoritarian principles of the Francoist regime, yet adapting them to the rapid social and economic transformation resulting from the unprecedented prosperity achieved during the years of developmentalism. Secondly, and according to the Campaigns and Festivals Section's chief, it sought to praise the cultural standard attained by the Spanish people thanks to the unceasing educational concerns of the dictatorship after more than ten years of FE's campaigns (Campos de España).[12]

Such broad propagandistic aims put a tacit ideological slant on every single show sponsored by the Spanish regime during 1964, even when the artists involved were not consciously willing to contribute to that aim. This happened particularly with the three music pieces commissioned by the MIT for the Concierto de la Paz (Concert of Peace), for which the contemporary avant-garde

---

12 Ramón Campos de España was in charge of the MIT's Campaigns and Festivals Section and appointed Deputy Commissioner of the "25 Years of Peace" Festivals.

musicians Miguel Alonso, Cristóbal Halffter, and Luis de Pablo enjoyed freedom to compose their works as long as they adapted to the "noblest of events, such as the one being commemorated" (qtd. in Contreras Zubillaga 183). Furthermore, the MIT did not only establish a National Council of Festivals and organize the first National Meeting of Festivals at the end of 1963 in order to prepare the 25 Year commemorative ceremonies, it also pursued closer cooperation with the cultural attachés that had been appointed to some strategic Spanish embassies for the occasion. The Operation Festivals, as the exuberant cultural campaign was called in the official documents, sought a strategic scheduling of diplomatic music exchanges—eased when possible by foreign funding—for the dissemination of Spanish culture abroad (MIT, "Acta").

As a result of such ambitious plans, it is highly significant that flamenco emerged as an intangible, semiofficial diplomatic means directed to rally a very specific target audience—Spanish emigrants—for a clear reason, namely, to bring them back into the fold of the motherland. In this context, the FE made the leap overseas to perform in Santa Isabel, the capital of Spanish Guinea (now Equatorial Guinea) in November 1964, in which flamenco was represented by the Spanish Ballet of María Rosa.[13]

Nevertheless, the dictatorship's biggest effort to increase the international impact of the 25 Years of Peace events was the visit of the Spanish Ballet of Mariemma to the Federal Republic of Germany (FRG) in July 1964. That endeavor, which was inspired by a cluster of international propaganda efforts, both at the state and the civil society level, was possible thanks to coordination among different institutions, such as the MIT, the German Arbeits- und Sozial-Ministerium (German Ministry of Labor, Employment, and Social Affairs), the Landeshauptstadt Düsseldorf Wirtschaftsförderungsamt (State Capital Düsseldorf's Business Development Office), the Instituto Español de Emigración (Spanish Emigration Institute, IEE), and the emigrants' Casas de España (Houses of Spain) in North Rhine-Westphalia. However, it was actually an actor, named Manuel Collado, who came up with the idea in March 1964. Collado was an important Spanish actor and stage manager. He maintained a close relation to MIT's authorities as his theater company participated annualy in the FE campaigns. Accustomed to German performing arts since he had studied in Germany years before, and because he had translated German authors into Spanish, Collado had no troubles obtaining permission from the MIT and the IEE to

---

13 On the documents on the performance of the Ballet Maria Rosa in Santa Isabel from 17-21 November 1964 see AGA, (3) 49.12, 44140.

negotiate *in situ* every detail of the tour with all involved parties beginning in May of that year (Collado, "Anteproyecto").

Collado's prompt report to the MIT from Germany testifies to constant administrative obstacles and funding problems, including the delayed disbursement of 5 million pesetas to nurture the project (Collado, Letter to Araujo). [14] Spanish authorities improvised some changes along the way. Firstly, after considering several venues for the show, including Bonn, Hamburg, and Frankfurt, the organizers selected Düsseldorf, Dortmund, and Mannheim as the festival's sites, following the recommendations of local artistic partners. These industrial cities and their surrounding urban areas were home to tens of thousands of Spanish workers who had emigrated since the late 1950s in search of better employment opportunities (Bundesanstalt 39-40). The numbers of this community in Germany speak for themselves: the FRG hosted 200,000 Spanish workers, which amounted to 45 percent of the total number of Spanish emigrants in Europe between 1959 and 1964 (Sanz Lafuente 293-305).

Secondly, Collado's first proposal of a FE in Germany, which consisted of a flamenco show with additional theater plays, classical music concerts, and exhibitions, was restructured into a simple performance of Spanish dance starring Mariemma. Her show comprised a condensed glance at the history of Spanish folk music, including regional Basque and Aragonese dances, Andalusian "fandango" and, of course, flamenco, with live music played by the Madrid Symphony Orchestra under the direction of Enrique Luzuriaga, who was also Mariemma's manager at the time (Cavia Naya). The German première of the film *Sinfonía Española* (Spanish Symphony, 1965), an audio-visual glorification of Spain as a tourist Mecca, enriched the event. The film, which was produced by American director Samuel Bronston, who had achieved widespread commercial success with the Hollywood productions *El Cid* (1961) and *The Fall of the Roman Empire* (1964). *Sinfonía Española* (all shot in Spain), was praised by Robles Piquer for "its artistic beauty . . . its positive insight into the old and modern Spain and its consideration as the feature film that has best visually described Spain with serious and significant contents" (Robles Piquer, Note to Fraga, 8 Apr.).[15]

---

14 Joaquín Araujo led the Programming Administration at the MIT's General Department on Festivals (Comisaría General de Festivales).

15 "la belleza cinematográfica de *Sinfonía Española*, su positivo enfoque respecto a la España de siempre y a la de hoy y el hecho de ser el mejor documental de largo metraje que ha fotografiado a España con un contenido serio y trascendente." Due to Ro-

As stated in the program handout designed and translated into German by Collado, Mariemma's flamenco performances between 14 and 19 July 1964 represented an "artistic mission" in the FGR. Since "Spain and its history are performed on the German stage," the event should serve as a "deep memory of the Homeland for our countrymen who live there and also for the German audience at the celebration of the 25 Years of Peace" (Robles Piquer, Note to Fraga, 8 Apr).[16]

In spite of the persuasive effect pretended by flamenco diplomacy, the selected target groups did actually notice the underlying political message that surrounded this propaganda initiative, expressing some reservations shortly after the FE was announced. When they first heard about Mariemma's visit to Germany, Spanish emigrants remembered some previous disappointing musical experiences promoted by the Spanish government—Coros y Danzas above all—which in their opinion did not correspond to their self-ascribed identity (Collado, "Informe General"). In Mannheim it was possible to gather enough Spanish immigrants willing to pay the low price tickets, but in Düsseldorf and Dortmund the organizers had to give away tickets to ensure a sufficient audience (Collado, Report to De la Hoz and Magariños).[17] On the reception of flamenco among Spanish emigrant communities in neighbouring Belgium, cultural studies have shed some light that allows us to deepen our case study. Even when immigrants from Spain were willing to see flamenco as a familiar musical genre, Spaniards in Belgium tended to remove any kind of biased Spanish nationalist connotation in flamenco, re-appropriating it as an ancestral cultural heritage and, mainly, a means of socializing and networking in the host country (Ruiz Morales). Either way, there is evidence that Mariemma's performance enjoyed greater success than Bronston's film in general terms (Collado, "Informe General").

A possible hostile reception of flamenco diplomacy in the German public opinion was clear enough to Collado, who recommended a subtle administrative procedure and avoided explicit references to the state sponsorship in order to prevent distortions or public alarm (Collado, Report to De la Hoz). All efforts were in vain. Some German press outlets strongly criticized the tour due to its

---

bles' compliments on the film, *Sinfonía* finally preceded each Festival during the 25 Years' celebrations.

16 "España y su historia se representan en el escenario alemán . . . recuerdo vivo de la Patria a nuestros compatriotas residentes en dicho país y al público alemán, con motivo de la conmemoración de XXV Años de Paz Española."

17 Fernando Magariños led the Assistance Abroad Section ("Sección de Asistencia Exterior") at the IEE.

ideological background. The journalist Kurt Krausbeck wrote on 23 June in the *Frankfurter Allgemeine Zeitung*:

We are not against Spanish artists and really want to live in peace with Franco. But celebrating his revolution in Germany is a slap in the face to every democrat for whom democracy is considered more than a temporarily useful form of governance. . . . A democracy that celebrates a *coup d'état* against democracy in Spain, does not show disrespect towards democracy? Will we celebrate "GDR" holidays in our National Theater in the future? (qtd. in Collado, "Informe General")[18]

According to the *Neue Rhein Zeitung*, Mariemma's performance in Düsseldorf proved how totalitarian states took such opportunities and exploited them for their own political goals. Despite these dissonances, the contemporary musical reviews reflected a consensual atmosphere of acceptance: "Flamenco up to Exhaustion," (qtd. in Aymamí)[19] titled the *Rheinische Post* an article in their 18 July issue, highlighting flamenco's emotional power in contrast to other neutral popular Spanish genres (Robles Piquer, Note to Fraga, 15 July). In addition, the *Neue Rhein Zeitung* described the festival as a great gift offered to both German and Spanish audiences (Aymamí).[20]

This partial success achieved by the first FE abroad encouraged the MIT to continue in the same way while diversifying music diplomacy towards unexplored strategic objectives of Spanish foreign policy. The next target area was the other side of the Iron Curtain, specifically the Soviet Union. Not surprisingly, flamenco played a significant role again.

The Spanish-Soviet cultural diplomacy program was initiated by the French impresario Fernand Lumbroso in November 1964, who was by then in charge of French-Soviet cultural exchanges. He outlined an attractive music businesss after an interview with MIT officials in Madrid in November 1964. The draft included

---

18 "Wir haben nichts gegen spanische Künstler und wollen mit Franco im Frieden leben. Aber seinen Putsch-Feiertag bei uns mitfeiern, das ist ein Schlag ins Gesicht jedes Demokraten, dem die Demokratie mehr als eine zeitenweise zweckmäßige Staatsform ist. . . . In einer Demokratie, die Feiertage erfolgreicher Putschisten gegen die Demokratie mitfeiern—heißt das nicht bekunden, wie wurscht und fremd einem Demokratie sei! Wird man künftig auch etwa der Feiertage der 'DDR' durch Feierstunden im Nationaltheater gedenken?"

19 "Flamenco bis zur Erschöpfung"

20 Luis Aymamí was in charge of migration affairs in Düsseldorf as a member of the staff of the Spanish Consulate.

a first visit to Moscow led by the Ballet of Antonio, one the most accomplished world-famous Spanish flamenco dancers at that time, and, in turn, a tour in Spain featuring the Ballet of the famous Russian choreographer Igor Moiseyev, which specialized in performing folkloric dances from the fifteen Soviet Republics. In Lumbroso's opinion, this bilateral initiative carried out by dance diplomats was to pave the way for further exchanges of soloists and classical concert performances between Spain and the Soviet Union (Lumbroso). Robles Piquer accepted Lumbroso's proposal immediately, arguing that Spain could gain a big advantage on the international stage with such strategic maneuver. The exchanges could help to urge the US government to invest in Spain in order to contain communism, since, according to Robles Piquer, "it is useful to have communists around when dollars are required" (Robles Piquer, Note to Fraga, n.d.).[21] In any case, nobody should be surprised by a rapprochement between Francoism and the USSR because in Robles's opinion, the "Russian soccer team has visited Spain before and played against its Spanish counterpart, who can be considered up to some extent as official as the Spanish Festivals, as well as an emblematic symbol of the nation" (Robles Piquer, Note to Fraga, n.d.).[22]

The Cold War atmosphere could indeed not be more favorable for a deepening of Spanish-Soviet diplomatic relations. Notwithstanding its alignment with the West, the Spanish government jumped on the *détente* bandwagon encouraged by the concurrent Vatican rapprochement towards the Eastern Bloc. Madrid and Moscow initiated a bilateral round of talks in Washington DC, in June 1964, leaving behind decades of misunderstandings in the UN. The outcome was an informal agreement for the promotion of Spanish-Soviet tourist and artistic exchanges as a first step towards a future multi-level rapprochement (Suárez Fernández 245-74). Two Spanish-Soviet press and naval agreements followed this first deal in September 1966 and February 1967, respectively.

Significantly, the deal was signed at the same time as Lumbroso put forth the Antonio-Moiseyev exchange in late November 1964. The project was set aside in March 1965, however, because the Soviet authorities offered unacceptable low fees to the Spanish ensemble. As a result, Antonio continued with his professional duties in Canada and the US, while the Spanish MFA demanded that the flamenco mission precede Moiseyev's tour as a key condition to a final

---

21 "es conveniente tener comunistas cuando se quiere tener dólares."
22 "Al fin y al cabo el equipo nacional ruso de futbol ha venido a España y ha jugado con el equipo nacional español, al que puede considerarse quizá tan oficial como a los Festivales de España y más representativo del país en ciertos aspectos."

agreement (De la Serna).[23] Everything may have come to nothing had it not been for the unexpected emergence of a private liason. The accomplished bullfighter and member of the Spanish political and cultural elites Luis Miguel Dominguín, who had addressed the Soviet cultural administration some months before in order to organize two bullfights in Moscow and Leningrad (Dominguín), was asked in December 1965 by the Soviet Ministry of Culture to mediate among the Spanish authorities, putting the dance exchange back on track again (Boni).[24]

After a long, arduous negotiation, Antonio was finally allowed to perform in eight Soviet cities, including Leningrad, Kiev, and Moscow between June and July 1966. His performances received all imaginable compliments from the audience and the press: "Antonio is a dancing Paganini" (qtd. in MIT, File 2),[25] declared Moiseyev after enjoying the dancer's accurate flamenco technique in Moscow. On 9 July, the *Literaturnaya Gazeta* similarly noted the aesthetic delight of the audience, claiming that Antonio depicted the talent of the entire Spanish people (MIT, File 2). The Spanish Ambassador to Paris reported on 23 June the evident contrast between the popular acclamation of Antonio's performance by the Soviet audience and the unenthusiastic reception of the American Ballet Theater tour that took place at that time (Cortina Mauri).

Subsequently, Moiseyev's ballet toured several Spanish cities as the grand finale to the FE campaign in August and September 1966. Spanish representatives monitored the visit very closely trying not to leave any detail to improvisation. For example, Antonio received Moiseyev and his company in his studio, the Spanish press covered every daily movement of the Soviet dancers, and visits to Seville's most famous *tablaos* (flamenco bars) and Basque industries were scheduled. To increase the political significance of the musical exchange, the secret police supervised the tour thoroughly (MIT, "Proyecto").[26] Seeking to fulfill the specific objectives of the dictatorship regarding the Soviet visit, the Dirección General de Seguridad (General Directorate of Security) infiltrated in the company of Moiseyev two musicians as local staff who acted as informants for the Spanish government. The dance diplomats were supposed to be overwhelmed by the Spanish endeavors to modernize the Spanish working class,

---

23 General Director of Cultural Relations at the MFA.
24 V. Boni was the Chief of Gosconcert, the Concert Asociation of the Ministry of Culture in the USSR.
25 "Antonio es el Paganini del baile."
26 Further newspaper clippings on the Moiseyev's visit to Spain in AGA, (3) 49.12, 44170.

"convincing them with facts that the workers could be better redeemed than in the ways proposed by the Soviets" (Arespacochaga).[27]

An ideological background dominated Francoist music diplomacy until the end of the dictatorship, as the Fourth International Dance Festival celebrated in Madrid between October and November 1975 revealed. At that time, the strict international isolation which burdened Franco's regime in the 1940s revived because of the last death penalties that were enacted by Franco in September 1975, only shortly before his own death. In the context of this extreme situation, performing flamenco on the stage of Madrid's Teatro de la Zarzuela implicitly assumed a political overtone once again. First of all, it is quite surprising that the Spanish representation at the event was run by Antonio as the leader of a new National Ballet of the Spanish Festivals. It was the first official Spanish dance company launched in 1974, long after flamenco had been associated with Spanish national authenticity. Moreover, the stage turned into a political space when La Scala Ballet and the Belgian Ballet du XXe Siècle, directed by Maurice Béjart, decided to protest against the recent executions by refusing to perform at the festival. Eventually, the show could go on thanks to the personal contacts from the MIT's managers such as Mario Antolín Paz, the MIT's General Director of Theatre who succeeded in programing different French, British, and American ballets at the last moment (Antolín Paz).

CONCLUSIONS

Flamenco diplomacy under Franco's dictatorsship consolidated as an official diplomatic practice that resorted extensively to private actors—namely, impresarios and popular flamenco stars. It was strengthened fundamentally when the MIT assumed a leading position in the implementation of the state music policy and the international promotion of Spanish popular culture from the 1950s onwards. The Ministry's administration tried to close the gap between classical and folk music developed in the years when Falange and Coros y Danzas were in charge of music policy, transforming the popular music styles into high culture. However, this pedagogical target failed: The popularization of elitist cultural manifestations did not actually mean that lower or middle-class audiences

---

27 "[C]onvencerles con realidades que, a la masa obrera, se la puede redimir mejor de lo que ellos propugnan por otros caminos." Juan Arespacochaga was the MIT's General Director of Touristic Promotion.

attended classical music shows which they could not afford—or which they did not really want to attend.

Beyond the Pyrenees, Franco's regime instrumentalized flamenco under the conviction that it would achieve immediate positive results for Spain's recognition and tourist developments. Some reasons explain this choice. On the one hand, the Roma community did not have a strong political organization, which was a pleasant advantage for the dictatorship's propagandistic aims in order to appropriate its culture heritage easier.[28] On the other hand, flamenco had already been commercialized since the late nineteenth century through *cafés cantantes* and *óperas flamenco*. This consumerist way of understanding flamenco, associated with all imaginable Andalusian clichés and romantic connotations—for example, depicting Andalusia as a land of bullfighters, bandits, and brave women—was shared by many people around the world. Thus, Franco's dictatorship reshaped flamenco into a cultivated form of "Spanish ballet," almost monopolized by flamenco, yet only as far as music and dance were concerned. Lyrics were set aside since they were not paramount to fulfill the main goal of Spanish tourism policy—namely, to leverage the image of a modernizing and unique nation recognized as a legitimate partner by the Western, and even the Eastern, bloc.

Regardless of the ambivalent reception of flamenco missions in some cases—for example, among the Spanish emigrants in the FRG—the most influential achievement under Franco's dictatorship was, in short, to transform flamenco into a "national ballet." Francoism created a National Flamencoist system based on the inclusion of flamenco in the national apparatus of public diplomacy. Domestically, the instrumentalization of flamenco resulted in its depoliticization, primarily because this asserted that flamenco represented the ancient roots of "Spanish" music history and a single "national" identity.

Finally, flamenco diplomacy brings us closer to the difficult balance between private diplomats' agency and state guidance in public diplomatic affairs, and more precisely to the current public diplomacy program fostered by the Spanish government, namely the Marca España ("About"). Not only does the collaboration of state and private actors on a shared international image of Spanish culture continue to be scarcely harmonic, but it also supports the old Francoist discourse of flamenco's allegedly Spanish essence (Perujo). Flamenco courses, agreements for a global dissemination of flamenco art, and the inclusion of flamenco on the

---

28 It was not until the 1970s that a group of "new flamenco" performers began to subvert the Francoist simplification of flamenco art, engaging regionalist political movements with an Andalusian inspiration (Grimaldos).

Representative List of the Intangible Cultural Heritage of Humanity in 2010 suggest that a long academic path awaits the study of flamenco diplomacy in the future.[29]

WORKS CITED

Ahrendt, Rebekah, et al., eds. *Music and Diplomacy from the Early Modern Era to the Present*. New York: Palgrave Macmillan, 2014. Print.

Álvarez Bolado, Alfonso. *El Experimento del Nacional-Catolicismo, 1939-1975*. Madrid: Cuadernos para el Diálogo, 1976. Print.

Álvarez Caballero, Ángel. "Del Nacionalflamenquismo al Renacimiento." *Los intelectuales ante el Flamenco: Los Complementarios 9-10, Cuadernos Hispanoamericanos* (1992): 109-20. Print.

Antolín Paz, Mario. Notes to the Minister of Information and Tourism Adolfo Martín Gamero, 22 Sep.-14 Oct. 1975. Archivo General de la Administración (AGA), Sección de Cultura, (3) 52.15, caja 88422. Print.

Arce, Julio. "On the Other Side of the Screen. Songs in Spanish Popular Cinema from Concha Piquer to Manolo Escobar." *Made in Spain: Studies in Popular Music*. Ed. Silvia Martínez and Héctor Fouce. New York/London: Routledge, 2013. 168-77. Print.

Arespacochaga, Juan. Report to Carlos Robles Piquer, 22 July 1966. AGA, (3) 49.12, 44148. Print.

Aymamí, Luis. Dispatch to the Minister of Foreign Affairs, Fernando María Castiella, 20 July 1964. AGA, (3) 49.12, 44140. Print.

Boni, V. Letter to Luis Miguel Dominguín, 18 Dec. 1965. AGA, (3) 49.12, 44148. Print.

Botti, Alfonso. *Nazionalcattolicesimo e Spagna Nuova (1881-1975)*. Milano: Franco Angeli, 1992. Print.

Bundesanstalt für Arbeitsvermittlung und Arbeitslosenversicherung. *Beschäftigung, Anwerbung, Vermittlung Ausländischer Arbeitnehmer: Erfahrungsbericht 1964*. Nürnberg: Bundesanstalt für Arbetisvermittlung und Arbeitslosenversicherung, 1964. Print.

Buch, Esteban, et al., eds. *Composing for the State: Music in Twentieth Century Dictatorships*. Abingdon/New York: Routledge, 2016. Print.

---

29 This work has been developed in the research project HAR2014-58695-R, funded by the Spanish Ministry of Economy.

Campos de España, Ramón. "Informe Sobre la Vinculación que en Relación con el XXV Aniversario de Paz Española Tendrá Lugar en los Festivales de España y Campañas de Divulgación Cultural" 24 Jan. 1964. To Enrique de la Hoz. AGA, (3) 49.12, 44167. Print.

Cavia Naya, Victoria. "El Ballet Español en Mariemma o la Amalgama de lo Tradicional en Ibérica (1964)." *Etno-Folk: Revista galega de etnomusicoloxía* 14-15 (2009): 390-426. Print.

Cazorla Sánchez, Antonio. *Fear and Progress: Ordinary Lives in Franco's Spain, 1939-1975*. Oxford: Wiley-Blackwell, 2010. Print.

Collado, Manuel. "Anteproyecto de Consulta para el Envío de Unos 'Festivales de España' a los Emigrados Españoles en Alemania," 16 Mar. 1964. AGA, (3) 49.12, 44140. Print.

---. "Informe General y Rendición de Cuentas de la Edición Especial de Festivales de España en Alemania," 28 Aug. 1964. AGA, (3) 49.12, 44140. Print.

---. Letter to Joaquín Araujo Dualde, 18 June 1964. AGA, (3) 49.12, 44141. Print.

---. Report to Enrique de la Hoz, 1 June 1964. AGA, (3) 49.12, 44140. Print.

---. Report to Enrique de la Hoz and Fernando Magariños, 21 July 1964. AGA, (3) 49.12, 44140. Print.

Contreras Zubillaga, Igor. "El Concierto de la Paz (1964): Three Commissions to Celebrate 25 Years of Francoism." *Composing for the State: Music in Twentieth Century Dictatorships*. Ed. Esteban Buch, et al. Abingdon/New York: Routledge, 2016. 168-86. Print.

Cortina Mauri, Pedro. Dispatch to Fernando María Castiella, 23 June 1966. AGA, (3) 49.12, 44148. Print.

Cruces Roldán, Cristina. "El Flamenco." *Conocer Andalucía: Gran Enciclopedia Andaluza del Siglo XXI, Vol. 6*. Ed. Gabriel Cano García. Sevilla: Tartessos, 2000. 146-217. Print.

De la Serna, Alfonso. Dispatch to Carlos Robles Piquer, 23 Oct. 1965. AGA, (3) 49.12, 44148. Print.

Delgado Gómez-Escalonilla, Lorenzo. *Imperio de Papel: Acción Cultural y Política Exterior durante el Primer Franquismo*. Madrid: Consejo Superior de Investigaciones Científicas, 1992. Print.

Delgado Gómez-Escalonilla, Lorenzo, et al., eds. *La Apertura Internacional de España: Entre el Franquismo y la Democracia, 1953-1986*. Madrid: Sílex, 2016. Print

Dominguín, Luis Miguel. Letter to V. Boni, 11 Feb. 1966. AGA, (3) 49.12, 44148. Print.

En un lugar de La Manga. Dir. Mariano Ozores, Screenplay by Mariano Ozores and Alfonso Paso. Perf. Manolo Escobar, Concha Velasco, and José Luis López Vázquez. José Frade PC/Arturo González PC, 1970. Film.

Escobar, Juan Gabriel García. *Moderno pero Español.* Belter Discos, 1970. LP.

Ferrer Cayón, Jesús. *El Festival Internacional de Santander (1932-1958). Cultura y Política bajo Franco.* Granada: Libargo, 2016. Print.

Folch, Enric. "At the Crossroads of Flamenco, New Flamenco and Spanish Pop: The Case of *Rumba.*" *Made in Spain: Studies in Popular Music.* Ed. Silvia Martínez and Héctor Fouce. New York/London: Routledge, 2013. 17-27. Print.

Fraga Iribarne, Manuel. *Memoria Breve de Una Vida Pública.* Barcelona: Planeta, 1980. Print.

García Delgado, José Luis, and Jiménez Juan Carlos. *Un siglo de España: La Economía.* Madrid: Marcial Pons, 1999. Print.

Gienow-Hecht, Jessica C. E., ed. *Music and International History in the Twentieth Century.* New York/Oxford: Berghahn, 2015. Print.

Goldbach, Theresa. "Fascism, Flamenco and Ballet Español: Nacionalflamenquismo." Master's Thesis. University of New Mexico, 2014. Print.

Gracia García, Jordi, and Ruiz Carnicer, Miguel Ángel. *La España de Franco (1939-1975): Cultura y Vida Cotidiana.* Madrid: Síntesis, 2001. Print.

Grimaldos, Alfredo. *Historia Social del Flamenco.* Barcelona: Península, 2010. Print.

Hayes, Michelle Heffner. *Flamenco: Conflicting Histories of the Dance.* Jefferson/North Carolina: McFarland, 2009. Print.

Jarvinen, Lisa, and Peredo-Castro, Francisco. "German Attemps to Penetrate the Spanish-Speaking Film Markets, 1936-1942." *Cinema and the Swastika: The International Expansion of Third Reich Cinema.* Ed. Roel Vande Winkel and David Welch. London: Palgrave, 2007. 42-57. Print.

Jevenois, Pablo de, and Juan M. Romero de Terreros, eds. *La Dirección General de Relaciones Culturales y Científicas, 1946-1996.* Madrid: Ministerio de Asuntos Exteriores, 1997. Print.

Library of Congress. Letter to Robles Piquer, 20 Oct. 1964. AGA, (3) 49.12, 44618. Print.

Lumbroso, Fernand. Letter to Joaquín Araujo, Enrique de la Hoz and Alfonso de la Serna, 24 Nov. 1964. AGA, (3) 49.12, 44142. Print.

Luqui, Joaquín. *Los Beatles que Amo.* Madrid: Nuevas Ediciones, 1977. Print.

Madridejos, Montse. "Carmen Amaya, *star* de Hollywood." *Revista de Investigación sobre Flamenco "La Madrugá"*, 6 (2012): 55-73. Print.

Marc, Isabelle. "La Diplomacia Musical Española: el caso de la Música Popular." *Análisis Real Instituto Elcano 61/2015*, 6 Nov. 2015. Web. 22 June 2017. <http://www.realinstitutoelcano.org/wps/portal/web/rielcano_es/contenido?WCM_GLOBAL_CONTEXT=/elcano/elcano_es/zonas_es/lengua+y+cultura/ari61-2015-marc-diplomacia-musical-espanola-musica-popular>.

Marca España. "About Marca España." Web. 22 June 2017. <http://marcaespana.es/en/about-marca-espana>.

Martínez Cabrejas, Guillermina. Letter to Manuel Fraga, 23 Dec. 1963. AGA, (3) 49.12, 44170. Print.

MIT. "Acta de la reunión de la Junta Coordinadora de Festivales," 17 Jan. 1964. AGA, (3) 49.12, 44166. Print.

---. Confidential Report to the Coordination Committee of the FE, 15 Oct. 1963. AGA, (3) 49.12, 44167. Print.

---. File 2 "Shows, Publicity, 1966." AGA, (3) 49.12, 44148. Print.

---. Notes on Advertising, 1965. AGA, (3) 49.12, 44168. Print.

---. "Proyecto de Actos y Atenciones previstos durante la estancia del Ballet Moiseyev (sic) en España." AGA, (3) 49.12, 44148. Print.

---. Report on the National Plans of the Spanish Festivals 1964, AGA, (3) 49.12, 44166. Print.

Moreda Rodriguez, Eva. "Hispanic-German Music Festivals During the Second World War." *The Impact of Nazism on Twentieth-Century Music*. Ed. Erik Levi. Vienna: Böhlau, 2014. 309-22. Print.

---. "'La Mujer que no Canta no es... ¡Ni Mujer Española!': Folklore and Gender in the Earlier Franco Regime." *Bulletin of Hispanic Studies* 89.6 (2012): 627-44. Print.

Orozco, Lourdes. "Flamenco: Performing the Local/Performing the State." *A History of Theatre in Spain*. Ed. Maria M. Delgado and David T. Gies. Cambridge: Cambridge UP, 2012. 372-90. Print.

Pack, Sasha D. *Tourism and Dictatorship: Europe's Peaceful Invasion of Franco's Spain*. New York and Houndmills: Palgrave, 2006. Print.

Pantaleoni, Angelo. "El Flamenco y la Cultura Oficial Española." *Revista Internacional* 6 (2005): 187-93. Print.

Payne, Stanley G. *Spanish Catholicism: An Historical Overview*. Madison: U of Wisconsin P, 1984. Print.

Paz, María Antonia, and Montero, Julio. *La Larga Sombra de Hitler: el Cine Nazi en España (1933-1945)*. Madrid: Cátedra, 2009. Print.

Perujo, Francisco. "El Flamenco Marca la Diferencia Cultural de España." *Retos de nuestra acción exterior: Diplomacia Pública y Marca España*. Ed. Rafael Rubio, et al. Madrid: Escuela Diplomática, 2012. 225-31. Print.

Richmond, Kathleen J.L. *Women and Spanish Fascism: The Women's Section of the Falange 1934-1959.* London: Routledge, 2003. Print.

Robinson, Harlow. *The Last Impresario: The Life, Times and Legacy of Sol Hurok.* New York: Viking Penguin, 1994. Print.

Robles Piquer, Carlos. Letter to Antoñita Moreno, 25 Nov. 1965. AGA, (3) 49.12, 44148. Print.

---. *Memoria de cuatro Españas: República, Guerra, Franquismo y Democracia.* Barcelona: Planeta, 2011. Print.

---. Note to Manuel Fraga Iribarne, 8 Apr. 1964. AGA, (3) 49.12, 44166. Print.

---. Note to Manuel Fraga Iribarne, 15 July 1964. AGA, (3) 49.12, 44140. Print.

---. Note to Manuel Fraga Iribarne, n.d., AGA, (3) 49.12, 44142. Print.

---. *Puntos de una política teatral.* Madrid: Ateneo, 1969. Print.

Ruiz Morales, Fernando C. "De Cante, Baile y Toque en la Emigración. Sociabilidad en Torno al Flamenco en Bélgica, 1956-1975." *Revista de Dialectología y Tradiciones Populares* 66.2 (2011): 433-54. Print.

Sanz Díaz, Carlos and José Manuel Morales Tamaral. "Selling a Dictatorship on the Stage: The 'Festivales de España' as a Tool of the Spanish Public Diplomacy during the 1960s and 1970s." Machineries of Persuasion: European Soft Power and Public Diplomacy during the Cold War AIAS Symposium. 19-20 Jan. 2017, Aarhus Institute of Advanced Studies, Aarhus, Denmark. Conference Paper.

Sanz Lafuente, Gloria. "Anexo 1: Estadísticas históricas de la emigración Asistida e IEE, 1956-1985." *Historia del Instituto Español de Emigración: La Política Migratoria Exterior de España y el IEE del Franquismo a la Transición.* Ed. Luís M. Calvo Salgado, et al. Madrid: Ministerio de Trabajo e Inmigración, 2009. 293-307. Print.

Stehrenberger, Cécile Stephanie. *Francos Tänzerinnen auf Auslandstournee: Folklore, Nation und Geschlecht im 'Colonial Encounter.'* Bielefeld: Trancript, 2013. Print.

Suárez Fernández, Luis. *Franco y la URSS. La Diplomacia Secreta (1946-1970).* Madrid: Ediciones Rialp, 1987. Print.

Tompkins, David G. *Composing the Party Line: Music and Politics in Early Cold War Poland and East Germany.* Indiana: Purdue UP, 2013. Print.

Viñas, Ángel. *En las Garras del Águila: Los pactos de Estados Unidos, de Francisco Franco a Felipe González (1945-1995).* Barcelona: Crítica, 2003. Print.

Washabaugh, William. *Flamenco: Passion, Politics, and Popular Culture.* Oxford/Washington: Berg, 1996. Print.

Part IV:
Representation and Participation

The Ethics and Politics of Empathy in US Hip-Hop Diplomacy
The Case of the Next Level Program

Kendra Salois

In the mid-2000s, the US State Department revised its historic musical diplomacy strategies, sending more genres abroad, linking to existing exchange programs, and increasing opportunities for musical interaction. The newest initiative, named Next Level, conducts workshops in the hip-hop arts for beginners and professionals alike while refining its domestic and foreign audiences. Unlike the mid-twentieth century "Jazz Ambassadors," Next Level (NL) seeks American musicians who identify as activists and teachers as much as emcees, deejays, dancers or beatmakers. NL's format and desired performers can be read as the latest iteration of best practices in person-to-person diplomacy. I argue it also expresses an ideological shift towards privileging musicians' affective labor—that is, their work on themselves and others to perceive an embodied interpersonal connection that transcends language—in and beyond musical performance.

Historians of the US Cultural Presentations Program (CPP), which sent jazz and art music ensembles abroad from 1954 through the 1970s for multi-country tours aimed at elite audiences, frequently focus on the ways that American musicians achieved their personal goals for meeting and playing with and for non-elites (see Eschen). Danielle Fosler-Lussier has recently argued that we should read these tour anecdotes not as moments of "subversion," but as accommodated, even appreciated, by State Department and Foreign Service personnel (*Cold War Diplomacy* 98-99). Regardless of how we interpret them, scholars agree that such moments and the CPP as a whole expressed all participants' understandings of themselves as active in one Cold War front. By contrast, the artists I have spoken with about their involvement in NL and other programs see themselves as transcending US diplomatic and policy goals, whether they agree with them or not, precisely through their own sincerity of intention (Salois "US Department").

This chapter argues that the Next Level program demonstrates what the State Department has learned from previous generations of musical diplomacy. With its small-scale workshops and hand-picked collaborations, NL has taken the unplanned encounters and unexpected consequences of earlier tours and made them the center of its programming strategy. Under this ideal, person-to-person musical diplomacy is mobilized not for the wholesale winning of hearts and minds—regardless of the cultural or class status of those hearts and minds—but for a micropolitics of empathy, where the goal is an affective sense of being mutually recognized and appreciated, if not understood.

This chapter discusses how NL's structure requires affective labor from its musicians. I focus on the kinds of intersubjective connections desired between American musicians, foreign musicians, and their target audiences. Ultimately, this chapter focuses on participants' intertwined musical and affective labor in order to move beyond framing "hip-hop diplomacy" solely as a contradiction, viewing it instead as an extractive application of the State Department's understandings of human and musical intersubjectivity.

US ARTS DIPLOMACY: PHILOSOPHY AND PRACTICE

US cultural diplomacy policy has been characterized by public-private partnerships, "policy incoherence...and political vulnerability" (Sablosky 31), and differing opinions within the foreign policy establishment since its inception in the 1920s and 1930s. As such, musical diplomacy has seen a succession of experiments, especially since its revival in the post-9/11 era. The forerunner of today's arts-diplomacy programs, the Cultural Presentation Program (CPP), was established in 1954. Debates dating to CPP's origins, including its founding board's preference for art musics, and its quick addition of internationally-known jazz ensembles to its roster of orchestras and chamber groups, constitute an important backdrop for present-day programming choices (Campbell; Eschen). Historians also emphasize the CPP's intention to demonstrate that US culture achieves its greatest potential through, not despite, its private markets (Monson 111).

Diplomacy practitioners and historians describe the decade after 1989 as a nadir in financial and political support for US cultural diplomacy (Bayles 235-36; see Bayles in this volume; Cull 180-83). The United States Information Agency (USIA), which was responsible for most arts diplomacy programming during the Cold War, shrank from 1978, when the Carter administration combined it with the State Department's Bureau of Educational and Cultural Affairs to create the United States International Communication Agency (USICA), through the 1980s and 1990s. In 1999, it was fully dissolved and its non-broadcasting programming integrated into the Department of State's Bureau of Educational and Cultural Affairs (Sablosky 32; Hayden 179).

After the attacks of 11 September 2001, a small boom in publications by scholars, practitioners, and advocates argued for a "new public diplomacy," described by Nicholas Cull as a response to changed factors including new political contexts, technologies, state and non-state actors, and theoretical approaches (Bayles 235; Cull xi-xii). Cultural programming was central to calls for renewed public diplomacy, as commentators pointed out its relatively low costs and the target youth audiences' desire for creative products. In 2005, the Rhythm Road program, now known as American Music Abroad (AMA), revived and expanded the mid-century "Jazz Ambassadors" model (Aidi; AMS Planning and Associates 21). AMA was the first of several new concert and exchange programs in music and dance. While the philosophical and theoretical underpinnings of new and old programs are similar, current arts diplomacy programming has also diversified its methods, its musical styles, and its targets, recognizing that no single musical export can meet the preferences of diverse youth audiences. Instead, realizing these audiences lack not American musical products but experience with actual Americans, programs like Next Level, OneBeat, and to some extent AMA focus on bringing individuals together for intensive short-term encounters.

Since their inception, US arts-diplomacy programs have relied on an apparent contradiction. On one hand, artists and audiences are perfectly capable of separating American people from American policy, and often willing to do so (Fosler-Lussier, "Music Pushed" 63).[1] On the other hand, that separation allows those who might disagree with US foreign policies to develop good will toward individual Americans. This in turn better prepares those audiences to accept American interests. In the words of the 1993 US Advisory Commission on Public Diplomacy (US ACPD), "US foreign and economic policies will be understood best . . . by those whose views are based on personal observation of American society and contact with a broad cross-section of Americans" (US ACPD 2, qtd. in Sablosky 38). To accept the notion of separate cultural and

---

1   Referring to both target audiences and American musicians, former NL site manager Paul Rockower remarked, "for the most part, people, I find, can differentiate between political representatives and people who are cultural representatives."

political spheres is in itself to accept a fundamental argument made by US diplomacy.

For Craig Hayden, this apparent contradiction confuses the legitimization of public diplomacy with the practice itself. He argues that US advocates often "conflate the compelling aspects of US values with the deployment of technologies that are perceived to be demonstrative of these values" (175). Hayden neatly encapsulates what Marshall Stearns and Dave Brubeck argued in the 1950s and 1960s, and what contemporary diplomatic and musical practitioners often argue today. According to this narrative, jazz and hip-hop do not merely sound American; the personal interaction their musical organization requires directly expresses central American values of individuality, mutual respect, dialogue, and debate in a democratic public sphere (Crist; Fosler-Lussier, *Cold War Diplomacy* 86).

Similarly, Hayden argues that "US public diplomacy [assumed] that . . . exposing foreign audiences to US values will illuminate a shared identification with US motives and policies. In this view, public diplomacy provides a kind of revelatory function—pointing foreign audiences toward the belief that American values and institutions are in fact their values" (180). By contrast, the Obama-era focus on diplomacy's methods of communication, rather than on a single strategic message, reveals a belief that "influence accrues not in the elaboration of arguments about the United States, but in the symbolic significance of diplomatic practices that aid . . . and connect" target populations (182).

Both of Hayden's comments fit two features of Next Level. First, the program emphasizes connecting different hip-hop communities, both in placing geographically distant American artists on teams together and in the Global Next Level All-Stars, the team of foreign artists formed from professionals in host countries and brought to the US for a two-week residency at the end of each edition. Second, narratives about hip-hop music frequently focus on its rapid rise to preeminence as a "global" popular form, combining an assumption of music's universality with a strongly held belief in hip-hop's particularity as a means of resistance and a demonstration of agency.[2] Deployed uncritically, such narratives

---

2   Hip-hop connection narratives, in which practitioners in widely disparate places understand systemic racism against African Americans as either practically resembling their own marginality or as a metaphor for their own struggles for recognition, strongly resemble Lauren Berlant's depiction of "intimate publics": "What makes a public sphere intimate is an expectation that the consumers of its particular stuff already share a worldview and emotional knowledge that they have derived from a broadly common historical experience. A certain circulation structures an intimate public, therefore: its consumer participants are perceived to be marked by a commonly

imply all hip-hop practitioners will immediately understand each other if only given the opportunity to connect. In this vision, NL is less a demonstration of an American way of life and more a service provider to small groups of influential artists in each country. Yet simultaneously, NL communicates the "global" relevance of American aesthetics and values precisely through the "revelatory function" of its networking platform.

STRUCTURING EMPATHY: THE NEXT LEVEL PROGRAM

Like other State Department arts-diplomacy programs, the Next Level program began with a call for applications from the Bureau of Educational and Cultural Affairs to non-profit groups to audition, arrange, and run the proposed trips. Mark Katz, Professor of Music at UNC-Chapel Hill in North Carolina, won the pilot grant in 2013; the grant has been renewed five times, including for the upcoming 2019 edition (Katz, Dec. 2016 and Feb. 2018). According to the ACPD's 2016 report, the program's 2013 budget was $960,000, with subsequent years funded at $800,000. This budget includes, but is not limited to, the costs of travel, accommodations, salary, and per diem for an average of 26 participants for two to three weeks each (US ACPD, *2016 Comprehensive Annual Report* 103).

During its first year, NL sent teams of American "artist-educators" to six countries—India, Bangladesh, Bosnia-Herzegovina and Montenegro, Serbia, Senegal, and Zimbabwe—to hold workshops in hip-hop emceeing, deejaying, composition or beatmaking, and dance. Like other programs, youth in countries or cities with significant Muslim populations are an important target audience. As Martha Bayles notes (255), unlike contemporary arts diplomacy programs that seek to reach mass audiences, such as American Music Abroad, DanceMotionUSA, or the regional Voice of America and Radio Sawa broadcasts, NL targets only pre-selected groups of youth and hip-hop devotees. Typically, the State Department confirms the cities each NL edition will visit before auditions occur for that grant year; NL organizers have input, but not a final say over

---

lived history; its narratives and things are deemed expressive of that history while also shaping its conventions of belonging; and, expressing the sensational, embodied experience of living as a certain kind of being in the world, it promises also to provide a better experience of social belonging—partly through participation in the relevant commodity culture, and partly because of its revelations about how people can live" (vii).

where to go (Katz "Hip-Hop Diplomacy"; Rockower). Site managers visit each host city prior to the teams' arrival to meet with embassy personnel and the heads of non-profit groups with whom the teams will work, to scout accommodations and locations, and to confirm their presence will not inflame any local rivalries. In each location, NL team members spend most of their time working with school-age youth, often with some practical exposure to the hip-hop arts.[3] Itineraries also leave time for team members to meet advanced students, take cultural excursions, and collaborate with local musicians and each other. Each trip culminates in at least one public performance by the team's students and one by the team itself.

NL's programming relies on teams of artists with strong teaching credentials as well as expert musicianship. The application for the 2015-16 year required "teaching ability and experience," "potential to use music or dance to promote peace and cultural exchange," and the "potential to thrive as cultural diplomats" ("Apply"). These application criteria also tend to encourage "conscious" artists, who explicitly use their music and lyrics for socio-cultural commentary. Likewise, foreign service personnel indicate that they are usually offered and prefer artists with a track record of social engagement, such as teachers, mentors, or non-profit entrepreneurs (Werberg).

The examples in the next section show that from audition to final performance to post-return media management, musicians' personal qualities of generosity, sincerity, and empathy are at the heart of a successful NL trip. I am most concerned with empathy, provisionally understood here as an affective recognition of the other as deserving of interest, investment, and care—and thus as equal, despite being dissimilar. As a concept, "empathy" is often deployed in a manner similar to "affect." It has enough of an implied conceptual core to be useful, but fuzzy boundaries and multiple theoretical genealogies permit wide variations in application. Lauren Berlant identifies a "metacultural ideal of liberal empathy" that expresses itself through "the ideal of a 'one people' that can absorb all differences" (55). This universalist discourse underpins much public diplomacy and is echoed by several interviewees.

As Martha Nussbaum (*Upheavals of Thought*) and Carolyn Pedwell ("Affective (self-) transformations"; *Affective Relations*) point out, different theories about empathy presuppose different emotional mechanics. Pedwell summarizes feminist and anti-racist definitions of empathy as concerned with "imaginative reconstruction," "perspective-taking," and "mutuality" (*Affective Relations* 51).

---

3   Katz notes that today, "the typical age range is 18-25," but teams occasionally partner with high schools (Feb. 2018).

These intertwine the rational, creative imagination and the affective, embodied dimension of understanding that imagination. By contrast, Sara Ahmed suggests a different process in her discussion of representations of queer lives. In her filmic and novelistic examples from the late twentieth century, queer subjects' happiness is derailed by the unhappiness of their loved ones, who themselves insist they are being empathetic when they fail to imagine happiness outside of conventional straight romantic lives (*Promise* 92-96). Ahmed uses these representations to insist on the inescapable otherness of the target of empathy, arguing that "empathy sustains the very difference that it may seek to overcome: . . . subjects 'feel' something other than what another feels in the very moment of imagining they could feel what another feels" (*Cultural Politics* 30).[4]

If commonplace discourses about empathy hold that it encourages people to see themselves as fundamentally similar, while critical theorists note that this can shade into appropriation or pity, how do diplomacy professionals deploy the idea? Pedwell distinguishes between theorists who see empathy as a "capacity, skill or tool," which can be instrumentalized by institutions and cultivated by the neoliberal subject invested in developing herself as a set of human resources, and those who see it as closer to affect, as an intersubjective "social relation or product of circulation" (*Affective Relations* 49). The latter, perhaps paradoxically, are more likely to understand the production of empathy as an economy of circulation with, like other economies, winners and losers.

EMPATHY AS AFFECTIVE LABOR

In what follows, I offer examples of the affective labor NL participants, including program organizers, must do throughout their trips. This work is not directed solely at workshop participants at the teams' field sites, but also at their team members, State Department personnel, and themselves. As effective teachers and "cultural diplomats," the musicians selected must demonstrate heightened interpersonal skills. They must be able to engage equally effectively, and on short notice, with a wide variety of strangers, including their musical colleagues from across the US, American and foreign embassy personal at their site, local

---

4   In her summary of feminist thinking around this issue, Clare Hemmings reminds us that "transnational feminist perspectives . . . have highlighted a further likely slip between empathy and pity in white Western consideration of 'global others' . . . and emphasised the struggles and loss of authority that real empathy requires" (152).

leaders at the institutions where they are placed, and youth workshop participants ranging from rank amateurs to devoted hip-hop heads.

While NL applicants are not asked to complete in-person interviews, expectations of applicants' personal engagement are shaped by and similar to those of other State Department-sponsored programs. As described by site manager and public diplomacy specialist Paul Rockower, the audition for American Music Abroad requires musicians to perform an emotional connection with their interviewers. Rockower noted "[t]here were some groups that were Grammy-nominated . . . they didn't get accepted because they were dour" during their auditions and interviews. That emotional connection was in part based on demonstrating a shared mission and reflecting organizers' own sense of the project's meaning and prestige. As he put it, "[y]ou don't want divas. You want people who will appreciate the opportunity." Further, musicians were asked to cultivate an empathetic response to the challenges of travel. Rockower recalled asking applicants to anticipate disastrous scenarios: "Pretend you're doing a program in Lebanon and you're on your way to a Palestinian refugee camp. . . . [When you arrive,] they've been sitting there for two hours and there's no power. What do you do?" Although this hypothetical two hours probably includes stressful situations for the musicians, team members are expected to desire to put the needs of the audience first, rather than being "divas."

Once musicians have completed their tour with NL or its sister programs, they are ineligible for subsequent editions for a minimum of three years ("Apply"). Should we consider NL and similar programs exploitative if these excellent artists cannot find a similarly remunerative opportunity, without the obligation to advance the US's diplomatic and political goals, in the private sphere? NL organizers themselves are sensitive to this possibility. Katz and his staff work to provide more secure employment and to sustain musicians' commitment to the program. During the second edition in 2015-16, teams went to El Salvador, Honduras, Tanzania, Thailand, and Uganda ("About"). According to Rockower, the Thailand trip was managed by an artist from the pilot year. By the summer of 2016, three artists had become site managers, with others expected to do so in future editions (Katz, July 2016). In addition, NL hires former participants for other roles in which they have expertise, such as videography. A former participant who also manages his own arts non-profit, dancer Junious Brickhouse, now serves as Associate Director (Katz, Feb. 2018).

Katz sees a responsibility to compensate hip-hop's artistic community in a sustainable way. As he explained in a public lecture during the pilot year, "I'm sure this is not the State Department's agenda, to employ hip-hop artists . . . but it is a part of my agenda. . . . I'm sending taxpayer dollars into the hands of hip-hop artists, and I think that's a good thing" ("Hip-Hop Diplomacy"). Additionally, Katz has

> long thought that it was important to bring hip-hop practitioners into the administration of the program. . . . One way to do that is to hire them as site managers. It's also a way of continuing that relationship and cultivating a strong and mutually beneficial relationship with the community that I interact with. . . . I can tell . . . that some artists will be excellent at site management—they have that skill set and that temperament. (July 2016)

By conflating "skills" and "temperament," Katz implies that managing personalities, reactions, and emotions is a major part of leading a team as a site manager.

In addition, NL organizers are careful to assemble inclusive teams for each trip. These not only show target audiences the diversity of musical styles, ages, religions, racial and/or ethnic backgrounds, sexual orientations, and gender identities in US hip-hop today, but demonstrate a commitment to the entire hip-hop community rather than a normative masculinist vision. During interviews, Katz, Rockower, and project manager Michael Cohen all emphasized the program's commitment to forming teams that included at least one woman. However, the ACPD data on NL show 30 percent female participation across the first three years, hinting at how difficult it is to achieve this goal at present (US ACPD, *2016 Comprehensive Annual Report*).[5] Keeping a diverse roster of musicians in the pool of potential labor in this way, while working around the rule against musicians going on multiple tours, is paradigmatic of what Carolyn Pedwell describes as the results of empathetic responses to differential life chances idealized by both critical scholars and international development professionals.

> [T]he radically 'unsettling' affective experience of empathy . . . is conceived as potentially generative of both personal and social change . . . [I]n these and other feminist and anti-racist texts, the suggestion is that, while 'we' might theorise social inequalities and commit ourselves to social responsibilities and obligations in the abstract, a transformation at the affective level is required to make 'us' actually feel, realise and act on them. ("Affective (Self-)transformations" 166)

---

5   Katz notes that "in the next [cycle] it will be 39 percent [female participation]" (Feb. 2018).

In this reading, Katz's goal of "continuing that . . . mutually beneficial relationship" is ultimately informed by affective connections to his interlocutors.[6]

In what follows, I will use the case of DJ 2-Tone Jones, a Washington DC-based artist who went on the first NL trip to India, to illustrate how NL's "artist-educators" are expected to manage their affective and musical labor abroad. Jones's background makes him an excellent choice for a team of "artist-educators" designed to introduce youth to hip-hop beyond internationally popular artists. His personal style is historicist in outlook, as evidenced by his published mixes and his Shaolin Jazz Project, which highlights the continuing influence of jazz on hip-hop by pairing jazz remixes with famous Wu-Tang a cappella raps. He is also active with a hip-hop non-profit called Words Beats & Life in Washington DC, coaching teenagers in deejaying and chess. In our interview, he described finding that the NL application reflected what he already does. He was also interested in "the approach of bringing together different artists who hadn't really worked with one another" to go abroad.

The team met for the first time in orientation in Washington DC in early summer 2015. The following month, they spent two weeks in Patna, the capital city of the Indian state of Bihar, working with children at a local high school. This was followed by one week at the US Consulate in Kolkata, working with more advanced students in their late teens to early twenties. As Jones explained to me, and as participants in other tours confirmed (Gann; Rockower), the very first trip of the pilot year was busier and more experimental than subsequent trips. The group worked with novice students three to four hours a day in order to prepare for their culminating performance. After hours, artists also rehearsed amongst themselves, preparing for their own performance at the end of the residency. They replicated that structure in Kolkata.

However, the team also had an additional mandate. The Consulate "wanted us to create six [public service announcements, PSAs] . . . three for radio, three for TV—that involved the youth in social issues they dealt with on a daily basis. We had to create those while teaching them while getting the performance together . . . and have the PSAs actually completed to actually display during the performance," recalled Jones (Wallace). As a dedicated teacher who frequently works with school-age children, Jones already had a strong idea of how long it would take absolute beginners to achieve a performance that was both rewarding

---

6   Note that this reading does not require a single kind of relationship between affective "transformation" and moral or ethical norms. I am not suggesting, for example, that Katz's desire to redistribute is not also based in a belief that it is the right thing to do.

for them and appropriately conversant in hip-hop conventions. According to him, the program did not allow for the latter goal:

We really had about 8 days with the kids . . . it's a hundred-plus degrees every day . . . and the artists who are leading this, we've never worked together. And we have to do our own performance. And we have to meet with local artists and put something together with them that will also be a part of this culminating [performance]. . . . So yeah, my average day might be waking up at 7 and then I might be going to bed at like 2 or 3 in the morning. (Wallace)

At the same time, Jones emphasized that he enjoyed working with the students in Patna. "If anything, [the kids] were better than my expectations," he commented. "They were just excited . . . about every day we were there." The equanimity with which Jones recalled the stresses and highlights of the three weeks, and his sense of being "kind of like the guinea pigs" (Wallace) on the program's first trip, demonstrated the precise blend of resilience, optimism, technical ability, and gratitude that the application process appears to seek.

EMPATHY ON STAGE

When they gathered to perform in the Kolkata Consulate at the end of the third week, team members still did not have strong expectations for how they would interact beyond basic hip-hop conventions. As Jones put it, "as a deejay, one of the people I should be able to feed off the most is the emcee, but I didn't hear her rap until the second week" (Wallace). Layering additional non-hip-hop musicians onto that lack of familiarity required complex musical negotiations at the moment of performance. Empathetic listening practices and affirming responses, understood here as affective "social relations" in Pedwell's sense, are vital to turning individual musicians' choices into an ensemble's coherent performance. To illustrate this, I will analyze specific moments from a video of the team's final performance. In this video, DJ 2-Tone Jones, producer Ko, and emcee Purple Haze collaborate with two Baul musicians, OneBeat alumna Malabika Brahma and her musical partner, percussionist Sanjay Bhattacherjee (Next Level USA 0:00-2:40).

    The video begins with Jones scratching into the percussion pattern that opens Main Source's 1991 hit "Looking at the Front Door," which is based in F minor. He launches the sample four measures before the song's famous vocables-based chorus. Ko is situated to the left of Jones; off screen, on the stage to the left,

Purple Haze and Malabika Brahma wait for their cue. Standing behind Ko and Jones, Bhattacherjee listens carefully for the right moment to enter. He makes tentative noises with his khamak, a tension drum, to find a pitch that will match the guitar in Jones' sample.[7] After two measures on the dominant pitch, Bhattacherjee lands on the tonic sounded by the bass guitar in the sample, while maintaining an off-beat pattern that echoes the guitar and hit-hat rhythms. Ko, who has been watching Jones and nodding along to this introduction, turns to his equipment to prepare to enter at the start of the eighth measure, or halfway through the chorus. At nearly the same time, emcee Purple Haze says "give us something Ko" as sixteenth notes beginning on the second half of the third beat of the eighth measure, so that her spoken "Ko" lands on the "and" of the fourth beat. At this cue, Bhattacherjee increases the volume of his strumming pattern in the ninth measure, his tonic pitch sliding slightly sharp. Ko's initial drum sounds land late; after two measures, he settles on a clap on the "and" of beats two and four.

Once a new eight-measure unit begins, Jones turns the volume down on his sample to highlight the other musicians. Ko glances back at Bhattacherjee, and they exchange a smile just as Malabika Brahma drifts into the frame as she moves to the beat. Throughout this and the next eight-measure units, Ko adds a syncopated bass-drum pattern of two dotted-eighths plus an eighth note, while Bhattacherjee occasionally throws in four eighth notes played on the beat to contrast this syncopation (0:00-1:09).[8]

Off camera, Purple Haze prepares to enter with the word "yeah" on the "and" of beat two of the sixth measure of a unit (approximately 1:04). Ko immediately drops the claps in his percussion pattern and Bhattacherjee fills the rest of the measure with on-beat strumming. Purple Haze then enters with the phrase "I used to be in love but no not anymore," so that the first syllable of "used" lands on the first beat of seventh measure, and "not" and "more" line up with Ko's bass-drum pattern. Combined, these give the effect of a late entrance, so that it sounds as if she rushes her first phrase to catch up. In her second line, "so I left my heart open where I once had it stored," with "left," "once," and "stored" lining up with dotted eighths in the bass-drum pattern throughout the eighth

---

7   Alternately known as a khamak (or khamaka) or ananda-lahari, this drum is usually hung from a shoulder strap and held under the arm. One or two strings threaded through the drum head are attached to a much smaller drum, held in the hand, with which the performer can change the strings' tension and pitch (Capwell 95).

8   As Mario Dunkel points out, Ko's bass-drum pattern gives the effect of 2/4 measures over the 4/4 of "Looking at the Front Door."

measure of the unit. During the next full eight-measure unit, Purple Haze settles into a straight eighth-note rhythm, contrasting the syncopated bass-drum pattern. Bhattacherjee transitions to a stable supporting pattern, letting the interplay between Purple Haze's phrases and Ko's changing drum samples be the focus of the unit. The camera focuses on Purple Haze as she directs her rap to Brahma, turning her body towards Brahma, smiling and looking at her even as Brahma gazes at the ground in an attitude of attentive listening. Both women keep time with their bodies, shifting their weight on subdivisions of the beat.

In the following eight-measure unit, Malabika Brahma's entrance precipitates new responses from each musician. Brahma enters on E, a major seventh above the tonic F sounded by the bass in "Looking at the Front Door." She ends her first phrase on the sixth degree above the tonic, or D-flat. Jones drops the Main Source chorus sample, in which the melodic phrase resolves to the dominant, avoiding potential dissonance. Bhattacherjee immediately fills in on the tonic for four measures. In her second phrase, Brahma climbs towards a higher register. In her third phrase, Brahma ascends to and holds a D-flat, which Bhattacherjee reinforces by playing it one octave below. Without the Main Source sample, this has the effect of establishing the sixth degree as a new tonic pitch. Purple Haze then initiates an exchange of lines in what I hear as the new key, singing "You know my heart, though you know I didn't tell you/How do you know me?" so that the ends of both lines fall on the new tonic pitch. Brahma and Purple Haze then cue each other to trade off phrases with eye contact, physical gestures, facial expressions, and verbal cues. After Brahma's phrase, Purple Haze repeats her line in her second entrance. However, beyond the camera's frame, Bhattacherjee shifts his accompaniment pattern back to the original tonic F immediately after Haze's line. As a result, Brahma takes the exchange in a different direction, rejoining with "I know" on a low F. As Purple Haze freestyles over the next measures, Brahma smiles and shakes her head while giving eye contact and focus to her, as Jones quietly brings back the chorus of "Looking at the Front Door." When Brahma enters again, she sings over the sample, using Purple Haze's melody from "you know my heart" as a cadence on the D-flat (1:32-2:40).

These moments demonstrate how difficult it is for seasoned musicians to anticipate unfamiliar collaborators' actions, read each other's cues, and decide what to do next, often within a subdivision of the beat. When I showed Jones this clip, he said, "This was one of the ones that was a little more thrown together in the moment. . . . All the others were things we might have tried in a jam session, whereas this was kinda like, 'uhh, hey I remember we did something the other day, do you remember?'" He offered that since he was not sure what would happen next, he thought "I can just do a basic beat, [Bhattacherjee] can just do whatever he's doing behind me." He noted that he did not feel the Baul musicians and the group had enough time to rehearse beforehand, but they "still made it work some kinda way" (Wallace).

Each decision discussed here has the potential to derail the performance. When Ko first enters, his slightly out-of-time sounds in his first two measures could confuse less able collaborators. When Bhattacherjee starts to vary his patterns, Ko looks back in a way that could be interpreted as either reinforcing or discouraging. When Purple Haze starts using shorter patterns that pull against the rhythms set up by Ko and Jones' sample, or when Brahma structures her melodic line around the sixth scale degree, both lead the backing musicians to reduce the texture to essential percussion.

In each case, the musicians respond to what they are hearing, even if it is not what they are listening for. For example, when I interpret Brahma's melody as a change of key, I am listening with the ingrained assumption that the bass line of "Looking at the Front Door" implies an unchanging tonal center, even when the sample itself is no longer audible. In a sense, I am unable to avoid hearing my own expectations, set up by the sample. The ensemble, however, fluidly moves between the F minor established in Main Source's chorus and Brahma's tonal center of D-flat, and between following the deejay or the khamak as the leading instrument. In a sign of the flexibility and intercultural adaptability that NL prizes in its musicians, both the hip-hop and Baul musicians in this example listen beyond genre conventions and affirm unexpected results.

Video analysis also demonstrates how the musicians use their roles in the group to promote effective turn-taking and expectations of reciprocity. In the moment of performance, the musicians manage their own reactions, their intergroup responses, and what they are showing to the audience all at once. Both vocalists, as the center of attention for the live audience, appear focused on making the audience feel comfortable with what is happening on stage. They maintain their composure and their smiles, literally reaching out to the audience with their gestures, and sharing space equally on stage even as they move from one side to the other. On the interaction between Purple Haze and Brahma, Jones commented, "there was a section of time where . . . I was like 'you know, where you guys going with this?' But. . . . They had a bond, they had a moment." Holding only microphones, the female vocalists use their relative freedom of movement to visualize their sonic dialogue, confirming their attention to and interest in each other's performances for both the instrumentalists and the audience. Likewise, the instrumentalists also constantly affirm each other's initiatives with non-verbal cues, even as their faces are turned to their instruments and their musical gestures may lead in a different direction. While the artists give a visual and sonic impression of confident spontaneity, on close listening one can hear the traces of a stressful, though rewarding, three weeks in their performance.

CONCLUSIONS

Next Level has turned a traditional weakness of arts diplomacy, the inability to judge performances' effectiveness with large audiences, into a strength. Although today's descendants of the mid-twentieth-century Cultural Presentations Program include more workshops and collaborations than the CPP was designed to do, they also still conduct multi-stop tours with audiences in the hundreds. To date, reviews of these programs' effectiveness rely on press clippings and anecdotes from embassy personnel. While these are often high-quality, well-contextualized data, they skew towards elite audiences and towards demonstrating the efficacy of the host embassies. In contrast, by targeting small groups preselected by the host embassy or consulate, or by the local school, NGO, or youth group, NL avoids having to adjudicate its impact on large audiences in the first place. Instead, as DJ 2-Tone Jones' example demonstrated, a successful Next Level trip negotiates a path through the occasionally conflicting goals of the embassy, the target institutions and students, and the artists themselves.

Despite differences these examples bring out within and between groups, everyone interviewed remains committed to the idea of forging a lasting connection and to the belief that they did so. NL completed its pilot year in April 2015 by bringing five foreign musicians to Washington DC and Chapel Hill, North Carolina. Dubbed the "Next Level Global All-Stars," they were among those who had collaborated with the NL teams on each tour. Each was chosen based on recommendations from NL organizers, the participating Embassy, and the NL musicians (Rockower). Like the US artists, the musicians chosen for the global residency were already active as professional musicians, teachers, advocates, media personalities, and/or activists. According to Mark Katz, the goals of the residency were to reunite selected foreign musicians with American participants and to offer an opportunity for one person from each country to create with the others (2014). In a blog post for the NL website, a staff member wrote, "Hip-hop represents a worldview where diversity is the norm, not the exception, and we strive to uphold that. . . . The same performance can even be meaningful to different people for different reasons, and this understanding has always been at the heart of our diplomatic mission" ("Amazing Journey").

Paul Rockower likewise described the Global All-Stars residency as "creating space in which diverse voices can be heard." But he also emphasized the difference between the goals of the NL organizers and those of the State Department, noting that for the latter, it was less about advancing hip-hop as an art form and more about training future leaders. As he put it, "That's why we do lots of workshops in entrepreneurship, in social activism, in conflict resolution . . . trying to give them more skills so they can . . . be involved in their communities." The organizers ran such workshops with the help of DC-based NL participants, including Jones, who joined a panel to discuss hip-hop pedagogy.

Based on their public comments, the members of the 2015 global residency were enthusiastic about the State Department's vision of hip-hop as social advocacy and entrepreneurship. In a roundtable in Washington DC on 10 April 2015, the All-Stars were asked what lessons they would bring home from the residency. Zimbabwean beat maker Nyari "FTR" Mazango said:

> The possibility that what I do, music, hip-hop, can connect me to so many people just as a medium in itself, I think is the biggest thing I can ever take from all this. . . . Because I can go back with it, and when I'm building community programs, . . . I can show them the possibility of connecting with so many people through the music itself.

Similarly, emcee Black Zang answered the same question with, "[In Bangladesh] we really can connect through hip-hop, we really can help each other . . . on any kind of issues."

In this way, Next Level may do its most profound work—or at least its most trackable work—on its American participants and their professional foreign counterparts who continue to reflect on their intercultural experiences, rather than on the youth who attend in-country workshops. Dr. Elliot Gann, a beatmaker and educational psychiatrist who joined the NL Senegal team in summer 2014, described telling his audience on a Senegalese radio show, "I wish every American could have the experience that I'm having." Toni Blackman, the first "hip-hop envoy" in the American Specialists Program and also part of the NL Senegal team, recently published her appreciation for the Dakaroise emcee Toussa, her collaborator and member of the global Next Level All-Stars in 2015, in a series of *Instagram* posts: "Toni & Toussa. Sounds like a great name for a café or the title of an EP. . . . It's so dope to see artists you helped mentor and/or coach soar. I'm so excited and proud." For his part, Jones described returning to DC with a cache of mid-century Bollywood recordings and a new interest in exploring the genre for beatmaking and collaboration.

What does a focus on affective labor, and empathy in particular, do for our understanding of artists' agency during Next Level or similar programs? My concern here is not whether artists' political speech is censored; every participant I have interviewed affirmatively stated they felt no pressure to be silent or avoid specific topics. Since the reorganization of USIA into USICA in 1978, safeguards have existed against cultural programs being co-opted by other parts of the State Department, and against compelling participants to act or speak on behalf of US foreign policy (Sablosky 32; Hayden 177).[9] Instead, I am interested in how artists are positioned and what makes them useful to the state.

Jones summed this up when I asked what he thought the State Department gets from Next Level.

Of course it is a way to better the US image abroad, that's the nature of the program. . . . These kids never thought in a million years that someone would pick them to work with hip-hop artists from the US. . . . Even if I found out there was some ulterior motive, I still would feel justified that these kids got something out of it. (Wallace)

Here, Jones takes for granted that the State Department is acting in its own interest, though he also said that he felt there were Department personnel with sincere interest in hip-hop music and culture. At the same time, the mutual attachment of teachers and students allows him to avoid asking or worrying about "ulterior motives."[10] In a similar vein, Jones appreciated that the program was "sending authentic artists," not necessarily "iconic" hip-hop artists, and placing a premium on teaching ability rather than fame. This individualized sincerity of intention allows hip-hop artists, who might not agree with US policy in the places they are going or in general, to join the program and make it work.

Additionally, the way that arts-diplomacy rhetoric positions artists who are working for these programs tends to erase their expertise and their labor as contributions. Precisely because artists are encouraged to say what they think, they are not encouraged to see themselves as representatives of the state or of the

---

9   I am not aware of an explicit policy regarding advertising NL's accomplishments to US citizens, but since the program routinely posts professionally edited videos to its own social media accounts, anyone in the personal and professional networks of NL and its current and former musicians can see program news through Facebook, Twitter, and elsewhere.

10 In our discussion, Jones recalled with a laugh that the team's Patna students "still reach out to us on Facebook. . . . I still get some of these random profile pictures on my page" (Wallace).

American people as a whole (though some do). Because they can run their workshops, demonstrations, and collaborations how they see fit, they are not encouraged to see themselves as employees of the state. Because they are selected as much for their personal qualities as for their musical abilities, they are not encouraged to see themselves as working, but rather as "doing what they love." Paradoxically, this devalues people's musical expertise and years spent honing their craft in favor of appreciating their generosity, flexibility, sincerity, empathy, or independence.[11] When this mode is embraced by musicians as well as State Department organizers, it serves to depoliticize the state's choice of hip-hop regardless of the performers' lyrical statements. Next Level and other programs stress the universalism of artists' affective labor instead of the systemic, race-based difference-making hip-hop arts so often identify and critique.

Next Level builds upon the now-commonplace "public diplomacy" paradigm by orchestrating moments of person-to-person diplomacy. Hip-hop's origin narrative, when told through institutions committed to color-blind policy, contributes to a belief in its power to overcome linguistic, religious, political, or cultural barriers shared by program organizers, workshop participants, and musicians themselves. As Rockower insisted in our discussion, "Hip-hop is universal. It's this empowering force in all of these different countries. . . . The value of this stuff—there's no metrics that will ever support it." I do not doubt the sincerity of this comment, but as in any genre, "empowerment" through hip-hop is dependent on local contexts and definitions of power.

In claiming that hip-hop transcends linguistic and political borders, the State Department deploys seductive assumptions about the universality of art. However, it does this through the paradoxical position hip-hop music occupies worldwide. While at home, US artists must continually reassert hip-hop's aesthetic value in order to combat systemic discrimination against the genre and African Americans. Abroad, Next Level relies on the affective labor of its teacher-artists to leverage hip-hop lovers' own narratives about the genre's role in supporting freedom and resistance. To return to Hayden's observations, NL thus serves a "relevatory function," confirming to both American and foreign participants a fundamental sameness of values understood as central to US public diplomacy

---

11 In reviewing this chapter, Katz suggested, instead, that NL participants are allowed to focus on their craft as musicians and teachers, "Instead of pressuring them to perform in areas in which they are not expert (speaking about US foreign policy, etc.)" (Feb. 2018). My point is not that NL participants should be expected to cultivate expertise in such traditional diplomatic skills, but that in practice, their affective labor is considered as or more important as their musical and teaching labor.

(180). This, in turn, serves to naturalize US cultural dominance and diminish questions about US domestic and foreign policy abroad.[12]

WORKS CITED

"About." *Next Level USA.* 2016. Web. 3 Jan. 2017. <http://nextlevel-usa.org/about/>.

"The Amazing Journey of the Next Level Global All-Stars Part I: Washington DC." *Next Level USA.* 2 May 2015. Web. 3 Jan. 2017. <http://nextlevel-usa.org/the-amazing-journey-of-the-global-next-level-all-stars-part-i-washington-dc/>.

"Apply to be a Next Level Artist-Educator." *Next Level USA.* 2016. Web. 2 Jan. 2017. <http://nextlevel-usa.org/apply/>.

Ahmed, Sara. *The Cultural Politics of Emotion*, Routledge, 2004. Print.

---. *The Promise of Happiness*. Durham: Duke UP, 2010. Print.

Bayles, Martha. *Through A Screen Darkly: Popular Culture, Public Diplomacy, and America's Image Abroad.* London: Yale UP, 2014. Print.

Berlant, Lauren. *The Female Complaint: The Unfinished Business of Sentimentality in American Culture.* Durham: Duke UP, 2008. Print.

Black Zang. "Global Next Level All-Stars." American University, Washington DC, 10 Apr. 2015. Panel Discussion.

Campbell, Jennifer L. *Shaping Solidarity: Music, Diplomacy, and Inter-American Relations, 1936-1946.* Diss. University of Connecticut, 2010. Print.

Capwell, Charles. *The Music of the Bauls of Bengal.* Kent State: Kent State UP, 1986. Print.

Cohen, Michael. Personal interview. 14 Jan. 2014.

Crist, Stephen A. "Jazz as Democracy? Dave Brubeck and Cold War Politics." *The Journal of Musicology* (26.2) 2009: 133-74. Print

Cull, Nicholas. *The Decline and Fall of the United States Information Agency: American Public Diplomacy, 1989-2001.* Palgrave Macmillan, 2012. Print.

Eschen, Penny M. von. *Satchmo Blows Up the World: Jazz Ambassadors Play the Cold War.* Cambridge: Harvard UP, 2004. Print.

---

12 The author would like to thank Mario Dunkel, Terence Kumpf, Sina Nitzsche, and Mark Katz for their comments on versions of this chapter, and to thank everyone interviewed for their time and comments.

Fosler-Lussier, Danielle. *Music in America's Cold War Diplomacy.* U of California P, 2015. Print.

---. "Music Pushed, Music Pulled: Cultural Diplomacy, Globalization, and Imperialism." *Diplomatic History* (36.1) 2012: 53-64. Print.

Gann, Elliot. Personal interview. 10 Nov. 2016.

Hayden, Craig. *The Rhetoric of Soft Power: Public Diplomacy in Global Contexts.* Plymouth: Lexington Books, 2011. Print.

Hemmings, Clare. "Affective Solidarity: Feminist Reflexivity and Political Transformation." *Feminist Theory* 13.2 (2012): 147-61. Print.

Katz, Mark. "Hip-Hop Diplomacy: Opportunities and Challenges." *YouTube*, University of Rochester Institute for Popular Music. 8 Oct. 2014. Web. 18 Oct. 2015. <https://www.youtube.com/watch?v=ubAZ_w5Vivg>.

---. Personal communication. 17 Feb. 2018.

---. Personal communication. 23 Dec. 2016.

---. Personal interview. 12 July 2016.

---. Personal interview. 7 Jan. 2014.

Monson, Ingrid. *Freedom Sounds: Civil Rights Call Out to Jazz and Africa.* Oxford: Oxford UP, 2007. Print.

Next Level USA. "BaulBeats at the American Cultural Center Kolkata (II)." *YouTube*, 15 July 2014. Web. 30 Dec. 2016. <https://youtu.be/4AVcBErWqQw>.

Nussbaum, Martha. *Upheavals of Thought: The Intelligence of Emotions.* Cambridge: Cambridge UP, 2003. Print.

Nyari "FTR" Mazango. "Global Next Level All-Stars." American University, Washington DC. 10 Apr. 2015. Panel Discussion.

Pedwell, Carolyn. *Affective Relations: The Transnational Politics of Empathy.* Palgrave Macmillan, 2014. Print.

---. "Affective (Self-)Transformations: Empathy, Neoliberalism and International Development." *Feminist Theory* 13.2 (2012): 163-79. Print.

Rockower, Paul. Personal interview. 20 Apr. 2015.

Sablosky, Juliet Antunes. "Reinvention, Reorganization, Retreat: American Cultural Diplomacy at Century's End, 1978-1998." *The Journal of Arts Management, Law, and Society* 29.1 (1999): 30-46. Print.

Salois, Kendra. "The US Department of State's 'Hip-Hop Diplomacy' in Morocco." *Music and Diplomacy from the Early Modern Era to the Present.* Ed. Rebekah Ahrendt, Damien Mahiet, and Mark Ferraguto. Palgrave Macmillan, 2014. Print.

@ToniBlackman. "Toni & Toussa." *Instagram*, 29 Dec. 2016. Web. 2 Oct. 2018. <https://www.instagram.com/p/BOnao6BAcTT/?taken-by=toniblackman&hl=en>.

---. "It's so dope to see artists you helped mentor and/or coach soar." *Instagram*, 29 Dec. 2016. Web. 2 Oct. 2018. <https://www.instagram.com/p/BOncJHnApbW/?taken-by=toniblackman&hl=en>.

US ACPD (US Advisory Commission on Public Diplomacy). *Public Diplomacy in a Changed World*. US Department of State, 1993. Print.

---. *2016 Comprehensive Annual Report on Public Diplomacy and International Broadcasting: Focus on FY 2015 Budget Data*. US Department of State, 2016. Print.

Wallace, Trey, aka DJ 2-Tone Jones. Personal interview. 29 Oct. 2015.

Werberg, Sam. Personal interview. 24 Aug. 2013.

Popular Musicking and the Politics of Spectatorship at the United Nations

James R. Ball III

> What is the place of the emotions in music? . . . [One view] holds that music is concerned with the "communication" or the "expression" or the "representation" of emotions . . . Common sense leads me to ask why people should devote so much of their lives and resources to the communication of emotions . . . and why, for that matter, listeners should be interested in having them communicated to them. *After all, we all have plenty of emotions of our own without having to feel other people's.*
> (Small 135-6, emphasis added)

Musicologist Christopher Small's work is often invoked to make romantic claims for music's capacity to forge community. In *Musicking*, the work from which my epigraph is drawn, he argues optimistically that music is a process in which performers and listeners each participate, a ritual that bonds people by celebrating their unique social worlds. Nonetheless, his glib argument against identifying the affective transmissions music engenders with its purpose pulses with charming anti-social cynicism. Small dismisses the theory that music facilitates the transfer of feelings between individuals, indicating his exhaustion with the often-invoked notion that art can make a better world by encouraging empathetic encounters between national and cultural others. Small's skepticism of aesthetic theories based in empathy offers a useful frame for reconsidering the use of music in diplomacy, especially in international institutions such as the United Nations.

Musical programs have often appeared at the UN, and music has long offered a set of handy metaphors to theories of international relations. In an early effort to theorize the work of the UN as performance, the Irish diplomat Conor Cruise O'Brien wrote that a resolution of the General Assembly "has the force of law in the same sense as has a sacred song: it provides spiritual encouragement and comfort and induces a sense of collective righteousness and of the legitimacy of a common endeavor" (19). At the UN, states performatively enact the contours of an international community, staging consensus and dissensus[1] in an effort to momentarily stabilize a particular configuration of states and peoples. As O'Brien implies, this work is also addressed to a global audience without diplomatic credentials in an effort to activate positive feelings regarding our species' shared humanity, responsibility, and purpose.

This chapter focuses on the divergent responses of multiple spectators addressed by the UN when it stages performances that incorporate popular music. I argue that the UN deploys musical performance as part of a broader project to transform the individual global citizens who follow the UN's work into docile subjects of global governmentality. However, this effort is undermined by the instability of the moment in which those individuals watch and listen. In what follows I will examine two scenes of what Small terms musicking: instances of performing or listening to music, an expanded category that recognizes that even spectatorship and audition constitute active participatory processes that make meaning. First, I will examine events produced by the UN Secretariat to commemorate the third International Happiness Day, held in 2015, which centered on the participation of the pop star Pharrell Williams. On that day, Williams straddled the line between two energetic audiences: a crowd of high school students who watched him from the floor of the General Assembly hall, and anxious UN functionaries who watched the crowd from the hall's green marble dais. Second, I will examine a New Year's concert mounted in the General Assembly in 2013, which featured a performance by Serbia's Viva Vox choir. Here I will focus on the Secretary-General as a highly-placed spectator who becomes a source of discomfort and offense for civil society groups and journalists who watch him in turn.

Among these other spectators, I will also locate my own gaze—my place as a spectator consuming these events through the UN's streaming web video service.

---

1 Dissensus is philosopher Jacques Rancière's term for a dispute that reveals inequality in spaces that claim to be egalitarian. He writes, "dissensus is not a conflict of interests, opinions, or values; it is a division put in the 'common sense': a dispute about what is given, about the frame within which we see something as given" (304).

I include my spectatorship not in an effort to generalize from my reactions, but rather to highlight their contingency. As ethnomusicologist Deborah Wong reflects on her own auto-ethnographic practice in the collection *Shadows in the Field*, "It's not impossible that your subjectivity and mine have points of overlap, but our responses are not, and can't be, equivalent" (80). My own reactions to these scenes of musicking vary widely from bemusement to aversion. I am primed to distrust sincerity, and occasionally cringe at the ways these events use pop stars, diplomats, and lay-persons. These reactions may well be a function of my privilege and position as a spectator. Nonetheless, this article is not about the contents of any individual spectator's experience, but an account of the instant of hailing whereby performance in international institutions impacts a spectator's subjectivity, interpellating that spectator as a subject of ideology. This instant will necessarily differ for each individual hailed.[2] I include my own first person accounts in an effort to theorize such moments even in their heterogeneity. As performance studies scholar Della Pollock asserts, "[t]his performative 'I' thus has a politics and an ethics. Performing displacement by error, intimacy, others, it moves beyond the atomization, alienation, and reproduction of the authorial self toward new points of identification and alliance" (252). My performative "I" is thus a consciously idiosyncratic refusal of identification with UN spectacle in service to thinking through other forms of affinity and organization.

At stake in this endeavor is a clearer view of the ways in which international institutions and the states that work within their confines exercise power via performance and spectatorship. The Secretary-General makes clear the central place of spectatorship in diplomacy at the UN; he facilitates spectatorship. His most explicit power is enshrined in the UN Charter's Article 99: "The Secretary-General may bring to the attention of the Security Council any matter which in his opinion may threaten the maintenance of international peace and security" (UN). The Charter calls on the Secretary-General to act as a global spectator. The Secretary-General trains the gaze of the UN Security Council on specific regions in conflict, a gaze followed often by the indirect application of economic

---

2   Here I follow Louis Althusser's theory of interpellation, as described in his essay, "Ideology and Ideological State Apparatuses." Althusser tells his readers that interpellation "can be imagined along the lines of the most commonplace everyday police (or other) hailing: 'Hey, you there!'" (118). While Althusser goes on to disclaim the theatricality of this example and the "temporal succession" it implies (118), the cases in this chapter insist on the utility of conceiving interpellation via the theatrical moments of hailing in which the implicit process of interpellation rises to the surface of consciousness.

and military force in the form of sanctions, peacekeeping, and related mechanisms. The UN's spectatorship is performative insofar as it is an integral part of a system of global governmentality that manages world populations by targeting "someone's body, soul, and behavior" (Foucault, *Security* 122). In other words, the UN acts on the world stage via spectatorship: by looking and not looking at particular individuals, populations, or territories, and by influencing what they can and cannot see in turn. In this context, the moment of interface between spectators and international institutions in performances of popular music at the UN provides an opportunity to reimagine the radical agency of even the most disenfranchised spectators on the world stage. Where powerful states mobilize performance on the world stage to emplace a spectator, in that spectator's reactions she or he may refuse to be placed.

INTERNATIONAL HAPPINESS DAY

In 1972, the King of Bhutan proposed a new indicator of national development, Gross National Happiness, or GNH, to be measured alongside indicators like Gross Domestic Product. GNH looks beyond what money can buy in the administration of the state by focusing regulative and legislative attention on four pillars: Sustainable and Equitable Socio-Economic Development, Conservation of the Environment, Preservation and Promotion of Culture, and Good Governance ("Four Pillars"). In Bhutan, a Gross National Happiness Commission is charged with mainstreaming these principles into national policies, orienting the apparatus of government towards the subjective wellbeing of citizens, monitoring their affective lives in regular nationwide surveys. These surveys consist of dozens of questions measuring and quantifying a respondent's psychological well-being, health, relationship with the environment, economic standard of living, and so on ("Gross National Happiness"). Internationally, GNH has also become an ideological export, a form of diplomatic cultural capital for Bhutan on the world stage. Advancing the cause of happiness, Bhutan placed the issue on the UN's agenda in 2011 through resolution 65/309, and a year later the General Assembly unanimously adopted resolution 66/281, also penned by Bhutan, proclaiming 20 March the International Day of Happiness. The resolution also emphasized the Secretary-General's important duties vis-à-vis global spectatorship by calling on him to bring the proclamation to "the attention of all Member States, organizations of the United Nations system and civil society organizations for appropriate observance" (UNGA 1).

International Happiness Day is hardly a distraction for the Secretariat: it provides an anchor for spectacles designed to encourage global spectators to sign on to UN priorities on issues like climate change and poverty eradication. As feminist scholar Sara Ahmed details in *The Promise of Happiness*, happiness also functions as a performative promise that "gives us a specific image of the future" suggesting "happiness lies ahead of us, at least if we do the right thing" (29). As a promise, happiness organizes and intensifies the energies of those to whom it is addressed. At the UN action is often accomplished through the use of performative speech, for instance, in the active language peppering the operational paragraphs of resolutions of the Security Council or General Assembly. Philosopher J. L. Austin's theory of the speech act (detailed in his lectures, *How to Do Things with Words*) may be even more broadly applied at the UN. International relations is a realm composed of diplomatic performatives: discrete, efficacious utterances deployed to affect the relations between states. A treaty, the threat of sanctions, an off the cuff remark by a head of state—each of these may function as a diplomatic performative, as an effort to remake the world through verbal performance. The promise of happiness is another diplomatic performative that works to interpellate states and citizens as good institutions and subjects on the world stage.

For the third observance of International Happiness Day in 2015, Secretary-General Ban Ki-moon released a brief video advertising programs run by the Secretariat in cooperation with groups like The UN Foundation, a non-governmental organization founded by Ted Turner to "connect people, ideas and resources to help the United Nations solve global problems" ("What We Do"). In the video the Secretary-General stands in front of a wall of neon pink flat screen monitors, imploring his audience in different languages to "be happy," while the best-selling song of 2014, pop star Pharrell Williams's "Happy," plays in the background (see fig. 9). The video launched multiple programs planned for 2015, including the #HappySoundsLike Campaign, a collaboration with streaming music platform Mix Radio, in which the public was invited to nominate songs to a global happiness playlist; an educational event in the General Assembly featuring Williams in conversation with environmental activists Philippe Cousteau and Sylvia Earle; and the Happy Party website (another co-production between Pharrell Williams and the UN Foundation, with support from Google) with which users could make animated gifs of themselves dancing along to "Happy" yet again.

Fig. 9: A screenshot of the UN promotional video "Ban Ki-moon Joins the #HappySoundsLike Campaign," featuring the Secretary-General.

Source: Courtesy of the United Nations.

At first glance Pharrell Williams's pervasive presence appears to be a product of the coincidence that Gross National Happiness found global purchase at the same time that Williams's hit song was climbing the charts. Extended reflection suggests a deeper affinity, however, between a discourse of happiness that is anti-consumerist on its face and a heavily commercialized popular music market. Even if some economists[3] are stymied by a "Happy Planet Index" that ranks the US in 150th place—"behind Burkina Faso," as *Foreign Policy Magazine* reported in 2009 (Yester)—it is not hard to be suspicious that Gross National Happiness in fact supports prevailing economic relationships. Gross National Happiness rewrites the terms with which populations are governed or managed while doing little to alter the structures of power underwriting the hierarchical distribution of states and their populations in the twenty-first-century.

Evident in the 2015 programs, implementing the Secretary-General's International Happiness Day mandate has required significant corporate sponsorship and has been largely facilitated by Ted Turner's UN Foundation. These partnerships entrench a twenty-first century neoliberal political order that prefers marketplace solutions when addressing civic issues. Where the raw measurement of wealth and production gives way to delicate assessments of individual and

---

3   See, for example, economist Arno Tausch's article "In Praise of Inequality? 'Happy Planet' Performance and its Determinants," and the economists quoted by Katherine Yester in *Foreign Policy Magazine*.

collective happiness, one still finds a market logic refining its tools for what philosopher Michel Foucault calls "governmentality . . . the way in which one conducts the conduct of men" (*Birth of Biopolitics* 187). Governmentality is an exercise of power not through direct applications of force, but by leveraging relationships between forces and managing populations by addressing their behaviors and dispositions (Foucault, *Security* 190-98). Gross National Happiness risks intensifying a global governmentality that sustains and obscures inequality, exploitation, and oppression. Even if the circulation of global capital is absent from an ideal theory of Gross National Happiness, neoliberal structures prove adept at incorporating the happiness discourse and infiltrating its material expressions. As a producer, songwriter, and performer with his own clothing lines and fragrances, Pharrell Williams, who ranked number 78 on *Forbes Magazine*'s 2015 list of the world's highest paid celebrities, embodies this contradiction.

While Gross National Happiness can be a positive and disruptive force in the field of economic and development policy, its implementation inevitably proves ambivalent where it becomes attached to the exercise of power via regimes of governmentality. Ahmed argues that "happiness is a form of world making" (2) and that it "becomes a duty" (7). Where she has warned against the "instrumentalization of happiness as a technique" (10), one might view the UN's International Happiness Day activities with similar suspicion. Here again, the role of the Secretary-General as a facilitator of spectatorship comes to the fore. The aforementioned General Assembly resolution 66/281 directs the Secretary-General to manage the attentions of states and civil society so that they might observe International Happiness Day appropriately. The Secretariat stages events designed to hail spectators into the duty of happiness, but these events also provide opportunities to feel otherwise.

I certainly felt otherwise. Each of the Secretariat's 2015 Happiness Day observances prompted my discomfort, but perhaps none so much as the Happy Party website Pharrell Williams, Google, and the UN Foundation produced (globalhappyparty.com). In this response, I am likely an outlier: judging from the endless sea of animated gifs of people dancing that composed the website (each uploaded by a visitor), it is clear that many others have enjoyed participating in the project. The site's looping music removes Williams's voice from the song to invite participation in performances that affirm the sentiment on offer: we are called to fill the space the lyrics have left behind. Without voice and lyrics only one index of the performing body remains, the clapping hands which refer one back to the song's missing verbal content: the repeated chorus of imperatives commanding the audience to "clap along if you feel like happiness is the truth . . . clap along if you know what happiness is to you . . . clap along if you feel like that's what you wanna do" (Williams). What these orders lack in severity they make up for with a presumed social pressure evinced by the parade of animated gifs collected for the event. These amplify the uncanny effects of the Happy Party: though many of the gifs feature people in groups, suggesting the scenes of community Happy Party produced locally, the overwhelming visual motif of the page is a uniform grid of squares in which the strobe-like rhythm of the shifting frames of each gif unifies globally diffuse dancers. Participants are atomized; they participate to be codified and arranged, assimilated uniformly under the banner of happiness. Though they seem to be having fun, I recoil from this scene of affective administration and refuse to be placed among them.

The UN Foundation and *National Geographic Magazine* brought Williams into the General Assembly Hall on Happiness Day to participate in an educational event on climate change. Greeting the cheering crowd of assembled youths he observed drily, "[s]o this is fun" ("International Day of Happiness Event"). His mild affect and intonation epitomized the wry response engendered by institutional efforts to inorganically command fun, from corporate team-building exercises to high school pep rallies. I also sensed an element of subversive sarcasm in Williams's presentation, a performance of cool his young audience seemed to embrace as their cheering swelled again. Williams's live appearance opened a moment of radical indeterminacy in which performer and spectators navigated and negotiated their relationships with one another and with the wider world. If I found the UN's calls for a modest and tightly controlled public participation in the International Day of Happiness off-putting, in the General Assembly that day other audiences refused to be placed in their own ways.

Maher Nasser, Director of the Outreach Division for the UN's Department of Public Information, opened the event with a call for participation that had clear limits: "Please use your cell phones. You can tweet, use social media. You can dance, but not on the tables." The audience broke into warm laughter ("International Day of Happiness Event"). Later, as Nasser attempted to organize the presenters for a photograph, the music video of "Happy" began playing in the General Assembly hall. The crowd of students left their seats to make their way to the General Assembly dais, staying off the tables. On his own initiative, Williams descended into the crowd, which now became a sea of smart phones pressing forward for a selfie with the celebrity (see fig. 10). The webcast of the event cut between images of the music video and the growing chaos in the Assembly hall, and after a minute Nasser could be heard again, booming over the song to entreat the crowd, "Please don't push, there are children who might get suffocated" ("International Day of Happiness Event"). The song was cut off and security guards pulled Williams and others back to the safety of the stage, from which they could exit the disorder.

Fig. 10: Pharrell Williams at the General Assembly during the special event on the occasion of the International Day of Happiness.

Source: Courtesy of UN Photo, Loey Felipe.

Two groups of spectators looked on one another at this event: a group of youths who transported the energy and conventions of a pop concert into the Assembly hall, and a security apparatus that watched them uneasily. The surging, self-organized crowd proved inappropriate, perhaps even subversive, in the serious diplomatic space of the General Assembly, and the representatives of authority on stage recoiled. While the disorder may have posed an immediate safety hazard to those present, it also posed an implicit threat to an institution striving to bring order to the world. A third spectator was also watching: I laughed a mirthless laugh at the ironic chaos streamed to me online, which seemed to parody the more consequential forms of crowd control for which the UN is often responsible in refugee camps or around demilitarized zones. Scholar, students, and security guards—spectators all—we materialized our relationship to an international order through the ways we watched.

According to Christopher Small, "[i]n the concert hall, as at any other kind of musical event there is an underlying kinship between the members of the audience . . . there are certain kinds of behavior they can expect of one another and other kinds that they need not" (41). Small indicates the nexus of space, spectatorship, and expectation that makes the power of crowds legible, the grounds on which heterogeneous and spontaneous responses take on social meaning. The General Assembly hall also activates expectations of behavior, whether it is playing host to a diplomatic or a musical performance. During its usual sessions, one expects dull speeches only occasionally ruptured by scenes of Soviet leader Nikita Khrushchev brandishing his shoe at the General Assembly podium in 1960, Saudi Arabia's UN Ambassador Jamil Baroody throwing a punch at the General Assembly President in 1973, or Israeli President Chaim Herzog tearing up a resolution equating Zionism with racism in 1975. All of these constitute theatrically excessive performative acts that take their meaning by virtue of their departure from the orderly norms of diplomacy.

Bringing musical performance into the General Assembly intensifies the norms governing audience behavior—how one acts and reacts takes on added performative force in the space of the Assembly hall. These added forces subvert the presumption of "underlying kinship" by rendering it a performative promise rather than manifest reality: something to be made that is always at risk of failure. The UN is founded on a similar performative promise, also always at risk of failure: "to save succeeding generations from the scourge of war" (UN). UN diplomats call on music to establish collective kinship as a desired horizon, organizing listeners into a unity reflected again in the concert of instruments or voices they watch. When alternative participatory formations emerge, such as the self-organized audience threatening to suffocate Pharrell Williams, they demonstrate the contingency and instability of the proposition. Deployed to generate affects (like happiness) that can foster community bonds, musical performance at the UN in fact opens a time and space that puts pressure on the processes that construct our social worlds.

NEW YEAR'S CONCERT OF THE 67TH SESSION OF THE GENERAL ASSEMBLY

Introducing Serbia's Viva Vox Choir in January 2013, Ban Ki-moon credited former Secretary-General Dag Hammarskjöld with innovating the tradition of musical performance at the UN in the 1950s. Ban spoke at a concert organized by the Permanent Mission of Serbia to the UN to celebrate Eastern Orthodox New Year and explicitly framed as a gesture of peace carried by elements intrinsic to the music presented. Turning to the performers, he noted that "tonight's performance should give us hope. The Viva Vox choir sings a cappella.

This style more than any other showcases the human voice. Voices can be used . . . to divide and oppress, or if they are used well, they can be used to heal and uplift, and harmonize" ("Viva Vox Choir"). Ban invokes a popular musical metaphor in the fields of diplomacy and international affairs, to affirm conceptual links between the harmony of voices or instruments, the harmony of the soul or spheres, and the harmony of nations or peoples. While contemporary scholarship has proven adept at deconstructing this metaphor, challenging the assumptions of universality that undergird it and the stable community it implies (see Ahrendt et al. 3-8, and Bayles in this volume), the concept of "harmonizing" remains a potent rhetorical device for policy-makers.

Speaking next, Vuk Jeremić, Permanent Representative of Serbia to the UN and the President of the General Assembly that year, continued Ban's theme: "Great music can cut across every boundary and touch every soul. It transcends differences. Irrespective of where we come from, it binds us together as human beings" ("Viva Vox Choir"). In their speeches, Ban and Jeremić indicate their attachment to an ideal of music that unites communities, performatively enacting common kinship among listeners. Yet each diplomat also noted that voices can oppress, that music transgresses political boundaries, and that sound penetrates the human body. If music forges community, it does so by mobilizing forces equally capable of dividing, destabilizing, and degrading the subjects on which they act.

The Viva Vox Concert in the General Assembly made clear the contradictions inherent in the UN's cosmopolitan promises; when melodies and lyrics prove contrapuntal, they imply the abyss separating aspirations towards global peace and the reality of competing nationalisms in international institutions. The Viva Vox Choir, according to their website, was formed in 2005 by a group of high school graduates and their former teacher and conductor, Jasmina Lorin. The group achieved international visibility in 2011 when their a cappella rendition of German industrial-metal band Rammstein's 1997 hit "Du Hast" went viral online ("Choir History"). Though Viva Vox is best known for their interpretations of popular music, for their performance at the UN they added what announcer Zoran Baranac described as "a few pieces that represent their national heritage" ("Viva Vox Choir"). These included "Tamo Daleko" (There, Far Away), a folksong composed during World War I; the nineteenth-century folksong "Ajde Jano" (C'mon Jana); and, most controversially, Stanislav Binički's "March on the Drina," written to commemorate the Serbian victory over Austria-Hungary in the Battle of Cer during World War I in 1914. The rest of the program included pop classics like ABBA's "Mamma Mia," novelty songs such as Monty Python's "Always Look on the Bright Side of Life," and representatives of a cosmopolitan commercial-cultural order, like Somali-Canadian rapper K'naan's "Wavin' Flag," which became popularized when Coca-Cola used it as a promotional anthem during the 2010 World Cup.

Viva Vox's rendition of John Lennon's 1971 hit "Imagine" formed the thematic heart of the program; Jeremić received resounding applause when he quoted it in his opening remarks. But "Imagine" also imported some sentiments into the General Assembly hall that rest uneasily with the explicit and implicit goals of the organization. The song's melodic tranquility and conventional harmonic structure mask the anarchic thrust of lyrics that implore listeners to "imagine there's no countries," "imagine there's no religion," and "imagine no possessions." Performing nationalist songs to celebrate Eastern Orthodox Christian New Year a few miles down the road from Wall Street, Viva Vox seemed unlikely to do any of these things. Perhaps this is why several of the songs they performed obscured their lyrical content. The concert opened with "Ameno," a song written by new-age group Era in a gibberish designed to sound vaguely religious. Later, "Imagine" was followed by "Baba Yetu" (Our Father), a 2005 composition by Christopher Tin in which the Lord's Prayer is sung in Swahili. And for the evening's encore presentation of Stanislav Binički's "March on the Drina," Viva Vox chose to substitute non-referential vocables for lyrics composed in 1964 that celebrate the expulsion of foreign invaders with stark images of blood flowing and streaming near the cold waters of the Drina.

With words absent, the singers emulated the martial instrumentation of drums and horns, shifting between fast and slow marching tempos. After three minutes the audience began clapping along to the driving rhythm, and the official UN webcast of the performance cut to a medium shot of Ban and Jeremić seated next to one another, clapping along as well. Here again, the Secretary-General's role as a highly-placed spectator was foregrounded in official records of the event (see fig. 11). After a moment, the cameras returned to the performers on stage, the clapping was drowned out by beat-boxing, the song ended, and the room erupted in applause. This scene precipitated a minor geopolitical incident: the day after the concert, the Congress of North American Bosniaks,[4] a non-governmental organization representing Bosnian communities in the US and Canada, delivered a letter to the Secretary-General condemning his participation in the evening's presentation because it had included the "infamous and offensive Serb nationalist song, 'March on the River Drina'" (Alibasic et al.). Two days later, a Bosnian-American reporter, Erol Avdović,

---

[4] The term Bosniak refers to those who identify with the Bosnian Muslim ethnic group, regardless of state of citizenship.

raised the issue again during the daily noon briefing by the Spokesperson for the Secretary-General, this time with specific reference to the fact that Ban was seen "applauding there" ("Daily Press Briefing"). On behalf of the Secretary-General, the spokesperson responded, "[w]e sincerely regret that people were offended by this song, which was not listed in the official programme. The Secretary-General obviously was not aware what the song was about or the use that has been made of it in the past" ("Daily Press Briefing").

Fig. 11: Secretary-General Ban Ki-moon and General Assembly President Vuk Jeremić watch the Viva Vox Choir perform.

Source: Courtesy of the United Nations.

According to the accounts of victims collected in the US State Department's Seventh Report on War Crimes in the Former Yugoslavia, "March on the Drina" served as a soundtrack to mass sexual violence during the Bosnian War in the 1990s. In Foča, the report asserts, Muslim "women knew the rapes would begin when ['March on the Drina'] was played over the loudspeaker of the main mosque" (US Department of State). It is not difficult to believe that the Secretary-General was indeed ignorant of the song's traumatic heritage, but this does little to ameliorate the inadequacy of the claims made by those who defended the song's inclusion in the event. From Baranac's introduction, which framed the performance as a reorientation of a once martial song to the project of peace, to Jeremić's later contention that offended parties were "twisting the meaning of our musical gift" (qtd. in Nichols), organizers of the concert and its participants demonstrated their inability to recognize the gestures and sounds that can reactivate historical traumas in the present. Where UN diplomats turn to music to sidestep the political pitfalls of words, they prove blind to politics performed and meanings carried by the structures those words inhabit. Once again, a live encounter on the world stage between spectators and performers disconcerted the smooth administration of international relations, undermining the performance of unity, agreement, and consensus that lends so much diplomacy its normative force.

Chief among those gestures verbose diplomats cannot account for is perhaps the sound of two hands clapping, especially those hands that clap along. This may be one reason why the Secretary-General proved much more the locus of offense in the incident than either Viva Vox or the Serbian Mission. Literary scholar Steven Connor describes clapping as "a form of bodily overflow into sound" (72) and hypothesizes its evolutionary origins in "the action of slapping and cuffing the body . . . an emblematic display on the body of the aggressor of what may be in the offing for his victim" (67-8). Perhaps American and Canadian Bosnian audiences focused on the Secretary-General's rhythmic clapping in their complaint because of a similar sense of implicit menace amplified by the song's historical uses. On the other hand, perhaps the Secretary-General's participatory spectatorship offended for the ways it transgressed hard-won political boundaries. In clapping along, an ostensibly benign gesture required by his office, Ban acquiesced to the intentional and unintentional meanings arranged on stage by Serbian diplomats and performers, and he re-transmitted those contents and their affective charge through the sounds produced when his hands came together to form a rhythm.

His individual act of clapping may also have unnerved Erol Avdović and others for the submission to a controversial collective it implied. Considering the acts of audiences to the theatre, performance studies scholar Baz Kershaw notes, "Applause is the moment in which the collective aims to assert itself over the individual, in which an imagined community is forged. So the pitch of applause—whether it is a standing ovation or a desultory clap—indicates different types of consensual abandon, a giving up of individual judgement: we lose something of ourselves in putting our hands together with others in public" (135). Insofar as any articulation of community also implies the necessary acts of exclusion that produce that community, the clap that claps along acknowledges the short distance between an audience unified in applause and the cacophonous clapping that might be used to chase away an object of fear. Much like the promise of happiness, unison applause becomes a duty and demand that forecloses on disagreement or dissensus. Thus an audience and performer—the Congress of North American Bosniaks and the Serbian Mission to the United Nations—entered into dispute over the contours and contents of an international community; a dispute that centered on the gestures and sounds made by the Secretary-General.

Feminist philosopher Julia Kristeva's formulation of abjection in *Powers of Horror* can offer much to an understanding of the import of aversive reactions to mass diplomatic spectacles. Abjection is both a psychological and a sociocultural function; it is a process that stabilizes an individual's sense of self and which polices the borders of a given community. According to Kristeva, "The abject and abjection are my safeguards. The primers of my culture" (2). Abjection is the process of casting off what might otherwise be considered constitutive of the subject, "I." Multiple affects index the scene of abjection: fear, disgust, shame, hate, and others. Where these erupt, the subject may be said to be in a process of self-stabilization, erecting and maintaining his or her psychological boundaries. As Kristeva puts it, "I experience abjection only if an Other has settled in place and stead of what will be 'me'" (10). In abjection, subjectivity emerges from a scene of self-alienation, where this Other is cast off and cast out.

In *National Abjection: The Asian American Body Onstage*, Karen Shimakawa also asserts "the paradigm of abjection as a national/cultural identity forming process" (3). However, Shimakawa engages abjection not as an exclusive psychoanalytic explanation for the formation of specific identities, but "as a descriptive paradigm in order to posit a way of understanding the relationship linking the psychic, symbolic, legal, and aesthetic dimensions of national identity" (4). Instances of audience aversion to geopolitical spectacle mark operations of (inter)national abjection. The offended reaction of Bosnian audiences may be located at a nexus where an individual's sense of psychological identity collides with the symbolic structures of public diplomacy in the legal ramifications of events staged in international institutions and the aesthetic experience of spectatorship.

Audiences that recoil in international institutions exhibit negative reactions to the performative production of Small's "underlying kinship." Kristeva notes, "Abjection . . . is the other facet of religious, moral, and ideological codes on which rest the sleep of individuals and the breathing spells of societies" (209). Abjection is the constitutive dark side of law, order, peace, and security. Abjection erupts in the space where the UN works to build or transform a global community that may not fit an individual's pre-existing sense of self. Audiences that recoil, become offended, or cringe exhibit necessarily visceral responses to cultural and political forces that smudge the boundaries of the subject. In these moments, the forces circulating between scenes of diplomatic performance show their effects on and in the bodies of spectators.

Steven Connor writes, "Clapping one hand on another dramatizes the fact that you are a subject and an object simultaneously, a doer and a done to; you fold yourself over yourself, you form an interface with yourself, which joins to the interface you form with others" (72). To Kershaw's annihilation of the individual by the collective in applause, we may add an individualized terror of bodily and psychological boundaries losing their solidity as palm meets palm. In clapping, the body ceases to be a discrete, whole, and stable entity. My argument that musical presentations in international institutions provide an especially potent opportunity for the negotiation and renegotiation of the contours of international community rests on recognizing the interrelationship between specific bodily configurations, shared or unshared affects and meanings, and the legal structures that make nations and states—an interrelationship made explicit by abjection. Where Kristeva acknowledges the horror of bodily disintegration ("The border has become an object. How can I be without a border?" 4), those who theorize clapping recognize its potential to reproduce that horror on a broader social scale.

As interface, the clapping body produces a sonic mesh that unites spectator and performer in shared rhythm or returned sentiment. Clapping knits together an audience in shared actions, and it even incorporates bystanders (like those watching the video online) when the sound reaches our ears. While these effects may be inconsequential in most musicking, at the UN they reiterate the vital work of the institution (making common cause among peoples divided), exposing the potential failure of that work. Both the spectator who claps and the spectator who does not (either at the live event or at mediated distances) intensify the social function of musicking, prompting confrontations between individuals and the forces that bind them together.

When I watch Ban Ki-moon clap along to "March on the Drina," I recoil for different reasons than Avdović or others who were offended. If abjection may be thought of alongside the uncanny, then the abject offers reminders that it was once a part of me; it reflects me, even in its difference, like a corpse. Watching Ban Ki-moon I find my own gaze doubled, uncannily, teleporting me into the scene. We are both spectators, and his acts of spectatorship surrogate my own, highlighting differential experiences of power on the world stage. Here I must recoil, I must cast off my recognition, I must be unsettled and displaced in order to remain psychologically sound. By clapping, the Secretary-General imports existential dread into geopolitical spectacle, the terror of identity lost when an individual subject becomes an object of collective administration, a constituent of a system of global governmentality that operates through spectatorship. Watching his consensual abandon, I become aware of the forms of social control that govern my world: I see myself and the power and limits of my own spectatorship.

The pressures of performance bear inordinately on the Secretary-General. According to the authors of *The United Nations and Changing World Politics*,

[t]he Secretary-General walks a tightrope, needing to appear independent and not simply a pawn of any or all of the [permanent members of the Security Council], but at the same time he must maintain the confidence and support of those same states. (Weiss et al. 11)

The Secretary-General performs for audiences at cross purposes, and so becomes, as Conor Cruise O'Brien once described Dag Hammarskjöld, "an attentive spectator of his own actions" (121)—self-alienated like the spectator become object in the act of applause. Elsewhere, O'Brien argues on behalf of the ritual and theatrical functions of the UN, which he casts as a secular Vatican on the East River where the Secretary-General acts as "the high priest of the shrine" (134). The papal analogy emphasizes the interstitial nature of the role, between great powers and the people as between god and (wo)man. The Secretary-General is an interface that acts on behalf of the Security Council, the General Assembly, and a nebulous international community. The Secretary-General is directed by powerful states to stage the surveilling gaze global governmentality requires. As a locus for multiple forms of spectatorship on the world stage, he generates energies that extend to global spectators, circulate among diplomats at the UN, or rebound back upon the Secretariat.

In his essay "The Standard Modes of Aversion: Fear, Disgust, and Hatred," philosopher Aurel Kolnai lists markers of the morally disgusting:

the *shirokaya natura* of the Russians [...]; inconsistency and irresponsibility; what the French call *inconscience*, overspontaneity, overpersonalness, softness, and sentimentalism; above all, what the Germans call *Verlogenheit*: that is, a character organically wedded to, a mental life diffusely steeped in, lying, dissembling, illusion, and self-deception. (103)

Kolnai's enumerations capture the many ways in which a diplomat's magnanimity toward cultural participation might prove unsettling: in its broadness, its sentimental sincerity, and its suspect theatricality. Kolnai's implicit emphasis on national difference is also remarkable insofar as his theory of disgust investigates the affective phenomena at the heart of scenes of abjection that make nations and states, racialize communities, and risk exploding into genocidal violence. That the Secretary-General's overgenerous participation in the Viva Vox concert offends Bosnian onlookers is not an example of misplaced outrage or an oversensitive response to a frivolous event. It is an integral and material moment in which international relations among people of different social and cultural frames are negotiated in autonomous reactions and calculated responses.

CONCLUSION

In the events investigated throughout this chapter, various audiences performed their resistance to the projects of social and political administration at the heart of the UN's work—to the unreflexive harmony it seeks. According to Sara Ahmed,

[h]armony would be a demand for accordance. This is why I would argue that the powers-that-be might want their subjects happy rather than sad [...]. The good encounter could be read as being how bodies stay in place or acquire a place in which they can stay, by agreeing with what they receive. The bad encounter can be read as how bodies refuse to be placed by disagreeing with what they receive. (213)

Ahmed accords a radical power to moments like those in which the UN's participatory events misfire and bodies refuse to be placed. Where one encounters and refuses the demand to be happy or clap along, one invites the rearrangement of psychological, physical, spatial, and social coordinates. Though I may join Christopher Small in arguing against empathy as the primary mechanism which music may offer diplomacy, I am not arguing against musical diplomacy at the UN. Rather, the utility and efficacy of music diplomacy must be noted elsewhere: in its counterintuitive effects, precisely when it misfires and results in infelicities.

According to Kolnai, "[i]t is as a disgusted self that I inscribe my quality and lineaments into the stuff of the world, and as a hating self that I set the seal of my personality on a universe reluctant and vulnerable like myself" (99). Scenes of public diplomacy at the UN may take on different meanings for different spectators, but all transmit their effects in the moment of encounter between a performance and its audiences. In our reactions we do things with even the most banal performances. As Ahmed puts it, "[t]o receive an impression is to make an impression" (40). In both positive and negative reactions, I become culturally, ideologically, and physiologically inscribed in the world, whether I am dancing on tables, taking a selfie, or clapping along. Watching others participate I become alienated from the processes that organize my social life, be they explicit, like public diplomacy, or implicit, like cultural abjection. A radical constituent power thus adheres to crowds assembled for the most scripted spectacles staged by the international institutions that administer global governmentality. Deploying popular music on the world stage, the UN invites audiences to recode the gestures with which it writes the world.

WORKS CITED

Ahmed, Sara. *The Promise of Happiness*. Durham: Duke UP, 2010. Print

Alibasic, Haris, Ajila Delkic, Emir Ramic, and Sanja Segerovic-Drnovsek. "Protest Letter to Ban Ki-moon, UN Secretary-General." *Bosniak.org*. Congress of North American Bosniaks. 15 Jan. 2013. Web. 24 June 2016. <http://www.bosniak.org/protest-letter-to-ban-ki-moon-un-general-secretary/>.

Althusser, Louis. "Ideology and Ideological State Apparatuses: Notes towards an Investigation," *Lenin and Philosophy and other Essays*. Trans. Ben Brewster. New York: Monthly Review Press, 2001. 85-126. Print.

Austin, J. L. *How to Do Things with Words*. 2nd ed. Ed. J. O. Urmson and Marina Sbisà. Cambridge: Harvard UP, 1975. Print.

"Choir History." *Viva Vox Choir*. Viva Vox Choir. 2015. Web. 24 June 2016. <http://www.vivavoxchoir.com/en/>.

Connor, Steven. "The Help of Your Good Hands: Reports on Clapping." *The Auditory Culture Reader*. Ed. Michael Bull and Les Back. Oxford and New York: Berg, 2003. 67-76. Print.

"Daily Press Briefing by the Office of the Spokesperson for the Secretary-General." *United Nations*. United Nations. 17 Jan. 2013. Web. 24 June 2016. <https://www.un.org/press/en/2013/db130117.doc.htm>.

Foucault, Michel. *Security, Territory, Population: Lectures at the College de France, 1977-1978*. Trans. Graham Burchell. Ed. Michael Senellart. New York: Palgrave Macmillan, 2007. Print.

---. *The Birth of Biopolitics: Lectures at the College de France, 1978-1979*. Trans. Graham Burchell. Ed. Michael Senellart. New York: Palgrave Macmillan, 2008. Print.

"Four Pillars and Nine Domains." *GNHCentreBhutan.org*. GNH Centre Bhutan. 2017. Web. 20 June 2017. <www.gnhcentrebhutan.org>.

"Gross National Happiness." *Grossnationalhappiness.com*. Centre of Bhutan Studies and GNH. 2017. Web. 20 June 2017. <https://www.grossnationalhappiness.com/>.

"International Day of Happiness Event." *UN Web TV*. United Nations, 20 Mar. 2015. Web. 24 June 2016. <http://webtv.un.org/watch/international-day-of-happiness-event/4129206146001>.

Kershaw, Baz. "Oh for Unruly Audiences! Or, Patterns of Participation in Twentieth-Century Theatre." *Modern Drama*. 44.2 (Summer 2001): 133-154. Print.

Kolnai, Aurel. *On Disgust*. Ed. Barry Smith and Carolyn Korsmeyer. Chicago and La Salle, IL: Open Court, 2004. Print.

Kristeva, Julia. *Powers of Horror: An Essay on Abjection.* Leon S. Roudiez, trans. New York: Columbia UP, 1982. Print.

Mahiet, Damien, Mark Ferraguto, and Rebekah Ahrendt. Introduction. *Music and Diplomacy from the Early Modern Era to the Present*. Ed. Rebekah Ahrendt, Mark Ferraguto, and Damien Mahiet. New York: Palgrave Macmillan, 2014. 1-16. Print.

Nichols, Michelle. "Serbian Military Song at U.N. Concert Sparks Bosnian Outcry." *Reuters.com*. 17 Jan. 2013. Web. 27 June 2016. <https://www.reuters.com/article/us-serbia-bosnia-un-song/serbian-military-song-at-u-n-concert-sparks-bosnian-outcry-idUSBRE90G1D520130117>.

O'Brien, Conor Cruise. *United Nations: Sacred Drama*. New York: Simon and Schuster, 1968. Print.

Pollock, Della. "The Performative 'I'." *Cultural Studies—Critical Methodologies*. 7.3 (2007): 239-55. Print.

Rancière, Jacques. "Who is the Subject of the Rights of Man," *The South Atlantic Quarterly*. 103.2/3 (Spring/Summer 2004): 297-310. Print.

Shimakawa, Karen. *National Abjection: The Asian American Body Onstage*. Durham and London: Duke UP, 2002. Print.

Small, Christopher. *Musicking: The Meanings of Performing and Listening.* Middletown: Wesleyan UP, 1998. Print.

Tausch, Arno. "In Praise of Inequality? 'Happy Planet' Performance and its Determinants." *Australian and New Zealand Journal of Public Health*. 35.6 (2011): 572-73. Print.

UN (United Nations). *Charter of the United Nations*. 26 June 1945. Web. 3 Mar. 2016. <https://www.un.org/en/charter-united-nations/>.

UNGA (United Nations General Assembly). Resolution 66/281 (A/RES/66/281). "International Day of Happiness," 28 June 2012. Web. 25 June 2016. PDF File. <https://www.un.org/ga/search/view_doc.asp?symbol=%20A/RES/66/281>.

US Department of State. "Seventh Report on War Crimes in the Former Yugoslavia." *US Department Of State Dispatch* 4.16 (19 April). Washington: GPO, 1993: 257-269. Print.

"Viva Vox Choir (Belgrade)-New Year's Concert of the 67th Session of the General Assembly." United Nations. *UN Web TV.* 14 Jan. 2013. Web. 24 June 2016. <http://webtv.un.org/watch/viva-vox-choir-belgrade-new-years-concert-of-the-67th-session-of-the-general-assembly/2094291812001/>.

Weiss, Thomas George, David P. Forsythe, Roger A. Coate, and Kelly-Kate Pease. *The United Nations and Changing World Politics*. 5th ed. Boulder: Westview Press, 2007. Print.

"What We Do: Campaigns and Initiatives." *United Nations Foundation*. 2013. Web. 24 June 2016. <http://www.unfoundation.org/what-we-do/campaigns-and-initiatives/>.

Williams, Pharrell. "Happy." *GIRL*. Columbia, 2013. MP3.

Wong, Deborah. "Moving: From Performance to Performative Ethnography and Back Again." *Shadows in the Field*. Ed. Gregory Barz and Timothy J. Cooley. Oxford: Oxford UP, 2008. Print.

Yester, Katherine. "Happy Math." *Foreignpolicy.com*. Foreign Policy Magazine. 14 Oct. 2009. Web. 1 Nov. 2015. <https://foreignpolicy.com/2009/10/14/happy-math/>.

From Sons of Gastarbeita to *Songs of Gastarbeiter*
Migrant and Post-Migrant Integration through Music and German Musical Diplomacy from the 1990s to the Present

Gesa zur Nieden

"Rap was communication-music as opposed to reference-music." This is how sociologist of music, Antoine Hennion, describes early US-American and European rap in one of his articles on mediators of music. By examining especially non-human mediators such as "scores, texts, sound, instruments, repertoires, staging, concert venues, and media," Hennion emphasizes the fact that the concern of rap "was not with music as a beautiful object or a purveyor of musical truth in a reconstituted collectivity […]. Instead what counted was the individual performance in the present with whatever means at hand and with success measured by how that performance is judged relative to the performances of one's rivals" (432).

According to this communication-based description, which highlights the dimension of battle and rivalry, rap music and hip-hop culture would not seem to be useful media of communication within transnational public diplomacy. Due to their centering of individuals and their competitive dimensions, rap and hip-hop seemingly oppose the diplomatic purpose of purveying a positive cultural image of a certain state based on "reference-music," even if recent public diplomacy scholars have pointed out the importance of direct and individual exchange with a "strong human factor" by focusing on so-called people-to-people exchange.[1] But despite the fact that rap music and lyrics might convey negative cultural images and "bad policies" that have to be avoided in public diplomacy (Scott-Smith 55), rap and hip-hop have been frequently employed in German public diplomacy of the last 20 years. This is certainly due to the current purpose of distributing the image of a culturally diverse nation in a global context: Since 1998, the German Ministry of Foreign Affairs and its connected institutions such as the Goethe Institute have utilized rap, hip-hop, and electronic music by German musicians with a recent history of migration to promote a modern image of Germany in a global age.[2] This includes the organization of concerts at various branch offices of the Goethe Institute, the preparation of educational material on rap songs for German lessons in France and Belgium, as well as the release of music collections by the first, second and third immigrant generations, remixed and recorded by young DJs under the title *Heimatlieder aus Deutschland* (Songs of Home from Germany).[3]

With regard to aesthetics, it seems as if the employment of rap and hip-hop only partly fits the actual definition of art within an "arts diplomacy" described by US researcher John Brown. While German rap music probably responds very

---

[1] Cf. the definition of Public Diplomacy by Cross (4). See also Scott-Smith (50-6). The immediate communication between people is also stressed in Deis (192-205).

[2] According to the annual reports of the Goethe Institute, their first rap project was organized in Cameroun in 1996, with Yaundö and the German lyricist Marcel Beyer. The first concert of German rappers with a recent migration history took place at the Goethe Institute in Brussels in 1998 with the crew Sons of Gastarbeita from Witten. A year later, two international joint programs included rap musicians from Germany: the workshops for German teachers "Rap in Deutschland" with rapper Spax and DJ Mirko and the exhibition "Migranten und Kulturpolitik" in Rotterdam with the participation of Selim Özdogan and Microphone Mafia from Cologne (see *Jahrbuch/Annual Report 1996/1997, 1997/1998* and *1998/1999*).

[3] The last years have witnessed a necessary and overdue debate over the terminology that is used in order to refer to the descendants of "guest workers" and other first-generation immigrants. While the terms "second-" and "third-generation immigrants" is still commonly used, social activists have advocated for the alternative of "new Germans," thus seeking to counter the process of Othering that is inherent in such concepts as second- and third-generation immigrants. Since many of the artists discussed here refer directly to the generation of "guest workers," this article uses the terms second- and third immigrant generations while being aware that these words do not question, in any way, their German citizenships and identities.

well to the purpose of personal communication and a demonstration of cultural diversity and humanity, it might not match the mental maps of global citizens regarding Germany in terms of music history as compared to the US. Indeed, following Brown, it is the romantic aesthetics of art that seems to guarantee the embeddedness of a nation in a global, humanist culture, since "arts diplomacy provides audiences with unique and memorable experiences" that are generated by "powerful impressions," "revelation," and "illumination." This kind of aesthetic approach seems to fit the repertoire of classical music by German composers while contradicting the alignment of German hip-hop with the concept of cultural, ethnic, and racial otherness of the Turkish-German population (Diessel; Ickstadt). Thus, how can diplomatic and cultural institutions integrate (politically motivated) rap and hip-hop into an art diplomacy that ensures personal experiences through "the kind of unique moments that make our lives worth living" (Brown 59)?

In what follows I will analyze Hennion's sociological statement on rap music as a medium of individual, mostly locally based communication in relation to the central concerns of (West) German public diplomacy between transnational information, dialogue, and a successful promotion of a modern image of Germany.[4] As Hennion does in his article, I will contextualize the employment of German-language rap music in German public diplomacy with other genres of popular music by members of the first, second, and third immigrant generations. I will cover the period from the 1980s to the present, looking at perspectives of both the musicians and (West) German institutions of foreign policy in the cultural realm to detect the principal aesthetics and cultural elements of rap music used in (West) German public diplomacy.

The chosen period of investigation allows me to historically contextualize the different intentions connected with German rap and other genres of German popular music composed and performed by the second immigrant generation: the children of so-called *Gastarbeiter* (guest workers), immigrants from Southern and Southeastern Europe, including Turkey, who responded to the German call for manpower between 1955 and 1973. Taking a person-oriented approach and a comparative look at the aesthetic values of rap music and its reception in comparison to other forms of popular music, I argue that German rap musicians in the 1990s with a recent migration history were called upon to underscore the democratic, young, and future-oriented image of a modern Germany as long as they set aside, or even erased, negative aspects of German history since the

---

4   For an overview of German public diplomacy see Zöllner (262-69). For an overview on concepts and key themes of public diplomacy see Ostrowski (19-36).

1930s. At present, the aesthetic value of projects on music by immigrants that are relevant to public diplomacy is increasingly based on a conception of music as a medium of a common cultural memory and a shared culture of remembrance in a post-migrant society, a fact that is paralleled by the mostly German citizenship and identities of the second immigrant generation.[5]

GERMAN RAP BETWEEN IMMIGRATION, INTEGRATION AND SOCIAL COMMITMENT

The history of German rap is strongly related to immigration, integration, social commitment, and cultural transfer in a culturally varied society.[6] In the 1980s German rap was established in West Berlin, Brunswick, Cologne, Frankfurt, Hamburg, Heidelberg, Kiel, and Dortmund, mostly by musicians with a migration history (Elflein 257, 261). When Germany was shaken by the many racist arson attacks on refugee centers during the 1990s, German rap and rock emerged as central media of antiracist commitment and the affirmation of Germany's so-called "multicultural" identity (Pennay 116-17). As Pablo Dominguez Andersen pointed out, the transfer of US-American rap to Germany was a means for mostly male members of the second immigrant generation to broach the issue of a constant lack of integration. While their English band names symbolized acculturation to the Western world, masking their Turkish, Greek, or Italian names, their German texts ironically contrasted the flow of German words with the language of Turkish *Gastarbeiter*, as in the song "Ahmet Gündüz" (1992) by Fresh Familee:

At work my boss say to me: *Kanacke*[7] how are you?
I tell him *Hastir lan*,[8]
but the asshole don't understand anything.
My son attend school, now knows how to write,
but teacher is a bastard, he gives him the lowest scores.[9]

---

5 For a critical view on the term "postmigrant" and on its history see Kosnick, (Introduction 7-10; "Ethnic Club Cultures" 199).
6 For the history of rap music in Germany see Pennay (111-33); Verlan and Loh; Loh and Güngör; Bennett (133-50); Androutsopoulos; Saied; Kautny (405-19).
7 Derogatory German slang term for Turkish and Southern European immigrants.
8 Fuck off in Turkish.

In this song from the album *Falsche Politik* (1993), the German boss's failure to understand the Turkish immigrant's German language outlines an overt rebellion by the Turkish-German rappers of the group against the socially, medially, and economically inaccessible structures in German everyday life.[10]

While this demand for respect is articulated with curse words that circumscribe the immigrant's presumed authentic experiences, three years later, the band Sons of Gastarbeita, a formation of young Lebanese-German and Philippine-German rap musicians in the Ruhr Area,[11] one of the biggest metropolitan regions in Germany, released a song that shows the same functional elements as "Ahmet Gündüz," including spoken German by Turkish *Gastarbeiter* and the denunciation of a collective lack of integration.

In contrast to "Ahmet Gündüz," however, the song points to the generational process of cultural rootedness rather than to actual experiences of social, political, and medial discrimination as the reason for rebellion.[12] First of all, the band name Sons of Gastarbeita mixes English and the Ruhr Area's vernacular to circumscribe the second immigrant generation in Germany (qtd. in Loh and Güngör 62). In their song "Söhne der Gastarbeita," the group's generationality is the core theme (*Du so*). Consisting of the lines "Sons of Guest Workaz / we are the sons of guest workers,"[13] the song's hook emphasizes the rappers' German, locally-rooted but culturally open identity ("a son of this region / regardless of tradition and religion").[14] The song also calls for the complete and permanent integration of the second immigrant generation into German society, a process that had been denied to their parents. The second verse, in which the rappers mimic the language of "guest workers," describes the idealized image of Germany many workers from countries such as Turkey, Greece, and Italy shared before their arrival in Germany, and which vanished into thin air once they had arrived. This positive but unrealistic image, emphasizing the importance of Germany for the second generation, becomes the song's central message in the second verse:

---

9   "In Arbeit Chef mir sagen: Kanacke hey wie geht's? / Ich sage *Hastir lan*, doch Arschloch nix verstehen. / Mein Sohn gehen Schule, kann schreiben jetzt, / doch Lehrer ist ein Schwein, er gibt ihm immer Sechs." (Kaya 79) All translations are my own unless noted otherwise.

10 For an interpretation pointing to the confrontation of different mentalities in the song see Kumpf (210-11).

11 For an overview of hip-hop culture in the Ruhr Area see Nitzsche (4-8).

12 For the mixture of German and Turkish in German rap also see Byrd (292-300).

13 "Sons of Gastarbeita/Wir sind die Söhne der Gastarbeiter."

14 "ein Sohn dieser Region/unabhängig von Tradition und Religion."

the struggle of first-generation immigrants is carried on by a progressive second generation who are rooted in Germany and who refer to this struggle as "creative resistance" ("kreativer Widerstand") to discrimination.

The rendering of German integration history via generationality is musically contextualized by a more mainstream soul beat and background singing. The female voices of the background chorus do not contrast, but rather complement the male shouting of the band name in the chorus, an outcry that is reminiscent of a political demonstration. With this musical arrangement, the Sons of Gastarbeita helped to popularize German post-migrant rap texts and styles beyond communities with a recent migration history and their focus on oriental music styles. In the 1990s, such a musical and textual orientation was embedded into the rise of German rap and rock as media of antiracist commitment and of what was commonly referred to as Germany's "multicultural" identity after the many racist arson attacks on refugee centers in 1991 (Hoyerswerda), 1992 (Rostock-Lichtenhagen), and 1993 (Solingen) (Sons of Gastarbeita, qtd. in Loh and Güngör 63).

In 2002, the group with its narrative of a new generation was officially honored by then German President Johannes Rau in the context of an "integration competition" that was organized by the Bertelsmann foundation (Bertelsmann-Stiftung 18). A privately-owned organization closely tied to the Bertelsmann media corporation, the Bertelsmann foundation had a special interest in the second immigrant generation (Bertelsmann-Stiftung 9). In their list of criteria for the choice of the winning projects they pointed to the significance of the musicians' own initiative and to the importance of direct exchange between local citizens from different cultural backgrounds at several times (Bertelsmann-Stiftung 17, 25). Moreover, the awarded projects embraced most of the central fields of public diplomacy, including language promotion, youth work, and cultural encounters/rapprochement (Bertelsmann-Stiftung 22). At the same time, the criteria covered typical aspects of public diplomacy evaluations such as efficient networking, sustainability, and range of influence (Bertelsmann-Stiftung 15). In the portrait of the band, music is ascribed a very wide range of influence in building communities and reaching out across various media (Bertelsmann-Stiftung 28).

Due to this overlap between the musical expression of a young generation and local or national public diplomacy, the Goethe Institute invited the Sons of Gastarbeita to perform and offer workshops to French students at the institute's branch offices in Brussels, Paris, Nancy, Lille, and Lyon in 1998, 1999, and

2008.[15] The Goethe Institute also integrated the group into their language courses by compiling an educational unit for German lessons in France on the song "Sons of Gastarbeita" (Dommel et al.). Those didactic materials not only accentuated the narrative of the young generation by providing an exercise where students had to write a story based on fragments of the lyrics; in the handout for German teachers, published online by the German language section of the Goethe Institute after 1998, the song was also directly linked to a very positive image of German *Landeskunde* (Area Studies):

In this context, the history of immigration in the German Federal Republic can be discussed (the 60s, the economic miracle, the Berlin Wall—workers from East Berlin could not come to West Berlin anymore, the lack of workforce in the highly industrialized Ruhr Area, the recruitment of Turkish workers). (Dommel et al., "6. Textarbeit 1")[16]

While the Goethe Institute's educational material narrates the 1970s, 1980s, and 1990s principally on the basis of the rappers' biographies, historical background information is limited to the 1960s economic boom, thus contradicting the original intention of the band who wanted to transfer historical knowledge on the contemporary life and structural disintegration of the first generation of *Gastarbeiter* (Sons of Gastarbeita qtd. in Loh and Güngor 63-5). In summary, the educational material used the lyrics to construct strategically suitable personalities while neglecting the performing musicians themselves who claimed to have studied the social conditions of first-generation *Gastarbeiter* in Germany and who had accumulated historical knowledge that was never taught at school (Sons of Gastarbeita qtd. in Loh and Güngor 63).

According to the teaching materials, these biographically constructed figures and their cultural mobility correspond to a global "reality" of migration (Dommel et al.,"1. Mit Wortkarten Geschichten schreiben").[17] To achieve such an understanding, the students are repeatedly asked to compare the statements in the song to the situation in France. Interestingly, these comparisons are mostly evoked when negative aspects, such as a lack of integration, are concerned:

---

15 For a brief overview of local promotions of hip-hop in the 1990s see Mager (267).

16 "Der Anlass ist gegeben, die Geschichte der Immigration in der BRD anzureißen (Die 60er Jahre, das Wirtschaftswunder, die Berliner Mauer – es kamen keine Arbeiter mehr aus Ost- nach West-Berlin, der Mangel an Arbeitskräften im hochindustrialisierten Ruhrgebiet, Anwerbung von türkischen Arbeitern)."

17 "Ihr werdet den Song anhören. Da geht es um eine Realität, die Menschen überall in der Welt betrifft."

[G]o deeper into the difficulties of the "guest worker": misery in the homeland, the dream of paradise, the hostility of Germans, and isolation within the "ghetto" that prevents them from properly acquiring good German. In the classroom discussion it becomes clear that such a situation is still extremely topical—even in one's own country. (Dommel et al., "7. Textarbeit 2")[18]

Thus, the handout constructs the rappers as members of a new generation only by constantly hinting to the fact that integration is a current topic in the entire world of "our times" (Dommel et al., "9. Textarbeit 4"). The artists' concert is mentioned only in testimonies by the participating schools that document the quantitative criteria for success. In one of those testimonies, for instance, a French teacher of German seeks to invite the rap group to her school for another concert after having attended a performance at the Goethe Institute:

Yesterday evening I attended the concert of the "Sons of Gastarbeita" with the pupils of the fifth bilingual English-German class and the presentation with the pupils' work done in two workshops in the morning of the same day at the very beginning; my pupils were caught with enthusiasm during the evening by the energy, the warmth, and the generosity of the musicians who allowed attendees to get on stage to dance—One of my pupils did a hip-hop performance and I found him quite talented!
We bought the CD and on our way back home my pupils again sang the refrain "Ich will mehr!" ("I want more")!!!
Thus I would like to know whether and under which conditions the Sons of G could come to our school to give comparable workshops and a concert. My colleague who gives music lessons has some musical instruments and we have various bigger rooms in the school building. How could such a thing be organized???
I would like to thank once again the Goethe Institute for this initiative and for the good gentle and intercultural spirit of this evening. (Sternberg, slide 22)[19]

---

18 "[D]ringt tiefer in die dargestellte Problematik des 'Gastarbeiters' ein: die Misere in der Heimat, der Traum vom Paradies, die Feindseligkeit der Deutschen, die Isolierung im 'Ghetto,' die einen guten Spracherwerb verhindert. Man erkennt im Klassengespräch, dass diese Situation auch heute noch—auch im eigenen Land—von höchster Aktualität ist."

19 "Je suis venue hier après-midi assister avec des élèves de cinquième 'bilingues anglais-allemand' au concert donné par les 'Sons of Gastarbeita' et à la présentation, au tout début des productions d'élèves ayant participé le matin-même à 2 ateliers; mes élèves ont été enthousiasmés par cet après-midi, par l'énergie, la chaleur et la généro-

In the didactic material the music of the song is only picked up in a little annotation that emphasizes the particular significance of the musical interpretation. The funky soul accompaniment is the reason why the chorus is—wrongly—interpreted as a complaint and not as a protest:

While working on a song the text should never be analyzed on its own. The interpretation confers a special meaning to it. Here we have a hip-hop rhythm that is continuously accompanied by instrumental funk and soul, not only in the instrumental passage but also in the sung stanzas. Funk and soul are melodious and sentimental. The refrain becomes a lament, at the end it is almost cried. . . . The instruments (especially keyboards and guitar) underline the lamenting character. Attention should be paid to the guitar solo in the interlude. How can the dying drum roll at its end be understood? (Dommel et al., "11. Das Lied hören")[20]

Characterizing the musicians as "faces of the future [who] refuse to be put down as exotic or 'mixed' people with personality and psychosomatic disorders" (Dommel et al., "5A. Wer sind die Sons of Gastarbeita").[21] Dommel et al. project

---

sité qui se dégageaient des musiciens- qui acceptaient que les jeunes montent sur la scène et y dansent- Un de mes élèves a fait une démonstration de hip-hop et je l'ai trouvé plutôt doué!"
Nous avons acheté le cd et pendant le trajet du retour mes élèves reprenaient le refrain 'ich will mehr!'!!! Jetzt wuerde ich gerne wissen, ob und unter welchen Bedingungen die Sons of G in meine Schule kommen koennten, um gleiche Workshops und ein Konzert zu planen; meine Musikkollegin verfuegt über ein Paar Instrument, wir haben mehrere grosse Räume in der Schule. Wie koennte sich das organisieren lassen??? (sic)
Ich bedanke mich nochmals für diese Initiative am Goethe-Institut und für den freundlich-interkulturellen guten Geist an diesem Nachmittag."

20 "Bei der Arbeit an einem Lied/Song sollte nie der Text allein behandelt werden. Die Interpretation gibt ihm besondere Bedeutung. Hier haben wir HipHop-Rhythmus, der ständig von instrumentalem Funk und Soul begleitet wird, nicht nur in den instrumentalen Passagen, sondern auch in den gesungenen Strophen. Funk und Soul sind melodiös und gefühlvoll. Der Refrain wird zur Klage, am Schluss fast geheult. . . . Die Instrumente (besonders Keyboards und Gitarre) unterstreichen den klagenden Aspekt. Zu beachten das Gitarrensolo im Zwischenspiel. Wie ist der absterbende Trommelwirbel am Schluss zu verstehen?"

21 "Gesichter der Zukunft . . . [die] sich nicht mehr als Exoten oder 'Mischlinge' mit Persönlichkeitskonflikten und psychosomatischen Störungen abstempeln."

what they deemed to be the sorrowful cultural identity of the rappers onto the music. In doing so, they tend to reduce the musicians to their ethnic identity rather than recognizing their artistic achievements.

Paralleling such an interpretation, a review on the Goethe Institute's intercultural activities published on the institute's website problematizes the fact that "the bands have not been invited because of their good music or excellent performances but because of the fact that they had non-German roots" (Verlan, "Breakdance").[22] The review then goes on to list Microphone Mafia, Sons of Gastarbeita, Islamic Force, and Asiatic Warriors as examples of such groups (Verlan, "Breakdance"). Sons of Gastarbeita confirmed this view themselves, criticizing the general lack of interest not only in their historical knowledge, but also in the aesthetic dimensions of their music (Loh and Güngür 63-75).

That the Goethe Institute's interpretation did not correspond to the rap group's self-determined understanding of their music is obvious if one regards the song against the backdrop of the band's oeuvre. The band's overall work can be characterized as a compromise between post-migratory engaged texts and the German middle-class rap music by such crews as Die Fantastischen Vier. For this compromise, they were repeatedly criticized by Turkish-German rappers who engaged with political themes in their music (Özdoğan 2).

Nevertheless, one might assume that the political commitment of Sons of Gastarbeita did not fit the needs of a German public diplomacy. In their song "März-Rap 1920" ("March Rap 1920") released in 2006, the group recalls the bloody workers' revolt of 1920 in the Ruhr Area to raise historical and political awareness. Based on the soul beat sample of "Söhne der Gastarbeiter," "März-Rap 1920" poetically retells the workers' rebellion with the help of historical recordings and calls for a collective awareness in order to warn against the one-sided orientation of political authorities. Awarding the band with the German records critics' prize, commentators praised "März-Rap 1920" as a successful analysis of a historical event and a reinvention of the political song genre ("Grenzgänger"). By seeking to build historical awareness of the social and class inequalities in the Weimar Republic, the Sons of Gastarbeita may have lost some of their appeal in the eyes of decision makers in the field of German public diplomacy. Instead, the two main band members, Ghandi Chaline and Germain Bleich, continued with rap projects in youth work in Germany that discussed genuine social issues like mobbing at school, the result of which practically contributed to further integration of German youths on various social levels.

---

22 "Die Bands wurden nicht eingeladen, weil sie gute Musik machten oder tolle Liveauftritte, sondern weil sie offensichtlich nicht-deutsche Wurzeln hatten."

HEIMATLIEDER: FROM ANTIRACIST COMMITMENT TO CULTURAL MEMORY

Compared to the Sons' rap concerts at Western European Goethe Institutes, the current official musical projects in the framework of German public diplomacy show a very different mixture of music, cultural identity, and political history. This is obvious in two contrasting examples: (1) the independent ethnographic initiative by the artists and authors Imran Ayata and Bülent Kullukcu, who both were born around 1970 in Germany and recently started an independent initiative in which they compiled a collection of German migratory music under the title *Songs of Gastarbeiter* (they released a compilation of migratory and post-migratory music that was distributed in Germany among first-generation immigrants) and (2) the project *Heimatlieder aus Deutschland*, a project piloted by the German Foreign Office presenting ensembles of traditional music and musicians with a migration background who are now active in Berlin and Augsburg. Collaborating with the labels Galileo Music and Karaoke Kalk, three albums entitled *Heimatlieder aus Deutschland* (Songs of Home from Germany, 2013), *New German Ethnic Music* (2013), and *Heimatlieder aus Deutschland Berlin/Augsburg* (Songs of Home from Germany Berlin/Augsburg, 2015) were released within the project ("CD und Vinyl").

Ayata and Kullukcu are popular mostly in academic circles and are currently touring to present their collection of songs recorded by first-generation immigrants in production studios in Germany and Turkey. On social media platforms, the authors post pictures of their hotel rooms, ironically relating them to their own artistic mobility, but also to the uncomfortable accommodation of their ancestors when they arrived in Germany as "guests." The photos of Gelsenkirchen, one of the poorest post-industrial towns in the Ruhr Area, for instance, ironically show off luxury items.[23] In this way, the artists comment ironically on dominant biographical narratives of and about first- and second-generation immigrants.

Based on political and historical research and on their own socialization, Ayata and Kullukcu's ethnographic project seeks to integrate an important part of German popular music history into the official historiography of German (popular) music. At the same time, the project might also constitute a material basis for an active generational memory of the 1950s and 1960s. The artists'

---

23 See Songs of Gastarbeiter, "Weil wir hin und wieder"; "Songs of Gastarbeiter, das ist keine Sosyete-Komfor-Zone" (sic); "Geht doch: Luxus in Gelsenkirchen"; "In Wiesbaden wieder zurück auf dem Gastarbeiterniveau"; "Hotel Fortuna, Essen."

ethnographic work is based on a politico-historical reflection of their own socialization and on archival research. Outside academic circles, Ayata and Kullukcu address both the social experience of the second generation of *Gastarbeiter* as well as the dominant German historicization of that experience. While they define the collected songs as "our songs," i.e. the songs of guest workers' children, in the booklet, the album cover of *Songs of Gastarbeiter* shows a beautiful view of a mountain landscape evoking the German concept of *Heimat* (homeland) (booklet). Interestingly, the various German-language "Anadolu rock" (Anatolian rock) songs contain a large amount of cultural allusions and ironies that result not only from the texts but from the music itself (Yener Ağabeyoğlu 62-3). The album, for instance, includes the song "Es kamen Menschen an" (People Arrived) by the Turkish rock musician and composer Cem Karaca. This choice is particularly interesting as Karaca was not a guest worker, but rather lived in Germany as a political exile in the 1980s.

Karaca's work, however, deals with the living conditions of first-generation immigrants. "Es kamen Menschen an" comments on Max Frisch's famous statement, "they called for workers, and human beings arrive" ("man hat Arbeitskräfte gerufen, und es kommen Menschen"):[24]

They [guest workers] have been quickly acknowledged in their home country
as foreign exchange earners,
but during this export of money and workers
they became strangers in their new world as in their old. (*Songs of Gastarbeiter*, booklet)[25]

Not only does Karaca recast Frisch's statement from his own perspective, he also underlines his musical authority by harking back to the Brechtian genre of the *Moritat* (street or murder ballad). This is most apparent in the deep brass sounds that enrich the generic rock music accompaniment with guitar, bass guitar, and

---

24 As Max Frisch states: "They say that [the guest workers] save one billion each year and send it to their homelands. That was not the idea. They save their money. In fact, you cannot really resent them that. But they are just there, a foreign infiltration by humans, although, as I said, one had merely asked for workers."
"[Die Gastarbeiter] sparen, heißt es, jährlich eine Milliarde und schicken sie heim. Das war nicht der Sinn. Sie sparen. Eigentlich kann man ihnen auch das nicht übelnehmen. Aber sie sind einfach da, eine Überfremdung durch Menschen, wo man doch, wie gesagt, nur Arbeitskräfte wollte." (Frisch 374).

25 "[Die Gastarbeiter] wurden in ihrem Heimatland / schnell als Devisenbringer anerkannt / doch bei diesem Arbeiter-Geld-Export / wurden sie Fremde hier wie dort."

drums in the intro. This style is combined with Karaca's voice that seems to imitate and ironically comment on the typical sound of German schlager, for example by the Austrian singer Udo Jürgens, simultaneously reminding the listener of songs like "Griechischer Wein" (Greek Wine) that transport a typical image of foreign Greek workers from a German perspective (see Huber 81-101). The ironic agglomeration of the German majority culture's conceptualizations of immigration is then contrasted by a second section with a saz-solo. In the solo, the saz, which is played double time over the unchanging rock beat, contrasts the rock rhythm with its rhythmically free playing; however, the solo also demonstrates the virtuosity of the musician playing the Turkish instrument, since the regular (half time) rock beat retakes its flow within the song only thanks to the double time of the saz. In summary, the song reflects not only great knowledge and critical awareness of German perspectives on immigration, but a competition between the two cultures that ironically emphasizes the simple regularity of the rock beat in contrast to the free rhythmic interpretation of the saz. With this irony, the musicians not only comment on contemporary German schlager, but also create an equitable involvement of two musical cultures.

Long before compiling songs by first-generation immigrants, Imran Ayata had emphasized his critique of a multicultural society. In his view, such a society's focus on ethnicity impedes serious exchange between people with different cultural backgrounds by neglecting many social, economic, and gender aspects (Ayata 275, 285). The same critique is inherent in the musical-theatrical piece *Ab in den Orientexpress* (Go, Take the Orient Express, 1984) in which Karaca participated as a musician and actor (Burkert and Böseke 1-2). This theatrical piece illuminates different social aspects and individual voices of Turkish and German characters in their social and cultural complexity. This complexity is reflected in a linguistic differentiation that also demonstrates the mental concepts related to the different characters: Turkish characters who speak Turkish, Germans who try to imitate the Turkish language, Turks speaking broken German, and Germans speaking a broken German because they think that Turks would understand them better. In this example, music is used as a placeholder for standardized spaces and mentalities that are constantly transcended by individual characters:

During the whole day Şahin Kadioğlu pushes his garbage can through the commercial center and tries to keep the ground clean of paper, cigarette butts, and chewing gum. The day before yesterday his boss gave him a new task. He has to clean the humidified fountain with swinging artificial palms and flowers two times a day. The constant background music by James Last has a particularly unpleasant effect in this place. At the café in the center of the mall, the loudspeakers seem to be turned up more loudly than in other places. The words "Mokka-Mekka" are placed in a brown-yellow writing above the bar, where Bernd's sister Claudia serves her clients.[26]

The irony of the piece is based on prejudices concerning the implied mental associations of immigrants and "natives." Thus, the musical irony in "Es kamen Menschen an" does not refer to a competition of virtuosity, but underlines the culturally experienced play with presumed cultural images. In this way, the authors and musicians of *Ab in den Orientexpress* emphasize the everyday life of immigrants and locals who belong to the same social reality. Like the historical compilation *Songs of Gastarbeiter*, *Ab in den Orientexpress* does not seem to have been used directly within German public diplomacy programs.

The current project *Heimatlieder aus Deutschland* presents a middle ground between the historiographically-oriented Sons of Gastarbeita and the musico-historiographically-oriented *Songs of Gastarbeiter*. As such, *Heimatlieder aus Deutschland* explicitly works to enlarge the term "home" in cultural and musical terms. In doing so, it contrasts the reduction to ethnicity that dominates the Goethe Institute's teaching materials analyzed above.

The output of the project is twofold: The first CD includes current so-called folk music ranging from Fado and Italian choirs to Turkish songs and Dalmatian klapa singing by different groups of German immigrants living in Berlin and Augsburg, while the second CD presents German DJs' remixes of those pieces under the label "New German ethnic music." Since the lyrics of the collected songs remain in their original languages, German is limited to the project's title. Instead, the DJs remix non-German spoken word samples into their songs and create their own beats, rhymes, and melodies from morphemes, syllabi, and word fragments. Very often, these fragments are used to accompany the steady beat of the remixes that contrasts the varied and complex rhythms of the original songs. Moreover, text fragments are used to expand the sound spectrum of musical

---

26 "Şahin Kadioğlu schiebt seine Müllkarre den ganzen Tag durch das Einkaufzentrum und bemüht sich, den Boden der Ladenstadt von Papier, Zigarettenkippen und Kaugummi sauber zu halten. Sein Vorgesetzter hat ihm vorgestern eine zusätzliche Aufgabe gegeben. Er muß den luftbefeuchtenden Springbrunnen mit den schwingenden Plastikpalmen und den künstlichen Blumen zweimal pro Tag reinigen. Die Musikberieselung durch James Last wirkt an dieser Stelle besonders unangenehm. Hier am Steh-Café, im Zentrum der Ladenstadt, scheinen die Lautsprecher weiter aufgedreht zu sein als anderswo. Mokka-Mekka steht in braun-gelber Schrift über der Theke, an der Bernds Schwester Claudia die Kundschaft bedient."

instruments to create smooth transitions from the original versions to the remixes.[27] With this kind of "musicalization" of language (or hybridization of language and music), the remixes are supposed to create a new genre of "New German ethnic music," thus symbolizing the "actual Germany," as former Secretary of State Frank Walter Steinmeier pointed out in a 2014 speech.

For the organizers of the Heimatlieder project, the remixes constitute a "thick description" of musical, linguistic, and cultural traditions that have been neglected by many Germans until today, simply because they did not understand them (Terkessidis and Kühling). According to the project organizers, the key group for understanding this kind of music are once again second-generation Germans who supposedly grew up with this music and have an emotional relationship to it. While the project defines music as a carrier of emotions and memories, it relies on elements central to nineteenth-century European musical aesthetics. According to the organizers of the project, those musical memories originate in the "guest workers'" practice of singing "songs of home" after their immigration to Germany. Such practice is said to "heal the fracture within the continuity of culture and memory that has been experienced by migrants and to re-contextualize themselves in the foreign country" (Terkessidis and Kühling).[28] At the same time, the project seeks to "erase the cultural articulations of the so-called first generation from the actually pejoratively understood context of folklore and puts it into a universal musical environment" (Terkessidis and Kühling).[29] The ethnomusicological annotations in the booklet accentuate this focus on a purely musical rather than a politically motivated cultural identity by pointing to the historical hybridization of Andalusian and Moroccan music, among other musical cultures.[30]

Such a historically wide-ranging agenda of transcultural history, cultural transfer, and exchanges is fundamental to the construction of a modern image of German culture: according to the organizers, the long-lasting intercultural

---

27 See "Milho Verde" (Trio Fado) and its remix by Guido Möbius, als well as the piece "Adalardan Bir Yar Gelir Bizlere" and its remix by Murat Tepeli (*Heimatlieder aus Deutschland*; *New German Ethnic Music*).

28 "[D]en durch die Migration erfahrenen Bruch in der Kontinuität von Kultur und Erinnerung zu kitten und sich im fremden Land sozusagen zu rekontextualisieren."

29 "entfernt die kulturellen Artikulationen der sogenannten Ersten Generation aus dem in Bezug auf Migration derzeit häufig pejorativ verstandenen Kontext von Folklore und stellt sie in ein universelles musikalisches Umfeld."

30 See the liner notes of "Saadi Bellouali Jani" and "Dini Din Allah" (*Heimatlieder aus Deutschland*).

exchange between different musical traditions and genres has the power to transform longstanding misunderstandings and stereotypes. In that sense, the description of a trip to Italy in the booklet can be read as an attempt to challenge existing gender roles:

Let's go to Italy! In 2005 the choir director Annunziata Matteucci travelled to Sardinia with thirty women to attend the famous Easter processions. In the small village Orosèi at the beautiful East coast (district Nuoro) she was amazed by a very special song of the local community: "Divina Consoladora" (Celestial Comforter). The song is traditionally performed at the feast of Saint Mary in September by four singers, the Tenores: "Celestial comforter of painful pains, give us a remedy for our sufferings." The Tenores taught the rare polyphonic singing technique to the women. Right after the journey the choir Donni Sò (They Are Women) was founded. Today 23 women between the ages of 30 and 60 sing in that choir. The music teacher Annunziata Matteucci wants to share the songs of the choir with the world and to preserve the particular treasure for future generations. (*Heimatlieder aus Deutschland*, booklet)[31]

By including this anecdote, the booklet to *Heimatlieder* emphasizes the fact that previously non-German traditions have been included as integral parts of German culture by transgressing gender categories and different generations. The fact that they are now used to represent Germany abroad not only exemplifies the success of a German "welcoming culture," but also takes on a new function as an instrument of German soft power. As Frank Walter Steinmeier has described Germany's new role in the twenty-first century:

---

31 "Auf nach Italien! 2005 reiste Chorleiterin Annunziata Matteucci mit dreißig Frauen nach Sardinien, um an den berühmten Osterprozessionen teilzunehmen. Im kleinen Ort Orosèi an der wunderschönen Ostküste (Provinz Nuoro) überraschte sie ein ganz besonderes Lied aus der dortigen Gemeinde: Divina Consoladora (Himmlische Trösterin). Es wird traditionell beim Marienfest im September von vier Sängern, den 'Tenores,' gesungen: 'Himmlische Trösterin des schmerzlichen Schmerzes, gib uns eine Medizin gegen unser Leiden.' Die Tenores brachten den Frauen die außergewöhnliche, mehrstimmige Gesangstechnik bei. Gleich im Anschluss an die Reise wurde der Chor Donni Sò gegründet, 'Frauen sind's': Heute singen hier 23 Frauen im Alter von 30 bis 60. Mit dem Chor möchte die studierte Musikpädagogin Annunziata Matteucci Lieder mit der Welt teilen und diesen ganz besonderen Schatz für künftige Generationen bewahren."

In the perspective of foreign affairs, we need open doors—and that is an argument that is often not considered: Imagine the world being a balance. In the coming decades the weight of Germany, Europe and the Western part of the world will be reduced and that of new players will increase—in Asia, South America, and also in Africa, and this will be true for all categories concerning "Hard Power": an increase of population, economic power, military power, political power. "Soft power" will be all the more important! It will be important that the things that we stand for will be attractive for the world: our concept of a free and open society, our idea of a social market economy.[32]

For the former German Minister of Foreign Affairs, the power of art, literature, and music lies in their capacity to generate "understanding," characterized by diplomatic collaboration, which he deems to be a basis also for everyday life:

Outside in the world there are indeed many crises. If we Germans want to participate, if we want to make a small contribution to peace—and we should follow this aspiration!—then first of all we have to be able to do the following: to understand the world! Understanding and comprehension are the basics for a true diplomatic solution.
But what is the premise for understanding?
Recently I visited India, together with a German author with Indian roots, Rajivinder Singh. And he told me: "To understand you need a view with six eyes. We should look at the world with our own eyes, with the eyes of the other and with a common view.
Such a view with six eyes starts with ourselves. Here, at home, we have to learn it.[33]

---

32 "Wir brauchen offene Türen aber auch aus außenpolitischer Sicht – und das ist ein Argument, das weniger oft beleuchtet wird: Stellen Sie sich die Welt als Waage vor. In den nächsten Jahrzehnten wird das Gewicht von Deutschland, Europa, dem Westen insgesamt abnehmen, und das von neuen Playern zunehmen – in Asien, Lateinamerika, auch in Afrika –, und zwar in allen Kategorien, die man 'Hard Power' nennt: Bevölkerungswachstum, Wirtschaftskraft, militärische Stärke, politisches Gewicht. Umso mehr kommt es auf 'Soft Power' an! Darauf, dass das, wofür wir stehen, attraktiv ist für die Welt: unser Modell einer freien und offenen Gesellschaft, unsere Idee einer sozialen Marktwirtschaft."
33 "Es gibt da draußen in der Welt wahrlich viele Krisen. Wenn wir Deutsche uns einbringen wollen, wenn wir ein kleines Stück beitragen wollen zum Frieden – und diesen Anspruch sollten wir haben! –, dann müssen wir zuallererst eines können: die Welt verstehen! Verstehen und Verständigung sind die Voraussetzung für jede echte diplomatische Lösung.
Aber was ist eigentlich die Voraussetzung für Verstehen?

The success of the project was documented in press reviews on the project's website, which accentuate the modernization of the terms "folklore" and *Heimat* as well as the power of music to transform laments into dance music ("Presse").

POPULAR MUSIC DIPLOMACY IN GERMANY BETWEEN REPRESENTATION AND PARTICIPATION

My analysis of popular music by musicians and groups with a recent migration history has illuminated three aspects which have shaped German public diplomacy from the late 1990s to today. First, the governmental bodies and private institutes responsible for cultural diplomacy, such as the Foreign Office and the Goethe Institute, tried to include current trends in popular music. All of the projects discussed in this chapter emerged out of a local political and social commitment or belonged to a specific current of cultural interest and/or expression. This is true for both the inclusion of the award-winning rap group Sons of Gastarbeita and the *Heimatlieder* project that contrasts the independent compilation *Songs of Gastarbeiter*.[34]

Second, contemporary German public diplomacy seems to prefer linear historical conceptions without interruption, and even music history to a social history of (failed) inclusion. In fact, German public diplomacy's emphasis on a historical intercultural hybridity diminishes the recognition and comprehension of irony as a means of participation and involvement within complex constellations of different mentalities. As a central element in the music of second generation immigrants, and as an important element of modern ethnography in a global, mediated age (Lethen 205-31), irony has been mostly erased by the political authorities in their public diplomacy strategies. Rather than trying to acknowledge irony, the projects that are funded by the Foreign Office have sought to integrate the first generation's nostalgia for their home-countries into the German music market via global music categories such as the newly invented genre of "new German ethnic music." As the new image of Germany is

> Kürzlich war ich in Indien. Mit mir war ein deutscher Schriftsteller mit indischen Wurzeln, Rajivinder Singh. Und er sagte: 'Zum Verstehen braucht man einen Blick der sechs Augen. Wir sollten die Welt mit unseren Augen sehen, mit denen des anderen – und mit einem gemeinsamen Blick.'
> Dieser Blick der sechs Augen beginnt bei uns selbst. Hier, zu Hause, müssen wir ihn lernen."

34 In 2013, Imran Ayata was invited by Mark Terkessidis ("Imran Ayata zu Gast").

global, multi-ethnic, and intercultural, German international public diplomacy seems to have acquired similar social and cultural policies that already exist in Germany.

Third, the definition of music used in the projects discussed above, differentiating between different genres such as rap, rock, electronic, and folk, generally fits the conventional aesthetic definition of "arts diplomacy" given by John Brown. Even in recent projects, popular music is supposed to take on the role of a language that is understandable for everybody and a carrier of emotions and memories. At the same time, its political and social dimensions—traceable in German migratory and post-migratory music from the 1980s to 2013—are promoted by the accompanying liner notes in booklets and by the musical performances themselves that accentuate an overall cultural hybridization. Here, processes of cultural transfer are used by agents of German public diplomacy to construct a linear and uninterrupted music history in order to balance participation and representation. Rather than integrating the social reality of immigration into the larger narratives of German music history, however, the contextualization of the music by first and second immigrant generation highlights the culturally diverse biographies of individuals for people-to-people exchanges. Thus, instead of the above named individual projects centered on ethnographic inquiries and private collections of records that create a distant view of cultural stereotypes in order to enhance discussion and self-reflection, the projects undertaken by German public diplomacy efforts paradoxically accentuate a holistic ethnic dimension over an accurate historical reality. This is the main difference between the grassroots compilation *Songs of Gastarbeiter* and its use within the larger, publicly funded *Heimatlieder aus Deutschland*.

Finally, in this context, rap music is a prosperous medium for public diplomacy, but only as long as it neglects its traditions and conventions as an Afro-diasporic cultural practice. German public diplomacy is less interested in the actual histories of popular music cultures than in their potential to show future-oriented, generationally-constructed cultural identities. At the same time, the academic interests of crews and bands such as Sons of Gastarbeita has prepared the groundwork for official, as well as independent, participatory projects of second immigrant generation within the framework of historical anthropology and ethnography. With regard to the background of the rich variety of existing projects on German migratory and post-migratory popular music, German public diplomacy will have to cope with the tension between "understanding" or "involvement" as well as between "history" and "memory" when creating representations of German culture through individual exchanges with a "strong human factor."[35]

WORKS CITED

Andersen, Pablo Dominguez. "Ahmet Gündüz. Migration, Männlichkeit und die diasporischen Ursprünge von HipHop in Deutschland und Europa." *Themenportal Europäische Geschichte* 2015. Web. 28 July 2016. <https://www.europa.clio-online.de/essay/id/artikel-3793>.

Androutsopoulos, Jannis, ed. *HipHop: Globale Kultur – lokale Praktiken*. Bielefeld: transcript, 2015. Print.

Ayata, Imran. "Kanak-Rap in Almanya: Über die schweren Folgen Deutschlands." *Angeworben-eingewandert-abgeschoben: Ein anderer Blick auf die Einwanderungsgesellschaft Bundesrepublik Deutschland*. Ed. Katja Dominik, Marc Jünemann, Jan Motte and Astrid Reinecke. Münster: Westfälisches Dampfboot, 1999. 273-87. Print.

Ayata, Imran and Bülent Kullukcu (AYKU). *Songs of Gastarbeiter Vol. 1*. TRIKONT US-0453. 2013. CD.

Baier, Frank and Sons of Gastarbeita. "März-Rap 1920." *1920: Lieder der Märzrevolution*. Die Grenzgänger und Frank Baier. Verlag Müller-Lüdenscheid, 2006. CD.

Bennet, Andy. *Popular Music and Youth Culture: Music, Identity and Place*. New York: Palgrave Macmillan, 2000. Print.

Bertelsmann-Stiftung, ed. *Auf Worte folgen Taten: Gesellschaftliche Initiativen zur Integration von Zuwanderern*. Gütersloh: Bertelsmann-Stiftung, 2003. Print.

Böseke, Harry, and Martin Burkert. *Ab in den Orient-Express: Neu erzählt nach dem gleichnamigen Theaterstück der beiden Autoren*. Kevelaer: Anrich extra, 1992. Print.

Burkert, Martin, and Harry Böseke. *Ab in den Orient-Express: Ein Stück zum Thema Ausländerfeindlichkeit*. Weinheim: Deutscher Theaterverlag, 1984. Print.

Byrd, Brenna Reinhart. "Stylized Turkish German as the Resistance Vernacular of German Hip-Hop." *The Cambridge Companion to Hip-Hop*. Ed. Justin A. Williams. Cambridge UP, 2015. 292-300. Print.

---

[35] The author would like to thank Mario Dunkel and Sina Nitzsche for their helpful comments on earlier versions of this chapter and Terence Kumpf for proofreading it.

Brown, John. "Arts Diplomacy: The Neglected Aspect of Cultural Diplomacy." *Routledge Handbook of Public Diplomacy.* Ed. Nancy Snow and Philip M. Taylor. New York: Routledge, 2009. 57-62. Print.

"CD und Vinyl." *Heimatlieder aus Deutschland.* 2016. Web. 6 July 2018. <http://www.heimatliederausdeutschland.de/cd-und-vinyl.html>.

Cross, Mai'a K. Davis. "Conceptualizing European Public Diplomacy." *European Public Diplomacy: Soft Power at Work.* Ed. Mai'a K. Davis Cross and Jan Melissen. New York: Palgrave Macmillan, 2013. 1-11. Print.

Deis, Christopher. "Hip-Hop and Politics." *The Cambridge Companion to Hip-Hop.* Ed. Justin A. Williams. Cambridge: Cambridge UP, 2015. 192-205. Print.

Diessel, Caroline. "Bridging East and West on the 'Orient Express': Oriental Hip-Hop in the Turkish Diaspora of Berlin." *Journal of Popular Music Studies* 13 (2001): 165-87. Print.

Dommel, Hermann, et al. "Sons of Gastarbeita – 'Söhne der Gastarbeita', ausgehend von einem Arbeitsvorschlag von Almuth Meyer-Zollitsch und Kornelia Bitzer-Zenner (Goethe-Institut Brüssel, 1998)." *Goethe Institut Paris.* Web. 28 July 2016. <www.goethe.de/resources/files/pdf63/Sons_of_Gastarbeita_Shne_der_Gastarbeita1_1.pdf>.

Elflein, Dietmar. "From Krauts with Attitudes to Turks with Attitudes: Some Aspects of Hip-Hop History in Germany." *Popular Music* 17.3 (1998): 255-65. Print.

Fresh Familee. "Ahmet Gündüz." *Falsche Politik.* Phonogramm, 1993. CD.

Frisch, Max. "Überfremdung I." *Max Frisch: Gesammelte Werke in zeitlicher Folge.* Vol. V 1964-1967. Ed. Hans Mayer. Frankfurt am Main: Suhrkamp, 1976. 374-76. Print.

"Grenzgänger und Frank Baier: 1920. Lieder der Märzrevolution." *Chanson. Liedermacher-Magazin.* 2006. Web. 6 July 2018. <www.chanson.de/download/presse_1920_cd.pdf>.

Heimatlieder aus Deutschland. Galileo Music Communication, 2013. CD.

Heimatlieder aus Deutschland Berlin/Augsburg. Galileo Music Communication, 2015. CD.

"Heimatlieder aus Deutschland." 2016. Web. 6 July 2018. <www.heimatliederausdeutschland.de/home.html>.

Hennion, Antoine. "Baroque and Rock: Music, Mediators and Musical Taste." *Poetics* 24 (1997): 415-35. Print.

Huber, Harald. "Griechischer Wein? Der Song als Heimat vielfältiger Kulturen." *Heimatlose Klänge? Regionale Musiklandschaften heute.* Ed. Thomas Phleps. Karben: CODA, 2002. 81-101. Print.

Ickstadt, Heinz. "Appropriating Difference: Turkish-German Rap." *Amerikastudien/American Studies* 44.4 (1999): 571-78. Print.

"Imran Ayata zu Gast bei Mark Terkessidis am Montag, den 10. Juni." *Trikont* 23 June 2013. Web. 6 July 2018. <trikont.de/blog/imran-ayata-zu-gast-bei-mark-terkessidis/>.

Goethe-Institut München. *Jahrbuch/Annual Report 1996/1997*. Ed. Goethe Institut, Munich 1997. Print.

---. *Jahrbuch/Annual Report 1997/1998*. Ed. Goethe-Institut, Munich 1998. Print.

---. *Jahrbuch/Annual Report 1998/1999*. Ed. Goethe-Institut, Munich 1999. Print.

Kautny, Oliver. "Immigrant Hip-Hop in Germany: The Cultural Identities of Migrants." *Hip-Hop in Europe: Cultural Identities and Transnational Flows*. Ed. Sina A. Nitzsche and Walter Grünzweig. Zürich: LIT, 2013. 405-20. Print.

Kaya, Verda. *HipHop zwischen Istanbul und Berlin. Eine (deutsch-)türkische Jugendkultur im lokalen und transnationalen Beziehungsgeflecht*. Bielefeld: transcript, 2015. Print.

Kosnick, Kira. Introduction. *Postmigrant Club Cultures in Urban Europe*. Ed. Kira Kosnick. Frankfurt am Main: Peter Lang, 2015. 7-34. Print.

---. "Ethnic Club Cultures: Postmigrant Leisure Socialities and Music in Urban Europe." *Speaking in Tongues: Pop Local Global*. Beiträge zur Popularmusikforschung 42. Ed. Dietrich Helms and Thomas Phleps. Bielefeld: transcript, 2015. 199-211. Print.

Kumpf, Terence. "Beyond Multiculturalism: The Transculturating Potential of Hip-Hop in Germany." *Hip-Hop in Europe: Cultural Identities and Transnational Flows*. Ed. Sina A. Nitzsche and Walter Grünzweig. Zürich: LIT, 2013. 207-26. Print.

Lethen, Helmuth. "Versionen des Authentischen: Sechs Gemeinplätze." *Literatur und Kulturwissenschaften: Positionen, Theorien, Modelle*. Ed. Hartmut Böhme and Klaus R. Scherpe. Hamburg: Rowohlt, 1996. 205-31. Print.

Loh, Hannes, and Murat Güngör, eds. *Fear of a Kanak Planet: HipHop zwischen Weltkultur und Nazi-Rap*. Höfen: Hannibal, 2002. Print.

Mager, Christoph. *HipHop, Musik und die Artikulation von Geographie*. Sozialgeographische Bibliothek 8. Heidelberg: Franz Steiner, 2007. Print.

New German Ethnic Music. Karaoke Kalk (Indigo), 2013. CD.

Nitzsche, Sina A. „Hip-Hop in Europe as a Transnational Phenomenon: An Introduction." *Hip-Hop in Europe: Cultural Identities and Transnational*

Flows. Ed. Sina A. Nitzsche and Walter Grünzweig. Zürich: LIT, 2013. 3-34. Print.

Ostrowski, Daniel. *Die Public Diplomacy der deutschen Auslandsvertretungen weltweit*. Wiesbaden: VS Verlag für Sozialwissenschaften, 2010. Print.

Özdoğan, Selim. "Der den Klang der Worte liebt." *Transit* 8.1 (2012): 1-5. Web. 8 Aug. 2016.

Pennay, Mark. "Rap in Germany: The Birth of a Genre." *Global Noise: Rap and Hip-Hop Outside the USA*. Ed. Tony Mitchell. Middleton: Wesleyan, 2001. 111-33. Print.

"Presse." *Heimatlieder aus Deutschland*. 2016. Web. 6 July 2018. <http://www.heimatliederausdeutschland.de/presse.html>.

Saied, Ayla Güler. *Rap in Deutschland: Musik als Interaktionsmedium zwischen Partykultur und urbanen Anerkennungskämpfen*. Bielefeld: transcript, 2012. Print.

Scott-Smith, Giles. "Exchange Programs and Public Diplomacy." *Routledge Handbook of Public Diplomacy*. Ed. Nancy Snow and Philip M. Taylor. New York: Routledge, 2009. 50-6. Print.

Sons of Gastarbeita. "Söhne der Gastarbeita." *Du so*. Kleff Records, 1996. CD.

Songs of Gastarbeiter. "Songs of Gastarbeiter, das ist keine Sosyete-Komfor-Zone" (sic). *Facebook*. 12 Oct. 2014. Web. 09 Sept. 2018. <https://www.facebook.com/SongsOfGastarbeiter/?fref=ts>.

---. "Geht doch: Luxus in Gelsenkirchen" *Facebook*. 29 Nov. 2014. Web. 09 Sept. 2018. <https://www.facebook.com/SongsOfGastarbeiter/?fref=ts>.

---. "Hotel Fortuna, Essen." *Facebook*. 28 June 2014. Web. 09 Sept. 2018. <https://www.facebook.com/SongsOfGastarbeiter/?fref=ts>.

---. "In Wiesbaden wieder zurück auf dem Gastarbeiterniveau." *Facebook*. 30 Nov. 2014. Web. 09 Sept. 2018. <https://www.facebook.com/SongsOfGastarbeiter/?fref=ts>.

---. "Weil wir hin und wieder gefragt werden." *Facebook*. 22 June 2014. Web. 09 Sept. 2018. <https://www.facebook.com/SongsOfGastarbeiter/?fref=ts>.

Steinmeier, Frank-Walter. "Wo beginnt Willkommenskultur." *Auswärtiges Amt*. 21 Oct. 2014. Web. 6 July 2018. <www.auswaertiges-amt.de/de/newsroom/141020-bm-ifa/266194>.

Sternberg, Julia. "In der Fremde daheim – à chacun ses étrangers." Goethe Institute Paris, 2008-2009. Power point presentation "Musik-Beiträge zum Projekt." Message to Gesa zur Nieden. 23 Sept. 2015. E-mail.

Terkessidis, Mark, and Jochen Kühling. "Projektansatz 'Heimatlieder aus Deutschland.'" *Heimatlieder aus Deutschland*. Web. 2 Nov. 2015. <http://

www.heimatliederausdeutschland.de/das-projekt/ansatz-und-entstehung.html >.

Verlan, Sascha, and Hannes Loh, eds. *25 Jahre Hip-Hop in Deutschland*. Höfen: Hannibal, 2006. Print.

Verlan, Sascha. "'Mit Breakdance in der Fußgängerzone...': vom Migrationshintergrund der Hip-Hop-Szene in Deutschland." *Schulprojekte – Multikulturelles Deutschland – Goethe-Institut*. 2011. Web. 6 July 2018. <http://www.goethe.de/de/kul/mus/gen/pop/hip/8573851.html>.

Yener Ağabeyoğlu, Nazlı. *Deutsch-türkische Rapmusik in Berlin: Soziokulturelle Faktoren bei der Selektion von Rap-Texten und auditiven Produktionsmethoden unter türkischstämmigen Jugendlichen in Deutschland*. Berlin: LIT-Verlag, 2014. Print.

Zöllner, Oliver. "German Public Diplomacy: The Dialogue of Cultures." *Routledge Handbook of Public Diplomacy*. Ed. Nancy Snow and Philip M. Taylor. New York: Routledge, 2009. 262-69. Print.

Public Diplomacy and Decision-Making in the Eurovision Song Contest

Dean Vuletic

In the 2013 Eurovision Song Contest (ESC) that was held in Malmö, Sweden, the Montenegrin hip-hop duo Who See and singer Nina Žižić performed the song "Igranka" (The Party), with Who See appearing on stage dressed as astronauts. It was a symbolic performance in a contest that has historically been used in cultural diplomacy to influence how Europeans see each other: as astronauts, Who See suggested how Europeans of different nationalities still often perceived each other as aliens despite the process of European integration, and even though the ESC has reflected how Europeans have commonly experienced fashions in popular culture and the development of technologies such as television. The term "vision" in the contest's name refers to the fact that the ESC has been conceived as a televisual event from its beginning. However, because entries in the contest have always represented states, they have also reflected the cultural diplomacy, nation branding, and soft power that shape how states are perceived internationally. The ESC has been especially beneficial for the cultural diplomacy of small states like Montenegro: the three-minute time-limit for entries is a relatively long opportunity for small states to regularly promote themselves to a worldwide audience numbering in the hundreds of millions.

Who should exactly determine how we *see* a state in the ESC has, however, been a matter of controversy ever since the contest was established in 1956. In the case of Who See, the group was internally selected by officials from the Montenegrin national broadcasting organization, RTCG (Radio Televizija Crne Gore, Radio and Television of Montenegro). The entries of other states in the 2013 contest were selected either directly by such officials or through a national selection process in which juries or the public voted for the winner. The ESC has always been a stage upon which political values have been contested through cultural diplomacy, be it through the whitewashing of authoritarian governments' international images or the promotion of the rights of sexual minorities. However, the extent to which the public has been allowed to participate in the national selections has particularly highlighted both the ESC's democratic exceptionalism in relation to other international mega events and a problematic relationship between national broadcasting organizations and the larger public with regards to democratic participation. While the democratic deficit is most obvious in the broadcasting organizations of authoritarian states, the debates over the role of public voting in the ESC demonstrate that it is an issue that liberal democracies have had to contend with as well.

This chapter focusses on issues of democracy in the ESC in terms of public participation in the national selection processes and the appropriation of the contest in the public diplomacy of governments. I herein also underline a distinction between cultural and public diplomacy. The term "public diplomacy" has usually been used to refer to diplomacy which is directed towards an audience—the "public"—with agents usually being national governments or international organizations, and their methods being more varied than just the cultural. In cultural diplomacy, however, the emphasis is on the "cultural" means—in other words, how artistic products are used to promote a state (Kim 318-9). As entries in the ESC are usually not selected by national governments but nonetheless still represent states, I consider them to be more an example of cultural rather than public diplomacy, although a national government often appropriates the ESC in its official public diplomacy policies when its state hosts the contest. However, the ESC is a rare case of direct democracy in cultural diplomacy, and this gives another spin to the term "public diplomacy," as the public actually plays a decision-making role, whereas in more conventional approaches to public diplomacy the public is a subject rather than an agent. While the receptive role of the public is usually given more consideration in studies on public diplomacy, I am here concerned with the role that the public is allowed to play in the creation of cultural diplomacy and the related tensions that the ESC has highlighted between decision-makers, including governments, national broadcasting organizations, and the larger public.

CULTURAL DIPLOMACY IN THE ESC

The ESC has historically been significant for cultural diplomacy because it has reached an unusually large audience and, being based on cultural trends and new technologies, the contest has been attractive because of its fashionability and modernity. Held annually in May, the ESC has included entries from almost every European state and has attracted around two hundred million viewers in recent years, making it one of the longest-running and most-watched television events worldwide. The ESC is organized by the European Broadcasting Union (EBU), which was established in 1950. The organization's active membership comprises national, public service broadcasting organizations from European states and the Mediterranean rim that are part of the European Broadcasting Area, a technical region defined by the International Telecommunication Union (ITU), a United Nations agency, for the purpose of allocating broadcasting frequencies. During the Cold War, Eastern European states had their equivalent international broadcasting organization, the International Organization for Radio and Television, but it dissolved in 1993 when the Central and East European broadcasting organizations joined the EBU. The EBU promotes cultural and technical cooperation between its members, especially through the Eurovision Network for program exchange that gives the ESC its name. The EBU has always been a technical rather than political grouping: indeed, it has never had political criteria for membership, be it for the accession or expulsion of members (Eugster 59).

While the rules of the ESC have undergone changes throughout its history, particularly with regards to its voting system, the contest's basis has remained the same: the national broadcasting organizations send artists and songs to compete against each other. The artists appear in the contest under the name of the states that the broadcasting organizations are from, so there is a direct—albeit, as we shall see, deceiving—association with the states. Juries from these states, and since the late 1990s public audiences as well, have submitted their votes to select the winner, whose state consequently earns the right to host the contest the following year. The voting results are analyzed in the international media, with a good result usually being equated with a positive international image for a state. On the other hand, poor results have often been discussed within the states themselves as being not only connected to the quality of the entry but also to broader issues, such as the international image of a state or any political controversies that it might be party to. Voting can also be controversial at the stage of the national selection of the ESC entry, the organization of which the EBU leaves up to the national broadcasting organizations. The latter sometimes choose to stage the national selection as a televised event based on the vote of a jury or the public, but officials from the national broadcasting organizations can also make the decision themselves—which can reflect both a desire to make participating in the ESC less financially costly as well as an elitist mistrust of the public's tastes.

Besides serving as a platform for the promotion of national interests, another dimension of the ESC that makes it important for cultural diplomacy is its engagement with the cultural, economic, and political concepts of Europe. The contest is quintessentially European: almost all parts of Europe have been represented in it at some point,[1] and states have often used their participation to express the Europeanist aspirations or pro-Western orientations of their foreign policies.

The ESC was established in 1956 in order to promote cultural and technical cooperation among Western European countries that were then pursuing their first steps towards economic and political integration through the European Coal and Steel Community, Euratom, the European Economic Community (EEC), and the North Atlantic Treaty Organization (NATO). The EBU has historically been closer to the Council of Europe (CoE) than to the European Union (EU) in terms of its symbolism, scope and style, especially with its focus on internationalism rather than supranationalism; the CoE and the EBU were also the first organizations that, in the mid-1950s, pioneered the use of the circle of twelve stars as a European symbol (Fornäs 117-8, 136).

However, despite the fact that it has functioned as a metaphor for European integration, the ESC has never been organized by either the CoE, the EEC or the EU, or any other European political organization. Not all of the ESC's participants during the Cold War were members of such organizations, either: ESC participants then included Israel, communist Yugoslavia, and neutral states such as Austria, Switzerland, and Finland. However, what all of these states had in common was that they were not part of the Eastern Bloc, even if they were not fully part of the Western one. Even Yugoslavia, which was still a one-party communist state with restrictions on media freedom, participated in the ESC because its alliance with the Soviet Union had been severed in 1948. And it did so alongside the anti-communist dictatorships of Franco's Spain and Salazar's

---

[1] The exceptions have been Liechtenstein and Vatican City: the former because it has not had a national, public service broadcasting organization, and the latter because it has likely not considered the contest to be appropriate for its cultural diplomacy. National broadcasting organizations from states with limited international recognition, such as Kosovo, have also not been allowed to enter the EBU because it only admits national broadcasting organizations whose states are members of the ITU. That the ESC has been seen as a desirable instrument of cultural diplomacy by states seeking wider international recognition was underlined by Kosovo's Deputy Foreign Minister, Petrit Selimi, who said in 2012 that "nothing is more important than the Song Contest in nation-building" (qtd. in European Broadcasting Union, "Kosovo").

Portugal, states which subsequently transformed into liberal democracies in the mid-1970s (Vuletic 82-4). Since the end of the Cold War, the ESC has continued to include national broadcasting organizations from states with authoritarian governments where media freedom is heavily restricted, including, for example, Azerbaijan, Belarus, and Russia. Belarus is now the only state in Europe that is represented in the ESC but is not a member of the CoE.

For both the preparation of an entry and, if it is victorious, the hosting of the contest the following year, the national broadcasting organizations responsible for arranging ESC entries have drawn on various experts to determine how to present their states, including ones from the music industry, tourism organizations and advertising firms. There has sometimes even been direct government involvement as well. The choices of artists, composers, lyrics, genres, themes, choreography, and costumes have thus been loaded with political meanings. For example, while an entry not sung in a state's native language and without folk elements may appear non-national or international in style, it can also be symbolic of a desire for European integration or international cooperation in the right political context. This was the case when Estonia won the 2001 ESC with the English-language pop song "Everybody." The song was performed by a duo that included Dave Benton, a black Dutch resident of Estonia, and its transnational character correlated to the final phase of Estonia's EU accession negotiations before the state joined that organization in 2004 (Jordan 77-83).

Issues of minority rights have furthermore been highlighted at the ESC through the performances of the representatives of ethnic, linguistic, racial, religious, and sexual minorities. In 1998, the transsexual Israeli singer Dana International won with her song "Diva," which promoted an image of Israel as diverse, open-minded, and tolerant. The artist and performance challenged the common representations of Israel in the European media as a state at war with its neighbors, occupying the Palestinian territories and violating the human rights of its Arab citizens. Dana International's success also prompted the Israeli government to develop a new tactic in its international promotion: to present itself as a state that is tolerant of sexual minorities, which critics have dubbed "pinkwashing" because they claim that it diverts attention from the human rights situation of Israeli Arabs and Palestinians (Gluhovic 203). During its promotional events at the 2012 ESC in Baku, the Israel Broadcasting Authority distributed a leaflet published by the Israeli Ministry for Public Diplomacy and Diaspora Affairs which promoted Israel as a state that is inclusive of its sexual minorities ("The True Face of Israel").

Other states have also sought to promote an image of themselves as more liberal or tolerant by including representatives of different ethnic groups and linguistic traditions in their ESC entries. For example, in 1999 Germany sent a group of Turkish German artists to the ESC in Jerusalem where they performed the song "Reise nach Jerusalem—Kudüs'e Seyahat" (A Journey to Jerusalem) in English, German, Hebrew and Turkish (Bohlman 218). When the German city of Düsseldorf hosted the ESC in 2011, each entry was introduced by a postcard that featured people from the entry's state who were visiting or working in Germany. These short clips promoted Germany as a state welcoming of migrants at a time when its conservative government was criticized for being too dominant in determining the EU's financial policies during the debt crisis that struck the continent in 2008.

While some entries in the ESC have taken international peace as their main theme, wars have also been a constant backdrop in the contest, from the Cold War to the wars in the former USSR, former Yugoslavia, and the Middle East after 1989. The tensions deriving from such wars have also been played out on the ESC stage from as early as the mid-1970s, when Greece and Turkey first debuted in the contest but protested against each other's entries in light of the political tensions related to the Turkish invasion of Cyprus (see Şahin in this volume). Armenia and Azerbaijan have also not given each other points in the contest's voting and have made political gestures concerning their conflict over Nagorno-Karabakh, while the Azerbaijani authorities have even questioned Azerbaijani citizens who have voted for Armenia in the ESC (Adams, "How Armenia").

However, cultural diplomacy at the ESC need not only reflect existing political tensions, but can even suggest different ways for states to relate to one another. For example, despite the political tensions that continue to exist among the states of the former Yugoslavia, they still tend to support each other in their voting, as studies on bloc voting in the contest have demonstrated (Gatherer 76-7). This may appear discordant with the recent history of the wars that they fought between themselves in the 1990s and the political problems that have consequently remained. However, their voting patterns are explained by the cultural affinities that these states share, especially through languages and the common cultural industries that were developed in Yugoslavia, which still transcend national boundaries to define a common market for popular music. When Serbia and Montenegro returned to the ESC in 2004, after having been excluded from the contest because of international sanctions for their roles in the wars in the former Yugoslavia in the 1990s, they received twelve points from other states of the former Yugoslavia that they had been at war with in the 1990s. This led Serbia and Montenegro's former foreign minister, Goran Svilanović, to describe this mutual support at the ESC as a positive development in relations between these states (Petruseva).

PUBLIC DEMOCRACY IN PUBLIC DIPLOMACY

How the ESC is conceived of as public diplomacy by governments is, however, a more complicated question than the aforementioned examples suggest. When I write that a state did this or that at the ESC, it might appear that this implies the involvement of the respective national government. This is usually not the case, however, and it is mostly deceptive to see an ESC entry as somehow representative of a national government. As described earlier, the EBU is the main organizer of the ESC, and its active membership is comprised of national broadcasting organizations that have a public service aim. These organizations, mostly from liberal democracies, are meant to function independently of government interference. In this case, a government would also not have control over the entry chosen to represent its state, for this is a matter for the national broadcasting organization to decide. However, the ESC entry appears on stage under the name of its state, not that of its national broadcasting organization, so the first association is that the entry is, for example, an Austrian, British or Italian one, and not from ORF (Österreichischer Rundfunk, the Austrian Broadcasting Corporation), the BBC (the British Broadcasting Corporation), or RAI (Radiotelevisione Italiana, Italian Radio and Television). Already in the contest's first decade, the EBU decided that the entries should be performed under the names of states because it felt that using the names of the national broadcasting organizations was too cumbersome and unattractive (European Broadcasting Union, "Planning Group Meeting"). As ESC entries are presented under the names of states, they are therefore examples of cultural diplomacy even though they are usually not produced with interference by national governments.

How the national broadcasting organizations have organized and selected their states' entries has often been controversial, especially when they have been perceived as doing so without a democratic mandate. As the ESC entry represents a state and the national broadcasting organization is financed by public sources, such as licensing fees and taxes, many citizens would like to participate in the process of selecting the entry. This procedure is often done through some sort of televised national selection process in which viewers determine the winner. Such public participation is also invited by the genre: popular music is, after all, characterized by a popularity based on commercial success. In this way, the ESC entry can be a rare example of cultural diplomacy that is the direct result of a national, democratic process in which the public directly selects a state representative. This is indeed an unusual phenomenon, for artists who represent their states in international competitions are usually not chosen by the public. Conversely, athletes who represent their states in international sports competitions like the Olympic Games or the FIFA World Cup do not, for example, have to face a public vote, but instead qualify on the basis of their talents measured by quantifiable criteria. However, in other international mega events in which the national selection is more subjective, such as for the Venice Art Biennale, cultural ministries or professional commissions usually conduct the selection process. And when it comes to examples of cultural diplomacy that are part of a government's foreign policy strategy, it is the democratically-mandated representatives of the government rather than the public who decide.

However, there are also cases in which the national broadcasting organization decides to select the entry for the ESC itself, with a technocratic committee made up of officials from the national broadcasting organization or experts from the popular music industry, and without input from the public. In recent years, national broadcasting organizations that have chosen to select their entries in this way have usually justified it by claiming that their television stations have needed to cut back on costs in light of the Great Recession, and that one of the ways to do so has been to cut down on the budget for the ESC. In many states, this has usually not been controversial, especially if the ESC has not been so domestically popular. National broadcasting organizations might also intervene if public tastes are considered too parochial to choose an internationally competitive entry:[2] ironically, in order to be successful and celebrated by national pride, an ESC entry should never be too national. However, the officials from national broadcasting organizations also have their own interests, predilections, and preferences. In some cases, public protests against such internal selections have compelled national broadcasting organizations to reverse their decisions: in

---

2   These debates also influenced the EBU's decision from 2009 to have mixed voting in the contest's semi-finals and final. The national public voting was seen as biased towards geographically neighbouring states and ones with shared cultural and political affinities, especially in states of East and Southeast Europe, although this has historically also been a phenomenon among Nordic states as well. The biggest five financial contributors to the contest, France, Germany, Italy, Spain and the United Kingdom, have since 2000 also been given a direct entry into the final, an issue that has prompted Turkey's national broadcasting organisation to withdrew from the ESC since 2013, considering that Turkey has a larger population than all of these states except Germany (Vuletic 156-60).

Ukraine, for example, the national broadcasting organization accordingly changed its internal selection of Vasyl Lazarovych for the 2010 ESC, with Alyosha subsequently winning a national selection that was based on jury and public voting. In a similar vein, the ARD (Arbeitsgemeinschaft der öffentlich-rechtlichen Rundfunkanstalten der Bundesrepublik Deutschland, Consortium of Public Broadcasters of the Federal Republic of Germany) had to retract its internal selection of Xavier Naidoo for the 2016 ESC since the popular singer was widely criticized for his right-wing political views (Lehming).

There was also criticism in Austria of ORF's internal selection of the bearded drag queen Conchita Wurst as the state's ESC representative in 2014 because of opposition to Wurst's gender presentation, with *Facebook* petitions opposing her selection and participation in the contest. In addition to objecting to her transvestism, such critics were also indignant that Wurst had not been selected by the Austrian public—to which the ORF responded that she had come second in a public vote in the national selection two years before and therefore had a democratic mandate. In her preparations for the ESC, Wurst was marketed as a symbol of diversity and tolerance, which aided Austria's international image that has often been tainted by far-right political figures. As a result, she was significant for Austria's cultural diplomacy even though she was not chosen by the government or the public, but rather by a group of liberal television officials who sought to present a more progressive national image. In the end, Wurst went on to win the ESC and her victory was well-received in Austria, with her domestic critics being marginalized: she was even received by the Austrian Chancellor, Werner Faymann, and Minister of Arts and Culture, Josef Ostermayer, upon her return to Vienna following her ESC win (Austrian Federal Chancellery). This was not, however, the first time that ORF internally selected an ESC entry with political connotations. Before the election of Kurt Waldheim as Austrian President in 1986, amidst controversy that he had concealed details about his role in the German army in the World War II, ORF sent an Austrian-Israeli singer, Timna Brauer, to the ESC. And when the far-right and anti-immigrant Austrian Freedom Party (Freiheitliche Partei Österreichs, FPÖ), led by Jörg Haider, joined the national coalition government in 2000, which prompted diplomatic sanctions against Austria by other EU member states, the ORF sent the Rounder Girls, a multiracial group composed of one white Austrian woman and two black female immigrants from the UK and the US, to sing a Motown-inspired song in English (Gura 68-70). In this way, the selection of an ESC entry can also play out over a domestic political battleground, as different political forces struggle to influence how their state—and their political programs—will be portrayed in the international arena.

The example of Wurst also demonstrated how governments in liberal democracies have tended not to take an interest in appropriating the ESC in their public diplomacy until their state has won. In authoritarian states that exercise control over the national media, the connection between the ESC and the government's public diplomacy is more direct. In Azerbaijan, for instance, participation in the ESC has been part of the government's broader campaign of public diplomacy in Europe, which has also included the "caviar diplomacy" of hosting and gifting officials from other European states and organizations. When it came to hosting the ESC in Baku in 2012, the First Lady, Mehrabin Aliyeva, was the head of the organizing committee while her son-in-law, Emin Agalarov, performed the interval act in the final. The 2012 ESC was the most expensive ever staged, after the one in Moscow of 2009, which again highlighted the importance that the Azerbaijani and Russian governments placed on the ESC for crafting their public image to international audiences (Adams, "Selling Azerbaijan"), especially as they sought to use it as a springboard for the hosting of other international mega events, such as the Olympic Games and the FIFA World Cup. European politicians urged the government of President Ilham Aliyev to also use Baku's hosting of the ESC to facilitate the state's democratization and improve its human rights record. When she presented Germany's voting results in the 2012 ESC, the German actress and comedian Anke Engelke emphasized that "it is good to be able to vote," thereby implicitly supporting the democratization of Azerbaijan. However, the legacy of the ESC has not left a lasting impact in this regard. Azerbaijan's media were still classified as "not free" by the human rights organization Freedom House in the years immediately following the 2012 ESC, and the state's international ranking regarding press freedom even worsened during that time (Freedom House 10). On the other hand, politicians from states that have been criticized by west European governments and organizations for their authoritarian systems have leveraged the same kind of criticism against the organization of the ESC. The president of Belarus, Aleksandar Lukashenko, for instance, attacked the voting in the ESC for being rigged and biased against Belarus—just as he had been criticized for not allowing free and fair elections in Belarus (BelTA).

The governments of most liberal democratic states represented in the contest, however, refrain from criticizing the ESC. In these states, governments are not meant to interfere with the operations of the national broadcasting organizations, meaning that they usually also stay out of the decision-making process for an ESC entry. In states in which the ESC is temporarily less popular, governments may also deliberately distance themselves from the contest to show that they are in touch with public opinion as well as to demonstrate that they are not wasting attention, funds, and time on such "frivolous" matters. However, governments in liberal democratic states usually do get involved in the ESC once their national entries have won. The first reason for this is that a victory is usually well-received in the winning state, even in one that was, until that point, not renowned for being enthusiastic about the contest, such as in Austria until Wurst's win in 2014. In this way, governments also try to capitalize on public euphoria. The second reason is that the hosting of the ESC requires significant financial resources that the national broadcasting organizations may not be able to provide without assistance from public or private sources. In this case, governments may step in to assist with the financial costs, and they would justify this intervention by claiming that it is in the national interest of public diplomacy to ensure that such a prominent international event is properly staged, as occurred in Estonia and Latvia when they hosted the ESC in 2002 and 2003, respectively (Jordan 85-8). A final reason why governments may get involved in hosting the ESC concerns local officials that lobby for their city to host the contest. Different cities in the host state usually present bids to stage the contest the following year, and it is at this point that local governments vie to promote their cities as potential ESC hosts—and as potential agents of their state's public diplomacy.

CONCLUSION

As a unique example of direct democratic involvement in shaping cultural and public diplomacy, the ESC has highlighted the tensions that exist between public and elite views of how a state should be represented. The national denomination of an ESC entry is deceiving, as the decision-makers behind it can lack broader political or public legitimacy. On the one hand, the ESC has been seen by different types of governments as a way to improve their own international images, especially in the case of authoritarian, dictatorial and/or one-party regimes, such as in Azerbaijan and Belarus in recent times or Greece, Portugal, Spain and Yugoslavia during the Cold War. On the other hand, it has been a way for other states to promote themselves as tolerant of ethnic, religious, gender, sexual, and migrant minorities. In many cases, the forging of such an image for a state has been the work of the national broadcasting organizations charged with organizing and selecting entries, although there has been more government involvement in states in which the national broadcasting organization has been more controlled by the government.

However, governments have generally become more involved in the ESC after their state has won the contest and plans need to be made for hosting the event the following year. Such victories usually appeal to the patriotic pride of citizens, even in states in which the contest was supposedly not so popular until then, as the recent case of Austria demonstrates. In addition, the hosting of the contest is regarded as an opportunity that can bring benefits for the international promotion of the state as well as the host city and region. In this regard, the ESC's significance for public diplomacy also involves different segments of a state's political structure, from national to local governments, as well as different public and private interests, from the national broadcasting organization to the commercial ambitions of the winning artists.

In the end, though, what is engrained in public opinion is that state X won the ESC in year Y because entries in the contest are always presented under the names of states. And this is why the significance of the ESC in cultural and public diplomacy is paradoxical: because it is always a state that is seen as the winner of the contest, even if the state itself has often done little to win it.

WORKS CITED

Adams, William Lee. "How Armenia and Azerbaijan Wage War Through Eurovision." *Time*, 11 Mar. 2012. Web. 30 Mar. 2018. <http://world.time.com/2012/03/11/how-armenia-and-azerbaijan-wage-war-through-eurovision/>.

---. "Selling Azerbaijan." *Time*, 14 May 2012. Web. 30 Mar. 2018. <http://content.time.com/time/magazine/article/0,9171,2113835,00.html>.

Austrian Federal Chancellery. "Bundeskanzler Faymann dankt Conchita: 'Ein Sieg für Toleranz, Liebe und Frieden.'" *Bundeskanzleramt Österreich* 18 May 2014. Web. 30 Mar. 2018. <http://www.oesta.gv.at/site/cob__55625/currentpage__0/6592/default.aspx.>.

BelTA. "Lukashenko: Eurovision is Totally Biased." *Belarusian Telegraph Agency*, 30 Apr. 2013. Web. 30 Mar. 2018. <http://eng.belta.by/president/view/lukashenko-eurovision-is-totally-biased-14871-2013>.

Bohlman, Philip V. *Focus: Music, Nationalism, and the Making of the New Europe*. 2nd ed. New York and Abingdon, Oxfordshire: Routledge, 2011. Print.

Eugster, Ernest. *Television Programming Across National Boundaries: The EBU and OIRT Experience*. Dedham, MA: Artech House, 1983. Print.

European Broadcasting Union. "Kosovo Seeks Full EBU Membership and Song Contest Slot." *EBU News*, 30 Mar. 2012. Web. 30 Mar. 2018. <https://www.ebu.ch/contents/news/2012/03/kosovo-seeks-full-ebu-membership.html>.

---. "Planning Group Meeting of Variety Programme Experts." (Geneva, 4 June 1964), 2. European Broadcasting Union Archives, Concours Eurovision de la chanson, Décisions 1. Print.

Fornäs, Johan. *Signifying Europe*. Bristol and Chicago: Intellect, 2012. Print.

Freedom House. *Freedom of the Press 2014*. Freedom House: New York and Washington DC, 2014. Print.

Gatherer, Derek. "Voting in Eurovision: Shared Tastes or Cultural Epidemic?" *Empirical Text and Culture Research* 3.1 (2007): 72-84. Print.

Gluhovic, Milija. "Sing for Democracy: Human Rights and Sexuality Discourse in the Eurovision Song Contest." *Performing the 'New' Europe: Identities, Feelings, and Politics in the Eurovision Song Contest*. Ed. Karen Fricker and Milija Gluhovic. Basingstoke, Hampshire, and New York: Palgrave Macmillan, 2013: 194-217. Print.

Gura, Caitlin. "Österreichs Abschneiden beim Eurovision Song Contest zwischen 2000 und 2013: Und dessen Auswirkung auf die österreichische Identität." *Eurovision Song Contest: Eine kleine Geschichte zwischen Körper, Geschlecht und Nation*. Ed. Christine Ehardt, Georg Vogt, and Florian Wagner. Vienna: Zaglossus, 2015: 65-90. Print.

Israeli Ministry of Public Diplomacy and Diaspora Affairs. *The True Face of Israel*. Jerusalem: Israeli Ministry of Public Diplomacy and Diaspora Affairs, 2012. Print.

Jordan, Paul. *The Modern Fairy Tale: Nation Branding, National Identity and the Eurovision Song Contest in Estonia*. Tartu: U of Tartu P, 2014. Print.

Kim, Hwajung. "Bridging the Theoretical Gap Between Public Diplomacy and Cultural Diplomacy." *The Korean Journal of International Studies* 15.2 (2017): 293-326. Print.

Lehming, Malte. "Eurovision Song Contest: Protest und Vorurteil." *Der Tagesspiegel*, 1 Dec. 2015. Web. 30 Mar. 2018. https://www.tagesspiegel.de/kultur/der-fall-xavier-naidoo-eurovision-song-contest-protest-und-vorurteil/12659116.html>.

Petruseva, Ana. "Old Foes Serenade Serbia in Istanbul." *Balkan Crisis Report* 499. 21 Febr. 2005. Web. 30 Mar. 2018. <https://iwpr.net/global-voices/old-foes-serenade-serbia-istanbul>.

Vuletic, Dean. *Postwar Europe and the Eurovision Song Contest*. London and New York: Bloomsbury Academic, 2018. Print.

List of Contributors

Ball III, James R., is Assistant Professor and Director of Undergraduate Studies at the Department of Performance Studies at Texas A&M University. He studies the politics of performance and the performance of politics, analyzing both the theatrical structures that underwrite public political events and aesthetic performances that intervene in political processes. His forthcoming book, *Theatre of State: A Dramaturgy of the United Nations*, considers the relationship between theatre and the United Nations and International Criminal Court. Ball's articles have been published in *Brecht Yearbook*, *e-Misférica*, and *TDR: The Drama Review*; he earned his PhD from NYU in 2012.

Bayles, Martha, is a columnist for *The American Interest* and the film and TV critic for the *Claremont Review of Books*. Her recent book, *Through a Screen Darkly: Popular Culture, Public Diplomacy, and America's Image Abroad* was described by *American Diplomacy* as "the freshest and most original treatment of US Public Diplomacy in many years." Her current work focuses on the threats to independent journalism around the world, and the importance of "voluntary restraint" in the American tradition of free speech. She is a fellow at the Institute for Advanced Studies in Culture at the University of Virginia, and since 2003 has taught humanities at Boston College.

Brown, Nicholas Alexander, is a conductor, musicologist, and producer based in Washington DC. He is the director of special productions and initiatives at Washington Performing Arts, and previously was a program specialist and a music specialist in the Library of Congress Music Division. He is the music director of The Irving Fine Society and president of the DC Library Association. Brown was a White House intern (Obama Administration) and is a contributor to the *Oxford Encyclopedia of the Bible and the Arts*. He holds a M. Mus in Musicology from King's College London, a MS in Library and Information Science at the Catholic University of America, and a BA in Music and History from Brandeis University.

Dunkel, Mario, is a *Juniorprofessor* (assistant professor) of music education at the Music Department of the Carl von Ossietzky University of Oldenburg. He holds a PhD in American studies from TU Dortmund University. His main research areas are music and politics, music and diplomacy, the history and practice of jazz, as well as transcultural music pedagogy. His articles have been published in *American Music*, the *European Journal of Musicology*, *Popular Music and Society*, and other journals. He is the principal investigator of the European research project "Popular Music as a Medium for the Mainstreaming of Populist Ideologies in Europe" (2019-2022, funded by the Volkswagen Foundation).

Feustle, Maristella, is the Music Special Collections Librarian at the University of North Texas. She oversees the processing and curation of over 120 special and archival collections in the UNT Music Library, including the personal archives of Willis Conover. She is a past chair of the Music Library Association's Preservation Committee, and a current member of the Society of American Archivists' Technical Subcommittee on *Describing Archives: A Content Standard*. She has presented on Willis Conover in Germany, Poland, Hungary, and the US, and is active as a jazz guitarist in the Dallas/Fort Worth area of Texas.

Ignácz, Ádám, is a musicologist. He was enrolled in the Philosophy Doctoral School of Eötvös Loránd University, Budapest, where he received his PhD in 2013. He has edited two volumes on the history of twentieth century Hungarian popular music and he has published articles in local and international journals and books on Russian music and musical life of socialist Hungary. Since 2013, he has worked as a research fellow for the Archives for Twentieth- and Twenty-First-Century Hungarian Music, Institute of Musicology, Hungarian Academy of Sciences. Since 2017, Ignácz has been editor-in-chief at the Hungarian music publishing house Rózsavölgyi & Co.

Kube, Sven, is a doctoral candidate in the Atlantic History PhD program at Florida International University. Kube investigates cultural industries and culture markets in their wider social, political, and ideological contexts. His dissertation reconstructs the history of the music industry in the GDR and investigates relations between VEB Deutsche Schallplatten and record companies in capitalist countries during the Cold War era. Sven completed a Master's program in American Studies at Dresden University of Technology. Research for his Master's thesis on Canadian Content regulations was funded by the Canadian government grant.

Mazzola, Alessandro, holds a PhD in Social and Political Science from the University of Liège, where he is a post-doc Research Associate at the Centre for Ethnic and Migration Studies (CEDEM). Alessandro's areas of expertise are the cultural production of minorities, the role of culture in social integration, political representation and participation with a focus on ethnic and immigrant minorities. His current research project focuses on the analysis of public opinion towards refugees and asylum seekers in Belgium and Europe.

Morales Tamaral, José Manuel, holds an MA in Late Modern and Contemporary History from the Complutense University of Madrid. His dissertation combines two research fields: diplomatic networks between Germany and Spain during the German Empire (1871-1918) and the origins of public diplomacy and cultural and press propaganda in Spain during the interwar period (1918-1936). His research interests include transnational unofficial actors, diasporic networks, cultural relations, and informal diplomacy.

Nathaus, Klaus, is a social historian and Associate Professor in Western contemporary history at the University of Oslo. In recent years, he has worked primarily on the production and consumption of popular music in Britain, West Germany and the United States in the twentieth century.

Nitzsche, Sina A., is the founder of the European Hip-Hop Studies Network. She teaches American Studies at the TU Dortmund University and at the Ruhr University Bochum. She co-edited *Hip-Hop in Europe: Cultural Identities and Transnational Flows*, *Breaking the Panel! Comics as a Medium*, and her forthcoming monography explores The Bronx in American popular culture. Her research interests include hip-hop studies, popular cultures, urban studies and media studies. This book project is inspired by, builds on, and expands her research at the Goethe Institutes New York City, Washington DC, and Bangkok as well as at the Austrian Embassy Bangkok.

Ritter, Rüdiger, studied Eastern European History, Musicology and Philosophy in Mainz, Dijon, Cologne, Volgograd and Kraków. He participated in several research projects on music, culture and politics in Eastern Central Europe in the ninetieth and twentieth centuries, such as "Collective Identity and History in Post-Socialist Discourses: Belarus, Lithuania, Poland, Ukraine" (University of Bremen), "Opposition by Cultural Transfer: Jazz in the Eastern Bloc" (Freie Universität Berlin), "Discourses on Europe in Polish *Drugi Obieg* Periodicals" (Research Unit Eastern Europe, Bremen) as well as "Productive Misunderstandings: The Reception of Willis Conover's Radio Broadcast *Music USA—Jazz Hour* in the Former Eastern Bloc."

Şahin, Nevin, holds a PhD in Sociology. Her research interests include sociology of music, migration and transnationality, historical musicology, sociology of religion and qualitative methodology. She conducted research among German-Turkish migrant women in Germany, Bulgarian-Turkish migrants in İstanbul, Mevlevi music circles, and she delivered presentations at conferences on public diplomacy, cosmopolitanism, global sociology, and Turkish and Greek music traditions. Her article "'Homeland' in 'Dreamland'? Space and Identity in *Göçmen Konutları*" was published in the edited book *Contemporary Turkey at a Glance: Interdisciplinary Perspectives on Local and Translocal Dynamics*.

Salois, Kendra, is an Assistant Professor of Ethnomusicology at American University in Washington DC. Her work focuses on the ethics, aesthetics, and political economy of transcultural encounters in hip-hop and North African popular musics. Her work appears in *Anthropological Quarterly*, the *Journal of Popular Music Studies*, and the Journal of World Popular Music, as well as the edited volumes *Music and Diplomacy from the Early Modern Era to the Present and Islam and Popular Culture*. Her book project explores the theories of citizenship advanced by Moroccan hip-hop artists, arguing the genre is central to Morocco's neoliberal transition.

Sanz Díaz, Carlos, is a Professor of Contemporary History at the Complutense University of Madrid. His recent publications include *Historia de las Relaciones Internacionales* and *La Guerra Fría (1947-1991)* (forthcoming). He is also co-editor of *La Gran Guerra en la España de Alfonso XIII* (forthcoming) and of *Das 'Gastarbeiter'-System nach dem Zweiten Weltkrieg: Westdeutschland und Europa*. His research focuses on Spanish foreign policy, scientific and cultural diplomacy, Spanish-German relations in the twentieth century, and transnational migrations since 1945.

Vuletic, Dean, is a historian of contemporary Europe who is based in the Department of East European History at the University of Vienna. He is the author of *Postwar Europe and the Eurovision Song Contest*, the first-ever scholarly monograph on the history of the Eurovision Song Contest, which he produced under a Marie Skłodowska-Curie Fellowship. He also regularly comments on the Eurovision Song Contest in international media. As a Lise Meitner Fellow, Vuletic currently leads the project "Intervision: Popular Music and Politics in Eastern Europe." He earned his PhD from Columbia University.

zur Nieden, Gesa, is a *Juniorprofessor* of Musicology at the Johannes Gutenberg University, Mainz. After completing her German and French doctoral studies on the Théâtre du Châtelet in Paris, she worked for the German Historical Institute in Rome. She was the German director of the ANR/DFG project "MUSICI" (2010-13) and of the HERA project "MusMig" (2013-16). Since 2018, she has been a leader of the DFG/NCN project "Pasticcio." Her research focuses mainly on music and mobility in early modern Europe and on ethnographical research on the contemporary reception of Richard Wagner and his music.

Index

11 September attacks, 66, 234
50 Cent, 167

a cappella, 75, 242, 264-5
ABBA, 70, 205, 265
abject, 23, 269-71, 273
affect, 23, 54, 233-4, 238-9, 241-2, 243, 249-50, 255, 258-9, 262, 264, 268-71
Afghanistan, 178, 181, 185, 189
Africa, 55, 109, 164-7
African American, 12-4, 36, 39, 41, 55, 108-9, 156, 164-7, 181, 204
Al Qaeda, 159
Allgemeine Musikalische Zeitung (AMZ), 33, 221
Amaya, Carmen, 213
American Society of Composers, Authors and Publishers (ASCAP), 39
Americanization, 30
Amiga, 203-206
Andalusia, 210-4, 219, 225, 291
Anglo-American, 36, 42, 198, 203
appropriation, 18-9, 30, 44, 93, 239, 302
Arab Middle East, 71, 166-7, 264, 305
Arab Spring, 167

arabesque, 79, 81
Armenia, 78, 306
Armstrong, Louis, 120, 156, 204
Asia, 21, 160, 169, 269, 293
Australia, 9
Austria, 177, 204, 265, 289, 304, 307, 309-12
Ayata, Imran, 284, 287-9
Azerbaijan, 305-6, 310-1

Balkans, 11
Ball III, James R., 23, 255-76
ballet, 181, 212, 216, 218, 222-5
ballet español, 216
Bangladesh, 168, 237, 248
Bayles, Martha, 12, 20-1, 43, 95, 155-73, 234-5, 237, 265
beat-boxing, 266
Beatles, the, 42, 178, 186, 204, 206, 216
beatmaker, 22, 233, 237, 248
bebop, 119, 121
Belarus, 98, 305, 310-1
Belgium, 18, 49-67, 71, 220, 278
Benton, Dave, 305
Berlin Wall, 19, 21, 156-7, 283
Bhutan, 258
bluegrass, 11, 169

322 | Index

blues, 38, 197, 203
Boko Haram, 159
Bosnia-Herzegovina, 168, 237, 266-9, 272
Brown, James, 178
Brown, Jim, 191
Brown, John, 278-9, 295
Brown, Nicholas Alexander, 21, 175-96
Brubeck, Dave, 100, 156, 236
Bulgaria, 147

cafés cantantes, 213, 225
Canada, 222, 266
canción española, 213
Carey, Mariah, 21, 163
Caribbean, 165-6
Cash, Johnny, 169, 206
Castro, Fidel, 179
Catholicism, 177, 210-3
Charles, Ray, 178
China, 158-62, 168
Christianity, 71, 169, 177, 184, 266
Chulaki, Michail, 136, 138-40, 148
Civil Rights Movement, 12-3, 108-9
classical music, 18, 31, 37-45, 97, 138-9, 143, 176-8, 198, 201-6, 212, 219, 222-5, 279
Columbia Records, 122, 184, 186, 191
communism, 20, 98, 103, 123, 133-6, 139, 144-8, 155-7, 179-85, 188-91, 197-8, 201, 204-7, 211, 222, 304
Communist Party of the Soviet Union (CPSU), 103, 133-6, 183-4, 189-90
Conover, Willis Clark, 19-20, 98, 100, 103-8, 117-31, 156, 164, 168
cosmopolitanism, 64, 133, 142, 144-5, 265-6
country music, 11, 21, 38, 168-9
Cream, 206

Cuba, 9, 177-80, 191
cultural Cold War, 13
cultural transfer, 30, 280, 291, 295
culturalization, 50
Cyprus, 75, 306
Czech Republic, 105, 147, 156-7, 200

dance music, 20, 38-40, 140-7, 203, 294
deejaying, 22, 165, 233, 237, 242-3, 246
democracy, 11, 24, 41-2, 53, 55-6, 95-101, 108-10, 127, 143, 155-62, 168-71, 178, 189, 197-8, 221, 236, 279, 302, 305-11
Denmark, 123
dervish, 16, 18, 69-87
Deutsche Schallplatten, 21, 199, 202, 206, 316
dictatorship, 163, 210-1, 215-8, 223-5, 304, 311
diplomacy:
  algorithmic, 15
  blue-collar, 21, 175-195
  Cold War, 19, 233, 236
  country music, 168-9
  cultural, 11-3, 19, 21, 49-57, 60, 64-6, 69, 86, 95, 184, 197-8, 211, 214, 216, 221, 234, 238-9, 294, 301-9
  digital, 15
  flamenco, 22, 211, 214, 217, 220, 224-6
  francoist, 211, 224
  jazz, 12-4, 20, 95, 98, 118, 126
  hip-hop, 22-3, 167-8, 233-4, 238, 241
  mediated, 15
  me-first, 15

P2P, 19, 22-3, 233-4, 250, 278, 295
public, 9-26, 69, 79, 95-7, 101-5, 117-9, 124, 138-9, 148, 155-6, 158, 160, 166-70, 209-10, 225, 235-40, 250, 269, 272-3, 277-82, 286-7, 290, 294-5, 301-7, 310-2
popular music, 12, 17, 43, 294
soft, 180
sound, 10, 37, 95
Twitter, 15
undiplomatic, 15
discrimination, 108-9, 156, 250, 281-2
Dunkel, Mario, 9-28, 40-1, 188, 244, 251, 296
Dvořák, Antonín, 34, 36

Eastern Bloc, 19, 95-110, 188, 197-9, 206, 222, 303-4
Eastern Europe, see Europe
Ebstein, Katja, 70
education, 16, 20, 23, 33-4, 51, 56-7, 60-2, 66, 98, 102, 105, 136-8, 147-9, 158, 162, 212, 215-7, 235-7, 248, 259, 262, 278, 283
Egypt, 180
El Salvador, 168, 240
electronic music, 278, 295
Ellington, Duke, 119-21, 156, 204
empathy, 22-3, 179, 233-4, 237-9, 241, 243, 249-50, 255, 272
England, 31, 34-5, 59
Erdoğan, Recep Tayyip, 76, 80
Erener, Sertab, 18, 69, 71-5, 77, 82, 84, 86
eroticism, 139, 164
Eschen, Penny M. von, 10-3, 30, 40, 97, 108, 154-5, 169, 193, 229-30
Estonia, 103, 125, 305, 311
Eterna, 202

ethnicity, 23, 38-40, 50, 61, 64-6, 72, 89, 164, 211, 241, 279, 286-91, 294-5, 305, 311
Europe:
    Eastern, 38, 95-110, 118, 124, 126, 133-4, 138, 147, 157, 166, 172, 188, 197-9, 206, 222, 225, 264, 266, 279, 303-4
    Southeastern, 279, 308
    Southern, 279
    Western, 30, 71, 204, 287, 304, 310
Eurovision Song Contest (ESC), 11-2, 18, 23-4, 69-77, 81-7, 301-12

Facebook, 168, 249, 309
fake news, 15
Fantastischen Vier, die, 286
festivals:
    Festival de Benidorm, 216
    Festivales de España, 214-7
    Fourth International Dance Festival, 224
    German-Spanish Festival, 212
    Havana Jam, 179-80
    International Festival of Santander, 214
    International Music and Dance Festival Granada, 212
    jazz festivals, 41, 101, 103-6, 110, 117-129
    July Fourth Disarmament Festival, 181-2
    Konya Festival, 75, 84
    Opera XXI, 59
    pan-European, 147
    protestival, 80
    Şeb-i-Arus Festival, 76, 83
    Talinn Jazz Festival, 20, 103, 117-29

World Festival of Youth and
  Students, 142, 146
Feustle, Maristella, 19, 117-29
Finland, 304
flamenco, 16, 22, 209-26
flamencoism, 22, 209-10
Flanders, 18, 49-66
folk, 13, 23, 36, 38, 73, 102, 134, 140-6, 157, 164, 188, 198, 203-4, 211-3, 222-4, 265, 290-1, 294-5, 305
folklore, 38, 211-3, 222, 291, 294
Fosler-Lussier, Danielle, 9-11, 13, 17-9, 30, 95, 97-8, 106, 110, 123, 183, 193, 229, 231-2
foxtrot, 146
Fraga, Manuel, 209, 215, 219-22
France, 9, 23, 59, 167, 278, 283, 308
Franco, Francisco, 22, 209-25, 304
freedom, 22-3, 96-101, 108-10, 123, 127, 148, 155-68, 181, 188-90, 199, 218, 246, 250, 304-5, 309-10
Fresh Familee, 280
Frisch, Max, 288

Galileo Music, 287
Gastarbeiter (guest workers), 23, 277-300
gender, 73-5, 81, 212, 241, 289, 292, 309, 311
Georgia, 175, 188
Germany, 21-2, 31-6, 40-4, 59, 95, 180, 197-206, 217-21, 278-283, 286-8, 291-5, 306-10
Gienow-Hecht, Jessica C. E., 10, 13, 30, 35-7, 69, 86, 95, 97, 110, 207
Gillespie, Dizzy, 11, 40, 120, 156-7
Goebbels, Joseph, 95
Goethe-Institut, 23, 33, 42, 278, 282-7, 290, 294

Goodman, Benny, 123, 126, 156
Great Britain, 197, 202, 206
Greece, 75, 281, 306, 311
Grieg, Edvard, 34
Guatemala, 30, 123

Hancock, Herbie, 9, 15-6
harmony, 17, 167, 265, 272
Heimatlieder aus Deutschland, 278, 287, 290-5
Hendrix, Jimi, 205
Herman, Woody, 119
hip-hop, see also rap, 11-3, 16, 21-3, 30, 164-8, 233-50, 277-9, 285, 301
Hitler, Adolf, 156
Holiday, Billie, 120, 221
Hollywood, 30, 158, 160, 219
Honduras, 168, 240
Houston, Whitney, 205
Hungary, 20, 104, 108, 123, 133-49, 265

identity, 11, 21-2, 24, 37-8, 49, 55, 60-6, 69, 83-6, 203, 210-3, 220, 225, 241, 269-70, 280-2, 286-7, 291, 295
ideology, 19, 21, 37, 42, 50, 53-6, 61, 64, 83-4, 96-7, 107-10, 118, 133, 136, 143-4, 146, 148, 178, 180, 185, 197, 203, 205, 217, 221, 224, 233, 257-8, 269, 272
Ignácz, Ádám, 12, 20, 133-53
immigration, see migration
imperialism, 18, 30, 44
India, 165, 168, 237, 242, 293
Indonesia, 167
infiltration, 19-20, 142, 147, 223, 261, 288
Instagram, 248

Index | 325

integration, 23, 34, 37, 51-2, 55, 117, 280-6
International Jazz Day (UNESCO), 9, 12-7
International, Dana, 305
Iran, 178
Islam, 77, 159-60, 163
Islamic State of Iraq and Syria (ISIS), 159
Islamist 159, 168
Israel, 180, 264, 304-5, 309
Italy, 281, 292, 308

Jackson, Michael, 164-5, 205
Japan, 9, 202
Jay-Z, 167
jazz, 5, 9, 11-7, 19-21, 23-6, 30-1, 37, 39-48, 57, 95-131, 134, 140-6, 151, 156-7, 160, 164, 168, 171-2, 181, 188, 193-4, 197, 201, 203, 204, 207-8, 233-6, 242, 251-2, 316, 318
jihad, 159, 170-1
Joel, Billy, 175-96
journalism, 31, 34, 37, 315
Jürgens, Udo, 289

K'naan, 266
Karaca, Cem, 288, 289
Karaoke Kalk, 287
Katz, Mark, 238, 240-2, 247, 250-1
Kazakhstan, 163
Kennedy, John F., 117, 185
Kenton, Stan, 119-20
Khrennikov, Tikhon, 144
Korea, 159
Krautrock, 42-3, 48
Kremlin, 134, 190
Kube, Sven, 6, 21, 197, 316
Kullukcu, Bülent, 287-8

Lazarovych, Vasyl, 309
Lennon, John, 9, 75, 195, 266
liberty, 155, 158, 160, 168
Libya, 163
Lil Wayne, 167
Lincoln, Abraham, 169, 171
Lopez, Jennifer, 163

Madonna, 73-4, 205
Mariemma, 209, 218-21
mass media, 30
Mazzola, Alessandro, 18, 49, 317
Middle East, 11, 160, 166-7, 171, 213, 306
migration, 23, 40, 111, 218, 221, 278-80, 282-3, 287, 289, 291, 294-6, 300, 317-8
Milyutin, Jury, 138-9, 146, 148,
modernism, 40, 121
Molchanov, Kirill, 138, 144-5, 148
Mongolia, 161, 167
Montenegro, 168, 237, 301, 306
Morales Tamaral, José Manuel, 16, 22, 209, 215, 317
Morocco, 26, 167, 252, 291, 318
MTV, 43, 165, 167
musicking, 23, 120, 130, 255-7, 270, 274
Muslim, 24, 71, 78, 166-7, 169, 237, 266-7

Naidoo, Xavier, 309
Nashville, TN, 168-9
Nathaus, Klaus, 17-8, 29, 40, 47, 66, 317
National Socialism, 107

nationalism, 15, 32, 34-5, 45, 50, 54-6, 62, 64-5, 70-1, 87, 111, 114, 178, 265, 304, 312
Nazi Germany, 95
Neo-Nazism, 179
Netherlands, the, 25, 55, 167, 202
Next Level, 170, 233-4, 236-7, 243, 247-52
Nieden, Gesa zur, 13, 16, 23, 277, 299, 319
nineteenth century, 32, 34, 40, 213, 255
Nitzsche, Sina A., 9, 252, 282, 296, 298-9, 317
North Africa, 167, 318
Norway, 34, 123

Obama, Barack, 9, 12, 179, 236, 315
Olympic Games, 162, 178
opera, 176, 197-9, 201-3, 209, 212-3, 217-8, 259, 269-70, 303-5, 310
óperas flamencas, 213
operetta, 39, 134, 146, 203
orientalism, 96, 213
Ottoman Empire, 83-4

Pakistan, 167
Parker, Charlie, 119
participation, 11-3, 22-3, 31, 35, 69-70, 73, 117, 185, 231, 241, 256, 261-2, 266, 271, 294-5, 302-10
Peru, 29-30, 44, 225, 229
Piquer, Carlos Robles, 215-6, 219-22
Poland, 96-7, 100-1, 103-6, 108-9, 112-3, 115, 123-4, 137, 147, 230, 316, 318
Police, the, 216
polka, 144
pop music, 12, 59, 77, 100, 134, 165-6, 189, 198, 203, 206

popular music studies, 10, 318
pornography, 159, 164
Portugal, 305, 311
Powell, Bud, 37, 119
Prague Spring, 104, 157
Presley, Elvis, 178, 205
program music, 117, 145
promotion, 14, 20, 23, 30, 38, 41, 57, 64, 97-8, 106, 119, 122, 136, 153, 181-2, 189, 212, 222, 224, 258, 260, 266, 279, 282-3, 302, 304-5, 312
propaganda, 10, 19, 24, 95-8, 124, 136, 157, 159-60, 162, 180-1, 188-90, 198, 210-11, 214, 218, 220, 317
punk, 11, 47
Putin, Vladimir, 9, 16, 159, 170
Python, Monty, 265

Queen, 206
queer, 239

R&B, 163, 178
race, 15, 108-9, 185, 250
racism, 55, 109, 156, 236, 264
radicalization, 166
rap, 21, 23, 164-7, 243, 245, 277-82, 284, 286-7, 294-5, 298-9
reggae, 11
regime, 6, 11, 21-2, 101, 106-7, 138, 148, 159, 168, 181, 184-5, 188-90, 209-10, 212, 217, 224-5, 261, 311
rhythm, 142-4, 146, 164, 167, 235, 244-6, 262, 266, 268, 270, 285, 289-90
Ritter, Rüdiger, 16, 19, 24, 95, 97-8, 100-1, 103, 105, 108
rock 'n' roll, 11, 30, 41, 100, 157, 186, 189, 216
rock, 6, 11, 21, 30, 37, 41-5, 78, 100, 104, 134, 156, 157, 160, 177, 179-

81, 184, 186-7, 189-91, 197-9, 201, 203-4, 216, 280, 282, 288-9
Rockower, Paul, 235, 238, 240-2, 247-8, 250
Russia 9, 16, 118, 128, 159, 168, 191

Şahin, Nevin, 13, 16, 18, 69, 83, 85, 306
Salois, Kendra, 12-3, 16, 22-3, 233
samba, 142
Santana, Carlos, 181
Sanz Díaz, Carlos, 16, 22, 209-30
schlager, 41, 203-4, 289
Scotland, 30, 34
Sekstet Komedy, 101
Senegal, 168, 237, 248
Serbia, 265, 268, 306
Siberia, 157
slow fox, 143
social media, 70, 249, 262, 287
Socialist countries, see Eastern Bloc and Soviet Union
Sons of Gastarbeita, 23, 277-8, 281-6, 290, 295
soul music, 282, 285-6
soundtrack, 30, 70, 75, 78, 146, 165, 216, 267
South America, 293
Soviet Union, 19, 20-2, 95-100, 105, 107-9, 118-9, 121-6, 133-41, 145, 147, 157, 175, 179, 181-92, 205, 217, 221-3, 304, 306
Sovietization, 20, 134-6, 138, 148, 198, 248
space, 21, 23, 36, 49, 56, 224, 246, 256, 261, 263-4, 269, 289, 318
Spain, 22, 209-16, 218, 219-23, 225, 304, 308, 311, 317

Stalin, Josef, 98, 100, 119, 134, 136, 143, 146-8
Stalinism, 20, 98-100, 107, 134, 136, 138-40, 147-48, 163
Sullivan, Arthur, 35
Supertramp, 206
Sweden, 75, 119, 301
swing, 119, 127, 142, 187, 289
Switzerland, 304

Taliban, 166
Tallinn Jazz Festival, see festivals
tango, 142, 146
Tanzania, 186, 240
Taylor, Billy, 120, 127
Taylor, James, 181
territorialization, 52
Thailand, 168, 240
totalitarianism, 149
traditionalism, 121
transatlantic, 30
transcultural, 22, 291, 316, 318
transdisciplinary, 10, 24
transformation, 10, 21, 31-2, 40-1, 64, 133-4, 136, 138, 140, 147-8, 158-9, 185, 217, 238, 241-2
transnational, 10, 18, 21, 24, 29-31, 34, 37, 40-41, 105, 277, 279, 305, 317-8, 239
Trinidad, 123
Trump, Donald, 16, 179
Turkey, 9, 11-2, 18, 69-71, 73-9, 81-2, 86-7, 279-81, 283, 286-90, 306, 308, 318
twentieth century, 11, 20, 29, 31, 37, 43, 157, 188, 233, 239, 316, 317-8
Twitter, 15, 179, 249

Uganda, 168, 240

Ukraine, 72, 309, 318
Union of Soviet Socialist Republics (USSR), see Soviet Union
United Kingdom, see also Great Britain, 42-3, 157, 167, 186, 308, 200, 202, 204, 206, 216, 224, 307, 309
United Nations (UN), 15-6, 23, 255-65, 267-73, 303, 315
United Nations Educational, Scientific and Cultural Organization (UNESCO), 9, 13, 15, 77, 81, 87
United States of America (USA, US), 7, 9, 11-4, 17-9, 21-2, 29, 31, 34-6, 38, 40, 42-3, 95-110, 117-9, 121-4, 128, 142, 145, 155, 156, 158-61, 164, 166-7, 169, 175, 177-82, 184, 186-91, 197, 204, 206, 213-4, 222, 233-7, 239-43, 247, 249, 250-1, 260, 266-7, 277-80, 317
Uzbekistan, 163

Vatican, 222, 271, 304
Velvet Underground, 157
Vietnam, 127, 181
Vietnam War, 184-5, 189
Viva Vox Choir, 23, 256, 264-5, 266-8, 271
Vuletic, Dean, 11, 23, 24, 305, 308

Wales, 34
Wallace, Trey, aka DJ 2-Tone Jones, 242-3, 246-7, 249
waltz, 143
West, Kanye, 21, 163
white (race), 21, 26, 40, 166, 179, 185, 239, 301, 309
White House, 9, 12, 315
Who See, 301
Williams, Pharrell, 256, 260-1, 263-4
working class, 175, 177-8, 180, 183-5, 188-9, 191, 223
World Cup (FIFA), 31, 266, 308, 310
world music, 164
World War I, 35, 39-40, 265
World War II, 10, 21, 24, 41, 52, 95, 98-9, 108, 118, 134, 135, 155-6, 198, 201, 309
Wurst, Conchita, 309-11

YouTube, 16
Yugoslavia, 23, 124, 267, 304, 306, 311

Zacharov, Vladimir, 138, 141, 148
Zappa, Frank, 157
Zimbabwe, 168, 237, 248
Žižić, Nina, 301
ZZ Top, 205

GPSR Authorized Representative: Easy Access System Europe, Mustamäe tee
50, 10621 Tallinn, Estonia, gpsr.requests@easproject.com

www.ingramcontent.com/pod-product-compliance
Lightning Source LLC
Chambersburg PA
CBHW070803040426
42333CB00061B/1803